MIGRATION
THEORY

MIGRATION
THEORY

Talking across Disciplines

Edited by
Caroline B. Brettell
James F. Hollifield

Routledge
a member of the Taylor & Francis Group
New York and London

Published in 2000 by
Routledge
29 West 35th Street
New York, NY 10001

Published in Great Britain in 2000 by
Routledge
11 New Fetter Lane
London EC4P 4EE

Routledge is an imprint of the Taylor & Francis Group.

Copyright © 2000 by Routledge

Printed in the United States of America on acid-free paper.
Design: Jack Donner

Library of Congress Cataloging-in-Publication Data

Migration Theory : talking across disciplines /
edited by Caroline B. Brettell and James F. Hollifield.
            p.   cm.
Includes bibliographical references.
ISBN 0-415-92610-6 (hb) — ISBN 0-415-92611-4 (pb)
1. Emigration and immigration. II. Brettell, Caroline. II. Hollifield, James Frank, 1954–

JV6035 .M545 2000
304.8—dc21   99–087915

Contents

Preface

As scholars and teachers, we are constantly engaged in writing and speaking. But in our haste to produce that next article or lecture, we do not always take the time to listen, especially to those working in sister disciplines. It is in the spirit of dialogue and in the hopes of gaining greater insight into the phenomenon of international migration that we started this project. The readers must judge whether or not we have succeeded in creating a dialogue and shedding light on why individuals move across national boundaries, how they are incorporated into host societies, and why some migrants may return to their countries of origin.

Migration is a subject that cries out for an interdisciplinary approach. Each discipline brings something to the table, theoretically and empirically. Anthropologists have taught us to look at networks and transnational communities, while sociologists and economists draw our attention to the importance of social and human capital and the difficulties of immigrant settlement and incorporation. Political scientists help us to understand the play of organized interests in the making of public policy; together with legal scholars, they show us the impact migration can have on the institutions of sovereignty and citizenship. Historians portray the migrant experience in all of its complexity, giving us a much greater empathetic understanding of the hopes and ambitions of migrants. Demographers have perhaps the best empirical grasp on the movement of people across boundaries, and they have the theoretical and methodological tools to show us how such movements affect population dynamics in the sending and receiving societies.

In bringing together this particular group of scholars, our ambition was to take a small step in the direction of creating a more unified field of study. With three exceptions, the papers that comprise this volume were originally presented at a meeting of the Social Science History Association. Although he did not present a paper, Peter Schuck attended the meeting and participated in the panel discussion. The chapters by Charles Keely on demography and Howard Chang on economics and law were added later. The authors carried on a lively discussion in the year or so that it took to bring this project to fruition. Other colleagues read and commented upon individual chapters, and to them we are grateful.

We also would like to thank those who had a direct hand in the production of the book. The editors at Routledge, Amy Shipper and Eric Nelson, worked diligently to shepherd the book from review to production. Noelle McAlpine of the Tower Center for Political Studies at Southern Methodist University helped us put the pieces of the manuscript together. Finally, we would like to thank all the contributors for being so patient and conscientious.

Migration Theory

Talking across Disciplines

Caroline B. Brettell and James F. Hollifield

Interest in international migration in the social sciences has tended to ebb and flow with various waves of emigration and immigration. The United States is now well into the fourth great wave of immigration. As we approach the end of the millennium, the immigrant population stands at a historic high of 26.3 million, representing 9.8 percent of the total population. Almost 14 million children under age eighteen living in the United States are either immigrants or have immigrant parents. Western Europe has experienced a similar influx of foreigners that began, in some countries, as early as the late 1940s. By the 1990s foreign residents were 8.2 percent of the German population, 6.4 percent of the French population, 16.3 percent of the Swiss population, and 5.6 percent of the Swedish population. In Canada, the establishment in 1967 of a point system for entry based on skills and the reunion of families has not only increased the volume of immigrants but also diversified their places of origin. The same is true for Australia where 40 percent of population growth in the post–World War II period has been the result of immigration. With the abandonment in the 1960s of the White Australia Policy barring non-European settlers, Australia has become a multicultural nation (Smolicz 1997). Even Japan, a country that has always had a restrictionist immigration policy began admitting foreign workers in the 1980s. Finally, the movement of large populations throughout the developing world, as refugees in Africa or "guest workers" in Asia and the Middle East, has led some analysts to speak of a global migration crisis (Weiner 1995).

Whether and where there might be a migration crisis remains an open question. But clearly the last half of the twentieth century has been an age of migration (Castles and Miller 1993). Scholars in all of the social sciences have turned their attention to the study of this extraordinarily complex phenomenon.[1] Yet, despite the volume of research interest in a host of academic fields, when members of the various disciplines meet, it is, as Silvia Pedraza

(1990:44) has so cleverly remarked, in much the same fashion as when "one sometimes arrives at a party and is . . . surprised to find out who else is there." It seems that only rarely do we talk across the disciplines.[2] Douglas Massey and his colleagues (1994:700–1) state the problem in succinct terms: "Social scientists do not approach the study of immigration from a shared paradigm, but from a variety of competing theoretical viewpoints fragmented across disciplines, regions, and ideologies. As a result, research on the subject tends to be narrow, often inefficient, and characterized by duplication, miscommunication, reinvention, and bickering about fundamentals. Only when researchers accept common theories, concepts, tools, and standards will knowledge begin to accumulate." Jan and Leo Lucassen (1997) argue that the deepest disciplinary canyon is between historians on the one hand, and social scientists, on the other. A canyon almost as deep separates those social scientists who take a top-down "macro" approach, focusing on immigration policy or market forces, from those whose approach is bottom-up, emphasizing the experiences of the individual migrant or the immigrant family.

This book represents an effort to bridge these canyons, particularly with respect to theorizing about international migration. Here, we have brought together in a single volume essays by a historian, a demographer, an economist, a sociologist, an anthropologist, a political scientist, and two legal scholars. Each was asked to assess and analyze the central concepts, questions, and theoretical perspectives pertaining to the study of migration in his or her respective discipline and in the intersection between disciplines. Most of the authors adopt a broad approach, but a few have chosen to situate their discussion in relation to a more focused debate. Rather than reaching for a unifying theory, as Massey et al. (1993) attempt to do,[3] in this introduction we examine the essays in this volume as a whole, noting convergence and divergence in how questions are framed, how research is conducted and at what levels and with what units of analysis, how hypothesis-testing proceeds, and ultimately how theoretical models are constructed. Our goal is dialogue and cross-disciplinary conversation about the epistemological, paradigmatic, and explanatory aspects of writing about and theorizing migration in history, law, and the social sciences. If this book moves the conversation in the direction of what Castles (1993:30) has called for—"the study of migration as a social science in its own right . . . strongly multidisciplinary in its theory and methodology" it will have achieved its objective.

FRAMING THE QUESTION

In the social sciences, students are taught that they must start any inquiry with a puzzle or a question, whatever the topic of study may be. Of course, the way in which that question is formulated or framed is dependent upon the discipline; and the construction of hypotheses also is driven by disciplinary con-

siderations. Intense disagreements and debates about the meaning and interpretation of the same body of data exist within single disciplines. Sometimes
there can be agreement across the disciplines on the nature of the problem, or
even on the methodology. However, agreement on a single explanation or
model is less likely; it is even rarer to find hypotheses that are truly multidisciplinary, drawing upon concepts and insights from several disciplines simultaneously. Each discipline has its preferred or acceptable list of questions,
hypotheses, and variables.

In the following table, we have constructed a matrix that summarizes principal research questions and methodologies, as well as dominant theories and
hypotheses for each of the disciplines represented in this volume. The matrix
is necessarily schematic and cannot include every question or theory; but it
provides a framework for establishing a dialogue across disciplines.

TABLE 1: MIGRATION THEORIES ACROSS DISCIPLINES

Discipline	Research Question(s)	Levels/Units of Analysis	Dominant Theories	Sample Hypothesis
Anthropology	How does migration effect cultural change and affect ethnic identity?	More micro/ individuals, households, groups	Relational or structuralist and transnational	Social networks help maintain cultural difference.
Demography	How does migration affect population change?	More macro/ populations	Rationalist (borrows heavily from economics)	Immigration increases the birth rate.
Economics	What explains the propensity to migrate and its effects?	More micro/ individuals	Rationalist: cost-benefit and push-pull	Incorporation depends on the human capital of immigrants.
History	How do we understand the immigrant experience?	More micro/individuals and groups	Eschews theory and hypothesis testing	Not applicable
Law	How does the law influence migration?	Macro and micro/ the political and legal system	Institutionalist and rationalist (borrows from all the social sciences)	Rights create incentive structures for migrants.
Political Science	Why do states have difficulty controlling migration?	More macro/ political and international systems	Institutionalist and rationalist	States are often captured by proimmigrant interests.
Sociology	What explains immigrant incorporation?	More macro/ ethnic groups and social class	Structuralist and/or functionalist	Immigrant incorporation is dependent on social capital.

For historians, who nowadays straddle the divide between the humanities and the social sciences, principal research questions are related to particular places and times. As Diner points out in her contribution to this volume, historians of migration tend to eschew theory and hypothesis testing, although their questions are similar to those of other social scientists—what are the determinants and consequences of population movement? In more precise terms, they ask who moves, when do they move, why do they move? Why do some people stay put? How do those who move experience departure, migration, and settlement? These questions are generally applied to single groups (or even individuals), rather than to a comparison across groups, an effort that would require, as Diner suggests, vast linguistic competence. In history, it is the narrative of how various groups settled, shaped their communities and constructed their identities that has taken precedence over the analysis of the migration process. On the issue of structure and agency, historians tend to focus more on individual migrants as agents. They are less concerned with explaining how social structures influence and constrain behavior.

Anthropologists tend to be as context-specific in their ethnographic endeavor, and much of their theorizing is idiographic. But their ultimate goal is to engage in cross-cultural comparisons that make possible generalizations across space and time, and hence nomothetic theory building. The ethnographic knowledge generated by anthropology "transcends the empirical" (Hastrup 1992:128) in its effort to arrive at a better understanding of the human condition.[4] Anthropologists are interested in more than the who, when, and why of migration; they want to capture through their ethnography the experience of being an immigrant and the meaning, to the migrants themselves, of the social and cultural changes that result from leaving one context and entering another. Brettell (in this volume) notes that this has led anthropologists to explore the impact of emigration and immigration on the social relations between men and women, among kin, and among people from the same cultural or ethnic background. Questions in the anthropological study of migration are framed by the assumption that outcomes for people who move are shaped by their social, cultural, and gendered locations and that migrants themselves are agents in their behavior, interpreting and constructing within the constraints of structure.

For sociology, as Heisler emphasizes in the opening sentences of her chapter, the central questions are: Why does migration occur? And how is it sustained over time? Sociologists share a common theoretical framework with anthropologists. Both are grounded in the classic works of social theory (Marx, Durkheim, and Weber), and each tends to emphasize social relations as central to understanding the processes of migration and immigrant incorporation. However, sociologists work almost exclusively in the receiving society, while anthropologists have often worked at the sending, receiving, or at both ends. The difference is a result of the historical origins of these two disciplines—

sociology in the study of Western institutions and society, anthropology in the study of "the other." Anthropology "came lately" to the study of migration and immigration, but in sociology it has been a topic of long-standing interest. Sociological questions are generally also outcomes questions. Although many sociologists are interested in the causes of migration, the discipline places great emphasis on the process of immigrant incorporation. Sociological theory has moved from postulating a single outcome (assimilation) to manifold outcomes that depend on such factors as social capital, labor markets, and a range of institutional structures. Heisler points to the significance of sociological research on the ethnic enclave economy and ethnic entrepreneurship. While anthropologists have emphasized the cultural construction and symbolic markers of ethnic identity, sociologists have emphasized the institutional manifestations of ethnic difference. Both are equally important, but they reflect a difference in disciplinary epistemologies and, hence, in how questions are framed. However, there is also a good deal of interchange and cross-reading between these two disciplines. One area where scholars in both fields come together is in their study of the social relations of immigration— specifically an assumption about the importance of social networks as both a causal and sustaining factor influencing the migration process.

The central question for demographers is the nature of population change. Births, deaths, and migration are the major components of population change. Drawing largely on aggregate data, they document the pattern and direction of migration flows and the characteristics of migrants (age, sex, occupation, education, and so on). This is what Keely (in this volume) labels the formal demography approach to migration. But he goes on to stress that demographers do not shun theory and explanation. Rather they draw upon theories from a range of social science disciplines to explain the social, economic, and political forces that shape and are shaped by migration flows. Thus, demographers by necessity have bridged the canyons between the disciplines. Demographers are as interested as historians, anthropologists, and sociologists in the questions of who moves and when, but to answer these questions, they engage in the construction of predictive models. As Keely phrases it, the demographer estimates the probability of an event (migration) happening to a particular proportion of the population. Demographers can and do forecast the future. Historians, anthropologists, and sociologists, by contrast, focus on actual behavior of individuals and groups in the past or in the present.

Economists also build predictive models. Chiswick's chapter in this volume offers an excellent example of how the question of "who migrates" and model building come together. He focuses specifically on a central debate within economics about migrant selectivity. The central question is: Under what conditions will the most favorable (in human capital terms and for labor market success) migrants be selected? Chiswick develops models that predict more or less positive selectivity under various conditions. This is a "supply-side" theory, rather than an outcomes theory, and it reflects the broader assumption that frames much of the research on migration within the discipline of economics—that individuals act rationally to maximize their utility (Faist 1997:249). Massey et al. (1993) label this the microeconomic model of individual choice.[5]

Again the contrast with anthropologists and historians, who would argue that economic factors cannot and do not fully predict population movement when they are divorced from social and cultural context, is strikingly apparent. Anthropologists in particular reject a universal rationality. Furthermore, anthropologists and historians are reluctant, if not averse, to framing questions in relation to evaluations of positive and negative inputs or outcomes. But economists (and economic demographers) are often called upon (by those who formulate policy) to assess the fiscal and human capital costs and benefits of immigration in precisely these evaluative terms. It therefore shapes many of the theoretical debates in their discipline (Borjas 1999; Huber and Espenshade 1997; Rothman and Espenshade 1992), not to mention broader debates about immigration policy. For example, in earlier work Chiswick (1978) addressed the economic assimilation rate of immigrants. He demonstrated that although immigrants start with earnings that are approximately 17 percent below that of natives, after 10 to 15 years of employment in the United States, they tend to surpass the average wage level and subsequently rise above it. This conclusion was challenged on the basis of more recent census data by economists such as George Borjas (1985), but Borjas's work in turn has been challenged by Chiswick (1986) and others (Duleep and Regets 1997a, 1997b). Economists and demographers have also explored the educational, welfare, and social security costs of immigrants (Passel 1994; Simon 1984), thereby responding to national debates that erupt from time to time in the political arena (National Research Council 1997).

Chiswick's chapter in this volume ends with a nod to the way that immigration laws and regulations shape selectivity factors (what he calls "rationing admissions"). A country that emphasizes skills as the primary criterion upon which to issue visas will experience a different pattern in the growth and composition of its immigrant population from that of a country that constructs a policy based on family reunification or refugee status. It is with attention to these questions that political scientists and legal scholars have entered as relative newcomers the arena of migration research.

As Hollifield emphasizes in his chapter, the questions for scholars of immigration within political science follow three themes. One is the role of the nation-state in controlling migration flows and hence its borders; a second is the impact of migration on the institutions of sovereignty and citizenship, and the relationship between migration, on the one hand, and foreign policy and national security, on the other; a third is the question of incorporation. Political science has paid attention to what sociologists and economists have written about social and economic incorporation and added to it the dimension of political incorporation—specifically questions of citizenship and rights, familiar themes for legal scholars as well (Schuck in this volume). It is worth noting, however, that Diner discusses a particular historical monograph, Salyer's *Law Harsh as Tigers*, that addresses similar issues for the Chinese who immigrated to the United States in the late nineteenth century. Salyer shows how these Chinese "sojourners" exercised their rights to challenge discriminatory laws.

Like sociologists, political scientists work largely at the receiving end, although one can find a few examples of those whose research has addressed emigration policy (rules of exit), rather than immigration policy (rules of entry), according to similar themes of control, but with a greater focus on development issues (Leeds 1984; Russell 1986; Weiner 1987, 1995). Whether they are looking at the sending or receiving societies, political scientists tend to be split theoretically. Some lean heavily toward a more interest-based, microeconomic (rational choice) approach to the study of migration (Freeman 1995, 1998; Kessler 1998), while others favor institutional, cultural, and ideational explanations for increases in immigration in the advanced industrial democracies (Hollifield 1992; Zolberg 1981).

Both traditions of inquiry can be found in the study of law as well, with one group of scholars (for example, Chang in this volume) taking a more rationalist, microeconomic approach to understanding migration, and another group (for example, Schuck in this volume; Legomsky, 1987) focusing on institutions, process, and rights as the key variables for explaining outcomes. As Schuck points out, most legal scholars are skeptical of the possibility for developing a "science of law"; and they devote most of their efforts to the analysis and assessment of caselaw. But in their work, both Schuck and Chang break with this atheoretical tradition as they attempt to explain how the law shapes the phenomenon of international migration, and how immigration in particular affects the American political economy. Schuck points to the difficulties of establishing a coherent regulatory regime for immigration and attempts to explain why there are such large gaps between immigration policy (the law on the books) and the implementation of policy (the law in action or in people's minds). His analysis is reminiscent of similar work in political science (Cornelius, Martin, and Hollifield 1994; Freeman 1995; Hollifield 1986), which seeks to explain the difficulties of immigration control in liberal democracies. The emphasis that Schuck places on the institution of rights as a key determinant of policy outcomes echoes work by political scientists and sociologists (Hollifield 1992; Jacobson 1996; Soysal 1994). Following the ideas of the sociologist, Robert Merton, Schuck suggests that the failure of immigration law may actually serve some latent social function: it helps to finesse or cover up the profoundly ambiguous attitudes of the American public toward illegal immigration, which Schuck describes as a "victimless crime."

In effect, Schuck argues that the law is extremely limited in what it can do to regulate international migration, and particularly illegal immigration, even though law plays a crucial role in constructing the "complex array of incentives that individuals and groups take into account in deciding whether, when, and where to migrate." On the one hand, legal admissions largely determine the types of naturalized citizens; on the other, the enforcement of immigration law is often constrained by cost or by liberal and human rights ideologies.

If Schuck borrows freely from the disciplines of political science and sociology, opting for an institutionalist or structural-functional approach to the study of migration, Chang's analysis of immigration law and policy is driven almost entirely by microeconomics, specifically trade theory. Like Chiswick, Chang takes a rationalist approach to understanding migration, and his primary concern is for the allocational and distributional effects of immigration policies. In contrast to Schuck, who worries about the impact of uncontrolled migration on the liberal polity and the rule of law, Chang, based on the assumption that an immigration regime should increase national economic welfare, argues for a more liberal body of immigration law in the United States. He suggests that maximum fiscal benefits from immigration can best be attained by applying fiscal solutions such as restrictions on immigrant access to transfer programs or "tariffs" imposed on immigrants to compensate the public treasury for transfers that we expect an immigrant to receive later. In the work of Schuck and Chang, we can see how the jurist's approach to the study of migration differs from that of many social scientists and historians. Legal scholars are less concerned with theory building and hypothesis testing, and more inclined to use the eclectic techniques of analysis in social science to argue for specific types of policy reform. Equally, they draw on detailed understandings of institutional and practical realities (mostly costs) to debunk general theories.

LEVELS AND UNITS OF ANALYSIS

Objects of inquiry and theory building are closely related to the levels and units of analysis. In migration research, these vary both within and between disciplines. An initial contrast is between those who approach the problem at a macrolevel, examining the structural conditions (largely political, legal, and economic) that shape migration flows; and those who engage in microlevel research, examining how these larger forces shape the decisions and actions of individuals and families, or how they effect changes in communities. World systems theory is one manifestation of the macro approach. Historians, Diner notes, know about world systems theory, but have tended to avoid it.[6] By contrast, in a range of social sciences, particularly sociology and anthropology, it has been influential (Portes 1997; Sassen 1996). However, as Hollifield points out, political scientists have tended to be critical of world systems theory and the types of globalization arguments that often flow from it. The logic of world systems theory is heavily sociological and structural, and it discounts the role of politics and the state in social and economic change. Mainstream scholars of international relations continue to place the state, as a unitary and rational actor, at the center of their analyses of any type of transnational phenomenon, whether it is trade, foreign direct investment, or international migration (Hollifield 1998).

Despite the importance of world systems theory to both sociology and anthropology, Heisler and Brettell suggest that more theorizing in these fields takes place at the microlevel, or at what Thomas Faist (1997) has recently labeled a "meso-level" that focuses on social ties.[7] By contrast, political science, with its central concern with the role of the state, operates more comfortably at the macrolevel. This is also true of the law, especially when law intersects with politics and economics. However, legal scholars equally focus on individual cases and on patterns of caselaw and hence operate at a microlevel of analysis as well. Economics also operates at both levels, depending on the research questions. Economists have not only theorized about how wage or employment opportunity differentials between sending and receiving societies affect general flows of populations but also about how such differentials influence individual or household cost/benefit and utilitarian decision making about migration. Demography is perhaps a special case because the primary unit of analysis for the demographer is the population. Hill (1997:244) has argued that the "easy definition of a population has blinded [demographers] to more complex thoughts about what holds people together and what divides them." In other words, the meso-level at which sociologists and anthropologists frequently operate to theorize about the maintenance or construction of kinship, ethnic, or community ties among immigrants is not of primary concern to demographers.

If the population is the unit of analysis for demographers, then for sociologists, anthropologists, and some economists it is the individual or the household. Recently, the sociologist Alejandro Portes (1997:817) has argued strongly in favor of something other than the individual as the unit of analysis. "Reducing everything to the individual plane would unduly constrain the enterprise by preventing the utilization of more complex units of analysis—families, households, and communities, as the basis for explanation and prediction." Brettell in fact traces a shift in anthropology from the individual to the household that accompanied the realization that individual migrants rarely make decisions in a vacuum about whether to leave and where to go and that immigrant earnings or emigrant remittances are often pooled into a household economy. Similarly it is in the distinction between individual decision making, on the one hand, and household or family decision making, on the other, that Massey et al. (1993) locate the difference between neoclassical microeconomic migration theory and the new economics of migration. New economics theorists argue that households send workers abroad "not only to improve income in absolute terms, but also to increase income relative to other households, and, hence, to reduce their relative deprivation compared with some reference group" (Massey et al. 1993:438; see also Mincer 1978; Stark 1991). This is an economic theory that, with a different unit of analysis, must take sociological and anthropological questions into consideration.

Economists asking a different set of research questions that are shared with sociologists often focus on other units of analysis—the labor market in the receiving society or the economy of a sending society. These generate different bodies of theory about dual and segmented labor markets, about aggregate income and income distribution, about the impact of capitalist development, about the political implications of emigrant remittances, or about global cities (Sassen 1991). In all cases, the needs and interests of entities other than the individual are of interest here.

Political scientists and legal scholars have generally entered into the debate at this point, taking as their primary unit of analysis the state. Bringing the state in as the unit of analysis by definition focuses attention specifically on international migration. As Keely points out, quoting Zolberg (1981), micro-analytic theories do not distinguish between domestic and international flows; nor do meso-level theories. The politics of the state (or states) are often behind refugee and illegal flows (Hollifield 1998; Zolberg, Suhrke, and Aguayo 1986). Rules of entry and exit formulated by the state regulate migration flows. State sovereignty and control are at issue in debates about citizenship, and since citizenship and sovereignty are cornerstones of the international legal system, migration always has the potential to affect international relations. In this case, the level of analysis may move (from the individual or the state) to the international system itself.

Contrasts between the perspectives of political science and those of anthropology are stark on the issue of the relationship between immigration and citizenship. Anthropologists are more concerned with the meaning of citizenship for the individual migrant—whether and how it is incorporated into a new identity—than are their colleagues in political science, who may be focused on the international systemic or national security implications of population movements. Sociologists, with their interest in institutions, have, it appears, aligned themselves more with political scientists and lawyers than with anthropologists on this particular question (Brubaker 1992). As Heisler points out, the theoretical focus in the citizenship literature, particularly in the European context, is primarily on the transformation of host societies and only secondarily on the immigrants. It is here that some intriguing interdisciplinary interchange could occur by combining different units of analysis (the state and the individual) and different questions (sovereignty and identity) (Kastoryano 1997). The utilitarian aspects of citizenship might also be a dimension of such interdisciplinary exploration. In their work on citizenship, for example, Peter

Schuck (Schuck and Smith 1985; Schuck 1998) and Rogers Smith (1997) explore the way in which naturalization law and policy (a state-level variable) affect the rate of political incorporation of newcomers.

DATA AND METHODOLOGY

The units of analysis in migration research are closely linked to matters of data and methodology. When the unit of analysis is the population, research is conducted at an aggregate level, using primarily census data, but sometimes also data from large surveys. Demographic data are abundant, discrete, accessible, and theorizing is itself driven by the data (Hill 1997). Keely emphasizes that demographers are perhaps most preoccupied with the accuracy of the data and with esoteric matters of method.[8] Because they use secondary data, they must be concerned with how migration and immigration were defined by those who collected the data. Sociologists and economists of migration, particularly if they are also trained as demographers, often use the same secondary data and engage in similar kinds of statistical methods of analysis. And yet, some sociologists and economists are equally aware of the limitations of census data. "They undernumerate undocumented migrants, they provide no information on legal status, and they are ill-suited to the study of immigration as a process rather than an event," writes Massey and colleagues (1994:700).

Sociologists and some economists also generate their own individual- or household-level data, generally using surveys of samples that can range from two hundred to two thousand. This is equally true of much anthropological research on migration, but anthropologists also generate primary individual- and household-level data through extended and sometimes arduous periods of ethnographic fieldwork and participant observation. While it may not be the basis for extensive theory construction, the life history method has been employed to some effect by anthropologists to access the rich texture of the lived experience of being a migrant and the cultural context of decision making.[9] Benmayor and Skotnes (1994b:15) are most articulate in outlining the way personal testimony "speaks . . . to how im/migrant subjects constantly build, reinvent, synthesize, or even collage identities from multiple sources and resources, often lacing them with deep ambivalence. Knowing something of the utter uniqueness of particular individual migrant experiences certainly enhances our generalizations about the group experience, but it also elicits humility about the adequacy of these generalizations and a realization that few actual individual lives fully conform to the master narratives."

In political science and the law, common methods often involve interviews with key politicians and lawmakers. They also involve a careful reading of texts, as well as statistical analysis of aggregate or individual-level data, depending on the types of questions that are asked. Policy analysis and political economy are often focused on aggregate data (Hollifield 1992), whereas studies of political and voting behavior, as well as public opinion, involve the use of individual-level survey data (DeSipio 1996). Legal scholars are less likely than economists or political scientists to use formal models or statistical analysis, relying instead on interpretation of caselaw, institutional analysis, and political history (Schuck 1998). But, with the theoretical and method-ological borrowing that goes on between law and economics or political science, legal scholars have come increasingly to draw on more formal meth-ods of data analysis.

Clearly, historical methods, which rely on archival sources, are quite distinct and well developed within that discipline. In recent years, of course, histori-ans and historical anthropologists have turned increasingly to quantitative methods of data analysis, which has in turn expanded and enriched the range of sources drawn upon to study migration and immigration. These include manuscript census data and ownership and housing records (Gabaccia 1984), population registers (Kertzer and Hogan 1989), official statistics containing aggregate data on emigration and immigration (Hochstadt 1981), passport reg-isters (Baganha 1990), ships' manifests (Swierenga 1981), and even local parish records (Brettell 1986; Moch and Tilly 1985). However, historians also use the kinds of documents to study migration that they have used for other historical projects—letters, autobiographies, newspapers and magazines, urban citizenship registers, sacred and secular court documents, tax and land records, settlement house and hospital admission records, organization book-lets, and oral histories (Baily and Ramella 1988; Diner 1983; Gjerde 1985; Mageean 1991; Miller 1985; Yans-McLaughlin 1990).

The diverse methods of history and the social sciences, and the various bodies of data that are used, yield different knowledge about migration. They access different voices and leave others out. They provide for different types of generalizations and hence different levels of theorizing. Bjeren (1997:222) outlines the implications of different methods for migration research. She writes:

> Large-scale social surveys are certainly necessary in migration research since it is only through such studies that the relative (quantitative) importance of different phenomena, the distribution of characteristics and their relationship between variables can be ascertained. However, the limitations imposed by the method of investigation must be respected for the results to be valid. The same holds true for detailed studies of social contexts, where the fascination of the complexity of life may make it difficult for the researcher to step back and free herself from the idiosyncrasies of an individual setting or situation.

If survey data miss some of the intersubjective meanings characteristic of social situations revealed in participant observation (Kertzer and Fricke 1997:18), research based on an intense examination of a limited number of cases (such as occurs in history and anthropology) can in turn limit generalization.

While method also involves comparison, in the study of migration, there are differences of approach within each discipline. As mentioned above, historians have tended to avoid comparisons mostly because they pose methodological challenges in terms of time and the skills necessary to command archival sources in different countries and distinct languages. The concept of "my group"—the Irish, the Italians, the Germans—described by Diner is also characteristic of anthropology, although the roots of anthropology as a discipline are in the comparative method. The anthropologist feels equally compelled to have command of the language of the immigrant population among whom he or she is conducting ethnographic fieldwork (participant-observation), be it the Portuguese in Paris, the Hmong in Minneapolis, or the Koreans in New York. When an anthropologist engages in comparison, it is often based on data gathered by another ethnographer and tends to be more impressionistic than systematic. There are, however, some examples of anthropologists who have studied the same national immigrant population in two different receiving societies and, hence, engaged in a process of controlled comparative analysis of quite specific questions that provide the foundation for the construction of middle-range theories of processes of migration and settlement (Brettell 1981; Foner 1985, 1998). Olwig (1998:63) notes, with reference to Caribbean migration, that comparative studies can generate quite distinct conclusions depending on the framework of analysis adopted.

> A framework which singles out for comparison the disparate experiences of migrating from a variety of Caribbean places of origin to their different respective (neo-) colonial metropoles leads to quite different conclusions than one which takes its point of departure in the multifaceted experiences of people who move from a single island society to a multiplicity of metropoles. The former form of comparison can have the effect of privileging the perspective of the metropoles ... however, if one takes as one's point of departure a particular island society, or even a particular family, one will see that there is a long heritage of moving to different migration destinations.

Foner (1998:48) suggests that the comparative approach to migration reveals "a number of factors that determine the outcome of the migration experience. . . . Cross-national comparisons allow us to begin to assess the relative weight of cultural baggage, on the one hand, and social and economic factors, on the other."

Some social scientists use historical analysis to frame their comparisons (Freeman 1979; Hollifield 1992; Perlman and Waldinger 1997). An excellent example is Robert Smith's (1997) comparison of the transnational practices of Italians who came to New York in the late nineteenth and early twentieth centuries with Mexican and other immigrants who have entered that city more recently. In particular, he notes differences in the longevity of community/ethnic organizations of the present by contrast with those of the past, the greater extent of participation in the development of sending communities, and an international political context and weaker anti-immigrant tenor that fosters continued ties with the homeland. But the comparison also allows him to argue that the "global nation is not a new idea" (Robert Smith 1997:123).

When historians of migration have themselves engaged in comparison, it is largely based on secondary sources used to complement primary research. (Campbell 1995). Thus, Gjerde (1996) has drawn on a range of works to write his masterful and ambitious analysis of the Midwestern immigrant experience in the nineteenth and early twentieth centuries. Similarly, Gabaccia (1994) uses a wealth of both primary and secondary sources to explore similarities and differences in the experiences of migratory women who came to the United States between 1820 and 1990. Historian Nancy Green (1997:59ff) rightly argues that only through comparison can we understand what is specific and what is general in migration and that "by changing the unit of analysis to compare immigrant groups to each other in their cities of settlement, we can focus on the intermediary—'mezzo'—level of analysis more pertinent to understanding the social construction of ethnic identities" (61). Historical comparisons that are "explicit, systematic, and methodologically rigorous" would, as Samuel Baily (1990:243) observes, "provide a corrective to the misleading assumption of U.S. exceptionalism," a problem raised in this volume by both Diner and Heisler. Indeed, Heisler calls most strongly for the development of cross-national comparative research. For her, the ocean that divides the study of immigration in Europe from that in the United States is perhaps as wide as the canyon that separates scholarship of the different disciplines— she calls for a bridge between Americanists and comparatists/globalists. Only through such comparison can the "national models" of migration be tested for cross-cultural validity. Portes (1997:819) has made a similar plea by suggesting that there are many questions that have flourished in the North American immigration literature that lack a comparative dimension.[10] The research of some European scholars of immigrant communities on ethnic enclaves and ethnic entrepreneurs in cities such as Amsterdam, Paris, and Berlin begins to address this problem.

While the case study is commonly used in all of the social sciences, much of the most important and pathbreaking work on migration has taken the form of systematic comparison, often with very sophisticated research designs using comparative method as a way of testing hypotheses and building theories. Some of the earliest work on immigration in political science and sociology involved systematic comparisons of politics and policy (Castles and Kosack 1973; Freeman 1979; Hammar 1985; Miller 1981; Schmitter 1979). These studies, which followed a most-similar-systems design, gave rise to a new literature in the comparative politics and sociology of immigration and citizenship (Bade and Weiner 1997; Brubaker 1992; Hollifield 1992; Horowitz and Noiriel 1992; Ireland 1994; Sowell 1996; Soysal 1994; Weiner and Hanami 1998). Such systematic, cross-national research has helped to illuminate similarities and differences in immigration and citizenship policy and to explain different outcomes. It is safe to say that the comparative method has been a mainstay of migration research across the social science disciplines, and it has resulted in some of the most innovative scholarship in the field.

IMMIGRATION AND INTEGRATION

For history, sociology, and anthropology, one of the dominant paradigms in migration theory is the assimilation model. As mentioned above, Heisler argues that this model, which predicts a single outcome, has given way to new models that predict a range of outcomes. This is best encapsulated in Portes and Rumbaut's (1990) complex model of incorporation. This model, formulated in relation to the United States, postulates outcomes for different groups according to contexts of reception that vary with reference to (1) U.S. government policy that passively accepts or actively supports; (2) labor market reception that is neutral, positive, or discriminatory; and (3) an ethnic community that is nonexistent, working class, or entrepreneurial/ professional. Heisler reviews the literature in sociology that deals quite specifically with the ethnic enclave economy and its role in either facilitating or delaying the process of incorporation. Sociologists who emphasize social capital (the social networks and social relationships of immigrants) tend to argue the former, while economists, like Chiswick in this volume, place greater emphasis on human capital criteria (schooling, professional qualifications, language proficiency, and the like) in facilitating incorporation.

Chiswick argues, in contrast to George Borjas, that higher levels of inequality in the country of origin do not lead to negative selectivity of immigrants, but rather to less favorable positive selectivity. In effect, according to Chiswick, even though immigrants may come from very poor countries, they are still favorably selected compared to those who stay behind, and are likely to add to the human capital stock of the receiving country and to assimilate fairly quickly. In this framework, immigrants' earnings are still likely to increase at a higher rate than the earnings of natives. Hence, economists and sociologists are focused on many of the same questions concerning the incorporation or assimilation of immigrants, even though their theories and methods are quite different (see Table 1).

A range of outcomes is equally manifested in the model of transnationalism that was first formulated by anthropologists but which has had an impact on migration research in several other disciplines including sociology and political science. The roots of transnationalism within anthropology can be found in earlier work on return migration that emphasized links with the homeland and the notion that emigration did not necessarily mean definitive departure in the minds of migrants themselves. But equally transnationalism implies that return is not definitive return. Furthermore, and as Heisler observes, for political sociologists the maintenance of home ties among European immigrants (a transnational perspective) was hardly surprising given policy that did not encourage permanent settlement. Even sending countries have developed transnational policies, encouraging, as in the case of Portugal and more recently Mexico, dual nationality to maintain a presence abroad as well as attachment to home. Although Diner does not address it in her chapter, there is also a body of historical work that has documented return movement in an era prior to global communication and cheap and easy mass transportation (Wyman 1993). Social scientists have yet to take advantage of this historical dimension to refine their understanding of contemporary flows. What precisely is different? Is transnationalism simply a characteristic of the first generation of contemporary migrants, or will it endure and hence mean something different in the twenty-first century from the return migration flows of the late nineteenth and early twentieth centuries? Are scholars of immigration talking about something totally new when they use the term "transnational space" (Faist 1997; Gutiérrez 1998)? Robert Smith (1997:111) argues that although the practices are not new, they are "quantitatively and qualitatively different . . . because, in part, of differences in technology as well as in the domestic and international politics of both sending and receiving countries." He also suggests that simultaneous membership in two societies does not mean coequal membership and that "local and national American identity [for the second generation] are most likely to be primary and the diasporic identity, secondary" (Smith 1997:112). Others would argue that there is something qualitatively different about the new culture that exists across borders and that powerfully shapes migrant decisions. Massey et al. (1994:737–38) link this new culture to the spread of consumerism and immigrant success that itself generates more emigration. Migration becomes an expectation and a normal part of the life course, particularly for young men and increasingly for young women. What emerges is a culture of migration.

Finally, one could argue that the growth of work on the second generation, particularly within the discipline of sociology, is a result of the rejection of the assumptions of assimilation theory (Perlman and Waldinger 1997; Portes and Zhou 1993; Portes 1996). Essentially, given postindustrial economies and the diversity of places of origin of today's immigrant populations, the path to upward mobility (and hence incorporation) will be much less favorable for the contemporary second generation than it was for the second generation of the past. Clearly, this is a topic of intense debate and another area of research and theory building dominated by research on U.S. immigrants that cries out for cross-national comparison and interdisciplinary perspectives that accurately assess the past as well as the present. Perlman and Waldinger (1997:894), for example, argue that "the interpretive stance toward the past, and toward certain features of the present situation as well, puts the contemporary situation in an especially unfavorable light." Later they point to the problem and implications of the absence of conversation across the disciplines on this topic: "Economists read Borjas, sociologists read their colleagues, and historians do not regularly read the literature produced by either discipline. Since Borjas's writings are also widely read and cited by policy analysts in connection with immigration restriction issues, this divergence of emphasis regarding the 'common knowledge' about long-term character of immigrant absorption should not be ignored" (Perlman and Waldinger 1997: 898–99). In fact, their close analysis of the historical evidence to illuminate contemporary trends is exemplary. They reveal continuities between the difficulties experienced by earlier immigrant groups and those of today that suggest "that the time frame for immigrant accommodation was extended and that we should not expect different today" (915).

Perhaps the controversial nature of the debate about the contemporary second generation, and the power of the transnational model, have placed the assimilation model back on the table. Alba and Nee (1997), for example, suggest that assimilation theory should be resurrected without the prescriptive baggage formulated by the dominant majority that calls for immigrants to become like everyone else. They argue that assimilation still exists as a spontaneous process in intergroup interactions. Certainly the current preoccupation in several fields with the transnational model may be a reflection of research that is largely focused on the first generation and that lacks a historical perspective. Toward the end of his essay in this volume Charles Keely observes that integration is a generational process of a population, not just a lifetime project of the immigrant group. Similarly, Herbert Gans (1997) has recently suggested that rejection of straight-line assimilation may be premature, given not only the different generations of immigrants studied by those who originally formulated the theory and by those carrying out contemporary research, but also differences in the background (outsiders versus insiders) of researchers themselves. This latter observation brings reflexivity, powerfully formulated within anthropology, to bear on sociological theory.[11]

BRIDGE BUILDING AMONG THE DISCIPLINES

Our discussion reveals that despite some strong statements to the contrary, there is already a good deal of interchange among the disciplines. Historians draw on many of the theories formulated by sociologists; demographers are attentive to both sociological and economic theory and, increasingly, to those emerging from political science; law has close affinity with all the social sciences and with history, while political science borrows heavily from economics and to a lesser extent from sociology and law; and anthropology shares much with both history and sociology. Although economists also borrow and work with other disciplines—demography, sociology, and history for example—they maintain a focus on their own methodology and models, especially the rational choice model. Proponents of rational choice might argue that this is an indication of how much more advanced economic modeling is, as a science, when compared with other social science disciplines. Detractors would say that economists are so wedded to the rationalist paradigm, they cannot admit that any other theoretical approach might be as powerful as a straightforward, interest-based, microeconomic model.

Our discussion also demonstrates clear divergences in which questions are asked and how they are framed, in units of analysis, and in research methods. Bridge building, in our view, might best proceed through the development of interdisciplinary research projects on a series of common questions to which scholars in different disciplines and with different regional interests could bring distinct insights drawn from their particular epistemological frameworks. How, for example, might anthropologists and legal scholars collaborate in the study of so-called cultural defenses (Coleman 1996; Magnarella 1991; Volpp 1994) that often involve new immigrants and how might the results of this work lead to refinements in theories about migration and change?

Bridge building also would entail identifying a common set of dependent and independent variables, so that it is clear what we are trying to explain and what factors we stress in building models to explain some segment of migrant behavior or the reaction of states and societies to migration. In this vein, we propose the following (suggestive) list of dependent and independent variables, broken down by discipline (see Table 2).

Clearly, we endorse the call for more cross-national interdisciplinary research projects (Castles 1993; Massey et al. 1998), whether at a micro- or a macrolevel of analysis. How, for example, are first-generation immigrants differentially incorporated (economically, politically, socially) in Germany as opposed to the United States, in Britain by comparison with France, in Australia by contrast with Canada, or in Singapore by comparison with Riyadh? Similarly, how and to what extent are immigrants, their children, and subsequent generations differentially incorporated in a cross-national context? A second topic crying out for interdisciplinary and cross-national examination is the impact (political, economic, social, cultural) of emigration and transnationalism on sending societies (Massey 1999). As noted above, primarily anthropologists and to a lesser extent historians have conducted the most work in the countries of emigration, but the questions asked must be expanded through the participation of those in other disciplines, particularly political science and economics. For example, some scholars have already noted how crucial migrants have become for national economies. Writing about the Dominican Republic, Guarnizo (1997:282–83) observes that "migrant's monetary transfers (excluding their business investments) now constitute the second, and according to some the first, most important source of foreign exchange for the national economy, and they are a sine qua non for Dominican macro economic stability, including monetary exchange rates, balance of trade, international monetary reserves, and the national balance of payments."

In countries of immigration, we foresee exciting collaboration on the question of citizenship between the political scientists and political sociologists who frame the question in relation to the nation-state and the rights of a democratic society, and the anthropologists who frame the questions in relation to ethnicity and the construction of identity. One of the central debates, emerging largely from within the field of economics but with resonance in law and political science, is between those who see a positive impact of immigration and hence propose an admissionist policy, and those who highlight the negative impact and advocate more restrictionist policy.[12] In his chapter here, Chang outlines the parameters of this debate and at the end, after presenting the case for a more liberal immigration policy, asks why liberalization has not occurred despite the likely benefits? He suggests that it may be because in the United States intolerance and xenophobia continue to shape the immigration policy of today as they have shaped that of the past. Economic models alone do not offer a complete explanation. Getting to the roots of anti-immigrant sentiments and their connection to the way nationals of the receiving society construct their own identities in relation to immigrants should be a prime research agenda for scholars of international migration. This would require the input of sociologists and anthropologists. Again it is a question that would

TABLE 2: MODELING MIGRANT BEHAVIOR AND ITS EFFECTS

Discipline	Dependent Variables	Independent Variables
Anthropology	Migrant behavior (emigration, integration)	Social and cultural context (transnational networks)
Demography	Population dynamics (distributions, levels, rates)	Migrant behavior as it affects population (e.g., fertility rates)
Economics	Migrant behavior (immigration and incorporation) and its economic impact	Wage/income differentials, demand-pull/supply-push, human capital, factor proportions
History	Migrant experience	Social/historical context
Law	Legal, political, social, and economic treatment of migrants	Law or policy
Political Science	Policy (admissionist or restrictionist) Outcomes (control and integration)	Institutions, rights Interests
Sociology	Migrant behavior (immigration and incorporation)	Networks, enclaves, social capital

be better served by cross-national and comparative research on the question of reception.

The broader implications of multidisciplinary and comparative approaches for theory are exciting to contemplate, particularly if bridges can be built between causal explanations and interpretive understandings, between statistical regularities and unique occurrences, and between the economic and structural forces that shape migrant behavior, and the individual agency that operates both harmoniously and disharmoniously in relation to those forces.

NOTES

1. Normally, a conceptual distinction is drawn between migration and immigration, the former referring to movement that occurs within national borders (internal migration) and the latter to movement across national borders (emigration or immigration). We use the term *migration* somewhat loosely here to refer to international migration, generally the emphasis of all the essays in this volume. However, from a theoretical perspective it is worth noting that economic theories of migration can often apply to either internal flows or international flows (Stark 1991). The same cannot be said for political scientists (for whom the state and state policies are a key question) or historians, anthropologists, and sociologists (for whom social and cultural context are significant). That said, anthropological research on migration began with the study of movement from countryside to city, but these were viewed as distinct social and cultural environments.

2. Hammar and Tamas (1997:13) observe that research is "frequently undertaken without consideration or consultation of related work in other disciplines" and call for more multidisciplinary research endeavors. Similarly, in a recent edited volume on Mexican immigration to the United States, Suárez-Orozco (1998) also calls for more "interdisciplinary dialogue." An early effort at interdisciplinary dialogue is Kritz, Keely, and Tomas (1981).

3. Portes (1997:10) argues that any attempt at an all-encompassing theory would be futile and that even the macro and the micro are not easily united into a single approach.

4. We must take issue with Bjeren (1997) who has argued that anthropologists never formulate theories divorced from context. While context is generally important, some theorizing moves away from it.

5. Keely discusses the excellent theoretical analysis in Massey et al. (1993). It is worth noting that in addition to the maximization of utility they also address the minimization of risk as a motivating factor for migration.

6. One example of a monograph in the historical literature that invokes both world systems theory and transnationalism is Friedman-Kasaba (1996). Her conclusion includes an analysis of theoretical debates.

7. Faist (1997:188) has usefully reformulated these three levels of analysis as the structural (the political-economic and cultural factors in the sending and receiving countries), the relational (the social ties of movers and stayers), and the individual (the degrees of freedom of potential movers). He also views macro- and micromodels as causal, while meso-models are processual. Hoerder (1997) offers a slightly different tri-level model: analysis of world systems, analysis of behavior among individual migrants from the bottom up, and analysis of segmentation and individual actions in terms of networks and family economies.

8. Caldwell and Hill (1988) have noted a similar "obsession" in other areas of demo-

graphic research and have consequently called for more micro approaches. Massey et al. (1994:700) see the focus in the literature on North American immigration on methodological and measurement issues as limiting to the advancement of theoretical understanding of what shapes and controls flows on migration.

9. Some examples are Brettell (1995), Hart (1997), Kibria (1993), Gmelch (1992), Olwig (1998), Stack (1996), and several of the chapters in Benmayor and Skotnes (1994a). Yans-McLaughlin (1990) writes about the use of subjective documents in history for similar purposes.

10. Massey et al. (1998) make such an attempt in a volume that compares the migration systems in North America, Western Europe, the Gulf region, Asia and the Pacific, and the Southern Cone region of South America.

11. For a contrary view, see Rumbaut (1997).

12. There are, of course, numerous policy analysts who hold a more nuanced middle position. Chiswick, in a personal communication to the editors, suggests that those holding this position might advocate a skill-based immigration policy based on the premise that different immigrant groups (by skill level) have different impacts on the receiving society. Such a policy would be admissionist toward those immigrants who offer positive benefits and restrictionist toward those who offer negative benefits.

REFERENCES

Alba, Richard, and Victor Nee. 1997. "Rethinking Assimilation Theory for a New Era of Immigration," *International Migration Review* 31: 826–74.

Bade, Klaus, and Myron Weiner. 1997. *Migration Past, Migration Future: Germany and the United States*. Providence/Oxford: Berghan Books.

Baganha, Maria Ioannis. 1990. *Portuguese Emigration to the United States, 1820–1930*. New York: Garland.

Baily, Samuel L. 1990. "Cross-Cultural Comparison and the Writing of Migration History: Some Thoughts on How to Study Italians in the New World," in Virginia Yans-McLaughlin, ed., *Immigration Reconsidered: History, Sociology, and Politics*, pp. 241–53. New York: Oxford University Press.

Baily, Samuel L., and Franco Ramella, eds. 1990. *One Family, Two Worlds: An Italian Family's Correspondence across the Atlantic, 1901–1922*. New Brunswick, N.J.: Rutgers University Press.

Benmayor, Rina, and Andor Skotnes. 1994a. *Migration and Identity*. Oxford: Oxford University Press.

———. 1994b. "On Migration and Identity," in Rina Benmayor and Andor Skotnes, eds., *Migration and Identity*, pp. 1–18. Oxford: Oxford University Press.

Bjeren, Gunilla. 1997. "Gender and Reproduction," in Tomas Hammar, Grete Brochmann, Kristof Tamas, and Thomas Faist, eds., *International Migration, Immobility and Development: Multidisciplinary Perspectives*, pp. 219–46. New York: Berg Publishers.

Borjas, George J. 1985. "Assimilation, Changes in Cohort Quality and the Earnings of Immigrants," *Journal of Labor Economics* 3: 463–89.

———. 1999. *Heaven's Door: Immigration Policy and the American Economy*. Princeton, N.J.: Princeton University Press.

Brettell, Caroline B. 1981. "Is the Ethnic Community Inevitable? A Comparison of the Settlement Patterns of Portuguese Immigrants in Toronto and Paris," *Journal of Ethnic Studies* 9: 1–17.

———. 1986. *Men Who Migrate, Women Who Wait: Population and History in a Portuguese Parish*. Princeton, N.J.: Princeton University Press.

————. 1995. *We Have Already Cried Many Tears: The Stories of Three Portuguese Migrant Women*. Prospect Heights, Ill.: Waveland.

Brubaker, Rogers. 1992. *Citizenship and Nationhood in France and Germany*. Cambridge, Mass.: Harvard University Press.

Caldwell, John C., and Allan G. Hill. 1988. "Recent Developments Using Micro-Approaches to Demographic Research," in John Caldwell, Allan Hill, and Valerie Hull, eds., *Micro-Approaches to Demographic Research*, pp. 1–9. London: Kegan Paul International.

Campbell, M. 1995. "The Other Immigrants: Comparing the Irish in Australia and the United States," *Journal of American Ethnic History* 14: 3–22.

Castles, Stephen. 1993. "Migrations and Minorities in Europe. Perspectives for the 1990s: Eleven Hypotheses," in John Wrench and John Solomos, eds., *Racism and Migration in Western Europe*, pp. 17–34. Oxford: Berg Publishers.

Castles, Stephen, and G. Kosack. 1973. *Immigrant Workers and Class Structure in Western Europe*. London: Oxford University Press.

Castles, Stephen, and Mark Miller. 1993. *The Age of Migration: International Population Movements in the Modern World*. New York: Guilford Press.

Chiswick, Barry. 1978. "The Effect of Americanization on the Earnings of Foreign-Born Men," *Journal of Political Economy* 86: 897–921.

————. 1986. "Is the New Immigration Less Skilled than the Old?" *Journal of Labor Economics* 4: 168–92.

Coleman, Doriane Lambelet. 1996. "Individualizing Justice through Multiculturalism: The Liberals' Dilemma," *Columbia Law Review* 96: 1093–1167.

Cornelius, Wayne A., Philip L. Martin, and James F. Hollifield, eds. 1994. *Controlling Immigration: A Global Perspective*. Stanford, Calif.: Stanford University Press.

DeSipio, Louis. 1996. *Counting on the Latino Vote: Latinos as a New Electorate*. Charlottesville: University of Virginia Press.

Diner, Hasia. 1983. *Erin's Daughters in America: Irish Immigrant Women in the Nineteenth Century*. Baltimore, Md.: Johns Hopkins University Press.

Duleep, Harriet O., and Mark C. Regets. 1997a. "Measuring Immigrant Wage Growth Using Matched CPS Files," *Demography* 34: 239–49.

————. 1997b. "The Decline in Immigrant Entry Earnings: Less Transferable Skills or Lower Ability?" *Quarterly Review of Economics and Finance* 37 (Special Issue on Immigration): 89–208.

Faist, Thomas. 1997. "The Crucial Meso-Level," in Tomas Hammar, Grete Brochmann, Kristof Tamas, and Thomas Faist, eds., *International Migration, Immobility and Development: Multidisciplinary Perspectives*, pp. 187–217. New York: Berg Publishers.

Foner, Nancy. 1985. "Race and Color: Jamaican Migrants in London and New York City," *International Migration Review* 19: 706–27.

————. 1998. "Towards a Comparative Perspective on Caribbean Migration," in Mary Chamberlain, ed., *Caribbean Migration: Globalised Identities*, pp. 47–60. New York: Routledge.

Freeman, Gary P. 1979. *Immigrant Labor and Racial Conflict in Industrial Societies: The French and British Experiences*. Princeton, N.J.: Princeton University Press.

————. 1995. "Modes of Immigration Politics in Liberal Democratic States," *International Migration Review* 19: 881–902.

————. 1998. *Toward a Theory of the Domestic Politics of International Migration in Western Nations*. South Bend, Ind.: The Nanovic Institute, University of Notre Dame.

Friedman-Kasaba, Kathie. 1996. *Memories of Migration: Gender, Ethnicity and Work in the Lives of Jewish and Italian Women in New York, 1870–1924*. Albany: SUNY Press.

Gabaccia, Donna. 1984. *From Sicily to Elizabeth Street: Housing and Social Change among Italian Immigrants, 1880–1930.* Albany: SUNY Press.

————. 1994. *From the Other Side: Women, Gender and Immigrant Life in the U.S. 1820–1990.* Bloomington: Indiana University Press.

Gans, Herbert J. 1997. "Toward a Reconciliation of 'Assimilation' and 'Pluralism': The Interplay of Acculturation and Ethnic Retention," *International Migration Review* 31: 875–92.

Gjerde, Jon. 1985. *From Peasants to Farmers: The Migration from Balestrand, Norway, to the Upper Middle West*: Cambridge: Cambridge University Press.

————. 1996. *The Minds of the West: Ethnocultural Evolution in the Rural Middle West, 1830–1917.* Chapel Hill: University of North Carolina.

Gmelch, George. 1992. *Double Passage: The Lives of Caribbean Migrants Abroad and Back Home.* Ann Arbor: University of Michigan Press.

Green, Nancy L. 1997. "The Comparative Method and Poststructural Structuralism: New Perspectives for Migration Studies," in Jan Lucassen and Leo Lucassen, eds., *Migration, Migration History, History: Old Paradigms and New Perspectives*, pp. 57–72. Bern: Peter Lang.

Guarnizo, Luis Eduardo. 1997. "The Emergence of a Transnational Social Formation and The Mirage of Return Migration among Dominican Transmigrants," *Identities* 4: 281–322.

Gutiérrez, David G. 1998. "Ethnic Mexicans and the Transformation of 'American' Social Space: Reflections on Recent History," in Marcelo M. Suárez-Orozco, ed., *Crossings: Mexican Immigration in Interdisciplinary Perspectives*, pp. 309–40. Cambridge, Mass.: Harvard University Press.

Hammar, Tomas, ed. 1985. *European Immigration Policy: A Comparative Study.* New York: Cambridge University Press.

Hammar, Tomas, and Kristof Tamas. 1997. "Why Do People Go or Stay?" in Tomas Hammar, Grete Brochmann, Kristof Tamas, and Thomas Faist, eds., *International Migration, Immobility and Development: Multidisciplinary Perspectives*, pp. 1–19. New York: Berg Publishers.

Hart, Dianne Walta. 1997. *Undocumented in L.A.: An Immigrant's Story.* Wilmington, Del.: Scholarly Resources Inc.

Hastrup, Kirsten. 1992. "Writing Ethnography: State of the Art," in Helen Calloway and Judith Okely, eds., *Anthropology and Autobiography*, pp. 116–33. London: Routledge.

Hill, Allan G. 1997. "'Truth Lies in the Eye of the Beholder': The Nature of Evidence in Demography and Anthropology," in David I. Kertzer and Tom Fricke, eds., *Anthropological Demography: Toward a New Synthesis*, pp. 223–47. Chicago: University of Chicago Press.

Hochstadt, Steve. 1981. "Migration and Industrialization in Germany, 1815–1977," *Social Science History* 5: 445–68.

Hoerder, Dirk. 1997. "Segmented Macrosystems and Networking Individuals: The Balancing Function of Migration Processes," in Jan Lucassen and Leo Lucassen, eds., *Migration, Migration History, History: Old Paradigms and New Perspectives*, pp. 73–84. Bern: Peter Lang.

Hollifield, James F. 1986. "Immigration Policy in France and Germany: Outputs versus Outcomes," *Annals of the American Academy of Political and Social Science* 485: 113–28.

————. 1992. *Immigrants, Markets, and States: The Political Economy of Postwar Europe.* Cambridge, Mass.: Harvard University Press.

————. 1998. "Migration, Trade, and the Nation-State: The Myth of Globalization," *UCLA Journal of International Law and Foreign Affairs* 3(2): 595–636.

Horowitz, Donald, and Gerard Noiriel. 1992. *Immigrants in Two Democracies: French and American Experience*. New York: New York University Press.

Huber, Gregory A., and Thomas J. Espenshade. 1997. "Neo-Isolationism, Balanced-Budget Conservatism, and the Fiscal Impacts of Immigrants," *International Migration Review* 31: 1031–54.

Ireland, Patrick. 1994. *The Policy Challenge of Ethnic Diversity: Immigrant Politics in France and Switzerland*. Cambridge, Mass.: Harvard University Press.

Jacobson, David. 1996. *Rights across Borders: Immigration and the Decline of Citizenship*. Baltimore, Md.: Johns Hopkins University Press.

Kastoryano, Riva. 1997. *La France, l'Allemagne et leurs immigrés: négocier l'identité*. Paris: Armand Colin.

Kertzer, David, and Dennis Hogan. 1989. *Family, Political Economy, and Demographic Change: The Transformation of Life in Casalecchio, Italy, 1861–1921*. Madison: University of Wisconsin Press.

Kertzer, David I., and Tom Fricke. 1997. "Toward an Anthropological Demography," in David I. Kertzer and Tom Fricke, eds., *Anthropological Demography: Toward a New Synthesis*, pp. 1–35. Chicago: University of Chicago Press.

Kessler, Alan E. 1998. "Distributional Coalitions, Trade, and the Politics of Postwar American Immigration," paper presented at the Annual Meeting of the American Political Science Association, Boston, Mass.

Kibria, Nazli. 1993. *Family Tightrope: The Changing Lives of Vietnamese Americans*. Princeton, N.J.: Princeton University Press.

Kritz, Mary M., Charles B. Keely, and Silvano M. Tomasi, eds. 1981. *Global Trends in Migration: Theory and Research in International Population Movements*. New York: Center for Migration Studies.

Leeds, Elizabeth. 1984. "Salazar's 'Modelo Económico': The Consequences of Planned Constraint," in Thomas C. Bruneau, Victor M. P. da Rosa, and Alex Macleod, eds., *Portugal in Development: Emigration, Industrialization, the European Community*, pp. 13–51. Ottawa: University of Ottawa Press.

Legomsky, Stephen. 1987. *Immigration and the Judiciary: Law and Politics in Britain and America*. Oxford: Oxford University Press.

Lucassen, Jan, and Leo Lucassen, eds. 1997. *Migration, Migration History, History: Old Paradigms and New Perspectives*. Bern: Peter Lang.

Mageean, Deirdre M. 1991. "From Irish Countryside to American City; The Settlement and Mobility of Ulster Migrations in Philadelphia," in Colin G. Pooley and Ian D. Whyte, eds., *Migrants, Emigrants and Immigrants: A Social History of Migration*, pp. 42–61. London: Routledge.

Magnarella, Paul J. 1991. "Justice in a Culturally Pluralistic Society: The Cultural Defense on Trial," *Journal of Ethnic Studies* 19: 65–84.

Massey, Douglas S. 1999. "International Migration at the Dawn of the Twenty-First Century: The Role of the State," *Population and Development Review* 25: 303–22.

Massey, Douglas S., Joaquin Arango, Graeme Hugo, Ali Kovaouci, Adela Pellegrino, and J. Edward Taylor. 1993. "Theories of International Migration: A Review and Appraisal," *Population and Development Review* 19: 431–66.

———. 1994. "An Evaluation of International Migration Theory; The North American Case," *Population and Development Review* 20: 699–751.

———. 1998. *Worlds in Motion: Understanding International Migration at the End of the Millennium*. Oxford: Clarendon Press.

Miller, Kerby. 1985. *Emigrants and Exiles: Ireland and the Irish Exodus to North America*. New York: Oxford University Press.

Miller, Mark J. 1981. *Foreign Workers in Western Europe: An Emerging Political Force*. New York: Praeger.

Mincer, Jacob. 1978. "Family Migration Decisions," *Journal of Political Economy* 86: 749–73.

Moch, Leslie Page, and Louise A. Tilly. 1985. "Joining the Urban World: Occupation, Family and Migration in Three French Cities," *Comparative Studies in Society and History* 25: 33–56.

National Research Council. 1997. *The New Americans: Economic, Demographic, and Fiscal Effects of Immigration*. Washington, D.C.: Commission on Immigration Reform and National Academy of Sciences.

Olwig, Karen Fog. 1998. "Constructing Lives: Migration Narratives and Life Stories among Nevisians," in Mary Chamberlain, ed., *Caribbean Migration: Globalised Identities*, pp. 63–80. New York: Routledge.

Passel, Jeffrey S. 1994. *Immigrants and Taxes: A Reappraisal of Huddle's 'The Costs of Immigration.'* Washington, D.C.: Urban Institute.

Pedraza, Silvia. 1990. "Immigration Research: A Conceptual Map," *Social Science History* 14: 43–67.

Perlmann, Joel, and Roger Waldinger. 1997. "Second Generation Decline? Children of Immigrants, Past and Present—A Reconsideration," *International Migration Review* 31: 893–922.

Portes, Alejandro. 1997. "Immigration Theory for a New Century: Some Problems and Opportunities," *International Migration Review* 31: 799–825.

———, ed. 1996. *The New Second Generation*. New York: Russell Sage.

Portes, Alejandro, and Rubén G. Rumbaut. 1990. *Immigrant America: A Portrait*. Berkeley and Los Angeles: University of California Press.

Portes, Alejandro, and Min Zhou. 1993. "The New Second Generation: Segmented Assimilation and Its Variants among Post-1965 Immigrant Youth," *Annals of the American Academy of Political and Social Sciences* 530: 74–96.

Rothman, E. S., and Thomas J. Espenshade. 1992. "Fiscal Impacts of Immigration to the United States," *Population Index* 58: 381–415.

Rumbaut, Ruben G. 1997. "Assimilation and Its Discontents: Between Rhetoric and Reality," *International Migration Review* 31: 923–60.

Russell, Sharon Stanton. 1986. "Remittances from International Migration: A Review in Perspective," *World Development* 41: 677–96.

Sassen, Saskia. 1991. *The Global City*. Princeton, N.J.: Princeton University Press.

———. 1996. *Losing Control? Sovereignty in an Age of Globalization*. New York: Columbia University Press.

Schmitter, Barbara E. 1979. *Immigration and Citizenship in West Germany and Switzerland*, unpublished Ph.D. dissertation, University of Chicago.

Schuck, Peter H. 1998. *Citizens, Strangers, and In-Betweens: Essays on Immigration and Citizenship*. Boulder, Col.: Westview Press.

Schuck, Peter H., and Rogers Smith. 1985. *Citizenship without Consent*. New Haven, Conn.: Yale University Press.

Simon, Julian. 1984. "Immigrants, Taxes and Welfare in the United States," *Population and Development Review* (March): 55–69.

Smith, Robert. 1997. "Transnational Migration, Assimilation, and Political Community," in Margaret E. Crahan and Alberto Vourvoulias-Bush, eds., *The City and the World: New York's Global Future*, pp. 110–32, New York: Council on Foreign Relations.

Smith, Rogers. 1997. *Civic Ideals: Conflicting Visions of Citizenship in U.S. History*. New Haven, Conn.: Yale University Press.

Smolicz. J. J. 1997. "Australia: From Migrant Country to Multicultural Nation," *International Migration Review* 31: 171–86.

Sowell, Thomas. 1996. *Migration and Cultures: A World View*. New York: Basic Books.

Soysal, Yasemin N. 1994. *Limits of Citizenship: Migrants and Postnational Membership in Europe*. Chicago: University of Chicago Press.

Stack, Carol. 1996. *Call to Home: African Americans Reclaim the Rural South*. New York: Basic Books.

Stark, Oded. 1991. *The Migration of Labor*. Cambridge: Basil Blackwell.

Suárez-Orozco, Marcelo M. 1998. *Crossings: Mexican Immigration in Interdisciplinary Perspectives*. Cambridge, Mass.: Harvard University Press.

Swierenga, Robert. 1981. "Dutch International Migration Statistics, 1820–1880: An Analysis of Linked Multinational Nominal Files," *International Migration Review* 15: 445–70.

Volpp, Leti. 1994. "(Mis)Identifying Culture: Asian Women and the 'Cultural Defense,'" *Harvard Women's Law Journal* 17: 57–101.

Weiner, Myron. 1987. "International Emigration and the Third World," in William Alonso, ed., *Population in an Interacting World*, pp. 173–200. Cambridge, Mass.: Harvard University Press.

———. 1995. *The Global Migration Crisis*. New York: HarperCollins.

Weiner, Myron, and Tadashi Hanami. 1998. *Temporary Workers or Future Citizens? Japanese and U.S. Migrations Policies*. New York: New York University Press.

Wyman, M. 1993. *Round Trip to America*. Ithaca, N.Y.: Cornell University Press.

Yans-McLaughlin, Virginia. 1990. "Metaphors of Self in History: Subjectivity, Oral Narrative, and Immigration Studies," in Virginia Yans-McLaughlin, ed., *Immigration Reconsidered: History, Sociology, and Politics*, pp. 254–90. New York: Oxford University Press.

Zolberg, Aristide R. 1981. "International Migration in Political Perspective," in Mary M. Kritz, Charles B. Keely, and Silvano M. Tomasi, eds., *Global Trends in Migration: Theory and Research in International Population Movements*. New York: Center for Migration Studies.

Zolberg, Aristide R., A. Suhrke, and S. Aguayo. 1986. "International Factors in the Formation of Refugee Movements," *International Migration Review* 20: 151–69.

CHAPTER 1

History and the Study of Immigration

Narratives of the Particular

Hasia R. Diner

In 1990 Roger Daniels, an immigration historian well worthy of his prominence in the field, tried to do something never before attempted. In his syn-
cretic book, *Coming to America: A History of Immigration and Ethnicity in
American Life*, he acknowledged the existence of migration theory and the
possibility that those who hoped to understand the experience of immigrants
to America ought to do so through some kind of theoretical lens. His reference to the work of the British demographer, E. G. Ravenstein, early in the
first chapter of *Coming to America*, in a section entitled "The Laws of Migration" seemed to herald a new era in the history of immigration history. Maldwyn Allen Jones's hardy *American Immigration*, first published in 1960 and
then reissued with an update in 1992, Alan Kraut's *The Huddled Masses*
(1982), and Thomas Archdeacon's *Becoming American* (1983) preceded
Daniels's as books that sought to encapsulate in a single volume "how people
have come from all over the world to North America and how they have formed
the population and society of the United States" (Archdeacon 1983:xi). These
earlier survey books unabashedly avoided referring to, contending with, or
confronting the existence of a body of scholarship called *migration theory*.

So, too, the monumental and authoritative *Harvard Encyclopedia of American Ethnic Groups* of 1980 made no mention of migration theory in either a
separate entry or in the general ones on "Immigration: Economic and Social
Characteristics" and "Immigration: Settlement Patterns and Spatial Distribution." In a way, the *Harvard Encyclopedia* set the tone by which American historians of immigration to the United States snubbed their collective noses at
theory. Immigration to America, the *Harvard Encyclopedia* noted, was of a
"magnitude . . . unmatched in the history of mankind" (Thernstrom and Orlov
1980). The historical geographer David Ward, who wrote the entry on modes
of settlement declared that immigrants to America created "distinctive loca-
tional patterns," and as such dismissed the possibility of fashioning some

overarching theories to explain phenomena (Ward 1980:496). Finally the reference volume provided a useful and comprehensive bibliography, and did so, organized by group, and with no theoretical books and articles included.

Daniels's inclusion of the phrase "migration theory," and his reference to Ravenstein therefore seemed to be going against the paradigm. He admitted, "One needs a kind of generalized conceptual framework within which the experiences of groups and individuals can be structured, compared and contrasted" (Daniels 1990:16). So, unlike other American historians who had tried their hand at the monumental task of writing in a single volume a history of overseas migrations to America, Daniels understood that the vast body of data about people, places, and time ought to be organized around some theoretical model or models.[1] He turned early on in his book to Ravenstein's essays written in 1885 and 1889 as "The Laws of Migration" and presented in the *Journal of the Royal Statistical Society.* "Remarkably," Daniels wrote, "most of Ravenstein's generalizations seem valid to contemporary scholars" (1990:16).

Oddly enough, however, Daniels never returned to Ravenstein, to any other theory or theorist of migration, and went on to author a solid, four hundred-page narrative about immigration devoid of a "generalized conceptual framework." He moved his book along the trajectory of time and group: "Pioneers of the Century of Immigration: Irish, Germans, and Scandinavians," "From the Mediterranean: Italians, Greeks, Arabs, and Armenians," "Eastern Europeans: Poles, Jews, and Hungarians," "Minorities from Other Regions: Chinese, Japanese, and French Canadians," represented some of the chapters within part II, "The Century of Immigration (1820–1924)," proving that for historians of American immigration "when" and "whence" remained the organizing questions.

Rather than charting a new moment in immigration history, Daniels offered the scholarly community another, solid, densely packed, information-laden book on the experiences of *all* of the American people, including the indigenous residents of North America, the forced African migrants who were brought as slaves, alongside the millions who left homes in Asia, Europe, South and Central America, the Caribbean, other parts of North America, the Middle East, from the late sixteenth century through the end of the twentieth. By implication it seems that Daniels wanted to break with tradition and use theory, but ultimately could not.

Daniels's dilemma grew out of the disjunction between history as an enterprise, immigration/ethnic history in particular, and the broad world of academic discourse of the 1990s. Emphasizing the need for interdisciplinarity, scholars in the humanities joined those in social sciences and invoked "theory" as they never had before. They sought expansive, but precise, language by which they could organize large bodies of data drawn from diverse sources and covering almost infinite situations. They engaged in the process of model building that undergirds the theoretical focus, and those models, once fashioned, can be applied to other fitting examples, other situations.

Daniels no doubt *wanted* to join the discursive moment of the 1980s and 1990s. But as a product, and producer, of the field of immigration history, he could not. American historians of immigration and ethnicity have by and large shied away from theory, even when they paid lip service to it. They confess to the intellectual benefits that would enrich their work if they would use it, and the academic cache that accompanies theoretical formulations. But, they continue down a well-trodden road, avoiding theory even as they acknowledge its salience to their project.

American historians' fundamental disinterest in theory is notable. They have, since Marcus Hansen in the 1930s called for a study of immigration (Hansen 1938, 1940), explored the same set of problems that sociologists, anthropologists, demographers, and economists have simultaneously studied. Like scholars in those "harder" fields, scholars whose right to call themselves "social scientists" has been unchallenged, historians have for seventy years been captivated by the almost universality of the migration experience and by a series of interlocking questions about it: Who moves? For how long? Why do some human beings get up and shift residence? Why do others stay put? Why do they migrate when they do? How do they decide where to go? How do they get there? How do they experience on a cultural level the act of leaving one place and relocating elsewhere?

But unlike the practitioners of those disciplines, historians have been disinterested in both creating "laws," to use Ravenstein's term, and in using existing ones to explain their data. Ironically the rise of history as an enterprise coincided with the first studies of migration as a theoretical issue. Scholars in the newly formed history departments in the newly formed universities of the late nineteenth century in England, Germany, and the United States had ample opportunity from the start to learn from their colleagues in the other newly constituted departments of political economy, sociology, and a bit later anthropology. Those scholars, down the hall as it were, understood, like Ravenstein, the significance of the historic dimension. Ravenstein in his formative articles claimed to have surveyed human migrations of the past, and after that immersion in history, he posited his "laws" governing human movements across time and place.

In the century since Ravenstein, an enormous corpus of scholarship from multiple social science disciplines has been available for historians to dip into. Harry Jerome in 1926, in a research project sponsored by the National Bureau of Economic Research, studied immigration to the United States and linked the ebbs and flows in the numbers to the ups and downs of the business cycle. Jerome acknowledged that although he could not find a perfect fit, he did see enough "general similarities in the appearance of the curves" to warrant a theory of why people migrated when they did. Written for policymakers, Jerome's study would have been cogent for even those unfamiliar with economic terms and formulas, yet none of the historians who have been precisely interested in this question have cited or employed his theory (Jerome 1926:240).

Likewise, just as Maldwyn Allen Jones was in the process of preparing *American Immigration*, William Petersen (1958) published "A General Typology of Migration," in the *American Sociological Review*. In 1966, at the moment when immigration and ethnic history as subfields (or a single subfield) within American history emerged, Everett S. Lee published "A Theory of Migration."[2] Both pieces offered, in language not intended just for disciplinary specialists, ideas about the timing, nature, and structure of immigrating populations. Neither piece garnered any attention from American historians who busily had embarked upon the enterprise of writing about Italian, Polish, Irish, Jewish, Swedish, Mexican, Greek, Chinese, Swiss (and so on) immigrants to America in general or to particular places therein.

Lee and Petersen constructed models that have been somewhat replaced by writings of a newer generation of migration scholars, and those theoretical innovations also lay in close reach of historians. Aristide Zolberg (1989), for example, wrote of the need to reconceptualize thinking about migration in light of the great human movements since the 1960s. His call to develop models based on analyses of global inequalities, the role of borders in limiting migrations, and the impact upon (potential) workers of "the dynamics of the transnational capitalist economy," could be applied to explaining the behavior of migrants not only in the contemporary world but also in centuries past. These forces, which could be included in the category of state theory and world systems theory, resonated to the experiences of many of the subjects that American immigration historians have studied. But they avoided these new theories as well as the more classic formulations.

What has developed could be seen as a huge chasm between the ways in which historians have worked as they tried to analyze the vast body of material that confronted them and the workings of social scientists interested in studying migration. In the same decade that American historians turned to the newly published *Harvard Encyclopedia of American Ethnic Groups* with its total absence of interest in the theory extant in the social scientific world, the *International Encyclopedia of Social Sciences* tackled migration and provided for historians a place to go to get a synopsis of current theory, should they want it. One of the authors of the social science reference work's entry on immigration (Peterson 1968) began his piece by defining migration and characterized prevailing ideas about the timing, modes, and typologies of migration as well as how to measure migrations. Brinley Thomas (1968), author of a highly respected book of the 1950s (Thomas 1954), focused on the economic aspects of migration. Importantly, in distinction to the historical enterprise, Thomas and Peterson made only the rarest references to particular groups and the extensive bibliographies; these two essays contained no entries on particular groups or places that either sent or received migrants.

Historians and social scientists obviously approach problems differently. The latter depend fundamentally on models. The former generally cringe at the idea. This disinterest may be endemic to most historians, shaped by their focus on the particular; their training, which requires them to stay close to empirical sources; and a basic orientation to *time* as a key factor. Historians search for transformative moments that divide the past into an analytic "before" and "after." Two Dutch historians who have worked on labor migrations within Europe used particularly dramatic imagery to describe how far apart historians and other social scientists stand when it comes to migration theory: "The migration landscape is full of canyons and fast running rivers. The deepest canyon separates social scientists from historians" (Lucassen and Lucassen 1997:10). The Lucassens rightly understood this distinction as existing between historians and social scientists. But American historians, those who study the history of the United States, emerge as particularly theoretically challenged when compared to Europeanists. Beginning in 1960, when Frank Thistlethwaite delivered a paper at the 11th International Congress of Historical Sciences in Stockholm in which he challenged the prevailing idea that migrations ought to be thought of as unilinear, straight-shot movements from one place to another and as indicators of crisis, European historians have attempted, more than their American counterparts, to turn to theory to explain their data. Following Thistlethwaite's lead are such European historians as Charles Tilly (1978), Leslie Page Moch (1992), James H. Jackson and Leslie Page Moch (1989), New Zealander J. D. Gould (1989), William McNeil and Ruth Adams (1978), and Nancy Green (1991).

Two exceptions of scholars of American immigration need to be mentioned. Dirk Hoerder, a German scholar, has studied German immigration to the United States. His work grew out of European historical traditions with their greater sensitivity to theory, at the same time that it has taken its place among the literature of United States history. Hoerder (1993, 1994) has demonstrated a strong interest in creating analytic categories around his data, framed by an interest in social scientific theories of migration. As such, Hoerder functions as a liminal figure, a Europeanist and an Americanist, and an Americanist who is a European.

Walter Nugent, however, in his 1992 analysis of migrations in the Atlantic world, *Crossings*, stands in a class by himself. Nugent, a relative latecomer to immigration history, had made a distinguished career for himself as a scholar of populism and late-nineteenth-century American political history. In *Crossings* he jumped off from Frank Thistlethwaite's call to cast aside the conventional categories of "emigrant" and "immigrant" and focused instead on the interconnected processes of migration. He particularly wanted to use the data on migrations to interrogate prevailing social science theories about modernization and its impact on demography. Throughout the book he challenged notions of ethnic and national particularism, group distinctions, the reigning assumptions that underlay much of American immigration history. From a theoretical stance, however, Nugent had a greater interest in modernization theory than in migration theory, and he addressed the latter lightly, as it informed his project of dismantling the former.

With the exception of Walter Nugent's book, the literature that makes up the field of American immigration history then stands out as nontheoretical when compared to European scholarship as well as when compared to the social sciences. How can one measure the disinterest of American immigration historians in the enterprise of theory? What standards might be invoked to prove that the goals of historians of immigration history in America and the goals of migration theorists have heretofore remained quite separate? Negative evidence, an absence of theory in the work of a particular cadre of historians would go to some length to show the disinterest, or conversely, the presence of theory would indicate that theoretical concerns inform the field.

One method for arriving at either of these, or the balance between them, might be to scan an array of books and articles produced in the field and examine such issues as: What other works did the authors cite? Which of those works fall into the category of theory? When and how often have authors incorporated theoretical models into their writings? Since our concern here is migration theory, as opposed to theories of ethnic group formation, ethnic identity, or cultural hybridization, we can also ask how much emphasis books in the field of immigration history give to the phenomenon of migration itself. Obviously for an essay of this length it would be impossible to survey all of the books and articles in the field, or even to sample them systematically. Rather a few stellar works will suffice. The Immigration History Society (which I discuss later in more elaborate detail) has offered the Theodore Saloutos Book Award every year since 1983. Intended to honor the best book published in a given year dealing with some aspect of the history of immigration, a few winners of the prize might be reasonable to examine for American historians' embrace of, or disregard for, theory.

George Sanchez's *Becoming Mexican American* garnered the Immigration History Society's highest accolade in 1994. This study of Mexican immigrants to Los Angeles in the period from 1900 until the end of World War II focused on "the related questions of cultural adaptation and ethnic identity." He noted in his introduction that his study revolved around a particular "cultural adaptation," which occurred, "without substantial economic mobility." In those same prefatory remarks he commented on the state of the field. He, like others of his cohort, felt called upon to interrogate previously fixed categories, among them, the notion that the place which immigrants left could be understood as definite and finite. Rather that entity called "Mexico" (or any other "back there") should be thought of as contested, fluid, and in the process of renegotiation. Sanchez further made the point, that "'Mexico,' maybe even more . . . than other nations, was a national community that had to be 'imagined' to exist, particularly given its racial and regional diversity" (Sanchez 1993:9–14).

Becoming Mexican American squarely confronted the immigration issue in the context of what has in American historical studies come to be called "borderland studies."[3] In the borderland, an amorphous zone of multiple populations spanning "fictive" borders, people came and went, constantly in the process of juggling identities and places of residence. Sanchez's Mexican immigrants to Los Angeles come and go. Even though they bade "farewell homeland," and went "across the dividing line," they remained engaged in the world of their premigration homes. When the policies of the U.S. government, or the vagaries of the American economy, as well as the needs of kin back home, intervened, they went back for some duration of time, and as such constantly engaged themselves with the question, "Where is home?"

Law Harsh as Tigers won the Soloutos Prize for 1995. Its author, Lucy Salyer, would no doubt *not* define herself as an immigration historian. Indeed, in the introduction to her book she exposed herself as a composite social and legal historian. Studying the ways in which Chinese immigrants to the United States struggled in, and against, the administrative agencies and federal courts to counteract the harsh restrictions imposed upon their immigration, Salyer confessed that she had stumbled upon immigration as a scholarly issue. She noted:

> I could not have predicted a decade ago that my research interests would lead me into immigration history. My primary aim was to explore the roots of the American administrative state in the Progressive Era. . . . I planned to analyze Federal judicial response to expansion of administrative power [in the Northern District of California]. But as I studied the court docket books, I was struck by the number of cases brought by Chinese litigants. (Salyer 1995:xiii)

Meticulous and complicated, *Law Harsh as Tigers* challenged some fundamental assumptions in immigration history. It dispelled the notion of the "passive" Chinese immigrants, depicted primarily as sojourners, who temporarily settled in America and made no cultural investment in learning the American system. Rather her subjects as individuals and particularly through their Triad (or tongs) societies, ably mastered the judicial process for their own advantage and mounted sophisticated legal campaigns to mitigate discrimination. Likewise, Salyer demonstrated the willingness of the courts to hear their voices. The harsh law had loopholes, and one judge after another found in favor of the plaintiffs, who had more rights than commonly assumed.

Unlike Sanchez, Salyer had little interest in immigration per se, despite the accolades which she won from among the ranks of immigration historians. Little in the book explained *who* those Chinese plaintiffs were, where they came from, why they chose to come to America, and why they waged such vigorous court battles to stay in a place they knew did not want them. Of the immigration process, which Sanchez explored in its complexity, Salyer offered little. Many of the Chinese immigrants fell into the "illegal" category. The California Chinese almost all came from one province, Kwangtung (Canton), and they lived in tightly drawn communities based around their surname or family societies. By implication Salyer built an argument around the idea of exceptionalism. The Chinese *were* exceptional immigrants. No other group of foreign nationals was the subject of such specific discriminatory legislation. Their need to learn how to manipulate the system grew out of their unique place in the American legal system.

The 1996 Saloutos Prize winner would have seemed the most likely to link the world of American immigration history to that of migration theory. Ewa Morawska won the award for her study, *Insecure Prosperity: Small-Town Jews in Industrial America, 1890–1914.* That expectation would have been based on two indicators about Morawska. First, a trained sociologist, Morawska revealed in an appendix, "(Self-)Reflection of a Fieldworker," that the most lasting impact upon her life as a scholar came from her doctoral work in Poland with Florian Znaniecki.[4] Znaniecki, she noted, taught her that "social life can and should be studied by rigorous scientific methods and explained by empirically testable theories." Likewise, she expressed an intellectual debt to Robert Merton, who called for social science based upon a "continuous dialogue between theory and data" (Morawska 1996:256).

Second, Morawska has been a major player in various efforts to bring about a marriage between history and social science. Fittingly, she lived in both worlds, nudging historians to think theoretically and sociologists to consider the implications of time- and group-specific circumstances. In a 1990 article, for example, she wrote of the yawning gap between the two:

> Although they ran parallel for considerable stretches, these two intellectual movements are not sufficiently aware of each other. Students in one discipline "discover" what has been acknowledged and treated in each other's research for quite some time. Not infrequently . . . I hear comments like that of an ethnic historian reacting to the latest "vogue" in immigration research. . . . "But we have known that for a decade!" And an immigration sociologist had a similar response to some new volume put out by ethnic historians: "Well, don't they ever read what we write?" (Morawska 1990:188)

Insecure Prosperity is a remarkable book. It compares Jews of a small, culturally parochial Pennsylvania steel town in their skeletal community, with their sisters and brothers in the infinitely more complex big cities like Pittsburgh and New York. It compares the Jews of Johnstown with Johnstown's other "others," the Slavic industrial laborers, whom Morawaska (1985) had analyzed in her earlier book, *For Bread with Butter.* Within the Jewish enclave of Johnstown she compared the earlier German Jewish residents with her subjects, the newcomers from Eastern Europe, just as she juxtaposed the experiences of children with those of their parents, and probed issues of change over time, by positing generational comparisons.

Insecure Prosperity did operate around a theoretical framework, or, as Morawska (1996:xvii–iii) put it, around a theoretical double "concentric circle." She explored the world of the Jews of Johnstown, compared around these many facets, through theories of "structuration," that is, the interplay of "human action" and "social environment." She unpacked the ways that Jews learned to "maneuver in their situation in the pursuit of the desired goals," employing ideas of Anthony Giddens (1976). Morawska's other theoretical circle focused on the theory of ethnicization, "a process of blending from inside the ethnic group of the old (country of origin) sociocultural patterns with the new—traditions and lifestyles of the dominant (host) society" (1996:xviii). Here, she admitted to being influenced by the well-established sociological model of the dichotomy between *Gemeinschaft* and *Gesellschaft.*

The theories that Morawska ignored, and the material that got short shrift, happened to be those involving the migration process. Surprisingly for the author of the words from *Immigration Reconsidered* about the almost hermetically sealed worlds occupied by immigration historians and immigration sociologists, little of the "stuff" of immigration made its way into the book. Her Jews lived on the edge of survival in Eastern Europe as part of the first chapter of the book. At the end of that chapter, in about four pages, they made their way to Johnstown. By the second chapter they were already recycling old economic relations with their Slavic neighbors and calling upon traditional commercial skills from back home and keeping alive a consciousness that life can always get worse. The migration process and theories that might be employed to explain it got lost.

Each one of the scholars could have either drawn from the theoretical literature on migration or been in the position to formulate their own kind of model.[5] Sanchez, for example, would have been well equipped to look back to Ravenstein or Everett Lee who specifically addressed issues of distance between the point of origin and the point of destination. Mexicans, like French Canadians, Jamaicans, and migrants from the Caribbean, differed from the Chinese immigrants Salyer studied or the Jews Morawska analyzed in that "back home" lay so close at hand. While Sanchez surely explored the back-and-forth phenomenon of the Mexicans in Los Angeles, he did not connect that possibility to either the experiences of others who migrated short distances or to the theoretical literature on precisely that subject. He could have turned to Zolberg whose theories about the impact of state policies indeed directly touched upon the lives of the subjects of *Becoming Mexican American.* Likewise, Morawska could have drawn upon theoretical literature about the size of the immigrant population—her east European Jews in Johnstown—in light of Lee or Peterson. In Morawska's analysis of the fabric of Jewish communal life in Johnstown, size counted for much. Lee and Peterson also used size in their typologies, yet their theories of migration based on size, did not show up here at all. Finally Salyer studied a group of people so eager to live in America that, despite the blatant racism which cast them as inferiors and put them outside of the orbit of citizenship, they continued to come and fought the system so that they could stay. Inherent in much of migration theory lies the issue of motivation: Why do some people at certain moments in the history of their particular homes choose to leave to resettle in certain particular, sought-after destinations? Again, Ravenstein, Lee, Peterson, and even more contemporary theorists like Zolberg presented much theoretical modeling Salyer could have employed—and possibly rejected—had she been interested in writing a book about immigration.

These three authors of Saloutos Prize–winning books share much in common with each other. They wrote outstanding books. Each challenged some long-held assumptions about an individual immigrant group in particular American settings. All three also rushed through the migration experience (or, in the case of Salyer, avoided it completely) in order to get to the heart of their project: the negotiation within the group, and between the group and the larger society, over the nature of identity and community. That being the shared vision, all three authors had no need to glean from the theoretical literature about immigration.[6]

Why would the scholarly group awarding the prize, the Immigration History Society (IHS), routinely choose to honor books that, their excellence notwithstanding, focus so little on the actual set of experiences surrounding immigration? The society was founded in 1965, and in its founding it clearly announced its commitment to the study of migration. It described itself as dedicated to "promote the study of the history of immigration to the United States and Canada from all parts of the world, including studies of the background of emigration in the countries of origin."[7] The next phrase in the IHS's statement of purpose may provide the clue to the conundrum about its decisions and about the field as a whole: it went on to include among its goals and foci, "to promote the study of ethnic groups in the United States, including regional groups in the United States, Native-Americans, and forced immigrants."

American historians of immigration, more than their European peers or their colleagues in the social sciences, are much more interested in ethnicity than in migration. For those who define themselves as immigration historians, who belong to the Immigration History Society, who sit on its prize committee (myself included), and who have written the books that make up the body of scholarship in the field, the narrative of how various groups settled, shaped their communities, and constructed their identities has taken precedence over the analysis of the migration process. That process appeared in the books and articles as a necessary prelude to that which really informed their imagination, the negotiation between identities, the formation of ethnicity.[8]

This phenomenon itself can be unpacked and used to explain the general indifference of American immigration historians to migration theory and the manipulation of models. First, the interest in ethnicity often, although definitely not always, has grown out of the reality that most of the scholars writing have chosen their own group as the subject of their research. They benefit from insider knowledge, and that intimate understanding of the inner life of "the group" often closes off the imperative to place it into a model or type. While they have written in a broad, humanistic framework, and not remotely as narrow chauvinists (an earlier brand of writing labeled "filiopietistic" has long been the model of what should be avoided at all costs), most immigration/ethnic historians in America have been convinced that the specific details of their group, or the group they have decided to study, are worthy of study in and of itself. Concern with the particular has *far* outweighed the interest in creating typologies, categories, or models.

As such, the field has been characterized by a group-by-group approach. Book and articles, dissertations, and the very organization of courses on the undergraduate and graduate level are based around the categories "Irish," "Chinese," "Norwegian," "Jewish," "Haitian," "Italian," "Polish," "Mexican," and the like. Over time the number of groups standing under the umbrella of American immigration scholarship has grown, but the basic mode of analysis has not. In each case, groups of scholars working on particular groups have emphasized in one way or another that their group's story truly stands out as different, notable, and particularly worthy of being told.

Because of this, few scholars have set out to write comparative histories, which would seem to be fundamental to a scholarly format for both the incorporation of existing theories and the creation of new ones.[9] So long as immigration historians set out to study the Italians of Buffalo, the Chinese of New York, or the Czechs of Chicago by themselves, theories of migration serve no real purpose. The experience of each group stands for itself and in and of itself ought to be studied. If, by contrast, historians would try to compare these three groups, then the fundamental structures of their migrations arrayed side by side and analyzed in a comparative framework would call for theory to explain differences or similarities. This comparative approach calls for models, whereas the group approach cannot employ them.

But American scholars of immigration history have refrained from comparative history for both practical and cultural reasons. In the first category, the scholar wanting to compare Italian, Chinese, and Czech immigrants, for example, would need linguistic competence in three radically different languages. Without the ability to read the sources, to deal with primary documents in their own context, the analysis would be derivative and of dubious value. On another level, most ethnic historians believe that the group they are studying deserves to be studied in its own name and that comparative studies often create invidious distinctions that have no place in scholarly discourse.

History itself, as a discipline, has by and large not been a hospitable locus for theory. Historians have been trained to think about time and place as the key variables by which to explain behavior. While historians have long been concerned with the same kinds of issues that anthropologists, economists, sociologists, and political scientists have struggled with—questions of how human beings have organized their lives and why they have done so in particular ways—historians work on the assumption that without knowing the particulars of where and when phenomena took place, no answers are possible. Historians fundamentally say, both directly and indirectly as reflected in the structure of the field, that context is everything and contexts differ from place to place, and change over time. As such, models cannot deal with the variations that the passage of time and the specifics of place mark upon peoples' behaviors. Historians operate close to the sources, and those sources have been grounded in particular moments in time, anchored to particular spots on the globe, and embodied in the experiences of particular people even as they moved from one of those settings to other new ones.

Furthermore, history, as a field that straddles the social sciences and the humanities, considers the narrative format the basic way of presenting its findings. While historians have since the middle of the 1960s and the rise of quantitative history, inspired by sociology, begun to embrace some of the modes of other disciplines, it remains a field committed to telling stories. Even the most notable products of the cliometric moment of the 1970s still presented to readers tales of particular people in particular places, Puritans in Dedham, steelworkers in Pittsburgh, slaves in their plantation communities, and very specific groups of immigrants, who would become "ethnics" creating their enclaves in America.

American historians have one more powerful legacy that prevents them from embracing theory. However much they resist and write against it, they still operate within the idea of American exceptionalism. More so than their European counterparts who seem much more comfortable seizing upon theory, juxtaposing the experiences of groups in widely divergent times and places, American historians remain loyally wedded to an American focus. Not surprisingly, and with few exceptions,[10] scholars of American immigration devote one chapter at most to "back home," a few pages (or, perhaps a short single chapter) to the physical process of migration and then devote the rest of their books to the American narrative, which is indeed what they wanted to study.

They have almost completely ignored the fact that immigrants, leaving the same towns and regions in the places of origin, dispersed themselves all over the world. Their analytic lenses have been trained on America and that has occluded the possibility of seeing migration in a broad global context, a prerequisite for thinking theoretically. As Donna Gabaccia (1997:177) noted in one of the few articles to depart from this practice, "Historians rightly approach global studies with trepidation. . . . Our discipline requires us to respect culture, context, and chronology." Again, American historians do so more than scholars based in other countries.

Therefore, the nature of history as a field, the particular perspective of American history, and the inner dynamics of American immigration history as a field has militated against a conjoining of the study of immigration to the United States and migration theory. The two have gone their separate ways. While they both may be the poorer for it, there is no reason to predict that in the immediate future they will find common ground.

NOTES

1. In the bibliographic essay to *From the Other Side: Women, Gender and Immigrant Life in the U.S., 1820–1990*, Donna Gabaccia (1994:176) directed "Students interested in theories of migration," to "begin with E. G. Ravenstein." She then offered three examples of "more recent work" concerned with theory. Unlike Daniels, Gabaccia did not organize her book around the "group" framework. But she too, despite references studded through the book about theory and theoretical questions, opted for themes in which group experiences would carry the narrative.
2. For an excellent compendium of representative articles dealing with migration theory, see Cohen (1996).
3. See Azaludúa (1987).
4. Znaniecki himself played a pivotal role in American immigration scholarship. He coauthored with W. I. Thomas a monumental five-volume study of Polish immigrants in Chicago, published between 1918 and 1920 (Thomas and Znaniecki 1984).
5. This group-by-group approach to immigration history in the United States is reflected in the full list of Saloutos Book Award winners, and not just the three analyzed here. Of those winners the only ones to deviate from the group approach have been Bailyn (1985), Fuchs (1990), Kraut (1993), and Jon Gjerde (1996). The rest since 1983 have been the study of a particular group in America. See Butler (1982), Wyman (1984), Miller (1984), Mormino and Pozzetta (1986), Ostergren (1987), Fischer (1988), Helweg and Helweg (1990), Hall (1991) and Gjerde (1993).
6. This same kind of group-oriented, empirically based scholarship also describes projects that have won the Immigration History Society's George E. Pozzetta Dissertation Research Award: for 1996, Russell Kazal, "Becoming Old Stock: Religion and the Waning of German-American Identity in Philadelphia, 1900–1930"; for 1997, Nancy C. Carnevale, "Living in Translation: Language and Italian Immigrants in the U.S., 1900–1968"; and for 1998, Richard Sukjoo Kim, "The Dialectics of Nationalism and Ethnicity: Korean Immigration to the United States and Transnational Politics, 1882–1945." Likewise, the winners of the Qualey Prize for the Outstanding Article to appear in the *Journal of American Ethnic History* prove the lack of interest in theory and the group approach. See Barry Chiswick, "The Labor Market Status of Hispanic Men" 7 (fall 1987); Victor A. Walsh, "'Drowning the Shamrock': Drink, Teetotalism, and the Irish Catholics of Gilded-Age Pittsburgh" 10 (fall 1990–winter 1991); K. Scott Wong, "Lian Qichao and the Chinese of America: A Re-evaluation of his Selected Memoir of Travels in the New World" 11 (summer 1992); Bettye Collier-Thomas and James Turner, "Race, Class and Color: The African American Discourse on Identity" 14 (fall 1994); Cheryl Greenberg, "Black and Jewish Responses to Japanese Internment" 14 (winter 1995).
7. The statement of purpose of the Immigration History Society appears on the inside of the cover of the society's journal, *Journal of American Ethnic History.*

8. In 1998, the Immigration History Society voted to change its name to the Immigration and Ethnic Society.
9. Perlmann (1988) and Kessner (1977) are two examples, but the body of scholarship like this is rare.
10. See, for example, Gjerde (1984).

REFERENCES

Anzaldúa, Gloria. 1987. *Borderlands/La Frontera: The New Mestiza.* San Francisco: Spinster/Aunt Lute.
Archdeacon, Thomas. 1983. *Becoming America: An Ethnic History.* New York: Free Press.
Bailyn, Bernard. 1985. *Voyagers to the West: A Passage in the Peopling of America on the Eve of the Revolution.* New York: Alfred A. Knopf.
Butler, Jon. 1982. *The Huguenots in America: A Refugee People in New World Society.* Cambridge: Harvard University Press.
Cohen, Robin. 1996. *Theories of Migration.* Cheltenham, UK: Edward Elgar.
Daniels, Roger. 1990. *Coming to America: A History of Immigration and Ethnicity in American Life.* New York: HarperCollins.
Fischer, David Hackett. 1988. *Albion's Seed: Four British Folkways in America.* New York: Oxford University Press.
Fuchs, Lawrence H. 1990. *The American Kaleidoscope: Race, Ethnicity and the Civic Culture.* Hanover, N.H.: University Press of New England.
Gabaccia, Donna. 1994. *From the Other Side: Women, Gender and Immigrant Life in the U.S., 1820–1990.* Bloomington: Indiana University Press.
———. 1997. "The 'Yellow Peril' and the 'Chinese of Europe': Global Perspectives on Race and Labor, 1815–1930," in Jan Lucassen and Leo Lucassen, eds., *Migration, Migration History, History,* pp. 177–96. Bern: Peter Lang.
Giddens, Anthony. 1976. *New Rules of Sociological Method: A Positive Critique of Interpretive Sociology.* London: Hutchinson.
Gjerde, Jon. 1984. *From Peasants to Farmers: The Migration from Balestrand, Norway to the Upper Midwest.* New York: Cambridge University Press.
———. 1996. *The Minds of the West: Ethnocultural Evolution in the Rural Middle West, 1830–1917.* Chapel Hill: University of North Carolina Press.
Gould, J. D. 1989. "European Inter-Continental Emigration, 1815–1914: Patterns and Causes," *Journal of European Economic History* 8 (3): 593–679.
Green, Nancy. 1991. "L'immigration en France et aux États-Unis, Historiographie comparée," *Vingtième Siècle* 20 (January–March): 67–82.
Hall, Gwendolyn Midlo. 1991. *Africans in Colonial Louisiana: The Development of Afro-Creole Culture in the Eighteenth Century.* Baton Rouge: Louisiana State University Press.
Hansen, Marcus Lee. 1938. *The Problem of the Third Generation Immigrant.* Rock Island, Ill.: Augustana Historical Society.
———. 1940. *The Immigrant in American History,* Arthur M. Schlesinger, ed. Cambridge, Mass.: Harvard University Press.
Helweg, Arthur M., and Usha M. Helweg. 1990. *An Immigrant Success Story: East Indians in America.* Philadelphia: University of Pennsylvania Press.
Hoerder, Dirk. 1993. *People on the Move: Migration, Acculturation, and Ethnic Interaction in Europe and North America.* Washington, D.C.: German Historical Institute.
———. 1994. "Changing Paradigms in Migration History from 'To America,' to World-Wide Systems," *Canadian Review of American Studies* 24 (2): 105–26.

Jackson, James H., and Leslie Page Moch. 1989. "Migration and the Social History of Modern Europe," *Historical Methods* 22 (1): 27–36.

Jerome, Harry. 1926. *Migration and Business Cycles.* New York: National Bureau of Economic Research.

Jones, Maldwyn Allen. 1992 [1960]. *American Immigration.* Chicago: University of Chicago Press.

Kessner, Thomas. 1977. *Beyond the Golden Door: Italian and Jewish Immigrant Mobility in New York City, 1880–1915.* New York: Columbia University Press.

Kraut, Alan M. 1982. *The Huddled Masses: The Immigrant in American Society, 1880–1921.* Arlington Heights, Ill.: Harlan Davidson.

———. 1993. *Silent Travelers: Germs, Genes, and the "Immigrant Menace."* New York: Basic Books.

Lee, Everett S. 1966. "A Theory of Migration," *Demography* 3 (1): 47–57.

Lucassen, Jan, and Leo Lucassen. 1997. "Migration, Migration History, History: Old Paradigms and New Perspectives," in Jan Lucassen and Leo Lucassen, eds., *Migration, Migration History, History*, pp. 9–38. Bern: Peter Lang.

McNeil, William, and Ruth Adams, eds. 1978. *Human Migrations: Patterns and Policies.* Bloomington: Indiana University Press.

Miller, Kerby A. 1984. *Emigrants and Exiles and their Irish Exodus to North America.* New York: Oxford University Press.

Moch, Leslie Page. 1992. *Moving Europeans: Migration in Western Europe since 1650.* Bloomington: Indiana University Press.

Morawska, Ewa. 1985. *For Bread with Butter: Life-Worlds of East Central Europeans in Johnstown, Pennsylvania, 1890–1940.* Cambridge: Cambridge University Press.

———. 1990. "The Sociology and Historiography of Immigration," in Virginia Yans-McLaughlin, ed., *Immigration Reconsidered: History, Sociology and Politics,* pp. 187–240. New York: Oxford University Press.

———. 1996. *Insecure Prosperity: Small-Town Jews in Industrial America, 1890–1940.* Princeton, N.J.: Princeton University Press.

Mormino, Gary R., and George Pozzetta. 1986. *The Immigrant World of Ybor City: Italians and Their Latin Neighbors in Tampa, 1885–1985.* Urbana: University of Illinois Press.

Nugent, Walter. 1992. *Crossings: The Great Transatlantic Migrations, 1870–1914.* Bloomington: Indiana University Press.

Ostergren, Robert C. 1987. *A Community Transplanted: The Trans-Atlantic Experience of a Swedish Immigrant Settlement in the Upper Midwest , 1835–1915.* Madison: University of Wisconsin Press.

Perlmann, Joel. 1988. *Ethnic Differences: Schooling and Social Structure among the Irish, Italians, Jews, and Blacks in an American City, 1880–1935.* New York: Cambridge University Press.

Peterson, William. 1958. "A General Typology of Migration," *American Sociological Review* 23 (3): 256–66.

———. 1968. "Migration: Social Aspects," in David Sills, ed., *International Encyclopedia of Social Sciences,* vol. 10, pp. 286–92. New York: MacMillan.

Ravenstein, E. G. 1885. "The Laws of Migration," *Journal of the Royal Statistical Society* 48: 167–227.

———. 1889. "The Laws of Migration," *Journal of the Royal Statistical Society* 52: 214–301.

Salyer, Lucy. 1995. *Law Harsh as Tigers: Chinese Immigrants and the Shaping of Modern Immigration Law.* Chapel Hill: University of North Carolina Press.

Sanchez, George J. 1993. *Becoming Mexican American: Ethnicity, Culture and Identity in Chicano Los Angeles, 1900–1945.* New York: Oxford University Press.

Thernstrom, Stephan, and Ann Orlov. 1980. *Harvard Encyclopedia of American Ethnic Groups*. Cambridge, Mass.: Harvard University Press.

Thistlethwaite, Frank. 1960. "Migration from Europe Overseas in the Nineteenth and Twentieth Centuries," XIème Congrés International des Sciences Historique, Stockholm 1960, *Rapports, V: Historie Contemporaine,* pp. 32–60. Gothenberg: Almquist and Wiksell.

Thomas, Brinley. 1954. *Migration and Economic Growth: A Study of Great Britain and the Atlantic Economy.* Cambridge: Cambridge University Press.

———. 1968. "Migration: Economic Aspects," in David Sills, ed., *International Encyclopedia of Social Sciences,* vol. 10, pp. 292–300. New York: MacMillan.

Thomas, William I., and Florian Znaniecki. 1984. *The Polish Peasant in Europe and America*, edited and abridged by Eli Zaretsky. Urbana: University of Illinois Press.

Tilly, Charles. 1978. "Migrations in Modern European History," in William McNeill and Ruth Adams, eds., *Human Migrations: Patterns and Policies*, pp. 48–68. Bloomington: Indiana University Press.

Ward, David. 1980. "Immigration: Settlement Patterns and Spatial Distributions," in Stephan Thernstrom and Ann Orlov, eds., *Harvard Encyclopedia of American Ethnic Groups,* pp. 496–508. Cambridge, Mass.: Harvard University Press

Wyman, Mark, 1993. *Round-Trip to America: The Immigrants Return to Europe, 1880–1930.* Ithaca, N.Y.: Cornell University Press.

Zolberg, Aristide R. 1989. "The Next Waves: Migration Theory for a Changing World," *International Migration Review* 23 (3): 403–30.

CHAPTER 2

Demography and International Migration

Charles B. Keely

The discipline of demography is generally divided into two main approaches to population phenomena: formal demography and social demography. Formal demography refers to the mathematical modeling of the population processes of birth, death, and migration. Social demography tries to untangle the determinants and consequences of population processes by focusing on the economic, social, and political causes and repercussions of births, deaths, and migration. The most characteristic example of formal demography is the life table, a mathematical description of what happens to a hypothetical group or cohort of 100,000 people who experience specified death rates at each age interval from birth to death. The life table depends on a series of hazard equations that describe the probability of going from one stage of life (or age group) to the next. The reciprocal of that probability is the probability of death or exiting from the original birth cohort of 100,000. In effect, the life table is a spreadsheet that provides information at each age group of how many people are still alive, the age-specific death rate for that age group, the total number of years lived by the original group, and so on. One can calculate the expectation of life at birth in number of years. In fact, the expectation of life at any age can be calculated for those who have survived to that age.

This abstract model of applying age specific death rates to a hypothetical birth cohort of 100,000 is the basis of practical applications like developing life insurance rates, measuring health outcomes, and other medical and public health interventions. Useful application depends on gathering accurate data on real populations to estimate actual age-specific death rates. Therefore, demographers are also interested in issues of data collection, such as accuracy, definition, and other topics involved in collection of population statistics. While all social scientists should be interested in the technical details of accurate data, demographers, like statisticians, probably pay somewhat more attention to these esoteric methodological issues. This is because demographic data are to a large extent derived from public data sources like censuses, vital events registration systems (birth, death, marriage, and divorce records), and administrative records from automobile registrations to welfare and Medicare usage. These data, in summary form with individual identifiers typically concealed, are public records used for a variety of policy and program objectives.[1]

Beginning in the nineteenth century and throughout the contemporary period, statisticians in the public domain have made giant leaps in professionalizing the collection, processing, and publication of social data collected by official bodies.[2] As can be seen in the example of the life table, demography's unit of analysis is generally a population. The focus is not so much on what happens to a specific individual, but rather what are the probabilities of events happening to a particular proportion of the population. The age-specific death rate for twenty- to twenty-four-year-old males, for example, does not tell us which specific young men died in the year in question, but instead that a particular percentage died. If the same death rate holds for that age-sex group, then in the following year it can be expected that a specific number of twenty- to twenty-four-year-old men will die without knowing the identity of particular individuals.

Formal demography also has made great strides in modeling the process of births in a population. Unlike death, birth has the added complication for modeling purposes that a women can give birth more than once in a lifetime, while death is a unique event. But births are also limited by the capacity of women to conceive and carry to term. So births are limited to the period between menarche and menopause for women and the incidence of those events vary around ages for young girls and older women at the beginning and end of their childbearing life. Additionally, pregnant women do not conceive while pregnant and for a variable period after giving birth (postpartum). The postpartum period varies among women due to their particular chemistry and is also affected by breastfeeding, which has a suppressant effect upon conception that varies by woman. It should be apparent that modeling fertility is more complicated than modeling mortality, but it is possible because probabilities can be specified that take account of individual variations in a large population. The focus on populations, rather than individuals, therefore, allows for more accurate knowledge of birth dynamics in a population due to a probability distribution of events for the population that vary among individuals.

Skipping over detail about fertility modeling in formal demography, it should be apparent that success in modeling fertility and mortality should lead to the ability to model the "natural history" of a population over time that experiences a set of age-specific birth and death rates. This has lead to stable population theory that allows analysis of what happens to a population's size, rate of growth or decline, and age structure through time. This allows too for population projections and for analyses of what changes in birth or death rates will do to a population over time. Early population projection techniques assumed a *closed population*, a population that experienced no in or out migration. This is referred to as *natural increase* (or decrease if mortality outstrips fertility for a period of time). More recently, attention to population projection techniques has incorporated migration assumptions and the formal properties of the impact of a constant rate or number of net migrants on a population have been analyzed (Coale 1972; Edmonston and Passel forthcoming; Espenshade, Bouvier, and Arthur 1982; Keely and Kraly 1978).

Demographers typically develop a series of projections (usually high, medium, and low variants, referring to assumed levels of fertility). The demographer or statistical agency is implying that it expects the high- and low-projected estimates to be realistic bounds around the "true" value. The medium level is usually a midpoint estimate between the high and low estimates. This tradition grew because most projections in the twentieth century, when these techniques were refined, were concerned with rapid population growth. Mortality was generally expected to remain close to prevalent levels or to decline slightly. The policy issue of interest was fertility levels (specifically whether they were going to decline) and the impact of high fertility on population size and age structures. The interest in rapid population growth was related to the impact of such growth on economic performance and development.

Note that projections are not necessarily forecasts or predictions. One can do an unrealistic projection to show the difference between a hypothetical scenario (such as immediate decline in fertility to replacement level in a developing country) and some other realistic scenario. The replacement fertility projection is not a forecast in any sense, but rather a heuristic device to illustrate the effect of a high fertility rate in a mathematical exercise. Within the tradition of providing a range of projections, the range is precisely that; the high and low levels are presented as realistic alternatives. In that case, any specific projection based on a fertility rate within the high and low range is possible and no particular projection should be assumed to be more probable.

Some demographers, however, and many users of population projection series use the medium as if it were the "most likely." For example, the abstract of an article about population projections from the Census Bureau written by Bouvier (1996) states: "According to the medium projection (or preferred scenario). . . ." In the introduction to another piece on these projections Bouvier and Martin (1993) note: "This projection is based on the Census Bureau's middle or most likely scenario." Although it may seem intuitively correct that the middle values are more likely, this is not statistically correct and can be fundamentally misleading. Because the person making a projection does not know what an essential value (such as a fertility rate) actually will be in the future, he or she is estimating what is considered to be reasonable bounds. Any level within those bounds is presented as a reasonable possibility, and no one value is considered as more likely than any other, including the midpoint estimate.

A careful analyst will also admit that even the bounds are estimates that experience might possibly prove to be incorrect.

Population projections, like all projections when they are used to forecast the future, are only as good as the assumptions about future rates and the accuracy of the information about the starting population projected into the future. A noted contemporary demographer, Nathan Keyfitz (1981), analyzed actual population projections from 1939 through 1968 from reputable organizations like the United Nations Population Branch, the World Bank, and the U.S. Census Bureau that used the best available techniques. Keyfitz concluded that because of unknowable changes in vital rates of births and deaths—and birthrates have the more powerful influence—projections beyond twenty years begin to become unstable in their accuracy, at least as measured by the success by such agencies to date.

Before moving to a discussion of international migration, it should be noted that demography includes a focus that tries to explain why the birth and death rates are at certain levels in a population and why they change. Social demography seeks to explain the causes of levels and trends in vital rates as well as to analyze the consequences and implications of changes in fertility, mortality, age and sex structure, and other characteristics of a population. Social demography borrows from other social sciences to provide the theories to test explanations of demographic phenomena. Demography, therefore, contributes to other social sciences by providing the formal models that quantify the operation of the properties of a population that is dynamic over time due to births, deaths, and two-way migration. In turn, demography borrows theoretical orientations of other social sciences to explain changes in parameters of models. Demographers are typically trained in another discipline, usually sociology or economics (and to a lesser but growing extent in political science or anthropology). Therefore, explanations, for example, of why birthrates change over time, typically rely on economic theories at both the macro- and microlevels and sociological theories related to changes in gender roles, family structure and formation, and other aspects of social structure. Political science brings in the role of government policy and its impact on taxation, medical innovation, public health, foreign aid, and other policy measures that both cause and are shaped by changes in demographic dynamics. The political dimension in the form of immigration law and policy is particularly relevant for international migration.

Demographers have a propensity to integrate the theoretical insights from different disciplinary perspectives. Of course, other social scientists approach the explanation of population phenomena in a holistic way, giving due notice to the insights from a variety of social science traditions. As a complex social phenomenon, population structure and change is not confined simply to economic or sociological variables, or any narrow disciplinary view. While great strides are made by the specialized development of individual social sciences, as has been the case in natural sciences, it is also clear that social phenomena have complexity and richness that require crossing disciplinary barriers to understand. When approaching human migration, therefore, the discipline of demography comes with a number of questions, tools, and approaches that have proved fruitful for analyzing the birth and death experiences of human populations.

Demographers typically approach any issue with questions about the data to be used. Although there are technical issues even about the definition of a death or a birth, generally the event is straightforward. What, however, is a migration? In its most basic referent, migration deals with a change of residence. This assumes there are identifiable old and new residences. If a person takes up a "temporary" residence, then there are complications. If residence means the place where one usually sleeps and takes some meals and keeps the daily needs for living, like clothes, then many people take up temporary residence from their usual place of abode. Going off to college and going to a summer home are examples of typical moves to a temporary residence. A decision has to be made whether to count such a move as a migration or not, typically involving some measure of time spent in the new residence. By contrast, short business trips and holidays are generally not classified as migrations. Data are collected on travel patterns because they are useful to the transportation and hospitality industries that cater to business travelers and vacationers. But a person's original intent to visit some place for a short period may turn into a very long stay or even a permanent move. Therefore, it sometimes happens that a migration, in the sense of a change in usual abode, has not clearly taken place until after a period of time lapses. Original intent is not always definitive.

There is not one correct answer to the question of what is a migration. Rather, a decision has to be made about definition that provides information useful to the collector and intended users of data, with due attention to trying to harmonize definitions across data sets to allow for comparability. In the case of international migration, each country has its own immigration laws and regulations. What is of interest to administrators and law enforcers across various countries is not always the same. Coming up with common definitions, data to be collected, and public reports to be made available is extraordinarily difficult (Kraly and Gnanasekaran 1987.) The United Nations Statistical Commission has recommended a stay of one year or more as a criterion of an international move, regardless of the specific visa category that permitted a change of residence that exceeded one year.

The study of migration generally focuses on changes or residence that involve crossing from one political unit to another, such as a county, a province, state, or international border. The focus on moves across political boundaries has both a theoretical and practical root. Practically, changes of residence across a political boundary are more liable to be recorded or counted. The existence of data requires that the move be important enough to some governmental or other agency that it gets counted. Some periodic national censuses, like the U.S. decennial census of population and housing, collect data on all changes of residence.[3] In that case, a change of usual residence is counted, even if a political boundary was not crossed. Administrative records about visas and entry and exit control at borders, which are collected for immigration control purposes, provide the bulk of data on the levels and characteristics of international migration. These data, it should be underscored, are collected for administrative and policing reasons, and not specifically to test research hypotheses about the determinants and consequences of migration.

Theoretically, moves over boundaries would seem to have more impact by changing the population characteristics of the old and new political units of the migrant's residence. When there is large-scale mobility in a population in general or in some specific time period, then social, economic, and political impacts can be great indeed. In the United States, for example, about 20 percent of the population changes residence in each ten-year period between censuses. Rapid suburbanization can have important impacts on the need for schools, social services, and other governmental requirements. In major cities of the United States, there has been a movement out of central cities by native born and an influx by immigrants. While the total size of the population changes is dampened by the opposite in and out flows, the age, socioeconomic characteristics, language usage, and many other aspects of social and economic life that affect cities can be greatly altered, not to mention taxation, housing stock, and other infrastructure that are powerfully affected by the population change. Migration, therefore, typically refers to change of usual residence that includes crossing a political boundary. Data can count the size of the movement in a given time period, the flow, or the cumulative number of migrants, the stock. The stock can be increased or decreased in any period by in and out migration or deaths to previous migrants.[4]

The example of the cities losing native-born population but gaining in immigrant population illuminates the importance of gross versus net migration. For any given area in a set period of time, there is usually migration in and out of the territory. Gross in-migration is the total number of people who enter an area; the gross out-migration includes those who leave; and net migration is the in migration minus the out migration. All these numbers can be important for policy or program purposes, as well as useful for analysis.

Because demographers focus on populations, the use of rates is important. Sometimes the word *rate* is used quite carelessly and can lead to confusion. A rate reflects the percentage of a population at risk that experiences the event in question. It is not always so easy to specify or quantify exactly who is at risk. Sometimes compromises are made. For example, a marital fertility rate refers to the births to married women divided by the number of married women times one hundred. We know, however, that some married women are either already pregnant or for another reason, like sterility, are not at risk of becoming pregnant in the time period. Nevertheless, the total married is used as the divisor because it would be impossible to determine exactly what proportion of married women is actually at risk. But the compromises often lead to more than minor quibbles. For example, the usual "divorce rate" reported is the number of divorces in a year divided by the number of marriages in that year. Clearly more people are at risk of divorce than just the newlyweds in that year. It could even happen that such a "rate" could exceed one hundred, if divorces outnumbered marriages in a given year. The usually reported "divorce rate" is really a ratio of divorces to marriages that took place in a year. Ratios can be very helpful for some analyses. But to use a ratio as a rate is incorrect and misleading. If the ratio of marriages to divorces, for example, is 1 to 1, it is incorrect to multiply the stock of married people by 100 percent and conclude that that will be the number of divorces for the currently married. Because there is one divorce for each marriage in one particular year does not mean that all marriages will end in divorce.

Demographers focus on another important distinction that can have major implications for analysis. The distinction is between a cohort and a period effect. A cohort is defined as all the people who experience an event in a specified time period. The baby boomers refers to the cohort of births from 1947 to 1967. Often a cohort refers to persons born in a given five- or ten-year period or who enter school or college in a given year. A cohort experiences a specific history that may affect them differently than another cohort born earlier or later. People born in the 1920s came of age during the Depression and experienced World War II as young adults. Baby boomers experienced a period of relative affluence as children and the Vietnam era as young adults. As these cohorts went through stages of their life cycles, they lived in different contexts.

Nevertheless, both cohorts went through life stages of early childhood, adolescence, marriage and family formation, and so on. Women who bore children in the baby-boom years experienced a period effect because both older and younger women had more children due to postwar "catch-up" fertility and the relative affluence of the 1950s and early 1960s. The baby boomers themselves, and their children, the Generation X, experienced a period effect of later marriage, delayed childbearing, and lower fertility than their parents and grandparents. Therefore, that a person lives through her twenties, thirties, and forties affects fertility, but so does the specific historical period when one is twenty, thirty, or forty. Baby boomers and their parents both experienced medical advances such as the widespread availability of antibiotics, inoculations for polio, better treatments for heart disease and cancers. Thus, both experienced a period effect that will have an impact upon longevity of each cohort because they were both alive, but at different ages, in the same period. Cohort and period effects are common in analyzing marital and fertility experience and causes of death.

Likewise, when one migrated and how old one was when he or she migrated can both affect adaptation. Migration is usually more likely for young adults, a fact that would be considered a cohort effect. But specific historical experiences may lead to increased or decreased migration of all age groups. War, restrictive immigration laws, economic depressions, or other circumstances may motivate more or less migration for all age groups and thus create a period effect.

Finally, demographers spend time analyzing the composition of a population, looking at age and sex structure, marital statuses, education and skills, dependency ratios (proportion of old and young non-working-age to the working-age population). Population characteristics and population structure affect not only demographic dynamics like fertility, mortality, and population growth but also the impacts on sending and receiving societies socially, economically, and politically. It is not enough to know how many migrate: one should also know important characteristics of the migrant population. For example, some propose to turn to immigration to supply younger workers in order to shore up pension systems of countries with aging populations. The "replacements" are not just workers; they also bring other characteristics and become members of society. The number of immigrants needed to "make up" for prior low fertility, which is what causes aging populations in the developed world, is large and must be admitted annually for a prolonged period. What seems like a simple, straightforward idea—use immigrants to solve social security funding problems—can lead to large-scale social change. It is a policy suggestion sure to lead to social and political controversy if vigorously pursued (see Coleman 1992 and 1995, for a discussion of Europe).

Social demographers borrow theories from other disciplines to explain international migration. A major difficulty often noted in the migration literature is developing a comprehensive theory that takes account of both voluntary and forced migration. This is a particularly vexing problem for international migration analysis because refugee flows (as well as other types of "involuntary" or "forced migration" like flight from natural disasters play a large role in the policy arena. The numbers are not trivial in the twentieth century.

Part of the difficulty is the names used for the phenomena. *Voluntary migration* is usually used synonymously with terms like *economic migration*. This is contrasted to *forced* or *involuntary migration* caused by man-made or natural disasters. Man-made disasters include the persecution of racial, ethnic, and religious groups or political dissenters and the flight due to the devastation of war. The problem is that all migration includes elements of choice and pressure. Not all people in groups targeted for persecution leave a country. Not all economic migration is without some coercion on the migrant's decision making. It is also clear that refugee flows are quickly followed by some returns (Larkin, Cuny, and Stein 1991). Why do some people return quickly, while others take longer or even struggle against ever returning?

Voluntary-involuntary and refugee-economic distinctions attempt to make hard and fast categories that fail to capture the complexity of human motivation and decision making. Nevertheless, refugees are a distinct class of persons in international law. States have signed international conventions that govern issues of protection and assistance to be afforded to refugees. Who is classified as a refugee by a state or by an international agency mandated to carry out international conventions makes a difference. What causes people to flee a country and to seek designation as refugees, which results in countries accepting obligations under international law, may be different from international migration caused primarily by natural disaster or for economic or social purposes like family reunion. The results or impacts for both sending and receiving countries can be dissimilar.

International migration is different in many respects from domestic migration. As Zolberg (1981:4) has stated: "Microanalytic theorists make no significant distinction between domestic and international migration. These theorists tend to treat barriers restricting exit or entry, deliberate recruitment efforts, or forced departures, as mere error factors which mar otherwise elegant, value-free equations." To a large extent, this continues to be the case.

Recent appraisals of international migration theory (Massey et al. 1993, 1994) analyze what is usually called economic migration—that is, more or less voluntary migration intended both as temporary and permanent to make money. The reviews do not tackle migration to flee persecution or war dangers. Nor do they take account of laws by sending or receiving countries that facilitate or inhibit international migration.[5] Massey et al. (1993), in the first of a pair of articles developed as a committee of the International Union for the Scientific Study of Population, describe theories that attempt to explain the origin and perpetuation of international migration. Theories about the initiation of international migration are categorized into four sorts of economic explanations and one political economy approach known as world systems theory.

Neoclassical macroeconomic theory explains migration flows as the result of wage differentials and the probability of obtaining a job in the form of unemployment rates. Neoclassical microeconomic theory focuses on the corresponding individual choice facing potential migrants in places with different wages and probabilities of finding work. What the migrant brings in the form of human capital also figures into the decision. The "new economics of migration," linked to a large extent with the work of economist Oded Stark, challenges neoclassical theory by moving the decision-making unit from the individual to family or household units. Migration is one of a number of options of a unit that allows it to control risks for the welfare of the whole unit. Particularly in less-developed countries, access to credit and well-institutionalized insurance markets lead a family or household unit to diversify its income generating portfolio (which members work where). Therefore, not only wage differentials but also risk diversification can come into play. Internal and international migration may be quite intertwined in the various risk strategies pursued by households. For policymakers, migration flows can be influenced not only by wages and availability of work but also by development of access to credit and insurance markets. In fact, policies that result in higher mean income may even produce more migration if poorer households do not share in the economic gain.

The dual labor market is the fourth economic theory reviewed by Massey et al. to explain the initiation of migration that focuses on the economies of the receiving countries. Dual labor market theory switches the focus from an individual or household decision-making level to the institutional context of economic structure and needs. Migration is the result of needs of industrial economies and not push factors in sending countries. The needs in industrial economies result from structural inflation, motivational problems stemming from the social meaning and mobility prospects connected with various occupations, economic dualism related to capital and labor costs in market economies, and the demography of labor supply.

Structural inflation refers to what would happen if the simpleminded idea were inaugurated of merely raising wages to recruit for unpleasant jobs. If such wages are raised, then managers' wages go up and workers in other higher prestige jobs would demand raises. Wage effects would ripple through the economy to reinstitute a wage hierarchy. Access to labor willing to work at relatively low wages allows all workers to be disciplined and wage levels to be held in check. Motivation relates to the issues of social prestige arising from specific jobs. When a job is at the bottom of the ladder with little status and few occupational mobility prospects, worker motivation becomes difficult. Migrants may have few problems with status if the job pays a wage that allows a migrant to send money home at higher rates than could be made at home. The standard of comparison for the migrant is not the host society. Likewise, a migrant may see low-paying, low-status jobs as a foot in the door. The job may be "dead end," but the migrant sees a brighter personal future in terms of job changing and upward mobility. The significant reference group and relative deprivation are typically different for immigrants than for native born. Economic dualism refers to using labor to increase or decrease production. Capital investment is consonant with meeting basic demand. Increased demand is met with more labor that can be laid off in slack demand periods. The cost of idled labor is borne by the worker who is unemployed. Idled capital is a cost to the producer. Migrants, therefore, are convenient to meet variations in demand, like seasonal variations, without needlessly tying up capital.

Finally, dual labor theorists note the relative unavailability of traditional sources of labor for low-status and low-paying jobs: women and teenagers. Changes in women's roles related to marriage, child rearing, and careers mean fewer women are available to take low-paying jobs until marriage or a first birth. Likewise, teens who took jobs for extra spending money and who derived status from their families and not after-school jobs are also less available. Sociodemographic changes related to female labor force participation and smaller birth cohorts means fewer persons in the traditional pools available. Migrants fill the bill.

World systems theory is a variety of political economy theory that proposes bifurcation of the world economy related to capitalist penetration from richer, industrial, market (capitalist) economies to poorer nations or the periphery. The search for land, raw materials, new markets, and labor upsets traditional economies and mobilizes labor for migration internally and internationally to meet the needs of core capitalist countries. Material and ideological links complete the relationship of dependency of periphery on the core. International labor flows in the opposite direction of flows of capital and goods to the benefit generally of the core. These economic theories take little note of controls on exit or entry by governments. It is assumed that the economic forces always trump in explaining migration flows, regardless of borders, laws, or restrictions.

Massey and his colleagues go on to explore theories that explain the continuation of migration flows once they have started. Network theories postulate that the existence of family, friends, and acquaintances in a receiving country reduces the costs and risks of migration by related people in the sending country. Therefore, changes in employment rates in a receiving country may be offset by having connections that make migration less costly to undertake and have increased assurance of getting a job through the help of one's networks. Additionally, once a flow has started, for-profit and not-for-profit organizations grow that want the flows to continue. These can form support groups for migrants and lobbying forces to permit continued migration. Finally, the theory of cumulative causation posits that each act of migration changes the social context, generally in the direction of increasing the probability of future migration. Income distribution, the organization of agrarian production reducing labor demand in sending areas, and a culture of migration all make future migration more likely.

All these theories are linked together in a perspective, sometimes labeled systems theory, which systematically describes the empirical generalization that over time stable patterns of international migration flows grow up between countries. Sometimes these are regional flows to one or a few countries and sometimes the flows are from distant sources related to the destination country by historical ties of colonialism, military alliances, or trading relationships. One can think, for example, of a migration system between the English-speaking Caribbean and England that transformed into a pan-Caribbean and U.S. pattern. One can speak of a Mediterranean migration system involving the Maghreb, southern Europe, and parts of southeastern Europe. Or a changing South African system is evolving based on prior relationships of labor mobility to South Africa, but developing in new political and economic ways with the political change away from apartheid.

In a later article, Massey et al. (1994) tried to test these theories in the context on the North American case, an example of a regional migration system. In a 1998 book, Massey et al. extended the test of theories to data from Europe, the Persian Gulf region, Asia and the Pacific, and South America. They conclude that each of the theories garners some evidence of support, although some had more than others. They rarely encountered negative evidence. Their biggest problem was a lack of evidence, often related to lack of appropriate data, rather than contrary evidence.

As mentioned previously, the theories that Massey et al. (1993, 1994, 1998) reviewed did not address political variables in any systematic sense. Weiner (1985) developed a way of analyzing the role of entry and exit rules and their impact on flows and the patterning of flows among different countries. He proposed five rules of entry and exit. Entry rules are: unrestricted entry; promotional entry rules; selective entry rules; unwanted or restrictive entry rules; and prohibition entry rules. Exit rules proposed are: prohibition exit rules; selective exit rules; permissive exit rules; promotional exit rules; and expulsive exit rules. The symmetry is clear. Weiner suggests a five-by-five table in which the twenty-five pairings permit classification. One can think of examples for the various boxes and develop hypotheses about the probability and frequency of flows and some characteristics like probable size and compositional elements of flows. The pairings of entry and exit rules can also usefully indicate something about the political systems of the countries and the relations among countries and a possible role for negotiation about migration issues in international relations. Weiner's attempt is to place migration in the wider context of international relations, a topic taken up by Mitchell (1992) and his coauthors looking at migration and international relations in the Americas and in this volume by Hollifield.

The political dimension of international migration suggests the perennial nettlesome problem of accounting for refugee flows. Independent work by Aristide Zolberg and Astri Suhrke led to their collaboration with Sergio Aguayo (1989) on a theoretical and descriptive study of contemporary refugee flows in the developing world. Building on this earlier work, Keely (1996) proposed a theory on refugee production and an explanation of the international community's response to refugee flows in the form of a refugee regime. The theory locates the genesis of refugee production in the structure and operation of the "nation-state" system and its inherent conflicts and instabilities. Refugee production is explained by the problem of states trying to reconcile and manage the contradiction of the norm of a single constitutive nation in each state with the reality of multinational states. Further, ideological differences on the structure of the state and society and the possibility of state failure and implosion combine to explain refugee flows in the legal sense that states use to define the class of people for whom international protection and assistance has been agreed. The international refugee regime is comprised of conventions, international organizations led by the UN High Commissioner for Refugees, nongovernmental organizations, and the host of practices and precedents built up since early collective action in 1921 under the League of Nations. This regime is supported by states to provide the protection and relief to persons who cannot obtain normal protection a state should provide its members. Thus the refugee regime, including the specifics of definitions used to allocate international protection and assistance, stems from states' failures to act as states are supposed to act. Resulting flows of unwanted migrants to escape violence and persecution are seen as a system failure and require collective action to try to contain and control and ultimately return the system to an equilibrium in which all people belong somewhere and in fact receive the protection of the state to which they belong.

The demography of refugees, in the sense of not only the numbers but also the fertility and mortality experiences under great duress, is only beginning to be addressed systematically (Reed, Haaga, and Keely 1998). One great difficulty is data collection under difficult circumstances, especially when human suffering would seem to dictate that data collection is a luxury. Better understanding and improved practices in reaction to extreme duress require attention to data collection and analysis using inventive and minimally intrusive ways to collect information to understand current situations and improve future performance.

Demography can help in the analysis of important social issues and proposed solutions. Three examples illustrate the policy contribution demography can make. Many industrial countries are concerned with the effects of low fertility on population age structure, and, by extension, on the labor force and the viability of government pension systems. Low fertility after the postwar baby boom has led to an aging of the population and concern whether a vital economy needs a younger age structure and whether there will be enough workers in the future to support retired persons collecting pensions from what are essentially income redistribution schemes. Suggestions to address the issue include raising the retirement age and increasing payroll taxes. Another is to increase immigration to help population growth (or stem its decline), have a younger workforce, and increase the ratio of workers to retirees.

Keyfitz (1981) pointed out that it would require very large numbers of immigrant over a long period to substitute for the effects of lowered fertility as experienced by contemporary industrial societies. Large, sustained immigrant flows could have a population impact similar to increased fertility in terms of population size and age structure. Large, sustained immigrant flows, however, are not politically sustainable because they would probably change other compositional aspects of a country's population, such as ethnicity, religion, or race, thus altering their identity. Periodically, one hears calls for immigration to counter the effects of low fertility. Coleman (1992, 1995, 1998), citing the work of others, makes the argument that large-scale immigration could lead to maintaining a country's population size, but it would not stop population aging. In a society with below-replacement fertility, a policy of maintaining population size through immigration would mean eventually that immigrants would become a larger part of society. A policy of maintaining a younger age structure would require even more immigration, resulting in large population growth. To maintain the current age structure in the European Union given current fertility and mortality, would require 4.5 million immigrants a year by 2007 and 7 million per year by 2024 (European Commission 1996, cited in Coleman 1998). Current immigration in the European Union is well below 1 million. Demographic analysis can show that a policy prescription to counter the effects of low fertility by immigration is not without other costly population and social impacts.

A second policy issue is the social impact of immigration on the racial and ethnic composition of a society. This line of argument and use of projections is more typical of the United States, but it has its European protagonists also. Generally attempts are made to estimate future proportions of racial and ethnic minorities if immigration at current levels continues (Edmonston and Passell forthcoming). Such projections have pitfalls in addition to the usual problems of estimating future fertility. Projections of ethnic and racial groups requires decomposing a society into each group and separately projecting them into the future. This requires estimates of future birth and death rates for each group, as well as estimates of the rates of intermarriage among the groups into the future and of rules for classifying racially and ethnically the offspring of intermarriage. One must also assume that current racial and ethnic categories, and their social meaning, will continue unchanged into the future just as they are today. For example, in order to project the Hispanic population in the United States to 2050, one must assume that "Hispanic" will continue to mean exactly what it means today socially. The history of ethnicity in the United States is not consonant with such an assumption. The social meaning of prior "minority groups" such as Italian, Jewish, and Catholic, have changed markedly from the heyday of immigration at the turn of the twentieth century, and even as late as the post–World War II period.

Complications related to changes in the social meaning of attributes of people calls into question simpleminded notions like "demography is destiny." Brimelow (1995) used that idea to oppose immigration on the grounds that immigrants were different—and by implication could never be like "us." The "us" in current debates refers to "Europeans," as opposed to Asians and Latin Americans who make up the bulk of today's immigrants to the United States. What is conveniently forgotten is that at the turn of the century, immigrants from Europe—Italians, Poles, Jews—were considered not just inferior but also as threats to the gene pool who would mongrelize the race. Such rhetoric has been abandoned, and in the meantime the "wretched refuse" has been transformed into "Europeans," the traditional source of the American population. To assume such social transformations cannot ever happen again and that today's minority groups will be forever fixed in American society requires a leap of faith.

What is the record on integration of immigrants and changes in behavior? Here demography can also provide useful information. If one looks at integration of immigrants in terms of generations, typically three generations in the United States has led to convergences in indicators such as educational attainment, fertility, income, and many other social indicators. Race has continued to be the great divide in American society. Social policy discussions on multiculturalism avoid the underlying issue, which is not cultural, but interaction and mobility in the workplace, in residence, and in family formation (intermarriage). Greater interaction—intermarriage is the litmus test—has led to greater homogenization of the earlier immigrants, who now appear to be European. As early as the 1950s, social commentators were worried about overhomogenization of the "organization man," the suburbs, and that great leveler, the wasteland of television. This contrasts with earlier concerns about the unassimilability of and genetic pollution caused by southern and eastern Europeans. Demographers and sociologists, along with historians, need to develop further dialogue across disciplines about immigrant integration. More work needs to done on second- and third-generation behavior of the more recent immigrant groups from Asia and Latin America. Too great a focus on the first or immigrant generation and underemphasis on the passage of time and its effects is too static an approach to the study of the effects of international migration on American society, or any society.

The social science of demography plays a broadly contributing role for the study of international migration. Its analytic tools stemming from formal demography provide insights into the effects of migration on population size, structure, and dynamics and provide modeling techniques related to stable population theory and population projections. The disciplinary penchant for attention to data quality helps provide analysts from other disciplines some assurance that issues of definition, collection, data reporting, and other technical matters are attended to. Attention to important fundamental distinctions, such as cohort and period effects or stocks and flows, come almost as second nature to demographic scholars. This helps instill some definitional and analytic precision and clarity in a field that is complex and hampered with data problems.

Data availability and quality are typically problematic for the study of international migration, as is frequently the case with much social science data, given the complex nature and ongoing character of social phenomena and the dependence on administrative data collected for purposes other than research. Attention to population variables often can enlighten by clarifying changes in the size or structure of the society undergoing concomitant social changes. Changes in birth cohorts or marriage patterns, for example, can affect labor supply and thus provide inducements to seek immigrant labor.

Because most demographers are also trained in another social science, they often cross disciplinary boundaries in search of theoretical explanations. Because social demography is theoretically eclectic, demographers studying migration are theoretically comfortable crossing disciplinary lines. International migration involves many aspects of society—the economic, the political, the social—therefore, the subject begs for interdisciplinary perspectives. It is no accident that many scholars of international migration are demographers. No one, of course, should look to demography to supply a unified theory of migration generally, or even of international migration. But, any satisfying theory will incorporate the insights and utilize the techniques of demographic analysis to understand what is, among other things, a basic component of the population dynamics of societies undergoing change.

NOTES

1. Suppression of individual identifiers is to ensure privacy, but note that, because demography focuses on a population as a unit of analysis, the probabilities of events or their consequences in the group, rather that the specific identity of individuals, are of interest. Therefore, public policy analysis and knowledge of social reality is consonant with the public value of individual privacy.

2. Statistical information can also be used for nefarious purposes, and statisticians collaborate in those projects. Seltzer (1998) details a less than proud history of cooperation with the Nazi final solution and, in contrast, but also the use of statistics at the Nuremberg trials.

3. The question typically takes the form of place of residence one or five years ago. Thus, any move in the period is recorded and comparison of the political unit of residence five years ago and at the time of the census allows for estimates of movements across boundaries. This sort of question misses migration by those who are deceased at the time of the census, those who moved before the one- or five-year reference period, or those who moved but returned to their original address within the one- or five-year period. Therefore, these questions underestimate total migration.

4. In some countries there is an interest in the stock of "foreigners." This loose term does not necessarily refer to the stock of migrants from foreign countries or the stock of those who are foreign born. It refers to noncitizens. In this case, the stock of foreigners can include children born in the country to noncitizen parents. Some countries are interested in foreigners in the sense of noncitizens. This would not be a count of the stock of international migrants, except in the case where not one international migrant became a citizen. Citizen and foreigner are not synonymous with migrant and nonmigrant. Therefore, in looking at statistics of any country, one must be aware of what is being reported: a count of net international migration, a count of citizens and noncitizens; or a count of native and foreign born (referring only to the physical locale of the birth and not whether the person born is citizen or foreigner).

5. This has not always been the case. See, for example, Kritz, Keely, and Tomasi (1981).

REFERENCES

Bouvier, Leon. 1996. "Quality of Life in the 21st Century: What the Latest Census Bureau Projections Mean for America." Backgrounder, *Center for Immigration Studies*, Washington, D.C.

Bouvier, Leon, and John L. Martin. 1993. "Four Hundred Million Americans! The Latest Census Bureau Projections." Backgrounder, *Center for Immigration Studies*, Washington, D.C.

Brimelow, Peter. 1995. *Alien Nation: Common Sense about America's Immigration Disaster*. New York: Random House.

Coale, Ansley J. 1972. "Alternative Paths to a Stationary Population," in Charles F. Westoff and Robert Parke, Jr., eds., *Demographic and Social Aspects of Population Growth*. Washington, D.C.: U.S. GPO. Vol. 1 of the reports of The Commission on Population Growth and the American Future.

Coleman, David. 1992. "Does Europe Need Immigrants? Population and Workforce Projections," *International Migration Review* 26: 413–61.

———. 1995. "International Migration: Demographic and Socioeconomic Consequences in the United Kingdom and Europe," *International Migration Review* 29: 155–206.

———. 1998. Seminar presentation, Notre Dame University.

Edmonston, Barry, and Jeffrey S. Passel. Forthcoming. "How Immigration and Intermarriage Affect the Racial and Ethnic Composition of the U.S. Population," in Frank D. Bean and Stephanie Bell-Rose, eds., *Immigration and Opportunity: Race, Ethnicity, and Employment in the United States*. New York: Russell Sage Foundation.

Espenshade, Thomas J., Leon F. Bouvier, and W. Brian Arthur. 1982. "Immigration and the Stable Population Model," *Demography* 19: 125–33.

European Commission. 1996. *The Demographic Situation in the European Union 1995.* Luxemburg: Office for Official Publications of the European Communities.

Keely, Charles B. 1996. "How Nation-States Create and Respond to Refugee Flows," *International Migration Review* 30: 1046–63.

Keely, Charles B., and Ellen Percy Kraly. 1978. "Recent Net Alien Immigration to the U.S.: Its Impact on Population Growth and Native Fertility," *Demography* 15: 276–83.

Keyfitz, Nathan. 1981. "The Limits of Population Forecasting," *Population and Development Review* 7: 579–93.

Kraly, Ellen Percy, and K. S. Gnanasekaran. 1987. "Efforts to Improve International Migration Statistics: A Historical Perspective," *International Migration Review* 21: 967–95.

Kritz, Mary M., Charles B. Keely, and Silvano M. Tomasi, eds., 1981. *Global Trends in Migration: Theory and Research on International Population Movements*. New York: Center for Migration Studies.

Larkin, Mary Ann, Frederick C. Cuny, and Barry N. Stein, eds. 1991. *Repatriation under Conflict in Central America*. Washington, D.C.: Center for Immigration Policy and Refugee Assistance, Georgetown University; Dallas, Tex.: Intertect Institute.

Massey, Douglas S., Joaquin Arango, Graeme Hugo, Ali Kouaouci, Adela Pellegrino, and J. Edward Taylor. 1993. "Theories of International Migration: A Review and Appraisal," *Population and Development Review* 19: 431–66.

———. 1994. "An Evaluation of International Migration Theory: The North American Case." *Population and Development Review* 20: 699–751.

———. 1998. *Worlds in Motion: Understanding International Migration at the End of the Millennium*. New York: Oxford University Press.

Mitchell, Christopher, ed. 1992. *Western Hemisphere Immigration and U. S. Foreign Policy*. University Park: Pennsylvania State University Press.

Reed, Holly, John Haaga, and Charles B. Keely, eds. 1998. *The Demography of Forced Migration: Summary of a Workshop*. Washington, D.C.: National Academy Press.

Seltzer, William. 1998. "Population Statistics, the Holocaust, and the Nuremberg Trials," *Population and Development Review* 24: 511–52.

Weiner, Myron. 1985. "International Migration and International Relations," *Population and Development Review* 11: 441–55.

Zolberg, Aristide R. 1981. "International Migrations in Political Perspective," in Mary M. Kritz, Charles B. Keely, and Sivano M. Tomasi eds., *Global Trends in Migration: Theory and Research on International Population Movements*, 3–27. New York: Center for Migration Studies.

Zolberg, Aristide R., Astri Suhrke, and Sergio Aguayo. 1989. *Escape from Violence: Conflict and the Refugee Crisis in the Developing World*. New York: Oxford University Press.

CHAPTER 3

Are Immigrants Favorably Self-Selected?

An Economic Analysis

Barry R. Chiswick

Economic migrants are those who move from one place of work and residence to another, either within a country or across international boundaries, primarily because of their economic opportunities, as distinct from refugees and those who move because of the migration decisions of others (*tied movers*). One of the standard propositions in the migration literature is that economic migrants tend to be favorably "self-selected" for labor market success. That is, economic migrants are described as tending, on average, to be more able, ambitious, aggressive, entrepreneurial, or otherwise more favorably selected than similar individuals who choose to remain in their place of origin. The favorable selectivity for labor market success of migrants would be less intense among those for whom other motives are important in their migration decision, such as tied movers, refugees, and those who move for ideological reasons (*ideological migrants*).

Whether migrants are favorably selected or not is important for understanding the economic and sociological consequences of migration for the sending (origin) and receiving (destination) regions, as well as for the migrants themselves. The more highly favorably selected are migrants, the more successful will be their adjustment in the destination, and the more favorable their impact on the destination economy and society. Moreover, the more highly favorably selected are the migrants, the greater, in general, will be the adverse effect of their departure on their origin. As a consequence, the extent of the favorable selectivity of migrants will affect the immigration policies of the destination and emigration policies of the origin. Immigration history, and as a result, the histories of the origin and destination regions, are thereby influenced by the selectivity of migrants.

In recent years there have been challenges to the general proposition of the favorable selectivity of migrants. In addressing this issue, this chapter first develops the human capital model for migration. It then considers alternative specifications of the migration model that are relevant for the issue of migrant selectivity. A review of some of the existing literature forms the basis for the discussion of the empirical testing of the model of migrant selectivity. The chapter closes with a summary and conclusion.[1]

THE HUMAN CAPITAL MIGRATION MODEL

Consider a simple human capital model of investment in migration (Sjaastad 1962; Becker 1964). Assume that wages in the origin and destination do not vary with the level of labor market experience. That is, for simplicity of exposition, it is assumed there is no on-the-job training and there are no post-migration human capital investments after the investment period. Also assume that there is a long (infinite) work life and that the costs of migration occur in the first period.[2] These migration costs include foregone earnings (C_f) and direct or out-of-pocket costs (C_d). Migration costs are defined broadly to include not merely the airfare or bus ticket and time in transit, but the full costs of relocating and adjusting both consumption and labor market activities from the origin to the destination.[3] The rate of return from migration can then be written (approximately) as:

$$(1) \qquad\qquad r = \frac{W_b - W_a}{C_f + C_d}$$

where W_b represents earnings in the destination and W_a represents earnings in the origin. Migration occurs if the rate of return from the investment in migration (r) is greater than or equal to the interest cost of funds for investment in human capital (i). The interest costs of funds is lower, the greater the person's wealth and access to the capital market.[4]

Assume first there are two types of workers, low-ability and high-ability workers, and that these ability levels are known without cost to the workers and potential employers.[5] The more able may have more innate ability or merely more schooling. Ability may have many dimensions, including ambition, intelligence, learning speed, entrepreneurial skills, aggressiveness, tenacity, and so on. Let r_l be the rate of return from migration to a low-ability person and let r_h be the rate of return to a high-ability person. If the low- and high-ability individuals have the same interest cost of funds, the person with the higher rate of return from migration will have the greater propensity to migrate. As a first step, assume that in the origin and destination wages are $100k$ percent higher for the more able (k measures the effect on earnings of higher ability); that is, the ratio of wages in the destination to wages in origin is independent of level of ability.[6] Then,

(2)
$$W_{b,h} = (1+k)W_{b,l}$$
$$and$$
$$W_{a,h} = (1+k)W_{a,l}$$

It is assumed that direct costs, which are the out-of-pocket costs associated with migration, do not vary with ability, $C_{d,h} = C_{d,l}$. Also assume that greater ability has no effect on efficiency in migration, but it does raise the value of foregone earnings. Then $C_{f,h} = (1+k)C_{f,l}$, where C_f is the foregone earnings. The rate of return to the high-ability person can be written as:

(3)
$$r_h = \frac{(1+k)W_{b,l} - (1+k)W_{a,l}}{(1+k)C_{f,l} - C_{f,l} + C_d} = \frac{W_{b,l} - W_{a,l}}{C_{f,l} + \dfrac{C_d}{(1+k)}}$$

Thus, the rate of return to the high-ability person (r_h) is greater than the rate of return to the lowest-ability person (r_l) as long as earnings increase with ability ($k > 0$) and there are positive out-of-pocket costs of migration ($C_d > 0$).

If there were no out-of-pocket costs associated with migration ($C_d = 0$), then $r_h = r_l$, and there would be no selectivity in migration on the basis of ability. Alternatively, suppose there were no labor market premium for a higher level of ability or a particular dimension of ability ($k = 0$). That is, this dimension of ability was not relevant in the labor market. Then, $r_h = r_l$, and there is no selectivity in migration on the basis of this dimension of ability. The smaller are the direct costs of migration (C_d) relative to the wage premium for higher levels of ability ($1 + k$), the smaller is

$$\frac{C_d}{(1+k)},$$

and hence the smaller is the differential in the rate of return to those of higher ability relative to those of lesser ability.

The preceding model assumed that greater ability enhances efficiency in the labor market in both the origin and destination. Now let us add another assumption: the more able are also more efficient in migration. Just as higher ability enhances productivity in the labor market, these same characteristics may enhance efficiency in investment in human capital. The same investment in migration may require fewer units of time and/or fewer units of out-of-pocket costs for the more able.

Since the opportunity cost of migration (C_f) is the product of time units (t) involved in migration multiplied by the value of time in the origin (W_a), opportunity costs can be written as $C_f = tW_a$. Efficiency can be expressed as the more able needing fewer time units to accomplish the same task $(t_h < t_l)$. Then, $C_{f,l} = t_l W_{a,l}$ and $C_{f,h} = t_h W_{a,h} = t_h(1 + k)W_{a,l}$, where $t_h < t$. This strengthens the argument that r_h is greater than r_l.

Note that even if there are no out-of-pocket costs $(C_d = 0)$, if the more able are more efficient in using time, relative skill differentials that do not vary across regions generate favorable selectivity in migration. That is, if $C_d = 0$, and $t_h < t_l$, using equation (3), when $C_{f,l} = t_l W_{a,l}$ and $C_{f,h} = t_h(1 + k)W_{a,l}$, then it follows that $r_h > r_l$.

The more able may also be more efficient in utilizing out-of-pocket expenditures $(C_{d,h} < C_{d,l})$ incurred in migration, just as they are more efficient in other activities. If direct costs exist and they are smaller for the more able $(C_{d,h} < C_{d,l})$, then the difference in the rate of return from migration is even greater than if there were no ability differences in using the out-of-pocket expenditures required for migration. If $C_{d,h} = (1 + \lambda)C_{d,l}$ where λ is a direct cost efficiency parameter, and $\lambda < 0$, then

$$(4) \qquad r_h = \frac{W_{b,l} - W_{a,l}}{C_{f,l} + \dfrac{C_{d,l}\,(1 + \lambda)}{(1 + k)}}$$

and r_h is larger relative to r_i the greater the efficiency in handling direct costs (the larger is λ in absolute value).

Thus, a human capital model, which assumes relative skill differentials are the same in the origin and destination generates favorable selectivity of migration in the supply of migrants if there are out-of-pocket (direct) costs that are not proportional to wages. This favorable selectivity is more intense if those who are more able in the labor market are also more efficient (able) in the migration process, either in using their own time or in using out-of-pocket expenditures.

It is reasonable to assume, however, that migrants will differ in the combination of own time (foregone earnings) and purchased inputs (direct costs) in the migration and readjustment process. The greater the value of foregone earnings (wages) and the greater a person's efficiency in using purchased inputs relative to their own time, the greater will be the relative use of purchased inputs over own time. Thus, high-ability migrants may appear to spend more on the migration process (out-of-pocket expenditures) and to use less time than those of lesser ability.

The model can be extended to consider situations in which the relative wage differentials are not the same across countries. Assume that there are no direct costs of migration $(C_d = 0)$ and that ability (human capital) does not affect efficiency in time use in migration $(t_h = t_l)$. Then,

$$(5) \qquad r_l = \frac{W_{b,l} - W_{a,l}}{t W_{a,l}} = \frac{1}{t} \left(\frac{W_{b,l}}{W_{a,l}} - 1 \right)$$

$$and$$

$$(6) \qquad r_h = \frac{W_{b,h} - W_{a,h}}{t W_{a,h}} = \frac{1}{t} \left(\frac{W_{b,h}}{W_{a,h}} - 1 \right)$$

Then the ratio of wages in the destination relative to the origin determines migration incentives. If the ratio of wages is the same, then the rates of return are the same and there is no skill selectivity in migration. If the ratio of wages across regions is greater for the high-ability, that is, W_b / W_a is greater for h than for l, then the high-ability have a greater incentive to migrate. If on the other hand, the ratio of wages across regions is greater for the low ability, then they would have a greater propensity to migrate, other factors being the same.

Several implications follow from this human capital model regarding the favorable selectivity of economic migrants—that is, those basing their migration decision on the conventionally measured rate of return from migration. The larger are the out-of-pocket costs of migration, the lower is the propensity to migrate, but the lower is the return migration rate and the greater is the propensity for favorable selectivity in migration.[7] This propensity for favorable selectivity is intensified if those who are more efficient in the labor market are also more efficient in the migration and adjustment process. This effect occurs if migrants are more efficient in using their own time, in using purchased inputs, or in combining their time and purchased inputs. If those with more human capital, for example, those with more schooling and greater proficiency in destination language skills, are more efficient in obtaining and interpreting information and in making decisions (greater allocative efficiency), then they would be more efficient in the migration process (Schultz 1975).

The favorable selectivity of migrants is even greater if the relative wage differential between the destination and origin (the ratio of wages in the destination to those in the origin) is greater for high-ability workers. The favorable selectivity is less intense if the ratio of wages in the destination to those in the origin is smaller for the high ability. Only if this latter effect is sufficiently large to offset the favorable selectivity effects of out-of-pocket costs and greater efficiency in the migration process will there be no selectivity in migration. In this framework, for there to be negative selectivity in migration, even more compressed wage differentials across regions are required for the high-ability relative to the low ability.

ALTERNATIVE MODELS

Several alternatives to the simple human capital model presented above have appeared in the literature to address the issue, either directly or indirectly, of the favorable selectivity of migrants. These include models based on asymmetric information, temporary migration, the Roy model, and noneconomic determinants of migration.

Asymmetric Information

Katz and Stark (1984, 1987) present a model of asymmetric information. Suppose potential migrants know their true productivity and employers in the origin have, over time, learned the workers' true productivity. Employers in the destination, however, cannot differentiate among high- and low-ability migrants. Employers in the origin pay workers wages in accordance with the worker's true productivity, while those in the destination pay workers according to the expected (average) productivity of migrants. High-ability workers will experience a smaller wage differential and higher foregone earnings than low-ability workers, and they will therefore have a smaller incentive to migrate. If employers can never detect true ability differences among migrant workers, there would be adverse selection. The increase in low-ability migration relative to high-ability migration would drive down the expected wage of migrants in the destination, further discouraging high-ability migration.

Employers in the destination would, of course, have an incentive to develop tests or techniques for distinguishing high- from low-ability workers. The lower the cost and the shorter the time interval for identifying ability, the lower the adverse selection effect from asymmetric information. Asymmetric information would appear to be most compelling for low-skilled jobs with a short duration (tenure on the job) that do not involve repeat occurrences. High-wage jobs would warrant investment in information about ability, if only through a trial investment/working period. This might take the form of hiring immigrant workers at low wages until true ability levels are revealed. Employers would then be able to discern the ability level of workers for jobs that have a long tenure or that involve repeat occurrences.

Short-Term Migrants

The model developed above assumed, for simplicity, that workers remained in the destination for a long period of time, and it implicitly assumed away location-specific human capital. Suppose, however, there is a short expected duration in the destination because of high expectations of voluntary return migration (guest worker or sojourner migration) or involuntary return migration (deportations) (Chiswick 1980, 1986b). Then migrants who made investments in destination-specific human capital would experience a capital loss when they leave the destination and their origin-specific human capital would have depreciated during their sojourn. Therefore, sojourner migrants or illegal aliens concerned about apprehensions and deportations would tend to avoid country-specific human capital investments and would tend to invest in internationally transferable human capital or very little human capital.

To the extent that there is a complementarity between country-specific and internationally transferable human capital, which is increased by location-specific licensing and certifications for professional and skilled jobs, temporary migrants would tend to have lower levels of both forms of human capital. This would result in lower skill levels among sojourner migrants and illegal aliens than among long-term (or permanent) legal migrants. This would give the appearance of less positive self-selectivity among short-term migrants (guest workers, sojourners, and illegal aliens) compared to permanent legal migrants.[8]

The Roy Model—Relative Skill Differentials

In a series of studies on selectivity in migration Borjas (1987, 1991) presents the Roy model (Roy 1951) as an alternative specification of the human capital model.[9] It is implicitly assumed that all migration costs are a constant proportion of foregone earnings, that there are no fixed (out-of-pocket) costs, and that ability has no effect on efficiency in migration. As a result, migration incentives are a function of the ratio of wages in the destination to the origin, as shown above in equations (5) and (6).

This application of the Roy model is a special case of the human capital model, as shown earlier. For the same wage structure (relative skill differentials) in the destination, a larger relative skill differential in the lower income origin implies a smaller destination to origin wage differential for higher-skilled workers, and hence a smaller incentive to migrate compared to lower-skilled workers. The reverse follows if there is a smaller relative skill differential in the origin. Borjas (1987:552) writes, "If the income distribution in the sending country is more unequal than that of the United States (and the correlation in earnings is positive and strong), emigrants will be chosen from the lower tail of the income distribution in the country of origin." This is not quite correct. As shown above, a larger skill differential in the origin than in the destination does not necessarily imply negative selectivity, but rather only less favorable positive selectivity.

In an empirical test of this model, Borjas (1987) regresses initial immigrant earnings and the improvement in immigrant earnings, as well as the emigration rate from the origin, on a measure of relative skill differentials in the origin. The measure of relative skill differentials Borjas used is the "Ratio of household income of the top 10 percent of the households to the income of the bottom 20 percent of the households" (Borjas 1987:545). This actually does not test for the effect of income inequality on positive or negative selectivity in international migration, but only for whether inequality in income in the origin is associated with a greater or lesser degree of selectivity, after controlling for other variables that reflect the effects on earnings in the United States of positive selectivity. This measure of household income inequality may be poorly related to the relevant variable, relative skill differentials. Controlling for other variables, the coefficient on the inequality variable is not statistically significant in analyses of immigrant earnings in the United States and in half of the specifications has a positive rather than the expected negative sign. Contrary to the conclusion, the test does not offer support for the hypothesis that immigrants from countries with greater skill differentials are drawn from the least able members of the origin labor force.[10]

In his reply to the Jasso and Rosenzweig (1990) critique of his paper, Borjas (1990:306) reiterates, "If earnings between the United States and the source country are positively and strongly correlated, positive selection is observed whenever the United States has more income inequality than the source country and negative selection is observed otherwise." In his new empirical test Borjas (1990: 307) uses as his measure of relative skill differentials a dummy variable for whether the origin country has an income distribution more unequal than the United States. The t-ratio of -1.8 is at the margin of statistic significance, although Borjas asserts confidently that his prediction is "confirmed by the results" (Borjas 1990:308). It is not clear why he changed the measure of inequality to a dichotomous variable or whether this measure of inequality in this and in the earlier study reflects skill differentials or other dimensions of household income inequality, such as the inequality in human capital and other assets, or differences in household labor supply. Moreover, the marginal t-ratio for inequality is in contrast to the very high t-ratios for the effect on immigrant earnings in the United States of origin country per capita income ($t = 6.4$) and the refugee variable, whether the origin is a communist country ($t = -3.6$).

Noneconomic Migrants

Conventionally defined economic variables are not the only determinants of migration. People also move for noneconomic reasons, including to accompany or join family members (tied movers), for real or perceived threats to their freedom or safety because of their class, religion, race, or other characteristic (refugees), and for ideological (including religious) reasons.[11] The favorable self-selectivity for labor market success would be expected to be less intense among those for whom migration is based primarily on factors other than their own labor market success. Studies of tied movers and refugees in comparison to economic migrants indicate that the former have higher unemployment rates and lower earnings than statistically comparable economic migrants (Chiswick 1978, 1979, 1980, 1982; Mincer 1978). The earnings disadvantages of tied movers and refugees are greater initially and diminish with duration of residence, but generally do not disappear.

Empirical Studies of Selectivity: Migrants and Return Migrants

A variety of studies have been conducted to test directly for the favorable-selectivity of migrants. A series of studies on internal migration in the United States and Canada have found that migrants tend to have higher levels of schooling than nonmigrants who remain in the place of origin and that the use of selectivity correction techniques indicates that they would have had higher earnings in the origin than nonmovers (see, for example, Baily 1993; DaVanzo 1976; Gabriel and Schmitz 1995; Islam and Choudhury 1990; Robinson and Tomes 1982; Vandercamp 1972).

There is less research on the issue of the selectivity of the emigration of in-migrants, of which a special case is return migrants, those who return to their origin. Migrants have a higher propensity for a subsequent move than do nonmigrants, other variables being the same. The former have already demonstrated a propensity to move, and have less human and social capital specific to the initial destination. Return migrants may have human and social capital specific to the origin that has not fully depreciated in their absence. Migrants may depart for a number of reasons, including new information about even better opportunities elsewhere, because ex post there is a realization that the destination did not live up to their expectations, or because economic or political circumstances in the origin or in the destination have changed. Moreover, they may depart because the initial move was intended to be temporary (sojourners), perhaps because they are target earners in the destination. These arguments and the statistical analyses suggest that on average migrants who subsequently emigrate will be somewhat less favorably selected than the original flow of economic migrants, but they appear to be more favorably selected than those who never moved.[12]

Beenstock (1996) studied the return migration of immigrants in Israel and found that it was greatest among those from the high-income Western democracies who were less successful in adjusting to Israel, among those who migrated as young adults and who did not have children. Return migrants had a lower proficiency in Hebrew (a destination-specific skill) and higher unemployment, other things the same, before they departed. Immigrants to Israel from the high-income Western democracies, primarily ideological migrants, have a high opportunity cost of remaining in Israel.

DaVanzo (1976) finds that for internal migration in the United States the return migrants respond to many of the same economic incentives as did the original migrants. Long and Hansen's (1977) study of black return migrants to the South suggests that both the original and return migration were selective in favor of those with more schooling. Rogers (1982) cites data indicating a variety of motives for return migration, including an original intention that the initial migration is only temporary. In an analysis of short-term interprovincial return migrants in Canada, Vanderkamp (1972) suggests that they were the less successful migrants. In a study of internal migration in the United States using the National Longitudinal Survey of Youth, Bailey (1993) finds a larger positive effect of a college education on initial migration than on return migration. He interprets this as implying that those with higher levels of education not only have higher rates of migration but also make fewer errors in their initial migration, suggesting greater efficiency in migration.

Nearly all of the studies of the selectivity of migrants focus on the level of earnings or schooling of migrants compared to nonmigrants in the origin or destination. Two exceptions are studies by Tidrick (1971) and Finifter (1976). Tidrick conducted a survey among Jamaican university students about their intention to emigrate and whether they would encourage others to emigrate. Using cross-tabulations she shows that both propensities were higher, the higher the social class of the student's family and the higher the student's level of ability. Finifter (1976) reports the findings from a series of Gallup Polls conducted in the United States from 1946 to 1971 that included a question on potential interest in emigrating among Americans. The propensity to express an interest in emigrating from the United States was greater among males, the currently unemployed, those "dissatisfied with the institutions of the American political system" (ideological emigrants), and those with a higher level of education, and declined with age (Finifter 1976:34–35). Both studies find a positive selectivity in the expressed interest in emigrating.

The Earnings of Migrants and the Children of Immigrants

One of the persistent findings regarding immigrants to the United States is that after a period of adjustment of about ten to fifteen years, male economic migrants earn more than adult men born in the United States of the same racial/ethnic origin, level of schooling, and other measure characteristics (see Chiswick 1979, 1980, 1986a).[13] Among refugees, by contrast, initial earnings are lower than among economic migrants, but the rate of improvement is greater and the gap diminishes over time, although it does not disappear with duration of residence. If refugees "catch up" to the earnings of otherwise similar native-born men this catch-up comes later than among economic migrants. Equally striking is that the native-born children of immigrants (second-generation Americans) tend to earn more than the native born with native-born parents (third- and higher-generation Americans) (Chiswick 1977, 1980, 1986b). Other things the same, within racial and ethnic groups, this earnings advantage is about 5 to 10 percent, or the earnings equivalent of about one extra year of schooling. These earnings advantages of immigrants and their native-born children occur in spite of the disadvantages of a foreign origin, including less country-specific knowledge or information and poorer proficiency in English, especially in the first generation.[14]

An analysis of the earnings of black internal migrants in the United States is instructive. Using data from the 1960 and 1970 Censuses of Population it has been found that black male migrants from the South to states outside of the South display similar earnings patterns as immigrants. The Census provides data on state of birth, state of residence five years ago, and current state of residence. Adult black men born in the South who have lived in the non-South, less than five years earn significantly less that those born in the non-South, other things being the same. By contrast, those born in the South who have lived in the non-South five or more years earn significantly more than statistically similar black men who were born in and remained in the nonsouthern States.[15] These findings are consistent with favorable selectivity in migration, with a period of adjustment required in the new (non-South) labor market.

These findings for international and internal migrants are consistent with the hypothesis that economic migrants are favorably self-selected for ability or human capital investment and that refugees are less intensely self-selected. When the favorable selectivity of economic migrants outweighs the disadvantages of a "foreign" origin (less-destination-specific human capital), the earnings of immigrants equal those of the native born and then surpasses that of the native born. Some of this favorable self-selectivity is transmitted to the immigrant's native-born children, although presumably with a regression to the mean, that is, the effect is dampened across generations.

SUMMARY AND CONCLUSIONS

This chapter has explored the theoretical issues and the empirical literature regarding the selectivity of migrants. Although the primary focus here is on international migration, reference is also made to internal and return migration. The analyses indicate a tendency toward the favorable self-selection (supply) of migrants for labor market success on the basis of a higher level of ability broadly defined. The favorable selectivity is more intense: the greater the out-of-pocket (direct) costs of migration and return migration, the greater the effect of ability on lowering the costs of migration, and the smaller are the wage differences by skill in the lower-income origin than in the higher-income destination. Favorable selectivity for labor market success can be expected to be less intense for noneconomic migrants, such as refugees, tied movers, and ideological migrants, and for sojourners (short-term migrants) and illegal aliens.

The theoretical analysis in this paper applies only to the supply of immigrants and not to the observed outcomes. The determinants of the demand for immigrants are also relevant for international migration as all nation-states have selection criteria for those they will admit. Among countries for whom entry restrictions are binding, the criteria for rationing immigration visas will influence the favorable selectivity of those who actually immigrate. Selection criteria can ration visas on one or more characteristics that enhance labor market earnings, such as schooling level, professional qualifications, age, and destination language proficiency, among other criteria. Alternatively, criteria can be used that are seemingly independent of skill level, such as kinship ties, refugee status, and lotteries. There will be a tendency for immigrants to be favorably selected under a given selection criteria. The former criteria, however, are likely to select, on average, a higher ability subset among those who would supply themselves as immigrants than would the latter criteria. The overall favorable selectivity of immigrants, therefore, depends on the favorable selectivity of the supply of immigrants and the criteria used to ration admissions.

NOTES

1. An earlier version of this chapter was presented at the American Economic Association Annual Meeting, New York, January 1999; an abridged version, "Are Immigrants Favorably Selected?" appeared in the *American Economic Review, Papers and Proceedings* 89 (2) (May 1999): 181–85. This chapter was written while the author was John M. Olin Visiting Professor, Center for the Study of the Economy and the State, Graduate School of Business, University of Chicago.

2. Under reasonable discount rates, increases in earnings received far into the future, say starting in thirty years, have a small present value. The length of the effective life can be considered infinite if the decision maker takes into account the higher earnings their descendants would receive if raised in the destination rather than in the origin. The sharp fall off of migration and other human capital investments with age among adults has less to do with the finiteness of the working life than with the rise in the opportunity cost of time with human capital investment, including on-the-job training or labor market experience, location-specific investments, and the incentive to make the most productive human capital investments (for which the internal rate of return is greater then the discount rate) sooner rather than later.

3. An analysis of the adjustment process is beyond the scope of this chapter. The adjustments relevant for the labor market include investments in schooling, on-the-job training, information and language, among other characteristics. See, for example, Chiswick 1978; Chiswick and Miller 1992; and Khan 1997.

4. The interest cost of funds or the discount rate would be the person's borrowing rate if at the margin the person is a borrower and is the lending rate if this is what the person does at the margin. The rate depends on the person's wealth and rate of time preference for consumption in the present relative to the future. Discount rates may therefore vary across individuals and by age for the same individual (see Hirshleifer 1958). For a model of the supply and demand for investment funds for investments in human capital, see Becker and Chiswick 1966.

5. Although for simplicity of exposition the discussion will be in terms of labor market earnings and ability, it can easily be extended to include efficiency in consumption. For the same nominal earnings, greater efficiency in consumption enhances real earnings.

6. If, for example, the more able earn, say, 20 percent more than the less able, then $k = 0.20$.

7. These out-of-pocket costs are frequently measured by distance. See, for example, Schwartz 1973.

8. This is consistent with analyses of illegal aliens in the United States that indicate those are disproportionately low-skilled workers, as measured by their level of educational attainment, English language proficiency, occupational status, and earnings. Illegal aliens appear to have lower earnings than workers with legal rights to work who otherwise have similar characteristics, presumably because of their limited job mobility, and shorter expected duration in the destination. See, for example, Rivera-Batiz 1999, and Kossoudji and Cobb-Clark 1998.

9. For a comment and reply on issues other than those raised here, see Jasso and Rosenzweig 1990; and Borjas 1990.

10. Cobb-Clark (1993), however, does find a marginally significant negative relation between income inequality in the origin and the earnings of immigrants in some of her equations in her study of immigrant selectivity among women in the United States. It is surprising that the effect is more pronounced for women than for men given that among women there is a larger proportion of tied movers. Given that the inequality measure is household income inequality, it is unclear whether female labor supply effects in the origin and destination are determining this relationship.

11. For the classic study of tied movers and tied stayers, see Mincer 1978. It is sometimes difficult to distinguish between ideological migrants and refugees. Many of the earliest settlers in the United States came for a fuller expression of their religious beliefs, and not necessarily because of persecution; hence, they would be ideological migrants. For a study of ideology and emigration from the United States in the post–WWII period, see Finifter 1976. Americans who went to the Soviet Union in the interwar period to build the new Soviet state were ideological migrants. North American Jewish immigrants in Israel would also be an example of ideological migrants (Beenstock 1996). While the latter earn more than other immigrants in Israel, overall and other variables the same, their real earnings are lower than what they would have received in the United States (Chiswick 1998).

12. See, for example, DaVanzo 1983; DaVanzo and Morrison 1986; Herzog and Schlottmann 1983; Long and Hansen 1977; Shumway and Hall 1996; Vandercamp 1972; Yezer and Thurston 1976.

13. Borjas (1985) argues that the appearance of a rise in earnings with duration of residence in cross-sectional data is due to a decline in the quality of more recent cohorts of immigrants. He does not deny the higher ability of earlier cohorts. Using different methodologies, Chiswick (1980, 1986a), Duleep and Regets (1996, 1997a, 1997b), and LaLonde and Topel (1992) show that Borjas (1985) misinterpreted the data and that there is no evidence of a decline in the earnings of immigrants relative to natives over successive cohorts during the post–WWII period, other variables being the same. By focusing on immigrant earnings at arrival, Borjas (1985) confused the steepening of human capital earnings profiles for immigrants and natives (a higher return to skill) and a reduction in the transferability of the skills of immigrants due to a shift in source countries of origin with a decline in immigrant quality (ability). For a similar earnings catch-up at the turn of the century, see Blau 1980. For an analysis of the catch-up in terms of employment and unemployment, see Chiswick and Hurst 1998. Lindstrom and Massey (1994) show that the emigration of the foreign born does not distort the assimilation of immigrants observed in the U.S. Census.

14. Preliminary results indicate that among native-born men those who speak a language other than or in addition to English at home, and who are disproportionately

second-generation Americans, have lower earnings, other things the same, than the native born who speak only English at home (Chiswick and Miller 1998).
15. See, for example, Chiswick 1980; Long 1974; Long and Heltman 1975; and Masters 1972.

REFERENCES

Bailey, Adrian. 1993. "A Migration History, Migration Behavior and Selectivity," *Annals of Regional Science* 27: 315–26.

Becker, Gary S. 1964. *Human Capital*. New York: NBER.

Becker, Gary S., and Barry R. Chiswick. 1996. "Education and the Distribution of Earnings," *American Economic Review* 56 (supplement): 358–69.

Beenstock, Michael. 1996. "Failure to Absorb: Remigration by Immigrants Into Israel," *International Migration Review* 30: 950–78.

Blau, Francine D. 1980. "Immigration and Labor Earnings in Early Twentieth Century America," in Julian L. Simon and Julie DaVanzo, eds., *Research in Population Economics* 2: 21–41.

Borjas, George J. 1985. "Assimilation, Changes in Cohort Quality and the Earnings of Immigrants," *Journal of Labor Economics* 3: 463–89.

———. 1987. "Self-Selection and the Earnings of Immigrants," *American Economic Review* 77: 531–53.

———. 1990. "Self-Selection and the Earnings of Immigrants: Reply," *American Economic Review* 80: 305–8.

———. 1991. "Immigration and Self-Selection," in John Abowd and Richard Freeman, eds., *Immigration, Trade and the Labor Market*, pp. 29–76. Cambridge: NBER.

Chiswick, Barry R. 1977. "Sons of Immigrants: Are They at an Earnings Disadvantage?" *American Economic Review* 67: 376–80.

———. 1978. "The Effect of Americanization on the Earnings of Foreign-Born Men," *Journal of Political Economy* 86: 897–922.

———. 1979. "The Economic Progress of Immigrants: Some Apparently Universal Patterns," in William Fellner, ed., *Contemporary Economic Problems, 1979*, pp. 357–99. Washington, D.C.: American Enterprise Institute.

———. 1980. *An Analysis of the Economic Progress and Impact of Immigrants*. National Technical Information Service, No. PB80–200454. Report prepared for the Employment and Training Administration, U.S. Dept. of Labor.

———. 1982. *The Employment of Immigrants in the United States*. Washington, D.C.: American Enterprise Institute.

———. 1986a. "Is the New Immigration Less Skilled than the Old?" *Journal of Labor Economics* 4: 168–92.

———. 1986b. "Human Capital and the Labor Market Adjustment of Immigrants: Testing Alternative Hypotheses," *Research in Human Capital and Development* 4: 1–26.

———. 1998. "Hebrew Language Usage: Determinants and Effects on Earnings Among Immigrants in Israel," *Journal of Population Economics* 11: 253–71.

Chiswick, Barry R., and Michael Hurst. 1998. "The Labor Market Status of Immigrants: A Synthesis," in Hermann Kurthen et al., eds., *Immigration, Citizenship and the Welfare State in Germany and the United States: Immigrant Incorporation*, pp. 73–94. Stamford, Conn.: JAI Press.

Chiswick, Barry R., and Paul W. Miller. 1992. "Language in the Immigrant Labor Market," in Barry R. Chiswick, ed., *Immigration, Language, and Ethnicity: Canada and the United States*, pp. 229–96. Washington, D.C.: American Enterprise Institute.

———. 1998. "The Economic Cost to Native-Born Americans of Limited English Language Proficiency," report prepared for the Center for Equal Opportunity, August.

Cobb-Clark, Deborah A. 1993. "Immigrant Selectivity and Wages: The Evidence for Women," *American Economic Review* 83: 986–93.

DaVanzo, Julie. 1976. "Difference between Return and Non-Return Migration: An Econometric Analysis," *International Migration Review* 10: 13–27.

———. 1983. "Repeat Migration in the United States: Who Moves Back and Who Moves On?" *Review of Economics and Statistics* 65: 552–59.

DaVanzo, Julie, and P. Morrison. 1986. "The Prism of Migration: Dissimilarities between Return and Onward Movers," *Social Science Quarterly* 67: 113–26.

Duleep, Harriet O., and Mark C. Regets. 1996. "The Elusive Concept of Immigrant Quality: Evidence from 1970–1990," Discussion Paper PRIP-UI-41, Program for Research on Immigration Policy. Washington, D.C.: Urban Institute.

———. 1997a. "Measuring Immigrant Wage Growth Using Matched CPS Files," *Demography* 34: 239–49.

———. 1997b. "The Decline in Immigrant Entry Earnings: Less Transferable Skills or Lower Ability?" *Quarterly Review of Economics and Finance* 37 (Special Issue on Immigration): 89–208.

Finifter, Ada W. 1976. "American Emigration," *Society* 13: 30–36.

Gabriel, Paul E., and Susanne Schmitz. 1995. "Favorable Self-Selection and the Internal Migration of Young White Males in the United States," *Journal of Human Resources* 30: 460–71.

Herzog, Henry W., and Alan M. Schlottmann. 1983. "Migrant Information, Job Search and the Remigration Decision," *Southern Economic Journal* 50: 43–51.

Hirshleifer, Jack. 1958. "On the Theory of Optimal Investment Decisions," *Journal of Political Economy* 66: 329–52.

Islam, Muhammed N., and Saud A. Choudhury. 1990. "Self Selection and Interprovincial Migration in Canada," *Regional Science and Urban Economics* 20: 459–72.

Jasso, Guillermina, and Mark R. Rosenzweig. 1990. "Self-Selection and the Earnings of Immigrants: Comment," *American Economic Review* 80: 298–304.

Katz, Eliakim, and Oded Stark. 1984. "Migration and Asymmetric Information: Comment," *American Economic Review* 74: 533–34.

———. 1987. "International Migration under Asymmetric Information," *Economic Journal* 97 (387): 718–26.

Khan, Aliya H. 1997. "Post-migration Investments in Education by Immigrants in the United States," *Quarterly Review of Economics and Finance* 37 (Special Issue on Immigration): 285–313.

Kossoudji, Sherrie A., and Deborah A. Cobb-Clark. 1998. "Coming Out of the Shadows: Learning about Legal Status and Wages from the Legalized Population," Department of Economics and School of Social Work, University of Michigan, mimeo.

La Londe, Robert J., and Robert H. Topel. 1992. "The Assimilation of Immigrants in the U.S. Labor Market," in George J. Borjas and Richard B. Freeman, eds., *Immigration and the Workforce: Economic Consequences for the United States and Source Areas*, pp. 67–92. Chicago: University of Chicago Press.

Lindstrom, David, and Douglas Massey. 1994. "Selective Emigration, Cohort Quality and Models of Immigrant Assimilation," *Social Science Research* 23: 325–49.

Long, Larry H. 1974. "Poverty Status and Receipt of Welfare Among Migrants and Nonmigrants in Larger Cities," *American Sociological Review* 39 (1): 46–56.

Long, Larry H., and Kristin A. Hansen. 1977. "Selectivity of Black Return Migration to the South," *Rural Sociology* 42 (3): 317–31.

Long, Larry H., and Lynne R. Heltman. 1975. "Migration and Income Differences between Black and White Men in the North," *American Journal of Sociology* 80 (6): 1391–1409.

Masters, Stanley H. 1972. "Are Black Migrants from the South to the Northern Cities Worse Off than Blacks Already There?" *Journal of Human Resources* 7: 411–23.

Mincer, Jacob. 1978. "Family Migration Decisions," *Journal of Political Economy* 86: 749–73.

Rivera-Batiz, Francisco L. 1999. "Undocumented Workers in the Labor Market: An Analysis of the Earnings of Legal and Illegal Mexican Immigrants in the United States," *Journal of Population Economics* 12: 91–116.

Robinson, Chris, and Nigel Tomes. 1982. "Self Selection and Interprovincial Migration in Canada," *Canadian Journal of Economics* 15: 474–502.

Rogers, Rosemarie. 1982. "Return Migration in Comparative Perspective," Fletcher School of Law and Diplomacy, Tufts University, mimeo.

Roy, A. D. 1951. "Some Thoughts in the Distribution of Earnings," *Oxford Economic Papers* 3: 135–46.

Schultz, Theodore W. 1975. "The Value of the Ability to Deal with Disequilibrium," *Journal of Economic Literature* 13: 827–46.

Schwartz, Aba. 1973. "Interpreting the Effect of Distance on Migration," *Journal of Political Economy* 81: 1153–69.

Shumway, J. Matthew, and Greg Hall. 1996. "Self Selection, Earnings and Chicano Migration: Differences between Return and Onward Migrants," *International Migration Review* 30: 979–94.

Sjaastad, Larry A. 1962. "The Costs and Returns of Human Migration," *Journal of Political Economy* 70 (Supplement): 80–93.

Tidrick, Kathryn. 1971. "Need for Achievement, Social Class and Intention to Emigrate in Jamaican Students," *Social and Economic Studies* 20: 52–60.

Vandercamp, John. 1972. "Return Migration: Its Significance and Behavior," *Western Economic Journal* 10: 400–65.

Yezer, Anthony M., and L. Thurston. 1976. "Migration Patterns and Income Change: Implications for the Human Capital Approach to Migration," *Southern Economic Journal* 42: 693–702.

CHAPTER 4

The Sociology of Immigration

From Assimilation to Segmented Integration,

from the American Experience to the Global Arena

Barbara Schmitter Heisler

Theory and research in international migration have centered on two basic sets of questions: Why does migration occur and how is it sustained over time? What happens to the migrants in the receiving societies and what are the economic, social, and political consequences of their presence? Historically sociologists have focused primarily on the second set of questions, leaving the first to economists and demographers. More recently, beginning roughly in the 1980s, however, sociologists have also paid increasing attention to the first set.

Immigration theory and research have a long history in sociology, compared to other social sciences. Harking back to the beginnings of the discipline in the United States, immigration and its consequences were among the central themes pursued by the Chicago School of Sociology.[1] Indeed, the assimilation perspective, pioneered by members of the Chicago School in the 1920s and 1930s and refined by their students in the following three decades, remained the dominant sociological paradigm until the late 1960s. Postulating assimilation as the eventual outcome of "all the incidental collision, conflict and fusions of peoples and cultures" resulting from migration (Park 1928), the assimilation perspective could not explain the "resurgence" of ethnicity and the persistence of racial inequality and conflict that were becoming increasingly apparent at that time.[2]

While earlier research by Reeves Kennedy (1944, 1952), Herberg (1956), and, in particular, Glazer and Moynihan (1963) had raised some questions concerning the Chicago School's optimistic contention that new immigrants would eventually move up the occupational hierarchy, lose their cultural distinctiveness, and blend into the dominant culture, it was not until the late 1970s and early 1980s that sociologists seriously challenged the dominant assimilationist trajectory. As immigration has become a pressing issue around the world, the past two decades have witnessed a virtual explosion of theory and research. Until the mid-1980s, however, most theoretically informed work focused on the United States, the sine qua non of immigration countries. Responding to the recognition that migration had become a worldwide phenomenon involving transformations on a global scale (Castles and Miller 1998), more recent work has increasingly included comparative, transnational, and global perspectives.

Although sociologists have not developed an encompassing theory of immigration, today the field is characterized by considerable theoretical vigor. Yet, a casual survey of the rapidly growing body of work produced by sociologists reveals a rather persistent, albeit gradually narrowing, division of labor between scholars who study American immigration and those who engage in more comparative research. As was the case for the Chicago School, scholars of American immigration are located at the center of the sociological enterprise, and although these scholars have developed a variety of new theories and models, the basic questions guiding their research do not differ substantially from those asked by the sociologists who first devoted systematic attention to immigration. On the whole, scholars who follow a more comparative research agenda have asked different questions, questions that have led them to make increasing contact with other social sciences, in particular, political science and anthropology; that is, they are much more likely "to talk across disciplines."

The purpose of this chapter is to provide a broad overview of the development and current state of sociological theory.[3] Given that the field is characterized by considerable diversity, I organize my discussion around the major theoretical perspectives. My discussion is informed by the conviction that a fuller understanding of the multifarious and increasingly important issues raised by international migration and its consequences calls for increased comparative and cross-disciplinary theory and analysis.

AMERICAN EXCEPTIONALISM? IMMIGRATION AND IMMIGRANT INCORPORATION IN THE UNITED STATES

As sociological theory of immigration and immigrant incorporation has moved away from the assimilation perspective in the 1970s, the models and concepts have changed considerably since Robert Park first formulated his race relations cycle (Park and Burgess 1921)[4] and W. I. Thomas and Florian Znaniecki wrote their seminal work *The Polish Peasant in Europe and America* (1927). Yet, the primary focus of research and the main questions asked by these students of American immigration still inform current work.

While more recent work has been more deliberately policy oriented, research and theory on immigration remain rooted in the social-problems-oriented approach associated with the Chicago School, which has been a persistent theme in American sociology. Thus, the driving research questions continue to center on the processes of immigrant incorporation (or nonincorporation, as the case may be). What has changed are the conceptualizations and understanding of these processes, from a single process leading to the eventual assimilation of all immigrants to the dominant American culture to what Alejandro Portes has called "segmented assimilation" (1995a; Portes and Zhou 1993), referring to assimilation into different existing cultures.[5] The main laboratories for empirical observations, which had already moved from Chicago to New York in the 1950s and 1960s, now include the new centers of immigration, Los Angeles and Miami.

More important for the discussion at hand, in the past twenty-five years we can identify several conceptual and analytic shifts in the study of immigrant incorporation in the United States: (1) a shift from focusing on immigrants and their efforts to adapt to their new environment, toward focusing on the interaction between immigrants and the structure of American society; (2) a shift from an undifferentiated and amorphous conceptualization of the latter to one that takes into account existing economic (in particular, labor market), ethnic and class structures and inequalities; (3) a shift from focusing primarily on cultural variables to emphasizing structural/economic variables, that is, the conditions of labor markets and the skills of immigrants; and (4) a shift from a single model identifying various steps or stages in the process of incorporation (i.e., assimilation) to the coexistence of several models, projecting a variety of conditions and possible outcomes.

These changes represent responses to the apparent failure of the assimilation model to explain the "resurgence" of ethnicity and the persistence of racial inequality and conflict in the late 1960s and early 1970s. Part of the failure can be attributed to the assumptions built into the assimilation model in particular the assumption of what Herbert Gans has called "straight-line assimilation" (Gans 1973, 1992).[6] Rejecting the assimilation model as ideologically rooted in Anglo conformity, naïve images of the melting pot and out of touch with contemporary realities (Alba and Nee 1997),[7] sociologists responded by developing several new models of immigrant incorporation. These models are decidedly more structural, focusing less on the immigrants themselves (e.g., on "the anguish of becoming American" [Agueros et al. 1971]), but on the process of interaction between host society institutions and structures and the characteristics of newcomers.

Although the claims made by the newer models have tended to be more modest and less sweeping, the question asked did not change substantially. What changed fundamentally were the images of the host society. While the assimilation perspective portrayed American society as a rather amorphous, homogeneous entity, an absorbent sponge, the newer theories gave shape to this amorphous entity. They pointed out that the sponge is structured and that the structure itself is subject to change.

Although Milton Gordon's (1964) influential multidimensional assimilation model identified several barriers to the assimilation process, the barriers identified were those associated with primary group affiliations. The larger institutional structures (e.g., labor markets, political, and educational institutions), identified as crucial barriers by the postassimilation models, were hardly considered important. Gordon also took for granted what immigrants were assimilating to—namely, middle-class American cultural patterns—which, in turn, remained largely unaffected, barring some minor changes at the margins, such as food or recreational patterns (Alba and Nee 1997).[8] In line with the then-dominant functionalist perspective on social mobility, Gordon perceived eventual assimilation and upward mobility as the movement of individuals, not groups. Thus, Gordon's model did not consider the possibility that entire groups may be moving or that ethnic boundaries themselves may be shifting over time.

While recognizing these obvious shortcomings of the assimilation model, recently several scholars have called for its rehabilitation (Alba and Nee 1997; Morawska 1994). Discarding the model's ideological baggage, and in particular the proposition that assimilation is a universal outcome, Alba and Nee have argued persuasively that the assimilation model remains useful for studying social processes that occur spontaneously. As part of "the theoretical tool kit" (Alba and Nee 1997:863), this model allows for the recognition that American culture is mixed and that elements of minority cultures are absorbed into the mainstream.[9]

THE RENAISSANCE OF ETHNICITY AND THE NEW IMMIGRATION: ENCLAVES AND NICHES

While the idea of the single "melting pot" suggested by the assimilationist perspective had been questioned by the research of Reeve Kennedy and Herberg in the 1940s and 1950s and subjected to further empirical analysis in the early 1960s (Glazer and Moynihan 1963), the more recent literature on immigrant incorporation suggests the existence of multiple "melting pots," or rather multiple processes, or modes of incorporation. Unlike the "triple melting pot" identified by Glazer and Moynihan in the 1960s, more recent conceptualizations of the processes of incorporation are not defined in religious/cultural terms, but rather in terms of economic activity, industry, labor markets and socioeconomic position. While the newer models differ from each other, their common essence is best captured by the concept "ethnic communities."

Taking their initial cues from the experiences of Asian immigrants, Edna Bonacich's middleman minority model (Bonacich 1973; Bonacich and Modell 1980) and Ivan Light's (Light 1972; Light and Bonacich 1988) ethnic entrepreneur/ethnic economy model represent the pioneering work in this area. More recent models are the ethnic enclave economy model and the ethnic niche model. Although "ethnic community" models are rooted in different theoretical perspectives and thus identify somewhat different types of ethnic community structures, they all recognize the ethnic community as a distinct mode of immigrant incorporation.

While the fact that some immigrant groups (in particular Chinese, Japanese, and Jews) were overrepresented in small-business activity had long been recognized, the middleman minority theory provided systematic answers to this fact. Eschewing a more obvious cultural explanation, Bonacich identifies the systematic exclusion of some immigrants from mainstream employment as the main cause for their position as small-scale traders and merchants. Positioned between mainstream producers and consumers, middleman minorities occupy a distinctive class position "that is of no special use to the ruling class," and act as a go-between to more subordinate groups (Bonacich 1980:14–15). Although Bonacich linked the success of middleman minorities to their social solidarity, as a Marxist she was more concerned with their distinctive class position. Using the model in their study of Japanese Americans, Bonacich and Modell (1980) found that the social solidarity that had helped to establish success in the first generation, was eroding in the second generation as many Japanese moved into the professions, suggesting that ethnic solidarity was primarily a temporary and situational phenomenon.

Less indebted to a Marxist perspective, Light's immigrant (ethnic) entrepreneur model (1979, 1984) more directly underlines the immigrant nature of ethnic enterprise, where the very experience of immigration produces a reactive solidarity (that did not exist before immigration) that becomes a resource for members of the group. Here, the sociocultural and demographic features of a group (e.g., entrepreneurial heritage, values, and attitudes), a multiplex of social networks and underemployed and disadvantaged coethnic workers, manifest themselves as ethnic resources that provide advantages to the group (Light and Rosenstein 1995).

Based on extensive research in the Cuban community in Miami, Alejandro Portes and his colleagues and students (Portes and Bach 1985; Portes and Manning 1986; Portes and Rumbaut 1990; Wilson and Portes 1980) developed the ethnic enclave economy model in the late 1980s. In contrast to the previous two models, the ethnic enclave economy model is rooted in dual or segmented labor market theory, which postulates the existence of two separate and distinct labor markets, a primary labor market of good jobs, decent wages, and secure employment and the secondary labor market of unskilled jobs, poor wages, and insecure employment (Edwards, Reich, and Gordon 1975; Piore 1979). Lacking the necessary skills for primary labor market employment and facing discrimination, immigrants are typically confined to employment in the secondary labor market where they are exploited as cheap labor and, in stark contrast to the assimilation perspective, have few opportunities for social mobility. For some immigrant groups, however, the ethnic enclave economy provides an alternative to the secondary labor market. Employment in the enclave economy offers some protection from the vicissitudes of the secondary labor market and a variety of advantages in terms of language and training opportunities (Portes and Bach 1985).[10]

The characteristics of the ethnic enclave economy differ from those associated with middleman minorities and immigrant entrepreneurs. Unlike the previous two models, an ethnic enclave economy is characterized by the spatial concentration of the immigrant group and by considerable within-group stratification. These characteristics give rise to clustered networks of businesses owned by group members. While ethnic business initially serves the culturally defined needs of coethnics, it branches out to serve the larger community. The key elements of ethnic enclaves are spatial clustering (Portes and Jensen 1989) and sectoral specialization (i.e., Cubans in Miami were found to be in five manufacturing sectors). Thus, unlike middlemen minorities or ethnic enterprise, the ethnic enclave economy is economically diversified, including all types of business, trade, and industrial production. Not all immigrations produce ethnic enclave economies. Indeed, studies suggest that they are rather difficult to create (Logan et al. 1994). Success depends on the size of the ethnic group, the group's level of entrepreneurial skills, capital resources, and the availability of less skilled coethnics.

Building on Lieberson's (1980) pioneering historical study of ethnic succession in urban labor markets, Roger Waldinger and his associates developed the ethnic niche model (Waldinger 1996; Waldinger and Bozorghmer 1996). This model is based on the observation that concentrations of immigrant employment are not limited to trade (as is the case for middleman minorities) or trade and small business (as is the case for ethnic enterprise), or trade and a variety of businesses (as is the case for the ethnic enclave economy), but can also be found in public-sector employment. In short, the existence of ethnic niches does not require immigrant entrepreneurs.

As is the case for the previous models, occupational ethnic niches develop from the interaction between the immigrant group and the larger society. Ethnic niches emerge when an ethnic group is able to colonize a particular sector of employment in such a way that group members have privileged access to new job openings, while restricting the access of outsiders. Ethnic niches emerge in every market economy where jobs are ranked according to the principles of desirability and availability.[11] In the United States, such rankings have been strongly influenced by a racial and ethnic pecking order, creating a queue. Immigrants are typically located at the bottom of the queue. Changes in the economy affect the queue, creating vacancies for social mobility and new spaces for new immigrants. Waldinger's research in New York and Los Angeles seems to demonstrate the continued importance of ethnic niches as a dimension of immigrant employment (Bailey and Waldinger 1991; Waldinger 1994).

In contrast to economic models of immigrant insertion into the labor market, the focus on immigrant networks, immigrant niches, and enclave economies give testimony to a fundamental sociological proposition: economic behavior is shaped by the overarching social relations and structures in which people are embedded (Weber 1965). To capture the fact that social expectations changed and even subverted the original intent of economic transaction, Granovetter (1985), used the term "embeddedness."[12] The additional distinction between "relational embeddedness," referring to personal relationships among actors and "structural embeddedness," referring to networks of social relations in which actors participate (1990), allows for the conceptualizations of relational and structural resources within social organization and for analyzing networks that may differ in size and density. Such embeddedness is the basis for the existence, creation, and reinforcement of social capital. First introduced into sociology by James Coleman (1988) and Pierre Bourdieu (1980), the concept of social capital has become a central component of recent theories. Broadly conceived, "social capital refers to the capacity of individuals to command scarce resources by virtue of their membership in social networks or broader social structures" (Portes 1995b:12). Applying these principles to immigrants, Portes and Sensenbrenner (1993) identified two main sources of social capital in immigrant communities: "bounded solidarity" and "enforceable trust." The former refers to principled group behavior that emerges specifically from the situational circumstances in which immigrants may find themselves in host societies. It is independent of earlier shared values. The latter refers to the ability of group goals to govern economic behavior based on expectations of higher community status and the fear of collective sanctions.

While ethnic entrepreneurship, ethnic enclaves, and ethnic niches illustrate the importance of group characteristics and the uses of ethnicity as a potential resource (in terms of networks and the social capital they generate), each of these models outlines a specific mode of incorporation. Indirectly these models also attest to the extraordinary diversity of contemporary immigration and the structural differentiation and flexibility of American society, generating a variety of new adaptations, processes, and outcomes.

To more fully capture the possible variations, Portes has developed a more inclusive and systematic model of immigrant incorporation that identifies twelve distinct outcomes, depending on the interaction of host society and immigrant characteristics (1995a, see also Portes and Rumbaut 1990). Moving from the macro- to the midlevel of the social structure, the model identifies three levels of immigrant reception: the level of government policy, the level of civil society and public opinion, and the level of the immigrant community. The first level identifies three possible policy responses, labeled "receptive," "indifferent," and "hostile." The receptive category applies to refugees who receive resettlement assistance; legal immigrants fall into the indifferent category; and the hostile category applies to populations whose entry and residence meets active opposition (i.e., undocumented immigrants). At the second level, each of the three government reception categories are divided into "prejudiced" and "nonprejudiced" reception, where prejudiced reception is accorded to nonwhite groups (the majority of recent immigrants), while white immigrants enjoy nonprejudiced reception. At the third level, Portes distinguishes between strong and weak ethnic communities. Strong communities are characterized by geographic concentrations and more diversified occupational structures including significant numbers of entrepreneurs (i.e., ethnic enclave economies), whereas weak ethnic communities are either small or predominantly composed of manual workers.

The model yields twelve distinct contexts of immigrant incorporation. The location of an immigrant group in a specific context shapes the limits and possibilities of individual and group action. Thus, for example, the context of legal Mexican immigrants is shaped by indifferent policies of government reception, prejudiced responses from civil society and public opinion and a weak ethnic community. Like Mexicans, Korean immigrants confront indifferent government reception and prejudiced responses from civil society, but they benefit from strong ethnic communities. As immigrant destinies depend on the specific context of incorporation, this model helps explain why Mexican immigrants (and most immigrants from Central America and the Caribbean) tend to occupy low socioeconomic positions and are less likely to be upwardly mobile.

CITIZENSHIP, GLOBALIZATION, AND TRANSNATIONALISM

The mass migration to Europe and the increased salience of international migration as a worldwide and global phenomenon (Castles and Miller 1998) gave impetus to new ways of thinking and a variety of new theories. Less concerned with the process of immigrant incorporation in one country (e.g., the United States) than with explaining the causes and consequences of immigration beyond the confines of a single country, these theories represent responses to the recognition that mass migration is self-perpetuating, transforming, systemic, and increasingly driven by global forces.

Although the permanent settlement of newcomers and the simultaneous loss of home country ties were never historical realities (Foerster 1919; Hoerder 1985; Piore 1979), the empirical realities of post–1965 immigration to the United States and the new mass migration to the advanced European countries first pointed to a new and growing semisettlement and an emerging transnationalism. The maintenance of home country ties and the semisettled condition of immigrants seemed hardly surprising in the European case, where most host countries did not encourage (and often actively discouraged) the permanent settlement of workers presumed to be temporary (Heisler and Schmitter Heisler 1986) and where many sending states actively supported the maintenance of ties in order to insure the continued flow of valuable remittances (Schmitter Heisler 1985). In the United States, pioneering research by

Massey et al. (1987) was among the first to identify the persistence and growing importance of economic, social, and political ties between Mexican immigrants and their Mexican communities of origin.

CITIZENSHIP: NATIONAL AND POSTNATIONAL

The largely unanticipated migration and settlement of large numbers of migrant workers in Europe's advanced industrial countries gave rise to comparative studies of citizenship and new theorizing about citizenship, nationhood, and the inclusion or exclusion of immigrants (Brubaker 1989, 1992; Faist 1995; Heisler and Schmitter Heisler 1991; Schmitter 1979). This topic had been of little concern in the United States where immigration had long been part of the "founding myths" and naturalization was relatively easy for legal immigrants and the children of immigrants became citizens by virtue of their birth on American territory (the principle of *jus soli*).[13] Characterized by different principles of citizenship, based primarily on descent (*jus sanguinis*), many European countries imposed significant (albeit varying from country to country) barriers to naturalization and restriction on birthright citizenship.

Sociological work on citizenship and inclusion has drawn on T. H. Marshall's seminal essay on citizenship and social class (1964). In addition to distinguishing between three types of citizenship—civil, political, and social—and tracing their respective historical trajectory in the British case, Marshall advanced the proposition that the development of citizenship rights has important consequences for social inequality and social cohesion: citizenship rights have served to attenuate inequalities of social class and helped to integrate previously excluded segments of society. Taking Marshall's proposition that citizenship rights are crucial to fostering the integration of previously excluded groups as her starting point in a comparative study of Germany and Switzerland (both countries with significant barriers to political citizenship), Schmitter argued that the more extensive social citizenship rights extended to immigrants in Germany would foster their greater economic and social and eventual political integration (1979). In her analysis, differences in social citizenship rights embedded in the welfare state facilitated migrants' integration into host society institutions, in particular labor markets and housing, and served as a resource for mobilization to gain more political rights.

In contrast, comparing Germany and France, Brubaker identified political citizenship as the crucial variable for immigrant incorporation. Conceptualizing the state as membership association, Brubaker argued that the starkly contrasting historical legacies of citizenship and nationhood in France (expansive, a territorially based community, and state-centered, assimilationist) and Germany (restrictive, a community of descent, ethnocultural, and "differentialist") led to differences in the civic incorporation of immigrants in these two countries. While Schmitter and more explicitly Hammar (1985,

1990) saw partial membership (Hammar uses the concept "denizenship" to denote the substantial social, civil, and even political rights accorded to long-term noncitizen residents in most advanced industrial democracies) as a possible alternative to full membership in the state, and hence a distinct "mode of incorporation," Brubaker identified such "partial membership," as characterized by the German case, as a deviation. Focusing on tracing the historical differences of citizenship and nationhood in the two countries, Brubaker paid little attention to the fact that these differences did not seem to affect the degree of integration into economic (labor market) and social institutions (housing, schooling).

In the context of expanding and deepening European integration and an increasing convergence in citizenship laws in France and Germany (Weil 1998), for members of European Union states, political citizenship in the countries in which they may reside has become largely irrelevant. While it continues to present some barriers to citizens of nonmember states, even in this case, long-term residency has been associated with substantial rights. The expansion of rights for noncitizens has been the focal point for postnational citizenship theorists (Bauböck 1994; Jacobson 1996; Soysal 1994). Postnational citizenship theorists have attributed such expansion to the development of international human rights standards, as laid down in bodies like the UN, the ILO, and the WTO, that guarantee a range of civil and social rights for noncitizens. Thus, Soysal (1994) has argued that refugee and human rights conventions signed by states have codified an international system based on the inviolability of the rights inherent in the "modern person" independent of rights inherent in the state. Legitimized by an international human rights discourse, rights and identities become increasingly decoupled from national citizenship, and the rights component of citizenship becomes reconfigured as the universal right of personhood, which is independent of nationality. Similarly, Jacobson (1996) has identified the international human rights regimes as a major force of change. For Jacobson, the lessening sovereign agency of states has been accompanied by a new regime of rights that reaches across national borders, and states are becoming an institutional forum for a larger international and constitutional order based on human rights.

Like Schmitter and Hammar, postnational citizenship theorists argue that full political citizenship and inclusion in the nation-state, may not be a necessary precondition for the protection and well-being or integration of long-term noncitizen residents. But rather than locating the extensive rights accorded to long-term noncitizen residents to the characteristics of Western democracies (e.g., the welfare state, the human rights clauses enshrined in their constitutions), they locate these rights beyond the individual nation-state. Indeed, postnational citizenship theories are part of a larger set of theories that attempt to explain international migration and settlement patterns in the context of global transformations.

GLOBALIZATION, TRANSNATIONALISM, AND STATE SOVEREIGNTY

The concepts of globalization, and in particular transnationalism and associated terms such as transnational community and transnational circuits, have gained increased prominence in all social sciences and hence are at the center of interdisciplinary concerns (see chapters by Brettell and Hollifield, this volume). Here, I limit myself primarily to the contributions made by sociologists.

Anthropologists have derived their understanding of transnationalism primarily in the context of kinship and network theories (Brettell, this volume). Thus, Basch and her collaborators defined transnationalism "as the process by which immigrants forge and sustain multi-stranded social relations that link their societies of origin and settlement" (1994:6). The pioneering research by sociologist Massey and his collaborators (Massey et al. 1987) also clearly identified the persistence and growing importance of economic, social, and political ties between Mexican immigrants and their communities of origin. An increasing number of empirical ethnographic studies by sociologists and anthropologists (Goldring 1992; Kyle 1995; Mahler 1995; Portes and Guarnizo 1991; Smith 1995) have identified similar ties, indicating that immigrant networks and the associated social capital are no longer confined to activities located primarily in the host society. Reaching across political borders, they are increasingly located in transnational spaces (Faist 1998; Pries 1997), where transnational social spaces "are combinations of social and symbolic ties, positions in networks and networks of organization that can be found in at least two spaces" (Faist 1998:217).

Working deductively from the perspective of world systems, and more recent and related globalization theories (Morawska 1990; Petras 1981; Portes and Walton 1981; Sassen 1988, 1991), some sociologists have linked the new global migrations and their consequences to the increasing penetration of the capitalist mode of production into more peripheral countries accompanied by new demands for cheap labor in core countries and the rapid globalization of economic and financial markets. Although the causes of migration may be primarily economic, in a globalized economy, once set in motion migration patterns are sustained and perpetuated by "well-established regional networks of trade, production, investment and communication" (Massey et al. 1998). The technological revolution, which has facilitated travel and communication across national borders, also supports the maintenance and expansion of transnational social networks created by the migrants themselves.

Although recent scholarship shows that immigrants coming to the United States did not cut their ties and "immigrant nationalisms did not simply go to the grave with the members of the migrating generation" (Jacobson 1995:5), theorists of transnational social spaces argue that current transnational practices differ significantly from those previous practices. They not only differ in terms of the frequency and quality of contacts and connections, they also differ structurally and politically. They are an integral part and supported by systems of increasingly dense commercial, financial, and cultural networks between sending and receiving countries that are embedded and part of a larger global system. In short, the new transnationalism is another manifestation of globalization.

Returning to questions of immigrant incorporation, what are the implications of transnational communities, or transnational social spaces for immigrant incorporation in receiving countries? Several scholars have suggested that transnational communities or transnational social spaces may represent a "strategy of survival and betterment" (Faist 1998:217), a separate and distinct mode of incorporation (Pries 1997). Referring specifically to the second generation, Portes suggests that the children of nonwhite immigrants who are overconcentrated in urban areas, lacking access to mobility ladders, may join an increasingly multicultural underclass, "a ticket to permanent subordination and disadvantage" (Portes 1998:52). "In this context, remaining ensconced in dense immigrant communities, especially those that have gone transnational in their strategy for economic adaptation, may not be a symptom of escapism, but rather a rational strategy for capitalizing on the moral and material resources that only these communities can make available" (Portes 1998:52). However, in his conclusion Portes strikes a cautionary note concerning the long-term implications of transnational communities, which, as he argues, cannot be assessed fully at this time. Whatever their long-term implications, the emerging work on transnationalism and transnational communities gives testimony and provides new insights into the extraordinary complexity of immigration processes at the end of the twentieth century.

While propositions concerning the emergence of transnational communities have been relatively uncontroversial and have been supported by a growing body of empirical research, the significant political consequences for core countries and for the traditional system of nation-states postulated by globalization theorists have generated considerable debate. This is particularly the case for the argument that globalization has significantly undermined state sovereignty and transformed the system of nation-states. Globalization theorists have argued that in a world of economic interdependence and globalization, supported by technological advances, states are becoming less and less able to control the flow of capital and labor. (For a detailed critical discussion, see Hollifield, this volume.) Bringing together both strands of the argument made by globalization theorists—the decline of state sovereignty and the rise of an international human rights regime—Sassen (1996) has argued more recently that the forces of globalization have undermined the traditional nation-state that had been built on the congruence between nation and state. As nation (defined in terms of belonging) and state (defined in terms of territory) become increasingly decoupled, national belonging and identity become increasingly detached from their historic moorings (Sassen 1996).[14]

Although theorists working from the theoretical framework of world systems and globalization have tended to give precedence to economic forces, and theorists of postnational citizenship have drawn on theories of citizenship and on the increasing role of international organizations, they arrive at similar conclusions. This is particularly the case for the new transnationalism. "Transnationalism is clearly in the air," as the editors of a recent volume on the topic have noted (Guarnizo and Smith 1998:3). Yet, I can only agree with Guarnizo and Smith's statement that "the very popularity and prominence in a variety of disciplines captured by this concept poses the risk of it becoming an empty conceptual vessel" (1998:4).

CONCLUSION

Although the above review is far from comprehensive, it demonstrates the considerable diversity and vitality in the area of immigration. Sociologists have built on previous work and, responding to changing world conditions, explored a variety of new directions. The latter have led to increased interdisciplinary contacts with other social sciences (in particular, anthropology and political science) moving in similar directions. Yet, overall the field is far from unified. I would agree with Alejandro Portes that the different components that have made up the field are "so disparate that they can only be unified at a highly abstract and probably vacuous level" (Portes 1997).[15]

While each of the theories and models discussed above has been subject to theoretical, conceptual, and empirical criticisms, in this chapter, I have purposely refrained from critiquing them. Instead, I would like to conclude with a constructive note by asking the question of how we might advance from here.

First, I would argue that sociologists build more bridges across the division of labor between "Americanists" and the "Comparativists/Globalists," that is, sociologists should talk more within their discipline. An obvious and recent bridge has been the recognition that immigrant communities have come to include significant transnational dimensions, which serve to create new forms of social capital (Smith 1998).[16] Yet, because recent work on transnationalism emerged from different theoretical roots than the more traditional approaches associated with models of immigrant incorporation and ethnic communities, so far there have been few attempts to use the theoretical and empirical insights of the former to elucidate and inform the latter, to develop a more comprehensive model of immigrant incorporation. For example, are transnational communities an additional and distinct mode of immigrant incorporation as some scholars have cautiously suggested (Faist 1998; Portes 1998; Pries 1997)? How do we relate transnational communities to other modes of incorporation—assimilation, ethnic enclave economies, ethnic niches, and ethnic entrepreneurs—with which they apparently coexist? Are transnational communities confined to migrants of the first generation or do they reach beyond into succeeding generations as Portes seems to suggest (1998)?

While theorists of transnationalism and globalization tend to identify global transformations as key causes for the newly emerging patterns of international migration and settlement, by relegating the state to the margins, they fail to consider the possible role played by sending countries as purposive actors attempting to shape the spaces of their transnational citizens. There has been a tendency to see transnational communities as created primarily from below, by migrants attempting to carve out new social spaces. Yet, as Robert Smith (1998) has argued, the role of sending countries should not be overlooked. Many sending states are actively promoting the reproduction of transnational subjects (the passage of dual citizenship laws by Mexico and the Dominican Republic are just one of many examples). The roles of sending states in shaping both transnational communities and postnational citizenship only beg for more detailed and, in particular, more comparative analysis. While there is nothing new about sending countries trying to influence the patterns of migration and the settlement of their citizens abroad (Schmitter 1984), the importance of "the home state—in its local, state and national incarnations—in creating transnational forms of political and social life, and in maintaining local, ethnic and national identities linked to the home country, has not diminished, but increased" (Smith 1998:200).

Building more bridges between Americanists and Comparativists automatically leads to more cross-disciplinary discourse as Comparativists and Globalists have tended to be more interdisciplinary. For example, there is an ongoing dialogue across disciplines among scholars working within globalization, transnational, and postnational perspectives. In the case of transnationalism, the dialogue is mostly among sociologists and anthropologists. While sociologists have been more inclined to examine transnationalism through macrosociological lenses and anthropologists have been far more concerned with micro- and midlevel processes, there is little disagreement on the growing importance of the transnational sphere in understanding the processes of migration and settlement.

As for the globalist and postnational perspectives, the dialogue is among sociologists and political scientists. Here, there is less agreement as political scientists have, by and large, been critical of the central claims made by postnationalists and globalists that the international human rights regime and economic globalization have substantially undermined state sovereignty, making states increasingly marginal actors in the process of migration and settlement (Freeman 1995; Joppke 1998; Hollifield 1998, 1999, this volume).

Finally, as European societies have displayed different histories, it is in this context that we could test some of the broad tenets of assimilation theory, devoid of its ethnocentric, American-centric context. A similar case could be made for the various ethnic community models.[17] Yet, such an endeavor must be approached cautiously. Just as the assimilation perspective did not pay much attention to the structural characteristics of American society, we cannot assume that the structural characteristics of American society are identical with those found in other advanced industrial societies. While the globalization perspective pays little attention to political and social differences between core countries subject to the same forces of globalization, the immigrant community models discussed above take the structural characteristics of American society as given. I suggest that applications of these models in different contexts could provide additional opportunities for refinement, modification, and innovation of these models. Along these lines, I have recently attempted to adapt Portes's model of immigrant incorporation (1995b) to the German context (Schmitter Heisler 1998). By taking account of the structural differences between German and American society, I conclude that the United States offers more and more diverse contexts for immigrant incorporation and with it more opportunities and fewer constraints than Germany.

NOTES

1. We may also mention Max Weber's research on the conditions of rural peasants and Polish migrant workers east of the Elbe River in Germany. For a summary, see Bendix 1962:14–30.
2. In a 1993 article, Nathan Glazer argues, "The failure of assimilation to work on blacks as on immigrants, owing to the strength of American discriminatory and prejudiced attitudes and behavior toward blacks, has been responsible for throwing the entire assimilatory ideal and program into disrepute" (122).
3. I am using the term *theory* rather loosely to include typologies and models that may not meet the strict definition of theory. For a good discussion of these issues, see Portes 1997.
4. The race relations cycle was based on the idea that immigrant groups, and, by implication, ethnic and racial groups more generally, typically go through several phases—contact, competition and conflict, accommodation, assimilation—where the end product is a melting with the larger society. In the final phase, group members acquire "the memories, sentiments and attitudes of other persons or groups, and, by sharing their experience and history, are incorporated with them in a common cultural life" (Park and Burgess 1921:735).
5. Assimilation may be a path into the white middle class, into the inner-city underclass, or into the ethnic immigrant community.
6. Critics of the straight-line assimilation assumption have argued that ethnicity may go through periods of re-creation (Greeley 1977; Yancey, Erikson, and Juliani 1976). In a later article, Gans introduced the concept "bumpy-line ethnicity," which suggests that the movement toward assimilation is punctured by periods of stagnation (1992).
7. Park's original model was fleshed out by his students Lloyd Warner and Leo Srole (1945) and further elaborated and extended by Milton Gordon (1964) to include several steps toward assimilation (the presumed outcome).
8. Gordon's seven-stage model had the advantage of lending itself to operationalization, but as Alba and Nee (1997) point out, the focus on primary group integration, overlooks the larger social processes.
9. Several historians have argued that assimilation theory is useful in understanding

past processes. See, in particular, Morawska 1994. See also Kazal 1995 and Barkan 1995. Anticipating criticisms that assimilation may have become a reality for European ethnic groups of the past, but hardly applies to new immigrants confronting different circumstances today, Alba and Nee (1997) make three important points. First, it is difficult to project the future of migration patterns. Second, we do not know whether assimilation would have taken place in absence of a halt to further mass immigration between the 1920s and 1965. Third, as they are socially constructed, racial distinctiveness and perceptions change over time. South Asians and people from the Caribbean Islands are examples.

10. Empirically, there is considerable debate concerning the claim made by ethnic enclave economy theorists that employees fare better in the enclave economy than in the secondary labor market. For a review of the empirical studies, see Light et al. 1994.

11. Waldinger defines ethnic niches as "an industry, employing at least one thousand people, in which a group's representation is at least 150 percent of its share of total employment" (1996:95).

12. The concept was first introduced by Karl Polanyi and colleagues (1957).

13. This is not to say that American scholars did not study citizenship, but that the topic has been treated primarily by legal scholars. See Hollifield, this volume.

14. Political scientists such as Freeman (1996) and Joppke (1998) tend to disagree with the two theses underlying the globalization perspective: the thesis of declining sovereignty and the thesis of pervasive restrictionism.

15. How far these two strands are removed from one another was demonstrated to me recently as a member of a jury to decide the Thomas and Znaniecki prize for the best book in international migration given by the ASA's section. I was the only member of the jury who included a comparative, transnational book among my top six choices from among the books submitted.

16. While there are also signs of such talking at the level of international conferences, so far these conferences tended to be confined to comparing country studies, rather than to generating new theoretical propositions.

17. This is not to say that scholars have not used these models. Existing applications, in particular of the immigrant entrepreneur model which is the most easily transferable across societies, have generally been uncritical in that they have simply transferred the model and sought to confirm it in a different context. From a theoretical perspective, it is more fruitful to explore possible deviations from the model.

REFERENCES

Agueros, Jack, et al. 1971. *The Immigrant Experience: The Anguish of Becoming American*. New York: Dial Press.

Alba, Richard, and Victor Nee. 1997. "Rethinking Assimilation Theory for a New Era of Immigration," *International Migration Review* 31: 826–74.

Bailey, Thomas, and Roger Waldinger. 1991. "Primary, Secondary, and Enclave Labor Markets: A Training System Approach," *American Sociological Review* 56: 432–45.

Barkan, Elliot. 1995. "Race, Religion, and Nationality in American Society: A Model of Ethnicity—From Contact to Assimilation," *Journal of American Ethnic History* 14: 38–101.

Basch, Linda, N. Glick-Schiller, and C. Blanc-Szanton. 1994. *Nations Unbound: Transnational Projects, Post-colonial Predicaments, and Deterritorialized Nation-States*. Langhorne, Pa.: Gordon and Breach.

Bauböck, Rainer. 1994. *Transnational Citizenship: Membership and Rights in International Migration*. Aldershot, U.K.: Edward Elgar.

Bendix, Reinhard. 1962. *Max Weber, An Intellectual Portrait.* Garden City, N.Y.: Doubleday.

Bonacich, Edna. 1973. "Theory of Middleman Minorities," *American Sociological Review* 38: 583–94.

———. 1980. "Class Approaches to Ethnicity and Race," *Insurgent Sociologist* 10: 9–23.

Bonacich, Edna, and John Modell. 1980. *The Economic Basis of Ethnic Solidarity: Small Business in the Japanese American Community.* Berkeley and Los Angeles: University of California Press.

Bourdieu, Pierre. 1980. "Le Capital Social: Notes Provisoires," *Actes et Recherches en Sciences Sociales* 31: 2–3.

Brubaker, Rogers, ed. 1989. *Immigration and the Politics of Citizenship in Europe and North America.* Lanham, Md.: University Press of America.

———. 1992. *Citizenship and Nationhood in France and Germany.* Cambridge, Mass.: Harvard University Press.

Castles, Stephen, and Mark Miller. 1998. *The Age of Migration: International Population Movements in the Modern World.* 2d ed. New York: Guilford Press.

Coleman, James. 1988. "Social Capital in the Creation of Human Capital," *American Journal of Sociology* 94: S95–S121.

Edwards, Robert, Robert Reich, and David Gordon. 1975. *Labor Market Segmentation.* Lexington, Mass.: D.C. Heath.

Faist, Thomas. 1995. *Social Citizenship for Whom? Young Turks in Germany and Mexican Americans in the United States.* Aldershot, U.K.: Avebury.

———. 1998. "Transnational Social Spaces out of International Migration: Evolution, Significance and Future Prospects," *Archive Européenne Sociologique* 39: 213–47.

Foerster, Robert. 1919. *The Italian Emigration of Our Times.* Cambridge, Mass.: Harvard University Press.

Freeman, Gary. 1995. "Modes of Immigration Politics in Liberal Democratic States," *International Migration Review* 29: 881–902.

Gans, Herbert. 1973. "Foreword," in Neil Sandberg, ed., *Ethnic Identity and Assimilation: The Polish Community*, pp. vii–xiii. New York: Praeger.

———. 1992. "The Second Generation Decline: Scenarios for the Economic and Ethnic Futures of Post-1965 American Immigrants," *Ethnic and Racial Studies* 15: 173–92.

Glazer, Nathan. 1993. "Is Assimilation Dead?" *Annals of the American Academy of Political and Social Sciences* 530: 122–36.

Glazer, Nathan, and Daniel Patrick Moynihan. 1963. *Beyond the Melting Pot: The Negroes, Puerto Ricans, Jews, and Italians of New York City.* Cambridge, Mass.: MIT Press.

Goldring, Luin. 1992. *Diversity and Community in Transnational Migration: A Comparative Study of Two Mexico-US Migrant Communities*, unpublished Ph.D. dissertation, Department of Rural Sociology, Cornell University.

Gordon, Milton. 1964. *Assimilation in American Life.* New York: Oxford University Press.

Granovetter, Mark. 1985. "Economic Action and Social Structure: The Problem of Embeddedness," *American Journal of Sociology* 91: 481–510.

———. 1990. "The Old and New Economic Sociology: A History and Agenda," in R. Friedland and A. F. Robertson, eds., *Beyond the Market Place*, pp. 89–112. New York: Aldine de Gruyter.

Greeley, Andrew. 1977. *The American Catholic: A Social Portrait.* New York: Harper and Row.

Guarnizo, Luis, and Michael P. Smith. 1998. "The Locations of Transnationalism," in Michael P. Smith and Louis Guarnizo, eds., *Transnationalism from Below*, vol. 6, pp. 3–34. *Comparative Urban and Community Research*, New Brunswick, N.J.: Transactions Publishers.

Hammar, Thomas, ed. 1985. *European Immigration Policy*. New York: Cambridge University Press.

————. 1990. *Democracy and the Nation State: Aliens, Denizens and Citizens in a World of International Migration*. Aldershot, U.K.: Avebury.

Heisler, Martin, and Barbara Schmitter Heisler, eds. 1986. *From Foreign Workers to Settlers? Transnational Migration and the Emergence of New Minorities. The Annals of the American Academy for Political and Social Science*. Beverly Hills, Calif.: Sage.

————. 1991. "Citizenship—Old, New and Changing: Inclusion, Exclusion and Limbo for Ethnic Groups and Migrants in the Modern Democratic State," in Jurgen Fijalkowski, Hans Merkens, and Folker Schmidt, eds., *Dominant National Cultures and Ethnic Identities*, vol. 1, pp. 91–128. Berlin: Free University.

Herberg, Will. 1956. *Protestant-Catholic-Jew*. New York: Anchor Books.

Hoerder, Dirk, ed. 1985. *Labor Migration in the Atlantic Economies: The European and North American Working Classes during the Period of Industrialization*, part III, "Acculturation Twice: Return Migration," pp. 353–434. Westport, Conn.: Greenwood Press.

Hollifield, James. 1998/99. "Migration, Trade, and the Nation-State: The Myth of Globalization," *UCLA Journal of International Law and Foreign Affairs* 3: 595–636.

Jacobson, David. 1996. *Rights Across Borders: Immigration and the Decline of Citizenship*. Baltimore, Md.: Johns Hopkins University Press.

Jacobson, Matthew. 1995. *Special Sorrows: The Diasporic Imagination of Irish, Polish and Jewish Immigrants in the United States*. Cambridge, Mass.: Harvard University Press.

Joppke, Christian. 1998. "Immigration Challenges the Nation State," in Christian Joppke, ed., *Challenge to the Nation-State: Immigration in Western Europe and the United States*, pp. 5–44. Oxford: Oxford University Press.

Kazal, Russell. 1995. "Revisiting Assimilation: The Rise, Fall and Reappraisal of a Concept in American Ethnic History," *American Historical Review* 100: 437–72.

Kennedy, Ruby Jo Reeves. 1944. "Single or Triple Melting Pot? Intermarriage Trends in New Haven, 1870–1940," *American Journal of Sociology* 49: 331–39.

————. 1952. "Single or Triple Melting Pot? Intermarriage in New Haven, 1870–1915," *American Journal of Sociology* 58: 56–59.

Kyle, David. 1995. *The Transnational Peasant: The Social Construction of International Economic Migration and Transcommunities from the Ecuadoran Andes*, unpublished Ph.D. dissertation, Department of Sociology, Johns Hopkins University.

Lieberson, Stanley. 1980. *A Piece of the Pie: Blacks and Immigrants since 1880*. Berkeley and Los Angeles: University of California Press.

Light, Ivan. 1972. *Ethnic Enterprise in America: Business and Welfare among Chinese, Japanese, and Blacks*. Berkeley and Los Angeles: University of California Press.

————. 1979. "Disadvantaged Minorities in Self-Employment," *International Journal of Comparative Sociology* 20: 31–45.

————. 1984. "Immigrant and Ethnic Enterprise in North America," *Ethnic and Racial Studies* 7: 195–216.

Light, Ivan, and Edna Bonacich. 1988. *Immigrant Entrepreneurs: Koreans in Los Angeles, 1965–1982*. Berkeley and Los Angeles: University of California Press.

Light, Ivan, and Carolyn Rosenstein. 1995. *Race, Ethnicity and Entrepreneurship in Urban America*. New York: De Gruyter.

Light, Ivan, et al. 1994. "Beyond the Ethnic Enclave Economy," *Social Problems* 41: 65–80.

Logan, John R., et al. 1994. "Ethnic Economies in Metropolitan Regions: Miami and Beyond," *Social Forces* 72: 691–724.

Mahler, Sarah. 1996. *American Dreaming: Immigrant Life on the Margins*. Princeton, N.J.: Princeton University Press.

Marshall, T. H. 1964. *Class, Citizenship and Social Development*. Garden City, N.Y.: Anchor Books.

Massey, Douglas, et al. 1987. *Return to Aztlan: The Social Process of International Migration from Mexico*. Berkeley and Los Angeles: University of California Press.

———. 1994. "An Evaluation of International Migration Theory," *Population and Development Review* 20: 699–751.

———. 1998. *World in Motion: Understanding International Migration at the End of the Millennium*. Oxford: Clarendon Press.

Morawska, Ewa. 1990. "The Sociology and Historiography of Immigration," in Virginia Yans-McLaughlin, ed., *Immigration Reconsidered: History, Sociology, and Politics*, pp. 187–240. New York: Oxford University Press.

———. 1994. "In Defense of the Assimilation Model," *Journal of American Ethnic History* 13: 76–87.

Park, Robert. 1928. "Human Migration and the Marginal Man," *American Journal of Sociology* 33: 881–93.

Park, Robert, and Ernest Burgess. 1921. *Introduction to the Science of Sociology*. Chicago: University of Chicago Press.

Petras, Elizabeth. 1981. "The Global Market in the Modern World Economy," in Mary Kritz et al., eds., *Global Trends in Migration: Theory and Research on International Population Movements*, pp. 44–63. New York: Center for Migration Studies.

Piore, Michael. 1979. *Birds of Passage*. New York: Cambridge University Press.

Polanyi, Karl, C. Arensberg, and H. Pearson. 1957. *Trade and Markets in the Early Empires*. New York: Free Press.

Portes, Alejandro. 1995a. "Children of Immigrants: Segmented Assimilation and its Determinants," in Alejandro Portes, ed., *The Economic Sociology of Immigration*, pp. 248–79. New York: Russell Sage.

———. 1995b. "Economic Sociology and the Sociology of Immigration: A Conceptual Overview," in Alejandro Portes, ed., *The Economic Sociology of Immigration*, pp. 1–41. New York: Russell Sage.

———. 1997. "Immigration Theory for a New Century: Some Problems and Opportunities," *International Migration Review* 31: 799–825.

———. 1998. "Divergent Destinies: Immigration, the Second Generation, and the Rise of Transnational Communities," in Peter Schuck and Rainer Münz, eds., *Paths to Inclusion: The Integration of Migrants in the United States and Germany*, pp. 33–57. New York: Berghahn Books.

Portes, Alejandro, and Robert Bach. 1985. *Latin Journey: Cuban and Mexican Immigrants in the United States*. Berkeley and Los Angeles: University of California Press.

Portes, Alejandro, and Luis Guarnizo. 1991. *Capitalistas del Trópico: La Immigración en los Estados Unidos y el Desarrollo de la Pequeña Empresa en la República Dominicana*. Facultad Latinoamericana de Ciencias Sociales, Programa Republica Dominicana, Johns Hopkins University.

Portes, Alejandro, and Leif Jensen. 1989. "What's an Ethnic Enclave? The Case for Conceptual Clarity," *American Sociological Review* 52: 768–71.

Portes, Alejandro, and Robert Manning. 1986. "The Immigrant Enclave: Theory and Empirical Examples," in Susan Olzak and Joane Nagel, eds., *Competitive Ethnic Relations*, pp. 47–66. New York: Academic Press.

Portes, Alejandro, and Ruben Rumbaut. 1990. *Immigrant America: A Portrait*. Berkeley and Los Angeles: University of California Press.

Portes, Alejandro, and Julia Sensenbrenner. 1993. "Embeddedness and Immigration: Notes on the Social Determinants of Economic Action," *American Journal of Sociology* 98: 1320–50.

Portes, Alejandro, and John Walton. 1981. *Labor, Class and the International System*. New York: Academic Press.

Portes, Alejandro, and Min Zhou. 1993. "The New Second Generation: Segmented Assimilation and its Variants among Post-1965 Immigrant Youth," *Annals of the American Academy of Political and Social Sciences* 535: 74–96.

Pries, Ludger. 1997. "Neue Migration im Transnationalen Raum," Transnationale Migration, *Soziale Welt*, Sonderband 12: 15–46.

Sassen, Saskia. 1988. *The Mobility of Capital and Labor.* Cambridge, Mass: Cambridge University Press.

———. 1991. *The Global City: New York, London, Tokyo.* Princeton, N.J.: Princeton University Press.

———. 1996. *Losing Control? Sovereignty in an Age of Globalization.* New York: Columbia University Press.

Schmitter Heisler, Barbara. 1979. *Immigration and Citizenship in West Germany and Switzerland*, unpublished Ph.D. dissertation, Department of Sociology, University of Chicago.

———. 1984. "Sending States and Immigrant Minorities: The Case of Italy." *Comparative Studies in Society and History* 26: 325–34.

———. 1985. "Sending Countries and the Politics of Emigration and Destination," *International Migration Review* 19: 469–84.

———. 1998. "Contexts of Immigrant Incorporation: Locating Dimensions of Opportunities and Constraints in the United States and Germany," in Hermann Kurthen, Jürgen Fijalkowski, and Gert Wagner, eds., *Immigration, Citizenship, and the Welfare State in Germany and the United States*, pp. 91–106. Stamford, Conn.: JAI Press.

Smith, Robert. 1995. *Los Ausentes Siempre Presentes: The Imagining, Making, and Politics of Transnational Community between Ticuani, Puebla, Mexico and New York City*, unpublished Ph.D. dissertation, Department of Sociology, Columbia University.

———. 1998. "Transnational Localities: Community, Technology and the Politics of Membership within the Context of Mexico-US Migration," in Michael Peter Smith and Luis G. Guarnizo, eds., *Transnationalism from Below*, vol. 6, pp. 196–238, *Comparative Urban and Community Research*. New Brunswick, N.J.: Transaction Publishers.

Soysal, Yasemin. 1994. *Limits to Citizenship: Migrants and Postnational Membership in Europe.* Chicago: University of Chicago Press.

Thomas, W. I., and Florian Znaniecki. 1927. *The Polish Peasant in Europe and America.* New York: Alfred A. Knopf.

Waldinger, Roger. 1994. "The Making of an Immigrant Niche," *International Migration Review* 28: 3–30.

———. 1996. *Still the Promised City? African-Americans and New Immigrants in Post-Industrial New York.* Cambridge, Mass.: Harvard University Press.

Waldinger, Roger, and Mehdi Bozorgmehr, eds. 1996. *Ethnic Los Angeles.* New York: Russell Sage.

Warner, Lloyd, and Leo Srole. 1945. *The Social System of American Ethnic Groups.* New Haven, Conn.: Yale University Press.

Weber, Max. 1965 [1922]. *The Theory of Social and Economic Organization*, translated by A. M. Henderson and T. Parsons, part I, pp. 88–115. New York: Free Press.

Weil, Patrick. 1998. "The State Matters: Immigration Control in Developed Countries." New York: United Nations, Department of Social and Economic Affairs, Population Division.

Wilson, Kenneth, and Alejandro Portes. 1980. "Immigrant Enclaves: An Analysis of the Labor Market Experience of Cubans in Miami," *American Journal of Sociology* 86: 296–319.

Yancey, William, Eugene Erikson, and Richard Juliani. 1976. "Emergent Ethnicity: A Review and Reformulation," *American Sociological Review* 41: 391–402.

CHAPTER 5

Theorizing Migration in Anthropology

The Social Construction of Networks, Identities, Communities, and Globalscapes

Caroline B. Brettell

In the late 1920s, while conducting fieldwork in Manus, New Guinea, Margaret Mead made note of the fact that young boys spent two, five, sometimes seven years away from their villages working for the white man. "This is the great adventure to which every boy looks forward. For it, he learns pidgin, [and] he listens eagerly to the tales of returned work boys" (Mead 1930:119). Similarly, 52 percent of the Chambri (Tchambuli) men between the ages of fifteen and forty-five were working as migrant laborers and therefore absent from the Papua, New Guinea, village where Mead was living in 1933. Despite these observations, Mead's ethnographic descriptions of life in New Guinea at this time are largely portraits of discrete and timeless cultures unaffected by the outside world.[1] This mode of representation was characteristic of the anthropology of Mead's time and of the functionalist paradigm that shaped much anthropological analysis until 1960. It was an anthropology that contained a "sedentarist bias" (Malkki 1995:208) and a rooted definition of culture, both of which explain why anthropology, by comparison with a range of other social science disciplines, did not give the study of migration high priority as an area of research until the late 1950s and early 1960s. As anthropologists progressively rejected the idea of cultures as discretely bounded, territorialized, relatively unchanging, and homogenous units, thinking and theorizing about migration became increasingly possible.

Ultimately, of course, anthropologists had to pay attention to migration because in those regions of the world that had traditionally been their arenas for ethnographic fieldwork—Africa, Oceania, and increasingly Latin America and the Caribbean—people were beginning to move in significant numbers from the countryside to the growing urban centers of the underdeveloped and developing world. In the city these rural villagers were finding employment as unskilled or semiskilled workers and living in neighborhoods with people of their own ethnic group or home community. The interest in migrants and migration grew in conjunction with the growth of both peasant studies and urban anthropology as anthropologists began to focus on peasants or "tribesmen" in cities (Mangin 1970; P. Mayer 1961; Plotnicov 1967; Sanjek 1990).

Since the 1970s, migration studies within anthropology have expanded significantly both with respect to the questions examined and the cross-cultural coverage.[2] Research has been extended to the populations of Europe, the United States, Australia, Southeast Asia, and the Middle East. Increasingly, international migrants, as well as those moving from town to town or city to city, have come under consideration. Numerous ethnographic monographs have been published—for example, on Jamaicans, Sikhs, Pakistanis, and Barbadians in England (Bhachu 1985; Foner 1979; Gmelch 1992; Werbner 1990); the Senegalese in Italy (Carter 1997); the Portuguese in France (Brettell 1995); Dominicans, Brazilians, Italians, Mexicans, Vietnamese, and El Salvadorans in the United States (Chavez 1992; di Leonardo 1984; Grasmuck and Pessar 1991; Mahler 1995a; Margolis 1994; Nash and Nguyen 1995); Palestinians in Honduras (Gonzalez 1992); Yemeni Jews in Israel (Gilad 1989); the Yoruba in northern Ghana (Eades 1980); and Shanghai Chinese in Hong Kong and London (Watson 1975)—culminating in a case studies series edited by Nancy Foner that includes volumes on Haitians (Stepick 1998), Asian Indians (Lessinger 1995), Hmong (Koltyk 1998), Vietnamese (Freeman 1995), and Soviet Jews (Gold 1995) in the United States.[3]

In anthropology, as in other disciplines, theorizing about migration has been shaped by a particular epistemology that generates a specific set of questions. For anthropology, a discipline sensitive to place but also comparative in its perspective, these questions have focused less on the broad scope of migration flows than on the articulation between the place whence a migrant originates and the place or places to which he or she goes. This includes exploration of how people in local places respond to global processes. Equally, anthropology's focus on culture, which includes the study of the interaction between beliefs and behavior, of corporate groups, and of social relationships, has resulted in an emphasis in migration studies on matters of adaptation and culture change, on forms of social organization that are characteristic of both the migration process and the immigrant community, and on questions of identity and ethnicity. In this chapter, I address the anthropological perspective on migration, beginning with a discussion of the formulation of typologies and moving from there to theories of articulation between sending and receiving societies, to a discussion of the social organization of migration and processes of adaptation and change that includes a consideration of the relationship between gender and migration, and finally to an analysis of connections between theorizing migration and theorizing identity and ethnicity.[4]

THE FORMULATION OF TYPOLOGIES

Since its beginnings as a comparative and cross-cultural science, anthropology has relied on typologies as a way to theorize about similarity and difference. Anthropologists have delineated distinct and diverse kinship and marriage systems, classified forms of religious behavior and belief, and distinguished between different types of economic exchange or political organization. Springing from this tradition, Nancie Gonzalez (1961) offered an early formulation of five types of migratory wage labor and looked at the impact of each of these on family organization. She argued that migration would be "reflected in social organization in different ways depending on the nature of the sociocultural system affected as well as the type of migration itself" (Gonzalez 1961:1278). The five types of migration identified by Gonzalez, based largely on her research in the Caribbean region, were "seasonal," "temporary nonseasonal," "recurrent," "continuous," and "permanent." Gonzalez's typology underscores the fact that population movements, especially those across international boundaries, cannot be defined exclusively as one-way and definitive. In the African context, anthropologists identified some migrants as weekly commuters, others as seasonal and circular movers, and still others as temporary sojourners or permanently displaced (Du Toit 1975). In the Asian context, similar variations in rural-urban migration patterns were identified in terms of the degree of commitment to the city (McGee 1975). All of these types encompass theories about the motivations for migration, about how migration is shaped by local, regional, national, and international economies, about the linkages between sending and receiving societies, and about the relationship between migration on the one hand and family structure and household strategies on the other.

Recently Gonzalez has added "conflict migration" (Gonzalez 1989, 1992) to the list of types of migration to describe population movement that is stimulated by violent conflict in the home society. Not only has she linked this type of migration to ethnicity (Gonzalez and McCommon 1989), a topic to which I return, but so-called conflict migration also raises the issue of whether and how to differentiate between migrants and refugees. The latter are assumed to be people who leave their home region involuntarily, but their experiences, once abroad, are not unlike those of migrants with the exception of their inability to return readily and freely to their homeland. Malkki (1995:496) has argued that "refugees do not constitute a naturally self-delimiting domain of anthropological knowledge" and that they can be theorized in much the same way as other displaced peoples. Du Toit (1990) has made a similar suggestion and called, in addition, for consideration of those involuntary migrants displaced by planned relocations.

If typologies delineate various migration strategies, then they also serve to

identify differing immigration policies of receiving societies and their relationship to the migrant experience (Callier-Boisvert 1987; Caspari and Giles
1986; Goodman 1987). Thus the post–World War II German concept of *gastarbeiter* (guest worker) came into common use to describe a particular
approach to foreign labor reminiscent of the United States *bracero* program
(Mandel 1989, 1990, 1991, 1994; Rhoades 1978b). In addition, the categories
of undocumented migrant worker or illegal alien have become well known
within the United States (Chavez 1990, 1991, 1992, 1994; Chock 1991), in
post–World War II Europe (as the illegal or clandestine immigrant), and in a
host of countries in the developing world. It is important to emphasize that
anthropologists, who perceive the disjunction between the ideal and the actual
as a fundamental characteristic of human experience, tend to look at immigration policy from the perspective of the immigrant who acts, adapts, and
often circumvents. This emphasis is equally shaped by a theoretical shift in
the discipline from an emphasis on structure to an emphasis on practice (Bourdieu 1977; Ortner 1984).

Since the late 1970s, in part in association with the emergence of the multi-
sited approach to fieldwork that George Marcus (1995) suggests is now characteristic of much contemporary anthropology, some scholars have studied
so-called return migration in different parts of the world (Brettell 1979;
Gmelch 1980, 1983, 1987, 1992; Guarnizo 1997; Kenney 1976; Lockwood
1990; Rhoades 1978a; Stack 1996; Taylor 1976; Thomas-Hope 1985). Gmelch
(1980) has drawn attention to typologies of return migration, a basic distinction being between emigrants who intend their departure to be permanent and
those who intend it to be temporary. Gmelch (1980) points out that most studies indicate that strong family ties, rather than economic factors (failure to
achieve financial success), are the major incentive for return. Stack (1996:xv),
for example, finds this to be the case among African Americans from northern cities who were "called back home" to the rural south. "The resolve to
return home is not primarily an economic decision but rather a powerful blend
of motives; bad times back home can pull as well as push. People feel an oblig-
ation to help their kin or even a sense of mission to redeem a lost community ... or simply a breathing space, a refuge from the maelstrom." In other
cases, for example Western Europe after 1973, migrants have been encouraged to return by the host society and offered specific monetary packages to
do so. Finally, return migration can be related to experiences of racism and
discrimination (Taylor 1976).

Return can also be part of the initial migration strategy, albeit frequently
postponed. Thus the concept of sojourner has been introduced as a distinct
type of migrant. For example, Margolis (1995:31) notes that Brazilians in the
United States see themselves as sojourners, target earners who are motivated
"by the desire to save money to meet some specific goal back home—buy a
house or apartment, a car or telephone, start a business, or perhaps return to

school." The question of settler or sojourner has also been raised in connection with Mexican immigrants (Chavez 1988) and is part of a literature on migration ideology that dates back to Philpott's (1973) research on West Indian migration (see also Dahya 1973; Rubenstein 1979). In the Portuguese case (Brettell 1979), this ideology is linked to the culturally embedded concept of *saudade*—nostalgia for the homeland. *Saudade*, Feldman-Bianco (1992:145) argues "is a cultural construct that defines Portuguese identity in the context of multiple layers of space and (past) time."

The ideology of return is conceptually similar to what Massey et al. (1993, 1994), drawing largely on anthropological research, have referred to as the culture of migration where migration is part of behaviors and values, a kind of rite of passage like baptism or marriage. For members of Mexican rural households, migration is a survival strategy that occurs at certain phases of a household cycle (Arizpe 1981). These peasant households control the circulation of their children in a form of relay migration. Holmes (1983) makes a similar argument in his reconceptualization of the European worker-peasant. He is able to show that migration is a strategy of great historical depth in some parts of the world, a strategy that has allowed peasant households to persist into the twentieth century. The life course or household life cycle approach to migration is characteristic of other research in European historical anthropology (Brettell 1986; Kertzer 1984).[5] In this historical work, as well as in work with contemporary societies, anthropologists have described a powerful relationship between different patterns of inheritance and patterns of migration (Douglass 1974; Iszaevich 1974).

Some of the research on return migration demonstrates that those who do return often remigrate, leading Margolis (1995), based on her research among Brazilian immigrants in New York City, to formulate the concept of "yo-yo migration" as yet another type. She contrasts this type of migration with cultural commuters or shuttle migrants "who regularly migrate back and forth between home and host country with no particular intention of staying in either place for good" (Margolis 1995:32). Since much of this research on return migration is conducted in both sending and receiving societies, it also examines both the impact of out-migration on those left behind and the reintegration of those who have returned after many years abroad (Gmelch 1992; Philpott 1970; Taylor 1976). Ruth Mandel (1990) describes the pain and disorientation characteristic of adolescent Turkish returnees, and in another essay she alludes to the creation of a new ethnic category for Turks who have repatriated—*Alamanyali*, the "Germanlike" (Mandel 1989). As such, rather than being accepted and respected, they are mocked. Similar categories exist for returned Portuguese migrants, be they the *brasileiros* of the nineteenth and early twentieth centuries, or the *franceses* of more contemporary times (Brettell 1979, 1986).

Anthropologists still rely on typologies to capture different migration strategies, but they also recognize that typologies generally offer a static and homogenous picture of a process that is flexible over the life course of an individual migrant or the domestic cycle of a household, varied within a population, and subject to change over time as larger contextual conditions change. Nevertheless, the typologies formulated by anthropologists have directed research to the diverse nature of the process and to the fundamental relationship between sending and receiving societies, whether conceived in the macroterms of a global economy or in the more microterms of social networks and emotional relationships that link households and individuals to both areas. They also help to achieve some of the comparative theoretical goals of the science of anthropology.[6]

ARTICULATING THE MICRO AND THE MACRO: MODERNIZATION THEORY, TRANSNATIONALISM, AND THE POLITICAL-ECONOMY OF MIGRATION

The delineation of types of migration is one way to theorize the way sending areas are articulated with receiving areas (Kearney 1986). The issue of articulation has been explored by anthropologists according to two distinct analytical approaches, one rooted in modernization theory and the other in an historical-structuralist perspective ultimately grounded in broader theory of political economy and the impact of global capitalism (Georges 1990; Kearney 1995).

Much of the early work on migration within anthropology was influenced by modernization theory and a bipolar framework for analysis that separated and opposed sending and receiving areas, and the push factors of out-migration from the pull factors of in-migration. This approach emerged, as Kearney (1986) has noted, from the folk-urban continuum model originally formulated by Robert Redfield (1941), a model that opposed city and country and contrasted two distinct ways of life, one traditional and one modern. Focusing on the motivations of individual migrants, some anthropologists working within a modernization theory framework have emphasized the rational and progressive economic decisions made in response to differentials in land, labor, and capital between where a migrant lives and the locale to which he or she has chosen to migrate. Wage labor is viewed by these individuals as offering more opportunities than subsistence farming (Mitchell 1969) and can, in fact, provide the cash needed to succeed in the rural context—to accumulate bride-price, provide a dowry, or buy a home. Others, arguing what DuToit (1990) has recently characterized as the "bright lights" theory (Gulliver 1957; P. Mayer 1961), have emphasized less the attraction of wage jobs than the excitement of urban life which draws young migrants, especially young men, to it.

One of the underlying assumptions of modernization theory was that the movement of people from areas that had abundant labor but scarce capital to areas that were rich in capital but short of labor would ultimately contribute to economic development in both sending and host societies. Modernization theory, in other words, encompassed an equilibrium model of development, the result of which would be a more equitable balance between resources and population pressure and the ultimate elimination of differences between rural-agrarian and urban-industrial areas. Migrants, through savings and investment, would become agents of change in their home communities. However, as much of the work on emigrant remittances and return migration has demonstrated, migrant savings are often spent on conspicuous consumer items, rather than for economic investment, and the skills learned abroad cannot be easily applied to the rural home context (Donnan and Werbner 1991; Gardner 1995; Gmelch 1980; Gregory and Cazorla 1987; Rhoades 1978a; Thomas-Hope 1985). Rather than being a form of development aid given by rich countries to poor countries, population movements have often resulted in migration-dependent communities and the generation of further migration through the diffusion of consumerism (Massey et al. 1994).

Although the push and pull elements of modernization theory still prevail to order discussions of why people migrate, the shortcomings of the equilibrium model of linear development with which modernization theory has been associated have stimulated interest in a historical-structuralist approach. This approach shifts attention from the motivations and adaptations of individual migrants to the macrolevel processes that shape and sustain population movements. As Lessinger (1995:71, 72) has recently phrased it, "Current research sees the impetus to migration as more complex both for individuals and for entire groups of people. Often push and pull factors operate simultaneously ... and there is no single profile of a typical migrant."

This historical-structuralist approach draws broadly on Marxist thought and more specifically on the work of dependency theorists such as André Gunder Frank (1967), and world systems theorists such as Immanuel Wallerstein (1974). It frames migration in the context of a global economy, core-periphery relations, and the development of underdevelopment. Within this perspective, concepts such as the international division of labor or the internationalization of the proletariat have emerged to describe the inequities between labor-exporting, low-wage countries and labor-importing, high-wage countries. Rather than stemming migration, development encourages it because development creates inequality and raises awareness about the larger society and hence enhances a sense of relative deprivation (Gonzalez and McCommon 1989). The net economic value of migration accrued to the city and not the countryside, to the core and not the periphery.

The unit of analysis in this body of theory is not the individual migrant, but rather the global market and the way that national and international economic and political policies, and particularly capitalist development, have disrupted, displaced, or even attracted local populations, thereby generating particular migration streams. Thus Eades (1987:13) argued more than a decade ago that "the anthropology of migrant labor . . . has become the anthropology of a world social order within which people struggle to make lives for themselves, sometimes helped, but much more often hindered, by the results of international flows of capital and the activities of states over which they have no control."

Dissatisfaction with what was almost exclusively, although perhaps unintentionally, a macroapproach that portrayed migrants not as active agents but as passive reactors manipulated by the world capitalist system, has resulted in a new form of theorizing about the articulation between sending and receiving societies, theorizing that is rooted in the concept of transnationalism. Transnationalism, which continues the critique of bipolar models of migration (Rouse 1992), is defined as a social process whereby migrants operate in social fields that transgress geographic, political, and cultural borders (Glick Schiller, Basch, and Szanton Blanc 1992:ix; see also Basch, Glick Schiller, and Szanton Blanc 1994). As a theoretical construct about immigrant life and identity, transnationalism aptly suits the study of population movements in a world where improved modes of transportation as well as the images that are transmitted by means of modern telecommunications have shortened the social distance between sending and receiving societies. Transnationalism emerged from the realization that immigrants abroad maintain their ties to their countries of origin, making "home and host society a single arena of social action" (Margolis 1995:29). From a transnational perspective, migrants are no longer "uprooted," but rather move freely back and forth across international borders and between different cultures and social systems (Georges 1990; Glick Schiller 1997; Glick Schiller, Basch, and Szanton Blanc 1992, 1995; Grimes 1998; Kearney 1991, 1995; Levitt 1998b; Rouse 1991; Smith 1993, 1997; Sutton 1987). These migrants bring change to localized communities not only through economic remittances but also social remittances (Levitt 1998b). Glick Schiller et al. (1995:49) argue that transnationalism in anthropology is "part of an effort to reconfigure anthropological thinking so that it will reflect current transformations in the way in which time and space [are] experienced and represented."

Transnationalism reflects the more general move in anthropology away from bounded units of analysis and localized community studies (Hannerz 1996, 1998; Ho 1993). Conceived as social action in "a multidimensional global space with unbounded, often discontinuous and interpenetrating sub-spaces" (Kearney 1995:549; see also Appadurai 1991 and Rouse 1995a), transnationalism is closely linked with broader interests emerging from postmodernist and feminist theory to theorize space and place in new ways (Feld and Basso 1996; Gupta and Ferguson 1992, 1997). Indeed, new thinking about the nature of community and how people become members of a community, including consideration of so-called border cultures (Alvarez 1995; Kearney 1991) and exploration of the relevance of Anderson's (1983) concept of the "imagined community" to immigration (Chavez 1991, 1994; Smith 1993), have been part of the new research on global space.[7] Gupta and Ferguson (1992:11) have argued that immigrants "use memory of place to construct imaginatively their new lived world," while Chavez (1991) views the imagining of community as two pronged—both from the point of view of immigrants and from the point of view of the host society. A sense of belonging emerges among the undocumented when they have "overcome feelings of isolation, developed a network of family and friends in the local community, acquired local cultural knowledge, and reconciled themselves to the possible threat of deportation" (Chavez 1991:272). Migrants themselves describe this process in terms of an emic (i.e., their own) notion of adaptation. Etically (i.e., from the analyst's point of view) Chavez draws on the idea of transition as formulated by Arnold Van Gennep to describe incorporation as a process of moving from outsider to insider. However, full incorporation, Chavez argues, requires that the larger society also "imagine" immigrants as members of their community.

Chavez's research is important because it focuses attention on issues of reception and representation of the "immigrant other." This topic has been explored from a number of different theoretical perspectives. Judith Goode (1990) reframes the relations between newcomers and established residents in a community in Philadelphia as host-guest relations and argues that hosts welcome newcomers "if they try to learn the rules" (126). In this community some of the immigrants are more educated and wield more economic power than the established residents, a difference that generates tension. Goode points to the contested arenas and military metaphors, such as "stand the ground," that residents use to express their concern. She also describes the expectations (including being a loyal American) that they hold for newcomers. Cole (1997), in a study of immigrants in Italy, calls for theorizing immigrant reception in relation to institutional or structural racism as well as class and regional identities, while Borneman (1998) draws on discourse analysis, theories of representation, and Goffman's (1963) work on stigma and labeling to explain the negative reception of Marielitos in the United States who were classified as communists, criminals, and homosexuals.[8] Finally, Koptiuch (1996) takes the question of reception in a somewhat different direction with an incisive, critical analysis of the legal strategy of "cultural defense" that characterizes some cases involving Asian immigrants that are brought into the courtrooms of the United States. Thus the attorney for a Hmong "tribesman" brought before a judge to answer criminal charges of kidnapping and rape of a Hmong college coed argues that his client is simply carrying out the cultural ritual of marriage by capture. Criminal charges in this case were dropped in favor of a lesser sentence. But, in Koptiuch's view, this is a form of paternalist and orientalist colonial discourse applied to the empire within. "From a spectacular collapse of space, time, and subjectivity, the law takes license to retrieve a non-historical, primitivized, feminized image of Asia that facilitates ... the denial of coevalness between Asia and the United States" (Koptiuch 1996:229). This work offers an excellent, albeit rare, example of how anthropology and the law have come together in the study of the implications of the persistence of cultural patterns among immigrants.

To conclude, transnationalism offers an alternative to and a critique of earlier manifestations of articulation theory that "posit a primeval state of autonomy (usually labeled precapitalist), which is then violated by global capitalism" (Gupta and Ferguson 1992:8). It has generated new ideas about the representation and incorporation of immigrants and the deterritorialization, if not the actual disintegration, of nation-states (Appadurai 1996; Gupta 1992; Hannerz 1992); and it lies behind efforts to merge migration studies with diaspora studies (Clifford 1997). Immigrants in the transnational and global world are involved in the nation-building of more than one state; thus national identities are not only blurred but also negotiated or constructed. "We live in a world where identities increasingly come to be, if not wholly deterritorialized, at least differently territorialized. Refugees, migrants, displaced and stateless peoples—these are perhaps the first to live these realities in their most complete form" (Gupta and Ferguson 1992:9). Some anthropologists have recently argued that the transnational arrangements constructed by "ordinary migrants, their families and their friends, have undermined both the political dominance exerted by the state and its cultural authority" (Rouse 1995a:358; see also Appadurai 1996 and Kearney 1991) and are therefore beginning to address the question of citizenship from a transnational perspective. Borneman (1997), for example, compares the exclusion from citizenship of immigrants in Germany who are legal residents and who have become culturally and linguistically German with the inclusion of ethnic Germans who have resided elsewhere in the world, sometimes for more than two centuries, and who are in fact linguistically and cultural distinct.

THEORIZING THE SOCIAL ORGANIZATION OF MIGRATION: KINSHIP, NETWORKS, GENDER, AND ETHNIC ENCLAVES

The anthropologist generally locates transnational processes within the lives of individuals and families and particularly in the personal, economic, and social connections that articulate the world they have left with the world they have entered (Goodson-Lawes 1993; Mahler 1995; Min 1998; Pessar 1995a; Wong 1998). In other words, if the roots of the discipline are in the study of kinship and social organization, then these roots are also at the core of migration research in anthropology and revolve in particular around the concept of social network, which gained importance as anthropologists turned their attention to the study of complex societies and urban populations (Boissevain and Mitchell 1973; Mitchell 1971, 1974).[9] Although considered by many to be no more than a tool of research and a method of analysis, in fact theories about how social relationships are forged and how social systems are constructed are at the foundation of network analysis.

In a wide range of cross-cultural contexts, anthropologists have examined the role of networks, based largely on ties of kinship and friendship, in the process of chain migration or what Wilson (1994) has recently labeled "network-mediated migration" (Butterworth 1962; Fjellman and Gladwin 1985; Gardner 1995; Graves and Graves 1974; Margaret Grieco 1995; Elizabeth Grieco 1998; Ho 1993; Kearney and Nagengast 1989; Kemper 1977; Massey et al. 1987). Often, these anthropologists have emphasized multiple destinations rather than a bipolar model linking one sending society to one receiving area (Du Toit 1990; Ho 1993; Uzzell 1976; Wilson 1994). "Network-mediated chain migration does not necessarily mean that prospective migrants or migrant families are given only one or a few options as to where they will go.... [M]igrants ... seek work first one place, then another, where they have kin and friends. In retrospect this can appear as a step migration pattern to an ultimate destination to which a migrant recurrently returns or where he/she finally settles in with or without his/her family" (Wilson 1994:272). Wilson goes on to argue (1994:275) that migration networks must be conceived as facilitating rather than encapsulating, as permeable, expanding, and fluid rather than as correlating with a metaphor of a rigid and bounded structure. She prefers this network approach to a market theory approach that involves immigrants in a cost-benefit analysis of the most favorable destination. Thus she concurs with the conclusion drawn by Massey et al. (1993:449) who suggest that networks can become self-perpetuating to migration because "each act of migration itself creates the social structure needed to sustain it. Every new migrant reduces the costs of subsequent migration for a set of friends and relatives, and some of these people are thereby induced to migrate, which further expands the set of people with ties abroad." The theory of network-mediated migration is quite distinct from theories rooted in the rational-choice and decision-making models preferred by some economists and political scientists. Indeed, it is only with a network-based model that Chapin (1992) could formulate her argument that lower-class emigrant tourists who return to the Azores for vacations stimulate the emigration of upper-class individuals.

Both transnationalism and the study of social networks have shifted the unit of analysis from the individual migrant to the migrant household (Briody 1987). Households and social networks mediate the relationship between the individual and the world system and provide a more proactive understanding of the migrant than that provided by the historical-structuralist framework. In other words, the effort to combine macro- and microperspectives of analysis through the filter of the household not only brings the migrant-as-decision-maker back into focus, but also reintroduces the social and cultural variables that must be considered in conjunction with economic variables. This synthetic approach permits an analysis of subtle differences between those local communities or social classes that become extensively involved in migration and those that do not. It also provides more understanding of how migration streams are perpetuated despite changes in economic and political policies that serve to constrain or halt them. Grasmuck and Pessar (1991:15, 13) have made the case most pointedly: "It is not individuals but households that mobilize resources and support, receive and allocate remittances, and make decisions about members' production, consumption and distribution of activities.... Social networks and households simultaneously mediate macrostructural changes, facilitate the migration response to these changes, and perpetuate migration as a self-sustaining social process."

While anthropologists have recognized the significance of networks of kinship and friendship to the process of migration, they have also paid a good deal of attention to and hence theorized about the role of networks in the process of settlement and adaptation in the society of immigration—that is, how networks provide social capital. Lomnitz (1977), for example, found that kinship networks were the basic units of production and consumption among rural-urban migrants in Mexico. In his work among undocumented Central Americans in Houston, Rodriguez observes the "larger the social network that serves for organizing undocumented migration, the greater are the social and economic resources that can be mustered for settlement, leading to greater household stability" (Rodriguez 1987:17; see also Anwar 1995; Benson 1990; Brettell and Callier-Boisvert 1977; Buechler 1976; Gold 1989; Grieco 1998; Lamphere, Silva, and Sousa 1980). Ho (1993) looks carefully at the sharing and reciprocity that occurs within kinship networks that cross national boundaries to create international families and a common practice of child fostering that aids migrants in achieving their goals (see also Nelson 1987; Soto 1987; Spiegel 1987). Finally, Werbner (1990), in a fascinating study of the relationship between labor migration and the gift economy, stresses the central role of networks not only in the processes of distribution and credit among Pakistani entrepreneurs in Manchester, England, but also as the foundation for complex relationships of gift exchange that bind the community together. "Through gifting migrants transform persons who are strangers into lifelong friends. Through such exchanges, not only men but whole households and extended families are linked, and exchanges initiated on the shop floor extend into the domestic and inter-domestic domain" (Werbner 1990:332; see also Werbner 1995 and White 1997). Although she does not invoke it directly, Werbner's analysis fits squarely into the interactionist theoretical approach that has its roots in Marcel Mauss's classic essay *The Gift*.[10]

Immigrant women are often at the center of these immigrant networks. They both initiate and maintain them (Kossoudji and Ranney 1984; Smith 1976; Stafford 1984; Werbner 1988; Yanagisako 1985; Zavella 1988). O'Connor (1990) describes the female-centered informal networks based on the Mexican tradition of *confianza* (trust) that emerge among Mexican women working in a wholesale nursery in California. These networks help immigrant women to cope successfully "with the conditions imposed by the Anglo-dominated political and economic structure" (O'Connor 1990:97), or to "discover ways to negotiate patriarchal barriers" (Hondagenu-Sotelo 1994:94). Married women in particular use them to facilitate their own migration, often without the knowledge of their husbands.

Despite Ravenstein's (1885) claim more than a century ago that women dominated short-distance population movements, women were generally ignored in the study of migration until quite recently.[11] If women were considered at all, then it was as dependents and passive followers of the initiating male migrant. Alternatively, women were the ones who waited in the countryside, assuming many of the responsibilities that had once been in the hands of men.[12] This particular conceptualization of the relationship between women and the process of migration suited modernization theory—women represented the traditional pole of the continuum and men the pole of modernity. Today it is apparent that not only are women often the first to migrate (sometimes they receive the initial job contract), but they also outnumber men in some international migration streams—for example, among Caribbean immigrants to the United States. Gender has been shown to be important in the decision to migrate (when, where, and who) as well as in the process of settlement in the receiving society.

Anthropologists have been at the forefront in theorizing about the significance of gender in migration (Brettell and deBerjeois 1992; Brydon 1987; Buijs 1993; Chavez et al. 1997; Goodman 1987; Ho 1993; Hondagneu-Sotelo 1992, 1994; Morokvasic 1984; Phizacklea 1983; Simon and Brettell 1986; Westwood and Bhachu 1988). This research focuses on the role and experiences of women in migration and on the changes that occur in family and kinship patterns as a result of migration (Foner 1997a; Kibria 1993). It examines the labor force participation of immigrant women (it is high), the impact of salaried employment on domestic roles and domestic power, health issues, and issues of political consciousness-raising. Much of this research can be squarely situated in relation to analytical models at the heart of feminist anthropology—the domestic-public model that explores women's status in relation to different spheres of activity and the model springing from Marxist feminism that addresses the interrelationship between production and reproduction. Among the questions explored are whether wage earning serves to enhance the power and status of immigrant women within their households, whether greater sharing of household activities emerges as a result of the work obligations of women, and how changes in employment, family structure, and lifestyle affect women's own assessments of their well being (Fernandez-Kelly 1990; Freidenberg et al. 1988; Hirsch 1999; Lamphere 1987; Meintel 1987; Mills 1998; Stafford 1984). Chai (1987a, 1987b), for example, explicitly applies the conceptual scheme of domestic/public to an analysis of Korean immigrant women in Hawaii. Middle-class and well-educated Korean women have been relegated to the domestic sphere in their home society, but as immigrants they take waged work outside the home. This wage earning "may lead to a more flexible division of labor, decision making and parental responsibility, as well as to less sex segregation in social and public places" (Chai 1987b:229). Korean women who tire of the menial jobs to which they are relegated in the public domain often revert to working in family-owned businesses and construct their own public domain with its own ladder of achievement within the Korean ethnic community. Bhachu (1988:76), in a study of the waged work of Sikh immigrant women in Britain, moves "beyond the simple thesis that wage labour equals liberation" to argue that "women's increased ability to develop more self-defined roles has been aided by their increased access to cash, which has allowed them to invest and consume in their own interests and for their own benefit." She also argues that specific cultural values and social patterns have undergone radical changes as a result both of migration and women's waged labor. Although the waged work of Dominican immigrant women in the United States leads to improved domestic social relations and ideology, "these household level changes do not in turn stimulate modifications in female workers's consciousness and demands for improved conditions in the workplace" (Pessar 1984:1189). By contrast, in Stockton, California, the informal economic activities in which Cambodian refugee women engage to generate extra earnings, as well as the fact that there are more job opportunities for women in this particular local economy, provide the basis for their emergent leadership roles within a community where they are the primary breadwinners (Ui 1991).[13]

The new sense of control that women gain as immigrants has raised questions for some anthropologists about the varying attitudes of men and women toward both life abroad and return migration. While some immigrant women yearn for the homeland (Goodson-Lawes 1993), research has more often demonstrated that women are often more reluctant to return to the sending society than are migrant men because it will mean giving up some of the advantages they have gained while abroad (Barou 1996). Gmelch and Gmelch (1995), in a comparative study of returnees to several countries of origin, found that women were less satisfied than men to be "home" and had greater problems of readjustment. They suggest that this is due not to differential motivations for return but to limited employment opportunities and specific social conditions that constrain women's social relationships. Goodson-Lawes (1993), in her study of Mexican women in Mexico and California, argues that the central issue is one of authority and power. In some cases women may feel that they have more power, even if more covert than overt, in their home village: "The type and extent of feminine authority wielded may be altered with immigration and thus affects the decision to emigrate or to return. In large part this decision can be understood as the product of a tension between desired control and imagined opportunity. When the possibilities of the North surpass, in a personal equation, the need to maintain a sense of personal control, one is enticed toward the border" (Goodson-Lawes 1993:293).

In general, anthropological research on immigrant women that is framed in relation to the domestic/public model, the opposition between production and reproduction, or issues of power and authority, all of which are central to feminist anthropological theory (Moore 1988, 1994), indicates a set of complex and varied responses to the necessity of balancing work and family life. In some cases greater equality between men and women is the result, in others it is not. The differences must be explained by a close examination of cultural factors (including gender ideology) and economic constraints. Recently, Pessar (1995b) has argued that the study of immigrant women challenges claims of feminist theorists about the nature of unpaid domestic work and the relationship between waged work and women's emancipation. Drawing from postmodern feminist theory, she adopts an inner subjectivity to stress that immigrant women do not necessarily view their situation as oppressive and that in fact many forge multiple and complex identities.[14]

Working within a political-economy theoretical framework, research on how the social position of immigrant women is affected by the social, economic, and political policies of states has also been a topic of research. Some theorists have described a "triple invisibility" for migrant women based on factors of class, ethnicity, and gender (Chavira-Prado 1992; Lamphere 1986; Marshall 1981; Melville 1988; Morokvasic 1983; Segura 1989). Segmented occupational structures funnel immigrant women into a few sectors of the economy, the garment industry and domestic service in particular (Fernandez-Kelly and Garcia 1985; Neale and Neale 1987; Repak 1995). Colen (1990) describes the West Indian household workers who had to put up with the long hours and myriad responsibilities to obtain their green cards with the help of an employer-sponsor. She argues that "a system of reproduction operates, encouraged by the state, which is highly stratified by class, race, place in a global political economy, and migration status" (Colen 1990:110). For some immigrant women the segmented labor market has meant downward mobility (Chai 1987a; Gold 1989; Margolis 1990). One Haitian woman complained, "The job I do is for an animal. It's the same day after day. I used to be a schoolteacher in Haiti. Now I'm doing a job that doesn't even require me to think" (Stafford 1984:181). Exploring the questions of gender, migration, and exploitation from a somewhat different angle, Margold (1995) describes the disintegration of self and the dismemberment of masculinity among Filipino male migrants in the Middle East who are referred to as "dogs" and "slaves," while Mills (1998) addresses how Thai female migrants negotiate gendered identities in relation to courtship and marriage in the context of the hegemonic forces of global capitalism. She concludes that "migrant women's encounters with dominant notions of Thai modernity engage them in the pursuit of new models of self-fulfillment and personal autonomy that focus their concerns on individual gendered dilemmas and choices rather than broader structures and relations of power" (Mills 1998:325).

While many immigrant women internalize the discrimination that ensues from this employment situation, others, in rarer instances, have become part of group-based political action (Giles 1991, 1992, 1993; Groves and Chang 1999; Ong 1987; Salzinger 1991). Much of this work is informed by broader thinking within feminist anthropology on formal and informal strategies of resistance that is itself shaped by the work of James Scott and by Anthony Giddens' theory of agency (Giddens 1984; Scott 1985; see also L. Abu-Lughod 1990; Moore 1994; Ortner 1995). It also challenges widely accepted notions that cultural constraints and a tight-knit ethnic enclave preclude immigrant women from engaging in political and leadership activities within and on behalf of their communities.

Of particular interest is Ui's (1991) study of female leadership in the Cambodian refugee community in Stockton, California. She argues that the rapid growth of the enclave has resulted in an expansion of service programs for Cambodians, which has in turn created employment opportunities that are disproportionately filled by women. These positions become the basis for obtaining economic and social power and hence leadership roles. Her conclusion offers a hypothesis that can be tested within other immigrant communities: "Despite traditional culture and gender roles, female leadership will develop and emerge when groups are in a situation in which ethnic identity and unity are strong, the employment opportunities for women are greater than those for men, and the intervention of the welfare state is significant" (Ui 1991:175).

Ui's study indicates that the concept of the ethnic enclave, addressed quite extensively by sociologists, is also of some importance to anthropological thinking about institution building, community formation, insertion into a particular urban economy and society, and the creation of ethnic space among immigrant populations (Harbottle 1997; Herman 1979; Kwong 1997; Werbner 1987; Wong 1998). Brettell (1981) has asked whether an ethnic enclave or community is inevitable in a broader comparative context, and points to immigration policy, laws about small business proprietorship, and the structure of cities as important variables to consider. Similarly, Werbner (1990), in research on Sikhs in Britain, addresses the question of whether and how enclave economies are formed, relating this process in some cases to the relative weight of ethnic versus class resources as principles of social organization within an immigrant community. Finally, based on research among Latinos in Washington, D.C., Pessar concludes that the emergence of social solidarity and an ethnic enclave is not inevitable and is unlikely where "immigrants do not face major hurdles to full participation in mainstream social and economic institutions" (Pessar 1995c:391).

Studies of ethnic enclaves in sociology are also linked with theories about the extent to which the ethnic economy and self-employment deter or promote immigrant incorporation and social and economic mobility. These are also questions explored by some anthropologists. Alvarez (1990), for example, challenging widely held notions that Mexican immigrants have a low level of involvement in entrepreneurship and the ethnic economy, outlines their activities in the Los Angeles produce industry. He finds it necessary to move beyond dual economy and labor market theory to anthropological theories about market hierarchies, formulated initially in the study of peasant societies in Asia and Latin America, in order to explain what has happened. Boissevain and Grotenbreg (1986) have examined variables such as experience and feeling about management, access to loyal and cheap labor, a patriarchal family structure, access to capital, the ability to control the administration of credit, access to a network of contacts, ambition and willingness to take risk, and a desire for independence to explain differences in the degree of self-employment among Surinamese of various ethnic backgrounds (Hindustani, Creole, Chinese, Javanese) who reside in Amsterdam. In another essay, Boissevain and Grotenbreg (1989) address the legal constraints on the self-employment of immigrants. Their research can be situated in relation to the theoretical debate within sociology (specifically in the work of Ivan Light and Edna Bonacich 1988) between cultural background and structural conditions as explanations for rates of entrepreneurship. They conclude that the harsh analytical distinction is inappropriate.

The work on ethnic enclaves and the ethnic economy within anthropology can also be related to a separate literature within urban anthropology that focuses on "the city as context" as an important framework within which to examine the process of adaptation and institution building among immigrant populations (Foner 1987a; Lamphere 1992; Rollwagen 1974a, 1974b; M. Smith 1974). In an attempt to "theorize the city," Low (1997) distinguishes between ethnic cities, gendered cities, and global cities. She delineates two different approaches in research on ethnic cities. One describes the ethnic city as a "mosaic of enclaves that are economically, linguistically and socially self-contained as a strategy of political and economic survival." The other focuses on ethnic groups defined "by their location in the occupational structure, their position in the local immigrant social structure, their degree of marginality, and/or their historical and racial distinctiveness as the basis of discrimination and oppression" (Low 1997:405; see also Low 1996). Low's formulations suggest a profitable new direction in research, one that reunites theories of migration and theories of urbanization.

THEORIZING MIGRATION/THEORIZING ETHNICITY AND IDENTITY

Clearly, anthropological studies of ethnic enclaves and entrepreneurship among migrant populations also underscore the close connections between theorizing migration and theorizing ethnicity. Indeed, Kearney (1995:559) has observed that "at the heart of current anthropological concerns with transnationalism, identity politics, migration, and human rights is the persistence, resurgence, or de novo emergence of ethnicity at a time when, according to modernization theory, it was to have been attenuated by robust nation states." He links the growing interest in the concept of identity and by extension ethnicity to the "implosion" of the concept of culture.[15]

Anthropological consideration of ethnicity has its origins in the research of the first generation of urban anthropologists working in Africa. Seminal work such as J. Clyde Mitchell's (1957) study of the Kalela Dance in Rhodesia (now Zambia), Epstein's (1958) monograph, *Politics in an Urban African Community*, and Abner Cohen's (1969) analysis of how Hausa traders used ethnicity for their own political and economic ends, challenged the assumption that detribalization was the inevitable outcome of the movement of rural dwellers to cities—clearly another critique of modernization theory. Much of this early work wrestled with the conceptual differences between "tribe" and "ethnic group" and resulted in the delineation of three distinct theoretical approaches to the study of ethnicity.[16] The primordialist approach, which prevailed until the 1960s, argues that ethnic identity is the result of deep-rooted attachments to group and culture; the instrumentalist approach focuses on ethnicity as a political strategy that is pursued for pragmatic interests; and the situational approach, emerging from the theoretical work of Frederik Barth (1969), emphasizes the fluidity and contingency of ethnic identity which is constructed in specific historical and social contexts (Banks 1996).

In studies of migration by anthropologists, the latter two approaches have attracted the most attention, not only because they suit the more emergent and interactive understanding of culture and the poststructuralist emphasis on the multiple and shifting basis of self-representation (Gupta and Ferguson 1997), but also because the act of migration brings populations of different backgrounds into contact with one another and hence creates boundaries. It is the negotiation across such boundaries, themselves shifting, that is at the heart of ethnicity.[17] Ethnicity is a strategic response, invoked in particular situations (Durham 1989). Thus, Lyman and Douglass (1973:350) have argued that to treat ethnic identity "as a group phenomenon in which recruitment of membership is ascriptive forecloses study of the process whereby individuals make use of ethnicity as a maneuver or strategem in working out their own life chances in an ethnically pluralistic social setting." This is precisely the approach that Rouse (1995b) takes in his study of Mixtec migrants from the *municipio* of Aguililla in central western Mexico who are residing in Redwood City, California. "Most Aguilillans who migrated . . . did not negotiate a shift from one set of identities to another but instead moved from a world in which identity was not a central concern to one in which they were pressed with increasing force to adopt understandings of personhood and collectivity that privileged notions of autonomous self-possession and a formal equivalence between the members of a group" (Rouse 1995b:370).[18] Lessinger (1995:6) follows a similar line of argument in her research on Asian Indians in the United States. "For many Indian immigrants and their children, ethnic group identity and ethnicity, have become the point of entry into U.S. society, and the vehicle for carving out a social role.... When Indians first migrate to the United States they think of themselves as Indians living abroad, then begin to envision themselves as Americans. Very quickly, however, they realize that U.S. society divides itself along ethnic and racial lines. A great many Indian immigrants conclude that it is preferable to develop an ethnic group identity rather than accept a racial categorization."

Negotiating race and ethnicity is also part of the Jamaican and Haitian immigrant experiences in the United States (Foner 1985, 1987; Stafford 1987) and has led several anthropologists to argue that race and ethnicity need to be considered together in any theoretical formulations of the construction of immigrant identity (Banks 1996; Goode and Schneider 1994; Williams 1989). Stepick (1998) describes how Haitian immigrant youth construct their identity in relation or in contrast to that of African Americans. He characterizes the first case as a "Haitian cover-up" and reveals some intriguing differences between boys who choose to be monocultural (either Haitian or African American) and girls who choose to be multicultural (both Haitian and African American).

Similar issues and approaches arise in research among immigrants in the European context. The identity of Sikh immigrants in Britain is crosscut by differences of class and caste as well as by differences between "twice migrants" and direct migrants (Bhachu 1993). Mandel (1989), emphasizing how social context influences the expression of identity, describes Greeks and Turks who are bitter enemies in the homeland but who join in a common purpose as immigrants in Germany. At issue, she suggests, "are the ways self and other articulate, historically and in the migratory situation, with shifting hierarchies of 'others'" (Mandel 1989:62). White (1997:754) comes to a similar conclusion, arguing that Turkish identities in Berlin "are forged from class, ethnic, and religious loyalties, from institutional and media ethnoscapes (created by Germans and by Turks themselves), from shared regularities of interpersonal expectations of generalized reciprocity, and in reaction to how Turks are defined (and redefined after reunification) by Germans." She focuses on the processual, community-building aspects of identity rather than on those that rely on fixed and external markers such as language. All these scholars of immigration suggest that ethnicity, which Ronald Cohen (1978:387) has defined (from the situational perspective) as "series of nesting dichotomizations of inclusiveness and exclusiveness," provides a foundation for constructing social cohesion and allegiance. It organizes and legitimizes responsive action. It is the "location and reason for the maintenance of a we/they dichotomization" [that has become], in Cohen's view (1978:385), "the crucial goal of research and theorizing."

However, some anthropologists have explored the symbols or ethnic markers around which such dichotomizations are formulated or constructed. Beriss (1990), for example, analyzes the so-called Foulard Affair, the 1989 incident in France in which three young girls were expelled from a school for wearing Muslim scarves in class. At the center of the conflict were the issues of French national identity and the integration of immigrants. Gross, McMurray, and Swedenburg (1996) explore the role of a musical genre, *rai*, not only in the construction of Franco-Maghrebi identities in Paris and Marseilles but also in the recasting of contemporary French identity in less exclusive and more syncretized form. Koltyk (1993) discusses how story cloths and home videos become the focus for the definition of self and the reinforcement of ethnic affiliation among Hmong refugees in the United States. Drawing on the theoretical work of Clifford and Marcus (1986), she views the videos in particular as a form of ethnic voice by which Hmong can write their own history and take control of their future, including the process by which they are integrated into American society. Finally, and in a somewhat different vein, Harbottle (1997) analyzes how Iranian immigrants in Britain who are involved in the catering trade disguise and protect their ethnicity through their work with specific types of non-Iranian food.

Mandel (1996), in an essay that links ethnic entrepreneurship to the symbols of ethnic identity, describes shopkeepers in Kreuzberg, the "little Istanbul" of Berlin, who have used the fear of *haram* (forbidden meat) as well as that which is obligatory or permitted (*helal*) to their advantage, the result being a proliferation of shops that cater exclusively to Turks and the creation of a Muslim space in Germany that is then subdivided by religion, either Sunni or Alevi. This "commercial self-sufficiency," she argues, "is another way the migrants have recreated the place for themselves, and in their own terms.... In this new place, by their own actions and decisions, they are setting new precedents, as they project an agency of their own design, reshaping the Kreuzbergs of Europe into novel and heterogeneous communities" (Mandel 1996:163–64). Along similar lines, Brettell (1977) has used the concept of ethnic entrepreneurship to discuss those individuals in a Portuguese immigrant neighborhood in Toronto, Canada, who serve as gatekeepers, maintaining the boundaries between an immigrant community and the larger city and culture in which it is located. She draws, in particular, on theories about patron-client relationships and cultural brokers to illustrate how ethnicity is manipulated and negotiated. From a more critical perspective, Kwong (1997:366) argues that within the Chinese community in New York ethnic solidarity "has increasingly been manufactured by the economic elite ... to gain better control over their co-ethnic employees." Employers convince their employees, many of whom are illegal immigrants, that the larger society is hostile and racist. In what he views as a form of class exploitation, these coethnic elites control the boundaries of the ethnic community and promote ethnic identity to serve their own ends.

Within the migrant spaces such as those described by Brettell and Mandel, immigrants engage in a host of community activities that become expressions of their ethnic identity. Anthropologists have been particularly interested in religious institutions and activities.[19] Ralston (1992), for example, has explored the role of religion in the formation of personal and social identity among South Asian immigrant women in Canada. In the absence of residential concentration, it is the collective activities in religious institutions that provide the context for ethno-religious consciousness. Indeed, she argues that in the context of a Canadian policy of multiculturalism religious activities may be more prominent as markers of identity abroad than they are at home. In a somewhat similar vein, Park (1989:290) suggests that many Korean immigrants "go from being non-religious to becoming believers." In New York City, where a new Korean church was founded every six days in the mid-1980s, the church provides an ethnic forum for socializing and status seeking. She contrasts the double role of Christian churches to both promote Americanization and preserve Korean identity with the emphasis on the preservation of Korean culture in Buddhist churches. In particular, Park explores the meaning of being "born again" and its links to spirit possession in Korean shamanistic ritual.

McAlister (1998) also explores the fusing of religious traditions in the context of transnationalism in her description of the participation of Haitian immigrants in the feast of the Madonna of 115th Street, a feast originated by Italian immigrants (Orsi 1985). Several other ethnographers have documented the survival, if not elaboration, of Afro-Caribbean, spirit-based religions such as Voodoo and Santería among West Indian immigrants in the United States (Brown 1991; Gregory 1987; Murphy 1988). Among the most interesting is Tweed's (1997) monograph on the shrine of Our Lady of Charity which serves the Cuban community in Miami. Tensions between prescribed religion and religion as practiced, between official Catholicism and Santería rituals are apparent. But Tweed's broader argument is that Cuban exiles see the shrine in Miami as a place to express diasporic nationalism and construct a translocal identity. Levitt (1998a) also draws on ideas about translocal identity to describe a transnational religious system connecting Dominican immigrants in Boston with their home island. These religious connections are part of what she labels social remittances, the "ideas, practices, identities, and social capital that flow from receiving to sending-country communities" (Levitt 1998a:76). Religious life in the home community has changed as a result of immigrant religious life, while the Catholic Church in Boston has succeeded where political and economic organizations have failed in forging pan-ethnic coalitions.

This interest in religion is also manifested in anthropological studies of ethnic festivals. Schneider (1990) has analyzed the ethnic parades of Poles and Puerto Ricans in Philadelphia as symbolic presentations that encode ideas about being an immigrant and being an American. Parade commentators stress unity and community self-identification as messages conveyed by these events.

Similarly, Kasinitz and Freidenberg-Herbstein (1987) have compared a West Indian American Day Carnival and a Puerto Rican Day Parade in New York as manifestations of ethnic pride and civic politics. Abner Cohen (1980, 1993) has studied similar festivals among West Indian immigrants in Britain. Finally, Werbner (1996) describes the processions of Muslim men to celebrate anniversaries of death and rebirth that wind their way through the streets of immigrant neighborhoods in Birmingham, Manchester, and London, England. Through these processions Muslims "stamp the earth with the name of allah" and thereby "make territorial claims in their adopted cities . . . and assert their equal cultural claims within the society" (Werbner 1996:182).[20] All of these studies challenge unidirectional theories of assimilation, add agency and fluidity to the process of adaptation, and reinforce the theory that ethnicity is culturally constructed. As Glick Schiller (1977) suggested more than twenty years ago, "ethnic groups are made, not born."

CONCLUSION

Although migrants around the globe have common experiences, migration itself is a complex and diverse phenomenon. Migrants can be differentiated by sex, class, ethnicity, the nature of their labor force participation, their reasons for migrating, the stage of the lifecycle at which they move, the form of the migration (internal, international, temporary, and so on), and the nature and impact of global economic and political policies that affect population movement. A consideration of all these factors, from a comparative perspective, offers the best understanding of the process of migration and of migrant culture. It assumes that migrants act and are "acted upon" with reference to their social, cultural, and gendered locations.

But for anthropologists whose central interest is in the human dimensions of this global process and the lived experience of being a migrant, there are further considerations that guide their research. These considerations have their roots in several key concepts of the discipline that in turn ground anthropological theory. Thus, the distinction between nature and culture is at the foundation of theories of ethnicity that reject a primordial and inherent identity in favor of one that is socially constituted. The connections between society and culture, as well as an understanding of community that has both local (micro) and global (macro) dimensions helps to explain how migrants as transnationals can operate in or between two (or more) worlds. An acceptance of the common disjunction between the ideal and the actual permits more complex formulations of the processes of change and adaptation that are part of being a migrant. An awareness of the differences between participant's models (the emic perspective) and observer's models (the etic perspective), lends subtlety to our knowledge of similarities and differences and solidity to our theories about the particular and the general in the experience of migration.

Furthermore, an observer's model rooted in the interaction between structure and agency accepts the fact that migrants shape and are shaped by the context (political, economic, social, cultural) within which they operate, whether in the sending society or in the receiving society.[21] Finally, the holistic perspective draws anthropologists to an exploration of a range of social and cultural phenomena (religious rituals, for example) that both have an impact on and are affected by migration.

Much of what is written by anthropologists on the subject of migration may, at first glance, be dismissed as largely descriptive ethnography, but a closer examination indicates that while generally "located" in the study of a specific migrant community or population, most of this research is implicitly, if not explicitly, theoretical. If a theory is defined as "an explanation of a class of events, usually with an empirical referent, providing insight into how and what is going on, and sometimes explaining why phenomena exist" (Barrett 1997:40), then much of this ethnographic work makes a significant and sometimes unique contribution to our theoretical conversations across the disciplines.

NOTES

1. For a discussion of the essentializing character of Mead's work, see Gewertz and Errington 1991. More recently, Lavie and Swedenburg (1996:2) have posed the question of what Margaret Mead would have "made of Samoan gangs in Los Angeles, or of the L.A.-Samoan gansta rap group the Boo-Yah Tribe, named after the Samoan term 'boo yah!' for a shotgun blast in a drive-by shooting."

2. This turning point was marked by the theme of the 1970 volume of the proceedings of the American Ethnological Society, *Migration and Anthropology*, edited by Robert F. Spencer. Five years later, two volumes dealing with migration were the result of the World Anthropological Congress (Du Toit and Safa 1975; Safa and Du Toit 1975). In these volumes, migration was linked to urbanization and development.

3. Other volumes in this series are Margolis 1998; Min 1998; Pessar 1995a; Mahler 1995; and Wong 1998. For a review, see Brettell 1999.

4. A preliminary and much shorter discussion of the study of migration in anthropology appeared in the *Encyclopedia of Cultural Anthropology* published by the Human Relations Area Files; see Brettell 1996.

5. Escobar, Gonzalez, and Roberts (1987:59) also argue that stage in the life- and household cycle can also influence the place of destination. For further discussion of the historical relationship between migration and the peasant household, see Moch 1992, and Brettell forthcoming.

6. Arguing in support of the role of typologies in anthropological theory, Schweizer (1998:74) claims that "types are theoretical idealizations that can be illustrated by empirical cases and that are approximated by other cases belonging to a given type. The typology is refined in light of new empirical and theoretical evidence obtained by research." This contrasts with Portes's (1997:806) assessment that typologies simply "assert differences without specifying their origins or anticipating their consequences." These varying points of view speak to the distinctions in the nature of both theory and method in anthropology and sociology.

7. Alvarez (1995) cites Linda Whiteford's (1979) early work on the extended community as the first to emphasize an unbounded and cross-border community. From

this point on, Alvarez suggests "it became the task of anthropologists to clarify how people arranged and located themselves in these binational and extended communities" (Alvarez 1995:457). Many of those scholars who were working with return migration in the 1970s were also thinking within a transnationalist framework, yet they were not using the concept itself (Brettell 1979; Buechler and Buechler 1975; and an essay or two in the volume edited by Rhoades 1979). Most recently, Foner (1997b) has asked what is actually new about transnationalism in a comparative analysis of immigrants to New York at the turn of the century with those in more recent decades.

8. For additional discussions, see some of the essays in Lamphere 1992. For additional research on the reception and representation of immigrants in European countries, see Grillo 1985; Mandel 1989; McDonogh 1992; and Zinn 1994.

9. J. A. Barnes (1954) first recognized the analytical utility of the concept of social network in his research on a Norwegian fishing community. Social networks received a good deal of attention from British social anthropologists working among urban migrants in Africa in the 1960s (Epstein 1961; Gutkind 1965; Mayer 1966; Mitchell 1971, 1974). For a more recent discussion of social network analysis as a "theory-net," see Schweizer 1998.

10. See Layton 1997, for a complete discussion of this approach within anthropology.

11. This is equally true of much historical research. Several excellent monographs focusing on immigrant women have emerged in recent years to compensate for this lack of attention (Diner 1983; Friedman-Kasaba 1996; Gabaccia 1994). Most recently, Hondagneu-Sotelo (1994) has correctly argued that gender is an analytic category that should equally be applied to an understanding of men's migration.

12. Examples of research that addresses how wives who remain behind manage remittances and maintain the reproductive and productive activities of the home community can be found in Brettell 1986; Connell 1984; Georges 1992; Hammam 1996; Hondagneu-Sotelo 1992. See also Donnan and Werbner 1991.

13. Several volumes in the "New Immigrant Series," edited by Nancy Foner, address gender issues. See Brettell and deBerjeois 1992, for a more thorough development of the scholarship on gender and migration within anthropology. Recently, Hirsch (1999:1346) has argued that a focus on "the causes of women's empowerment has limited our understanding of gender and migration." We miss, she suggests, the interrelatedness of wage labor, on the one hand, and broader cultural and legal differences of life in the receiving society, on the other. Furthermore, we tend to assume that migration is always beneficial to women, which may not be the case.

14. See L. Abu-Lughod 1993 for a good example of the postmodern feminist approach.

15. For recent discussions of the concept of cultural identity, see Bammer 1994; Gupta and Ferguson 1992; Rouse 1995b; Williams 1989.

16. For a more thorough discussion than can be offered here, see Banks 1996. Earlier reviews can be found in R. Cohen 1978; Jenkins 1986; Reminick 1983. See also Wallman 1978, 1986. R. Cohen (1978:384), in particular, addresses the difference between "tribe" and "ethnic," the former characterized as isolated, primitive-atavistic, non-Western, bounded, systemic, and objectively identified; the latter characterized as nonisolated, contemporary, universally applicable, a unit in relation to others where the degree of systemic quality varies, and both objectively and subjectively identified. While the traditional/modern dichotomy underlies these differences, it is nevertheless apparent how the transfer from thinking about tribes to thinking about ethnic groups was influenced by a reconceptualization of the concept of culture.

17. Wallman (1986:229–30) has argued that anthropologists looking at ethnic relations "take account of the effect of context on the marking and meaning of ethnic difference, and since it is impossible to understand contextual factors without noticing

change, it is the variability of ethnic boundaries which catches the anthropologist's eye, and the logic of ethnic boundary processes which holds the profession's attention. . . . Differences between groups of people turn into ethnic boundaries only when heated into significance by the identity investments of either side." For another application of this approach, see Talai 1986.

18. In what is quite apparently a challenge to an outsider perspective and to the question of rights pursued by some political scientists, Rouse (1995b) suggests that few of these Mixtec migrants construed their problems in terms of prejudice and discrimination or by recourse to the language of rights.

19. Several of the authors who have contributed monographs to the "New Immigrant Series" edited by Nancy Foner include sections that deal with the significance of religious institutions in the formation of community and ethnic identity. Of course this interest in religion is not unique to anthropologists. Historians have also written about the role of religious institutions among immigrants in America. A recent book edited by Warner and Wittner (1998) includes a number of interesting chapters by scholars with diverse disciplinary backgrounds.

20. Anthropologists have also looked at the impact of returning migrants on the revitalization of festivals in the home community. See Brettell 1983; Cruces and Diaz de Roda 1992; Kenna 1992; and Levitt 1998a. Two ethnographic films, *Mayordomia: Ritual, Gender and Cultural Identity in a Zapotec Community* and *Oaxacalifornia*, also deal with this topic. Feldman Bianco's film *Saudade*, about Portuguese immigrants in New Bedford, Massachusetts, opens with the celebration of the Day of Portugal in that community.

21. Ortner (1996:12) conceptualizes this interaction as "the challenge to picture indissoluble formations of structurally embedded agency and intention-filled structures, to recognize the ways in which the subject is part of larger social and cultural webs, and in which social and cultural "systems" are predicated upon human desires and projects."

REFERENCES

Abu-Lughod, Lila. 1990. "The Romance of Resistance: Tracing Transformations of Power through Bedouin Women," *American Ethnologist* 17: 41–55.

———. 1993. *Writing Women's Worlds: Bedouin Stories*. Berkeley and Los Angeles: University of California Press.

Alvarez, Robert M. Jr. 1990. "Mexican Entrepreneurs and Markets in the City of Lost Angeles: A Case of An Immigrant Enclave," *Urban Anthropology* 19: 99–124.

———. 1995. "The Mexican-US Border: The Making of an Anthropology of Borderlands," *Annual Review of Anthropology* 24: 447–70.

Anderson, Benedict. 1983. *Imagined Communities: Reflections on the Origins and Spread of Nationalism*. London: Verso.

Anwar, Muhammad. 1995 "Social Networks of Pakistanis in the UK: A Re-evaluation," in Alisdair Rogers and Steven Vertovec, eds., *The Urban Context: Ethnicity, Social Networks and Situational Analysis*, pp. 237–57. Oxford: Berg.

Appadurai, Arjun. 1991. "Global Ethnoscapes: Notes and Queries for a Transnational Anthropology," in Richard Fox, ed., *Recapturing Anthropology*, pp. 191–210. Santa Fe, N.M.: School of American Research Press.

———. 1996. "Sovereignty without Territoriality: Notes for a Postnational Geography," in Patricia Yaeger, ed., *The Geography of Identity*, pp. 40–58. Ann Arbor: University of Michigan Press.

Arizpe, Lourdes. 1981. "Relay Migration and the Survival of the Peasant Household," in

Jorge Balan, ed., *Why People Move: Comparative Perspectives on the Dynamics of Internal Migration,* pp. 187–210. Paris: Unesco Press.

Bammer, Angelika, ed. 1994. *Displacements: Cultural Identities in Question.* Bloomington: Indiana University Press.

Banks, Marcus. 1996. *Ethnicity: Anthropological Constructions.* New York: Routledge.

Barnes, J. A. 1954. "Class and Committees in a Norwegian Island Parish," *Human Relations* 7: 39–58.

Barou, Jacques. 1996. "Portugais d'Auvergne: D'une identité villageoise à l'autre," *Revue d'Auvergne* 3: 147–59.

Barrett, Stanley R. 1997. *Anthropology: A Student's Guide to Theory and Method.* Toronto: University of Toronto Press.

Barth, Frederik, ed. 1969. *Ethnic Groups and Boundaries: The Social Organization of Cultural Difference.* London: George Allen and Unwin.

Basch, Linda, Nina Glick Schiller, and Cristina Szanton Blanc. 1994. *Nations Unbound: Transnational Projects, Postcolonial Predicaments, and Deterritorialized Nation-States.* Utrecht: Gordon and Breach Publishers.

Benson, Janet E. 1990. "Households, Migration and Community Context," *Urban Anthropology* 19: 9–29.

Beriss, David. 1990. "Scarves, Schools and Segregation: The Foulard Affair," *French Politics and Society* 8: 1–13.

Bhachu, Parminder. 1985. *Twice Migrants: East African Sikh Settlers in Britain.* London: Tavistock.

———. 1988. "Apni Marzi Kardhi Home and Work: Sikh Women in Britain," in Sallie Westwood and Parminder Bhachu, eds., *Enterprising Women: Ethnicity, Economy and Gender Relations*, pp. 76–102. London: Routledge.

———. 1993. "Twice and Direct Migrant Sikhs: Caste, Class and Identity in Pre- and Post-1984 Britain," in Ivan Light and Parminder Bhachu, eds., *Immigration and Entrepreneurship*, pp. 163–83. New Brunswick, N.J.: Transaction Press.

Boissevain, Jeremy and Hanneke Grotenbreg. 1986. "Culture, Structure and Ethnic Enterprise: The Surinamese of Amsterdam," *Ethnic and Racial Studies* 9: 1–22.

———. 1989. "Entrepreneurs and the Law: Self-employed Surinames in Amsterdam," in June Starr and Jane Collier, eds., *History and Power in the Study of Law: New Directions in Legal Anthropology,* pp. 223–51. Ithaca, N.Y.: Cornell University Press.

Boissevain, Jeremy, and J. Clyde Mitchell, eds. 1973. *Network Analysis.* The Hague: Mouton.

Borjas, George. 1989. "Economic Theory and International Migration," *International Migration Review* 23: 457–87.

Borneman, John. 1997. "State, Territory and National Identity Formation in the Two Berlins, 1945–1995," in Akhil Gupta and James Ferguson, eds., *Culture, Power, Place: Explorations in Critical Anthropology*, pp. 93–117. Durham, N.C.: Duke University Press.

———. 1998. "Emigrées as Bullets/Immigration as Penetration; Perceptions of the Marielitos," in John Borneman, *Subversions of International Order: Studies in the Political Anthropology of Culture*, pp. 249–72. Albany: SUNY Press.

Bourdieu. Pierre. 1977. *Outline of a Theory of Practice.* Cambridge: Cambridge University Press.

Brettell, Caroline B. 1977. "Ethnicity and Entrepreneurs: Portuguese Immigrants in a Canadian City," in George Hicks and Philip Leis, eds., *Ethnic Encounters: Identities and Contexts*, pp. 169–80. Belmont, Calif.: Wadsworth.

———. 1979. "Emigrar para Voltar: A Portuguese Ideology of Return Migration," *Papers in Anthropology* 20: 1–20.

———. 1981. "Is the Ethnic Community Inevitable? A Comparison of the Settlement

Patterns of Portuguese Immigrants in Toronto and Paris," *Journal of Ethnic Studies* 9: 1–17.

———. 1983. "Emigração, a Igreja, e a Festa Religioso no Norte do Portugal; estudo de um caso," *Estudos Contemporâneos* 5: 175–204.

———. 1986. *Men Who Migrate, Women Who Wait: Population and History in a Portuguese Parish.* Princeton, N.J.: Princeton University Press.

———. 1995. *We Have Already Cried Many Tears: The Stories of Three Portuguese Migrant Women.* Prospect Heights, Ill.: Waveland Press.

———. 1996. "Migration," in David Levinson and Melvin Ember, eds., *Encyclopedia of Cultural Anthropology*, vol. 3, pp. 793–97. New York: American Reference Publishing Company (Henry Holt and Company).

———. 1999. "New Immigrants to America: Contributions to Ethnography and Theory," *Identities* 5: 603–17.

———. Forthcoming. "A Society in Motion: Migration and the European Family, 1750–1914," in Marzio Barbagli and David I. Kertzer, eds., *History of the European Family.* New Haven, Conn.: Yale University Press.

Brettell, Caroline B., and Colette Callier-Boisvert. 1977. "Portuguese Immigrants in France: Familial and Social Networks and the Structuring of Community," *Studi Emigrazione/Études Migrations* 46: 149–203.

Brettell, Caroline B., and Patricia A. deBerjeois. 1992. "Anthropology and the Study of Immigrant Women," in Donna Gabaccia, ed., *Seeking Common Ground: Multidisciplinary Studies of Immigrant Women in the United States*, pp. 41–64. Westport, Conn.: Greenwood Press,

Briody, Elizabeth K. 1987. "Patterns of Household Immigration into South Texas," *International Migration Review* 21: 27–47.

Brown, Karen McCarthy. 1991. *Mama Lola: A Vodou Priestess in Brooklyn.* Berkeley and Los Angeles: University of California Press.

Brydon, Lynne. 1987. "Who Moves? Women and Migration in West Africa in the 1980s," in Jeremy Eades, ed., *Migrants, Workers, and the Social Order*, pp. 165–80. London: Tavistock.

Buechler, Hans C., and Judith-Maria Buechler. 1975. "Los Suizos: Galician Migration to Switzerland," in Helen I. Safa and Brian Du Toit, eds., *Migration and Development: Implications for Ethnic Identity and Political Conflict*, pp. 17–30. The Hague: Mouton.

Buechler, Judith-Maria. 1976. "Something Funny Happened on the Way to the Agora: A Comparison of Bolivian and Spanish Galician Migrants," *Anthropological Quarterly* 49: 62–69.

Buijs, Gina, ed. 1993. *Migrant Women: Crossing Boundaries and Changing Identities.* Oxford: Berg.

Butterworth, Douglas. 1962. "A Study of the Urbanization among Mixtec Migrants from Tilaltongo in Mexico City," *America Indígena* 22: 257–74.

Callier-Boisvert, Colette. 1987. "Working-class Portuguese Families in a French Provincial Town," in Hans Christian Buechler and Judith-Maria Buechler, eds., *Migrants in Europe: The Role of Family, Labor, and Politics*, pp. 61–76. Westport, Conn.: Greenwood Press.

Carter, Donald. 1997. *States of Grace: Senegalese in Italy and the New European Migration.* Minneapolis: University of Minnesota Press.

Caspari, Andrea, and Wenona Giles. 1986. "Immigration Policy and the Employment of Portuguese Migrant Women in the UK and France: A Comparative Analysis," in Rita J. Simon and Caroline B. Brettell, eds., *International Migration: The Female Experience*, pp. 152–77. Totowa, N.J.: Rowman & Allenheld.

Chai, Alice Yun. 1987a. "Adaptive Strategies of Recent Korean Immigrant Women in Hawaii," in Janet Shristanian, ed., *Beyond the Pubic/Domestic Dichotomy:*

Contemporary Perspectives on Women's Public Lives, pp. 65–100. Westport, Conn.: Greenwood Press.

———. 1987b. "Freed from the Elders but Locked into Labor: Korean Immigrant Women in Hawaii," *Women's Studies* 13: 223–33.

Chapin, Frances W. 1992. "Channels for Change: Emigrant Tourists and the Class Structure of Azorean Migration," *Human Organization* 51: 44–52.

Chavez, Leo R. 1988. "Settlers and Sojourners: The Case of Mexicans in the United States," *Human Organization* 47: 95–107.

———. 1990. "Coresidence and Resistance: Strategies for Survival among Undocumented Mexicans and Central Americans in the United States," *Urban Anthropology* 19: 31–61

———. 1991. "Outside the Imagined Community: Undocumented Settlers and Experiences of Incorporation," *American Ethnologist* 18: 257–78.

———. 1992. *Shadowed Lives: Undocumented Immigrants in American Society.* Fort Worth, Tex.: Holt, Rinehart and Winston.

———. 1994. "The Power of the Imagined Community: The Settlement of Undocumented Mexicans and Central Americans in the United States," *American Anthropologist* 96: 52–73.

Chavez, Leo, F. Allan Hubbell, Shiraz I. Mishra, and R. Burciaga Valdez. 1997. "Undocumented Latina Immigrants in Orange County, California: A Comparative Analysis." *International Migration Review* 31: 88–107.

Chavira-Prado, Alicia. 1992. "Work, Health, and the Family: Gender Structure and Women's Status in an Undocumented Migrant Population," *Human Organization* 51: 53–64.

Chock, Phyllis. 1991. "'Illegal Aliens' and 'Opportunity': Myth-Making in Congressional Testimony," *American Ethnologist* 18: 279–94.

Clifford, James. 1997. *Routes: Travel and Translation in the Late Twentieth Century.* Cambridge, Mass.: Harvard University Press.

Clifford, James, and George E. Marcus, eds. 1986. *Writing Culture: The Poetics and Politics of Ethnography.* Berkeley and Los Angeles: University of California Press.

Cohen, Abner. 1969. *Custom and Politics in Urban Africa.* London: Routledge and Kegan Paul.

———. 1980. "Drama and Politics in the Development of a London Carnival," *Man* 15: 65–87.

———. 1993. *Masquerade Politics: Explorations in the Structure of Urban Cultural Movements.* Berkeley and Los Angeles: University of California Press.

Cohen, Ronald. 1978. "Ethnicity: Problem and Focus in Anthropology," *Annual Review of Anthropology* 7: 379–403.

Cole, Jeffrey. 1997. *The New Racism in Europe: A Sicilian Ethnography.* Cambridge: Cambridge University Press.

Colen, Shellee. 1990. "Housekeeping for the Green Card: West Indian Household Workers, the State, and Stratified Reproduction in New York," in Roger Sanjek and Shellee Colen, eds. *At Work in Homes: Household Workers in World Perspective,* pp. 89–118. Washington, D.C.: American Ethnological Society, Monograph #3, American Anthropological Association.

Connell, John. 1984. "Status or Subjugation? Women, Migration and Development in the South Pacific," *International Migration Review* 18: 964–83.

Cruces, Francisco, and Angel Diaz de Roda. 1992. "Public Celebrations in a Spanish Valley," in Jeremy Boissevain, ed., *Revitalizing European Rituals*, pp. 62–79. London: Routledge.

Dahya, B. 1973. "Pakistanis in Britain. Transients or Settlers," *Race* 14: 241–77.

Di Leonardo, Micaela. 1984. *The Varieties of Ethnic Experience: Kinship, Class, and Gender among California Italian-Americans.* Ithaca, N.Y.: Cornell University Press.

Diner, Hasia R. 1983. *Erin's Daughters in America: Irish Immigrant Women in the Nineteenth Century.* Baltimore, Md.: The Johns Hopkins University Press.

Donnan, Hastings, and Pnina Werbner, eds. 1991. *Economy and Culture in Pakistan: Migrants and Cities in a Muslim Society.* New York: St. Martin's Press.

Douglass, William A. 1974. *Echalar and Murelaga: Opportunity and Rural Exodus in Two Spanish Basque Villages.* New York: St. Martin's Press.

Durham, William H. 1989. "Conflict, Migration, and Ethnicity: A Summary," in Nancie Gonzalez and Carolyn S. McCommon, eds., *Conflict, Migration and the Expression of Ethnicity*, pp. 138–45. Boulder, Colo.: Westview Press.

Du Toit, Brian. 1975. "A Decision-Making Model for the Study of Migration," in Brian Du Toit and Helen I. Safa, eds., *Migration and Urbanization: Models and Adaptive Strategies*, pp. 49–74. The Hague: Mouton.

———. 1990. "People on the Move: Rural-urban Migration with Special Reference to the Third World: Theoretical and Empirical Perspectives," *Human Organization* 49: 305–19.

Du Toit, Brian, and Helen I. Safa. 1975. *Migration and Urbanization: Models and Adaptive Strategies.* The Hague: Mouton.

Eades, Jeremy. 1980. *The Yoruba Today.* Cambridge: Cambridge University Press.

———, ed. 1987. *Migrants, Workers, and the Social Order.* London: Tavistock.

Epstein, A. L. 1958. *Politics in an Urban African Community.* Manchester, Eng.: Manchester University Press.

———. 1961. "The Network and Urban Social Organization," *Rhodes-Livingstone Journal* 29: 29–62.

Escobar, Agustin, Mercedes Gonzalez, and Bryan Roberts. 1987. "Migration, Labour Markets, and the International Economy: Jalisco, Mexico, and the United States," in Jeremy Eades, ed., *Migrants, Workers, and the Social Order*, pp. 42–64. London: Tavistock.

Feld, Steven, and Keith H. Basso, eds. 1996. *Senses of Place.* Santa Fe, N.M.: School of American Research Press.

Feldman-Bianco, Bela. 1992. "Multiple Layers of Time and Space: The Construction of Class, Ethnicity and Nationalism among Portuguese Immigrants," in Nina Glick Schiller, Linda Basch, and Cristina Blanc Szanton, eds., *Towards a Transnational Perspective on Migration: Race, Class, Ethnicity and Nationalism Reconsidered*, vol. 645, pp. 145–74. New York: Annals of the New York Academy of Sciences.

Fernandez-Kelly, Maria Patricia. 1990. "Delicate Transactions: Gender, Home, and Employment among Hispanic Women," in Faye Ginsburg and Anna Lowenhaupt Tsing, eds., *Uncertain Terms: Negotiating Gender in American Culture*, pp. 183–95. Boston: Beacon Press.

Fernandez-Kelly, Maria Patricia, and Anna M. Garcia. 1985. "The Making of an Underground Economy: Hispanic Women, Home Work and the Advanced Capitalist State," *Urban Anthropology* 14: 59–90.

Fjellman, Stephen M. and Hugh Gladwin. 1985. "Haitian Family Patterns of Migration to South Florida," *Human Organization* 44: 301–12.

Foner, Nancy. 1979. *Jamaica Farewell.* London: Routledge and Kegan Paul.

———. 1985. "Race and Color: Jamaican Migrants in London and New York City," *International Migration Review* 19: 706–27.

———. 1987a. "Introduction: New Immigrants and Changing Patterns in New York City," in Nancy Foner, ed., *New Immigrants in New York*, pp. 1–33. New York: Columbia University Press.

———. 1987b. "The Jamaicans: Race and Ethnicity among Migrants in New York City," in Nancy Foner, ed., *New Immigrants in New York*, pp. 195–217. New York: Columbia University Press.

———. 1997a. "The Immigrant Family: Cultural Legacies and Cultural Changes," *International Migration Review* 31: 961–74.

———. 1997b. "What's New About Transnationalism? New York Immigrants Today and at the Turn of the Century," *Diaspora* 6: 355–76.

✓   ———. 1999. "Anthropology and the Study of Immigration," *American Behavioral Scientist* 42: 1268–70.

Frank, Andre Gunder. 1967. *Capitalism and Underdevelopment in Latin America*. New York: Monthly Review Press.

Freeman, James M. 1995. *Changing Identities: Vietnamese Americans 1975–1995*. Boston: Allyn and Bacon.

Freidenberg, Judith, G. Imperiale, and M. L. Skovron. 1988. "Migrant Careers and Well-Being of Women," *International Migration Review* 22: 208–25.

Friedman-Kasaba, Kathie. 1996. *Memories of Migration; Gender, Ethnicity and Work in the Lives of Jewish and Italian Women in New York, 1870–1924*. Albany: SUNY Press.

Gabaccia, Donna. 1994. *From the Other Side: Women, Gender, & Immigrant Life in the United States 1820–1990*. Bloomington: Indiana University Press.

✓   Gardner, Katy. 1995. *Global Migrants, Local Lives: Travel and Transformation in Rural Bangladesh*. Oxford: Clarendon Press.

Georges, Eugenia. 1990. *The Making of a Transnational Community: Migration, Development, and Cultural Change in the Dominican Republic*. New York: Columbia University Press.

———. 1992. "Gender, Class, and Migration in the Dominican Republic: Women's Experiences in a Transnational Community," in Nina Glick Schiller, Linda Basch, and Christina Szanton Blanc, eds., *Towards a Transnational Perspective on Migration: Race, Class, Ethnicity, and Nationalism Reconsidered*, vol. 645, pp. 81–99. New York: Annals of the New York Academy of Sciences.

Gewertz, Deborah, and Frederick Errington. 1991. "We Think, Therefore They Are? Occidentalizing the World," *Anthropological Quarterly* 64: 80–91.

Giddens, Anthony. 1984. *The Constitution of Society*. Cambridge, Eng.: Polity Press.

Gilad, Lisa. 1989. *Ginger and Salt: Yemeni Jewish Women in an Israeli Town*. Boulder, Colo.: Westview Press.

Giles, Wenona. 1991. "Glass, Gender and Race Struggles in a Portuguese Neighborhood in London," *International Journal of Urban and Regional Research* 15: 432–41.

———. 1992. "Gender, Inequality and Resistance: The Case of Portuguese Women in London," *Anthropological Quarterly* 65: 67–79.

———. 1993. "Clean Jobs, Dirty Jobs: Ethnicity, Social Reproduction and Gendered Identity," *Culture* 13: 37–44.

Glick Schiller, Nina. 1977. "Ethnic Groups are Made, Not Born: The Haitian Immigrant and American Politics," in George Hicks and Philip Leis, eds., *Ethnic Encounters: Identities and Contexts*, pp. 23–35. Belmont, Calif.: Wadsworth.

———. 1997. "The Situation of Transnational Studies," *Identities* 4: 155–66.

Glick Schiller, Nina, Linda Basch, and Christina Szanton Blanc. 1992. "Transnationalism: A New Analytical Framework for Understanding Migration," in Nina Glick Schiller, Linda Basch, and Christina Szanton Blanc, eds., *Towards a Transnational Perspective on Migration: Race, Class, Ethnicity, and Nationalism Reconsidered*, vol. 645, pp. 1–24. New York, Annals of the New York Academy of Sciences.

———, eds. 1992. *Towards a Transnational Perspective on Migration: Race, Class, Ethnicity, and Nationalism Reconsidered*. New York: New York Academy of Sciences.

———. 1995. "From Immigrant to Transmigrant: Theorizing Transitional Migration," *Anthropological Quarterly* 68: 48–63.

Gmelch, George. 1980. "Return Migration," *Annual Review of Anthropology* 9: 135–59.

———. 1983. "Who Returns and Why: Return: Migration Behavior in Two Atlantic Societies," *Human Organization* 42: 46–54.

———. 1987. "Work, Innovation and Investment: The Impact of Return Migration in Barbados," *Human Organization* 46: 131–41.

———. 1992. *Double Passage: The Lives of Caribbean Migrants Abroad and Back Home.* Ann Arbor: University of Michigan Press.

Gmelch, George, and Sharon Bohn Gmelch. 1995. "Gender and Migration: The Readjustment of Women Migrants in Barbados, Ireland, and Newfoundland," *Human Organization* 54: 470–73.

Goffman, Erving. 1963. *Stigma.* Englewood Cliffs, N.J.: Prentice-Hall.

Gold, Steven J. 1989. "Differential Adjustment among New Immigrant Family Members," *Journal of Contemporary Ethnography* 17: 408–34.

———. 1995. *From the Workers's State to the Gold State: Jews from the Former Soviet Union in California.* Boston: Allyn and Bacon.

Gonzalez, Nancie L. Solien de. 1961. "Family Organization in Five Types of Migratory Wage Labor," *American Anthropologist* 63: 1264–80.

———. 1989. "Conflict, Migration, and the Expression of Ethnicity: Introduction," in Nancie Gonzalez and Carolyn S. McCommon, eds., *Conflict, Migration and the Expression of Ethnicity*, pp. 1–9. Boulder, Colo.: Westview Press.

———. 1992. *Dollar, Dove and Eagle: One Hundred Years of Palestinian Migration in Honduras.* Ann Arbor: University of Michigan Press.

Gonzalez, Nancie, and Carolyn S. McCommon, eds. 1989. *Conflict, Migration and the Expression of Ethnicity.* Boulder, Colo.: Westview Press.

Goode, Judith. 1990. "A War Welcome to the Neighborhood: Community Responses to Immigrants," *Urban Anthropology* 19: 125–53.

Goode, Judith, and J. A. Schneider. 1994. *Reshaping Ethnic and Racial Relations in Philadelphia: Immigrants in a Divided City.* Philadelphia, Pa.: Temple University Press.

Goodman, Charity. 1987. "A Day in the Life of a Single Spanish Woman in West Germany," in Hans Christian Buechler and Judith-Maria Buechler, eds., *Migrants in Europe: The Role of Family, Labor, and Politics,* pp. 207–19. Westport, Conn.: Greenwood Press.

Goodson-Lawes, J. 1993. "Feminine Authority and Migration: The Case of One Family from Mexico," *Urban Anthropology* 22: 277–97.

Grasmuck, Sherri, and Patricia R. Pessar. 1991. *Between Two Islands: Dominican International Migration.* Berkeley and Los Angeles: University of California Press.

Graves, Nancy B., and Theodore D. Graves. 1974. "Adaptive Strategies in Urban Migration," *Annual Review of Anthropology* 3: 117–51.

Gregory, David D., and Jose Cazorla. 1987. "Family and Migration in Andalusia," in Hans Christian Buechler and Judith-Maria Buechler, eds., *Migrants in Europe: The Role of Family, Labor, and Politics,* pp. 149–88. Westport, Conn.: Greenwood Press.

Gregory, S. 1987. "Afro-Caribbean Religions in New York City: The Case of Santeria," in Constance Sutton and Elsa Chaney, eds., *Caribbean Life in New York City: Sociocultural Dimensions,* pp. 307–24. New York: Center for Migration Studies.

Grieco, Elizabeth. 1998. "The Effects of Migration on the Establishment of Networks: Caste Disintegration and Reformation among the Indians of Fiji," *International Migration Review* 32: 704–36.

Grieco, Margaret. 1995. "Transported Lives: Urban Social Networks and Labour Circulation," in Alisdair Rogers and Steven Vertovec, eds., *The Urban Context: Ethnicity, Social Networks and Situational Analysis*, pp. 189–212. Oxford: Berg.

Grillo, Ralph. 1985. *Ideologies and Institutions in Urban France: The Representation of Immigrants.* Cambridge: Cambridge University Press.

Grimes, Kimberly M. 1998. *Crossing Borders: Changing Social Identities in Southern Mexico.* Tucson: University of Arizona Press.

Gross, Joan, David McMurray, and Ted Swedenburg. 1996. "Arab Noise and Ramadan Nights: *Rai*, Rap, and Franco-Maghrebi Identities," in Smadar Lavie and Ted Swedenburg, eds., *Displacement, Diaspora, and Geographies of Identity*, pp. 119–55. Durham, N.C.: Duke University Press.

Groves, Julian McAllister, and Kimberly A. Chang. 1999. "Romancing Resistance and Resisting Romance: Ethnography and the Construction of Power in the Filipina Domestic Worker Community in Hong Kong," *Journal of Contemporary Ethnography* 28: 235–65.

Guarnizo, Luis Eduardo. 1997. "The Emergence of a Transnational Social Formation and the Mirage of Return Migration among Dominican Transmigrants," *Identities* 4: 281–322.

Gulliver, P. H. 1957. "Nyakusa Labour Migration," *Rhodes-Livingstone Institute Bulletin* 21: 32–63.

Gupta, Akhil. 1992. "The Song of the Non-aligned World: Transnational Identities and the Reinscription of Space in Late Capitalism," *Cultural Anthropology* 7: 63–79.

Gupta, Akhil, and James Ferguson. 1992. "Beyond 'Culture': Space, Identity and the Politics of Difference," *Cultural Anthropology* 7: 6–23.

———. 1997. "Culture, Power, Place: Ethnography at the End of an Era," in Akhil Gupta and James Ferguson, eds., *Culture, Power, Place: Explorations in Critical Anthropology,* pp. 1–29. Durham, N.C.: Duke University Press.

Gutkind, Peter C. W. 1965. "African Urbanism, Mobility and the Social Network," *International Journal of Comparative Sociology* 6: 48–60.

Hammam, Mona. 1986. "Capitalist Development, Family Division of Labor, and Migration in the Middle East," in Eleanor Leacock and Helen I. Safa, eds., *Women's Work: Development and Division of Labor by Gender,* pp. 158–73. South Hadley, Mass.: Bergin and Garvey.

Hannerz, Ulf. 1992. "The Global Ecumene as a Network of Networks," in Adam Kuper, ed., *Conceptualizing Society*, pp. 34–56. New York: Routledge.

———. 1996. *Transnational Connections: Culture, People, Places.* New York: Routledge.

———. 1998. "Transnational Research," in H. Russell Bernard, ed., *Handbook of Methods in Cultural Anthropology*, pp. 235–56. Walnut Creek, Calif.: Altamira Press.

Harbottle, Lynn. 1997. "Fast Food/Spoiled Identity: Iranian Migrants in the British Catering Trade," in Pat Caplan, ed., *Food, Health and Identity*, pp. 87–110. New York: Routledge.

Herman, Harry Vjekoslav. 1979. "Dishwashers and Proprietors: Macedonians in Toronto's Restaurant Trade," in Sandra Wallman, ed., *Ethnicity at Work*, pp. 71–90. London: MacMillan Press.

Hirsch, Jennifer S. 1999. "En el Norte la Mujer Manda: Gender, Generation, and Geography in a Mexican Transnational Community," *American Behavioral Scientist* 42: 1332–49.

Ho, Christine G. T. 1993. "The Internationalization of Kinship and the Feminization of Caribbean Migration: The Case of Afro-Trinidadian Immigrants in Los Angeles," *Human Organization* 52: 32–40.

Holmes, Douglas. 1983. "A Peasant-Worker Model in a Northern Italian Context," *American Ethnologist* 10: 734–48.

Hondagneu-Sotelo, Pierrette. 1992. "Overcoming Patriarchal Constraints: The Reconstruction of Gender Relations among Mexican Immigrant Men and Women," *Gender and Society* 6: 393–415.

———. 1994. *Gendered Transitions: Mexican Experiences of Immigration.* Berkeley and Los Angeles: University of California Press.

Iszaevich, Abraham. 1974. "Emigrants, Spinsters, and Priests: The Dynamics of Demography in Spanish Peasant Societies," *Journal of Peasant Studies* 2: 292–312.

Jenkins, Richard. 1986. "Social Anthropological Models of Inter-ethnic Relations," in John Rex and Dick Mason, eds., *Theories of Race and Ethnic Relations,* pp. 170–85. Cambridge: Cambridge University Press.

Kasinitz, P., and J. Freidenberg-Herbstein. 1987. "The Puerto Rican Parade and West Indian Carnival: Public Celebrations in New York City," in Constance Sutton and Elsa Chaney, eds., *Caribbean Life in New York City: Sociocultural Dimensions*, pp. 327–49. New York: Center for Migration Studies.

Kearney, Michael. 1986. "From the Invisible Hand to Visible Feet: Anthropological Studies of Migration and Development," *Annual Review of Anthropology* 15: 331–404.

———. 1991. "Borders and Boundaries of State and Self at the End of Empire," *Journal of Historical Sociology* 4: 52–74.

———. 1995. "The Local and the Global: The Anthropology of Globalization and Transnationalism," *Annual Review of Anthropology* 24: 547–65.

Kearney, Michael, and Carole Nagengast. 1989. *Anthropological Perspectives on Transnational Communities in Rural California*. Davis: California Institute for Rural Studies.

Kemper, Robert V. 1977. *Migration and Adaptation: Tzintzuntzan Peasants in Mexico City*. Beverly Hills, Calif.: Sage Publications.

Kenna, Margaret E. 1992. "Mattresses and Migrants: A Patron Saint's Festival on a Small Greek Island Over Two Decades," in Jeremy Boissevain, ed., *Revitalizing European Rituals*, pp. 155–72. London: Routledge.

Kenney, Michael. 1976. "Twentieth Century Spanish Expatriate Ties with the Homeland: Remigration and its Consequences," in Joseph B. Aceves and William A. Douglass, eds., *The Changing Faces of Rural Spain*, pp. 97–122. New York: Schenkman.

Kertzer, David I. 1984. *Family Life in Central Italy, 1880–1910.* New Brunswick, N.J.: Rutgers University Press.

Kibria, Nazli. 1993. *Family Tightrope: The Changing Lives of Vietnamese Americans*. Princeton, N.J.: Princeton University Press.

Koltyk, Jo Ann. 1993. "Telling Narratives through Home Videos: Hmong Refugees and Self-Documentation of Life in the Old and New Country," *Journal of American Folklore* 106: 435–49.

———. 1998. *New Pioneers in the Heartland: Hmong Life in Wisconsin.* Boston: Allyn and Bacon.

Koptiuch, Kristin. 1996. "Cultural Defense and Criminological Displacements: Gender, Race, and (Trans)nation in the Legal Surveillance of U.S. Diaspora Asians," in Smadar Lavie and Ted Swedenburg, eds., *Displacement, Diaspora, and Geographies of Identity*, pp. 215–33. Durham, N.C.: Duke University Press.

Kossoudji, Sherrie A., and Susan I. Ranney. 1984. "The Labor Market Experience of Female Migrants: The Case of Temporary Mexican Migration to the U.S," *International Migration Review* 18: 120–43.

Kwong, Peter. 1997. "Manufacturing Ethnicity," *Critique of Anthropology* 17: 365–87.

Lamphere, Louise. 1986. "From Working Daughters to Working Mothers: Production and Reproduction in an Industrial Community," *American Ethnologist* 13: 118–30.

———. 1987. *From Working Daughters to Working Mothers: Immigrant Women in a New England Community*. Ithaca, N.Y.: Cornell University Press.

———, ed. 1992. *Structuring Diversity: Ethnographic Perspectives on the New Immigration*. Chicago: University of Chicago Press.

Lamphere, Louise, Filomena M. Silva, and John P. Sousa. 1980. "Kin Networks and Strategies of Working-Class Portuguese Families in a New England Town," in Linda Cordell and Stephen Beckerman, eds., *The Versatility of Kinship*, pp. 219–49. New York: Academic Press.

Lavie, Smadar, and Ted Swedenburg. 1996. "Introduction: Displacement, Diaspora, and Geographies of Identity," in Smadar Lavie and Ted Swedenburg, eds., *Displacement, Diaspora, and Geographies of Identity*, pp. 1–25. Durham, N.C.: Duke University Press.

Layton, Robert. 1997. *An Introduction to Theory in Anthropology*. Cambridge: Cambridge University Press.

Lessinger, Johanna. 1995. *From the Ganges to the Hudson: Indian Immigrants in New York City*. Boston: Allyn and Bacon.

Levitt, Peggy. 1998a. "Local-level Global Religion: The Case of U.S.-Dominican Migration," *Journal for the Scientific Study of Religion* 37: 74–89.

————. 1998b. "Social Remittances: Migration Driven Local-Level Forms of Cultural Diffusion," *International Migration Review* 32: 926–48.

Light, Ivan, and Edna Bonacich. 1988. *Immigrant Entrepreneurs: Koreans in Los Angeles, 1965–1982*. Berkeley and Los Angeles: University of California.

Lockwood, Victoria S. 1990. "Development and Return Migration to Rural French Polynesia," *International Migration Review* 24: 347–71.

Lomnitz, Larissa. 1977. *Networks and Marginality: Life in a Mexican Shantytown*. New York: Academic Press.

Low, Setha M. 1996. "The Anthropology of Cities: Imagining and Theorizing the City," *Annual Review of Anthropology* 25: 383–409.

————. 1997. "Theorizing the City: Ethnicity, Gender, and Globalization," *Critique of Anthropology* 17: 403–409.

Lyman, Stanford M., and William A. Douglass. 1973. "Ethnicity: Strategies of Collective and Individual Impression Management," *Social Research* 40: 344–65.

Mahler, Sarah J. 1995a. *American Dreaming: Immigrant Life on the Margins*. Princeton, N.J.: Princeton University Press.

————. 1995b. *Salvadorans in Suburbia: Symbiosis and Conflict*. Boston: Allyn and Bacon.

Malkki, Liisa H. 1995. "Refugees and Exile: From 'Refugee Studies' to the National Order of Things," *Annual Review of Anthropology* 24: 495–523.

Mandel, Ruth. 1989. "Ethnicity and Identity among Guestworkers in West Berlin," in Nancie L. Gonzalez and Carolyn S. McCommon, eds., *Conflict, Migration, and the Expression of Ethnicity*, pp. 60–74. Boulder, Colo.: Westview Press.

————. 1990. "Shifting Centers and Emergent Identities: Turkey and Germany in the Lives of Turkish Gastarbeiter," in Dale Eickelman and James Piscatori, eds., *Muslim Travelers: Pilgrimage, Migration, and the Religious Imagination*, pp. 153–71. Berkeley and Los Angeles: University of California Press.

————. 1991. "Foreigners in the Fatherland: Turkish Immigrants Workers in Germany," in G. Guyerin-Gonzales and C. Strikwerda, eds., *The Politics of Immigrant Workers: Labor Activism and Migration in the World Economy since 1830*. New York: Holmes and Meier.

————. 1994. "'Fortress Europe' and the Foreigners Within: Germany's Turks," in Victoria A. Goddard, Josep R. Llobera, and Cris Shore, eds., *The Anthropology of Europe: Identities and Boundaries in Conflict*, pp. 113–24. Oxford: Berg.

————. 1996. "A Place of Their Own: Contesting Spaces and Defining Places in Berlin's Migrant Community," in Barbara Daly Metcalf, ed., *Making Muslim Space in North America and Europe*, pp. 147–66. Berkeley and Los Angeles: University of California Press.

Mangin, William. 1970. *Peasants in Cities: Readings in the Anthropology of Urbanization*. Boston: Houghton Mifflin Company.

Marcus, George. 1995. "Ethnography in/of the World System: The Emergence of Multi-sited Ethnography," *Annual Review of Anthropology* 24: 95–117.

Margold, Jane A. 1995. "Narratives of Masculinity and Transnational Migration: Filipino

Workers in the Middle East," in Aihwa Ong and Michael G. Peletz, eds., *Bewitching Women, Pious Men; Gender and Body Politics in Southeast Asia*, pp. 274–98. Berkeley and Los Angeles: University of California Press.

Margolis, Maxine. 1990. "From Mistress to Servant: Downward Mobility among Brazilian Immigrants in New York City," *Urban Anthropology* 19: 215–30.

———. 1994. *Little Brazil: An Ethnography of Brazilian Immigrants in New York City.* Princeton, N.J.: Princeton University Press.

———. 1995. "Transnationalism and Popular Culture: The Case of Brazilian Immigrants in the United States," *Journal of Popular Culture* 29: 29–41.

———. 1998. *An Invisible Minority: Brazilians in New York City.* Boston: Allyn and Bacon.

Marshall, Paule. 1981. "Black Immigrant Women in Born Girls, Brownstones," in Delores Mortimer and Roy S. Bryce Laporte, eds., *Female Immigrants in the United States*, pp. 1–13. Washington, D.C.: Smithsonian Press.

Massey, Douglas S., Rafael Alarcon, Jorge Durand, and Humberto Gonzalez. 1987. *Return to Aztlan: The Social Process of International Migration from Western Mexico.* Berkeley and Los Angeles: University of California Press.

Massey, Douglas S., Joaquin Arango, Graeme Hugo, Ali Kouaouci, Adela Pellegrino, and J. Edward Taylor. 1993. "Theories of International Migration: A Review and Appraisal," *Population and Development Review* 19: 431–66.

———. 1994. "An Evaluation of International Migration Theory: The North American Case," *Population and Development Review* 20: 699–751.

Mayer, Adrian C. 1966. "The Significance of Quasi-groups in the Study of Complex Societies," in Michael Banton, ed., *The Social Anthropology of Complex Societies*, pp. 97–122. London: Tavistock.

Mayer, Philip. 1961. *Townsmen or Tribesmen.* Cape Town: Oxford University Press.

McAlister, Elizabeth. 1998. "The Madonna of 115th Street Revisited: Vodou and Haitian Catholicism in the Age of Transnationalism," in R. Stephen Warner and Judith G. Witnner, eds., *Gatherings in Diaspora. Religious Communities and the New Immigration*, pp. 123–60. Philadelphia, Pa.: Temple University Press.

McDonogh, Gary. 1992. "The Face Behind the Door: European Integration, Immigration, and Identity," in Thomas Wilson, ed., *Cultural Change and the New Europe*, pp. 143–65. Newbury Park, Calif.: Sage Publications.

McGee, T. G. 1975. "Malay Migration to Kuala Lumpur City: Individual Adaptation to the City," in Brian Du Toit and Helen I. Safa, eds., *Migration and Urbanization: Models and Adaptive Strategies*, pp. 143–78. The Hague: Mouton.

Mead, Margaret. 1930. *Growing Up in New Guinea.* New York: Mentor Books.

Meintel, Deidre. 1987. "The New Double Workday of Immigrant Workers in Quebec," *Women's Studies* 13: 273–93.

Melville, Margarita. 1988. *Mexicans at Work in the United States.* Houston, Tex.: Mexican American Studies Program, University of Houston.

Mills, Mary Beth. 1998. "Gendered Encounters with Modernity: Labor Migrants and Marriage Choices in Contemporary Thailand," *Identities* 5: 301–34.

Min, Pyong Gap. 1998. *Changes and Conflicts: Korean Immigrant Families in New York.* Boston: Allyn and Bacon.

Mitchell, J. Clyde. 1957. "The Kalela Dance: Aspects of Social Relationships among Urban Africans in Northern Rhodesia," *Rhodes Livingstone Papers,* no. 27. Manchester, Eng.: Manchester University Press.

———. 1969. "Structural Plurality, Urbanization and Labour Circulation in Southern Rhodesia," in J. A. Jackson, ed., *Migration*, pp. 156–80. Cambridge: Cambridge University Press.

———. 1971. *Social Networks in Urban Situations.* Manchester, Eng.: Manchester University Press.

————. 1974. "Social Networks," *Annual Review of Anthropology* 3: 279–99.

Moberg, Mark. 1996. "Transnational Labor and Refugee Enclaves in a Central American Banana Industry," *Human Organization* 55: 425–35.

Moch, Leslie Page. 1992. *Moving Europeans: Migration in Western Europe Since 1650.* Bloomington: Indiana University Press.

Moore, Henrietta. 1988. *Feminism and Anthropology.* Minneapolis: University of Minnesota Press.

————. 1994. *A Passion for Difference.* Bloomington: Indiana University Press.

Morokvasic, Mirjana. 1983. "Women in Migration: Beyond the Reductionist Outlook," in Annie Phizacklea, ed., *One-Way Ticket: Migration and Female Labour*, pp. 13–31. London: Routledge and Kegan Paul.

————. 1984. "Birds of Passage Are also Women," *International Migration Review* 18: 886–907.

Murphy, Joseph. 1988. *Santería: An African Religion in America.* Boston: Beacon Press.

Nash, Jesse W., and Elizabeth Nguyen. 1995. *Romance, Gender, and Religion in a Vietnamese-American Community: Tales of God and Beautiful Women.* Lewiston, N.Y.: Edwin Mellen Press.

Neale, Rusty, and Virginia Neale. 1987. "As Long as You Know How to do Housework: Portuguese-Canadian Women and the Office-Cleaning Industry in Toronto," *Resources for Feminist Research* 16: 39–41.

Nelson, Nici. 1987. "Rural-Urban Child Fostering in Kenya: Migration, Kinship Ideology, and Class," in Jeremy Eades, ed., *Migrants, Workers, and the Social Order*, pp. 181–98. London: Tavistock.

O'Connor, Mary. 1990. "Women's Networks and the Social Needs of Mexican Immigrants," *Urban Anthropology* 19: 81–98.

Ong, Aihwa. 1987. *Spirits of Resistance and Capitalist Discipline: Factory Women in Malaysia.* Albany: SUNY Press.

Orsi, Robert Anthony. 1985. *The Madonna of 115th Street: Faith and Community in Italian Harlem, 1880–1950.* New Haven, Conn.: Yale University Press.

Ortner, Sherry. 1984. "Theory in Anthropology since the Sixties," *Comparative Studies in Society and History* 26: 126–66.

————. 1995. "Resistance and the Problem of Ethnographic Refusal," *Comparative Studies in Society and History* 37: 173–93.

————. 1996. "Making Gender: Toward a Feminist, Minority, Postcolonial, Subaltern, etc., Theory of Practice," in Sherry Ortner, *Making Gender: The Politics and Erotics of Culture*, pp. 1–20. Boston: Beacon Press.

Park, Kyeyoung. 1989. "'Born Again': What Does it Mean to Korean-Americans in New York City," *Journal of Ritual Studies* 3: 287–301.

Pessar, Patricia R. 1984. "The Linkage between the Household and Workplace of Dominican Women in the U.S," *International Migration Review* 18: 1188–1211.

————. 1995a. *A Visa for a Dream: Dominicans in the United States.* Boston: Allyn and Bacon.

————. 1995b. "On the Homefront and In the Workplace: Integrating Immigrant Women into Feminist Discourse," *Anthropological Quarterly* 68: 37–47.

————. 1995c. "The Elusive Enclave: Ethnicity, Class, and Nationality among Latino Entrepreneurs in Greater Washington, D.C.," *Human Organization* 53: 383–92.

Philpott, Stuart B. 1970. "The Implications of Migration for Sending Societies: Some Theoretical Considerations," in R. F. Spencer, ed., *Migration and Anthropology*, pp. 9–20. Seattle, Wash.: American Ethnological Society.

————. 1973. *West Indian Migration.* London: London School of Economics Monograph.

Phizacklea, Annie. 1983. *One-Way Ticket: Migration and Female Labour.* London: Routledge and Kegan Paul.

Plotnicov, Leo. 1967. *Strangers to the City: Urban Man in Jos, Nigeria*. Pittsburgh, Pa.: University of Pittsburgh Press.

Portes, Alejandro. 1997. "Immigration Theory for a New Century: Some Problems and Opportunities," *International Migration Review* 31: 799–825.

Ralston, Helen. 1992. "Religion in the Life of South Asian Immigrant Women in Atlantic Canada," *Research in the Social Scientific Study of Religion* 4: 245–60.

Ravenstein, E. G. 1885. "The Laws of Migration,*" Journal of the Royal Statistical Society* 48: 167–277.

Redfield, Robert. 1941. *The Folk Culture of Yucatan*. Chicago: University of Chicago Press.

Reminick. Ronald. A. 1983. *Theory of Ethnicity: An Anthropologist's Perspective*. Lanham, Md.: University Press of America.

Repak, Terry A. 1995. *Waiting on Washington: Central American Workers in the Nation's Capital*. Philadelphia, Pa.: Temple University Press.

Rhoades, Robert E. 1978a. "Intra-European Migration and Rural Development: Lessons from the Spanish Case," *Human Organization* 37: 136–47.

———. 1978b. "Foreign Labor and German Industrial Capitalism 1871–1978: The Evolution of a Migratory System," *American Ethnologist* 5: 553–75.

———, ed. 1979. "Return Migration," *Papers in Anthropology*, vol. 20. Department of Anthropology: University of Oklahoma.

Rodriguez, Nestor. 1987. "Undocumented Central Americans in Houston: Diverse Populations," *International Migration Review* 21: 4–26.

Rollwagen, Jack. 1974a. "Introduction: The City as Context, A Symposium," *Urban Anthropology* 4: 1–4.

———. 1974b. "The City as Context: The Puerto Ricans of Rochester," *Urban Anthropology* 4: 53–59.

Rouse, Roger. 1991. "Mexican Migration and the Social Space of Postmodernism," *Diaspora* 1: 1–23.

———. 1992. "Making Sense of Settlement: Class Transformation, Cultural Struggle, and Transnationalism among Mexican Migrants in the United States," in Nina Glick Schiller, Linda Basch, and Christina Szanton Blanc, eds., *Towards a Transnational Perspective on Migration: Race, Class, Ethnicity, and Nationalism Reconsidered*, vol. 645, pp. 25–52. New York: Annals of the New York Academy of Sciences.

———. 1995a. "Thinking Through Transnationalism: Notes on the Cultural Politics of Class Relations in the Contemporary United States," *Public Culture* 7: 353–402.

———. 1995b. "Questions of Identity: Personhood and Collectivity in Transnational Migration to the United States," *Critique of Anthropology* 15: 351–80.

Rubenstein, Hymie. 1979. "The Return Ideology in West Indian Migration," *Papers in Anthropology* 20: 21–38.

Safa, Helen I., and Brian Du Toit, eds. 1975. *Migration and Development: Implications for Ethnic Identity and Political Conflict*. The Hague: Mouton.

Salzinger, Leslie. 1991. "A Maid by Any Other Name: The Transformation of 'Dirty Work' by Central American Immigrants," in Michael Burawoy et al., eds., *Ethnography Unbound: Power and Resistance in the Modern Metropolis*, pp. 139–60. Berkeley and Los Angeles: University of California Press.

Sanjek, Roger. 1990. "Urban Anthropology in the 1980s: A World View," *Annual Review of Anthropology* 19: 151–86.

Schneider, Jo-Anne. 1990. "Defining Boundaries, Creating Contacts: Puerto Rican and Polish Presentation of Group Identity through Ethnic Parades," *Journal of Ethnic Studies* 18: 33–57.

Schweizer, Thomas. 1998. "Epistemology: The Nature and Validation of Anthropological Knowledge," in H. Russell Bernard, ed., *Handbook of Methods in Cultural Anthropology*, pp. 39–87. Walnut Creek, Calif.: Altamira Press.

Scott, James. 1985. *Weapons of the Weak: Everyday Forms of Peasant Resistance.* New Haven, Conn.: Yale University Press.

Segura, Denise A. 1989. "Chicanas and Immigrant Women at Work: The Impact of Class, Race and Gender on Occupational Mobility," *Gender and Society* 3: 37–52.

Simon, Rita James, and Caroline B. Brettell. 1986. *International Migration: The Female Perspective.* Totowa, N.J.: Rowman and Allanheld.

Smith, M. Estellie. 1974. "A Tale of Two Cities: The Reality of Historical Differences," *Urban Anthropology* 4: 61–72.

———. 1976. "Networks and Migration Resettlement: Cherchez la Femme," *Anthropological Quarterly* 49: 20–27.

Smith, Robert. 1993. "Los Ausentes Siempre Presentes: The Imagining, Making and Politics of a Transnational Community between New York City and Ticuani, Puebla," Papers on Latin American and Iberian Studies. New York: Columbia University.

———. 1997. "Transnational Migration, Assimilation, and Political Community," in Margaret E. Crahan and Alberto Vourvoulias-Bush, eds., *The City and the World: New York's Global Future*, pp. 110–32. New York: Council on Foreign Relations.

Soto, Isa Maria. 1987. "West Indian Child Fostering: Its Role in Migrant Exchanges," in Constance Sutton and Elsa Chaney, eds., *Caribbean Life in New York City: Sociocultural Dimensions*, pp. 131–49. New York: Center for Migration Studies.

Spiegel, Andrew. 1987. "Dispersing Dependents: A Response to the Exigencies of Labour Migration in Rural Transkei," in Jeremy Eades, ed., *Migrants, Workers, and the Social Order*, pp. 113–29. London: Tavistock.

Stack, Carol. 1996. *Call to Home: African Americans Reclaim the Rural South.* New York: Basic Books.

Stafford, Susan H. Buchanan. 1984. "Haitian Immigrant Women: A Cultural Perspective," *Anthropologica* 26: 171–89.

———. 1987. "The Haitians: The Cultural Meaning of Race and Ethnicity," in Nancy Foner, ed., *New Immigrants in New York*, pp. 131–58. New York: Columbia University Press.

Stepick, Alex. 1998. *Pride against Prejudice: Haitians in the United States.* Boston: Allyn and Bacon.

Sutton, Constance. 1987. "The Caribbeanization of New York City and the Emergence of a Transnational Sociocultural System," in Constance Sutton and Elsa Chaney, eds., *Caribbean Life in New York City: Sociocultural Dimensions*, pp. 15–30. New York: Center for Migration Studies.

Talai, V. 1986. "Social Boundaries within and between Ethnic Groups: Armenians in London," *Man* 21: 251–70.

Taylor, Edward. 1976. "The Social Adjustment of Returned Migrants to Jamaica," in Frances Henry, ed., *Ethnicity in the Americas*, pp. 213–30. The Hague: Mouton.

Thomas-Hope, Elizabeth. 1985. "Return Migration and its Implications for Caribbean Development: The Unexplored Connection," in Robert Pastor, ed., *Migration and Development in the Caribbean: The Unexplored Connection.* Boulder, Colo.: Westview Press.

Tweed, Thomas A. 1997. *Our Lady of the Exile: Diasporic Religion at a Cuban Catholic Shrine in Miami.* New York: Oxford University Press.

Ui, Shiri. 1991. "'Unlikely Heroes': The Evolution of Female Leadership in a Cambodian Ethnic Enclave," in Michael Burawoy et al., eds., *Ethnography Unbound: Power and Resistance in the Modern Metropolis*, pp. 161–77. Berkeley and Los Angeles: University of California Press.

Uzzell, Douglas. 1976. "Ethnography of Migration: Breaking Out of the Bipolar Myth." Houston, Tex.: Rice University, Program of Development Studies.

Wallerstein, Immanuel. 1974. *The Modern World-System: Capitalist Agriculture and the*

Origins of the European World Economy in the Sixteenth Century. New York: Academic Press.

Wallman, Sandra. 1978. "The Boundaries of Race: Processes of Ethnicity in England," *Man* 13: 200–17.

———. 1986. "Ethnicity and the Boundary Process in Context," in John Rex and David Mason, eds., *Theories of Race and Ethnic Relations*, pp. 226–45. Cambridge: Cambridge University Press.

Warner, R. Stephen and Judith G. Wittner, eds. 1998. *Gatherings in Diaspora: Religious Communities and the New Immigration.* Philadelphia, Pa.: Temple University Press.

Watson, James. 1975. *Emigration and the Chinese Lineage: The Mans in Hong Kong and London.* Berkeley and Los Angeles: University of California Press.

Werbner, Pnina. 1987. "Enclave Economies and Family Firms: Pakistani Traders in a British City," in Jeremy Eades, ed., *Migrants, Workers, and the Social Order*, pp. 213–33. London: Tavistock.

———. 1988. "Taking and Giving: Working Women and Female Bonds in a Pakistani Immigrant Neighbourhood," in Sallie Westwood and Parminder Bhachu, eds., *Enterprising Women: Ethnicity, Economy, and Gender Relations*, pp. 177–202. London: Routledge.

———. 1990. *The Migration Process: Capital, Gifts, and Offerings among British Pakistanis.* New York: Berg.

———. 1995. "From Commodities to Gifts: Pakistani Migrant Workers in Manchester," in Alisdair Rogers and Steven Vertovec, eds., *The Urban Context: Ethnicity, Social Networks and Situational Analysis*, pp. 213–36. Oxford: Berg.

———. 1996. "Stamping the Earth with the Name of Allah: Zikr and the Sacralizing of Space among British Muslims," in Barbara Daly Metcalf, ed., *Making Muslim Space in North America and Europe*, pp. 167–85. Berkeley and Los Angeles: University of California Press.

Westwood, Sallie, and Parminder Bhachu, eds. 1988. *Enterprising Women: Ethnicity, Economy, and Gender Relations.* London: Routledge.

White, Jenny. 1997. "Turks in the New Germany," *American Anthropologist* 99 (4): 754–69.

Whiteford, Linda. 1979. "The Borderland as an Extended Community," in F. Camara and Robert Van Kemper, eds., *Migration across Frontiers: Mexico and the United States*, pp. 127–37. Albany: Institute for MesoAmerican Studies, State University of New York at Albany.

Williams, Brackette F. 1989. "A Class Act: Anthropology and the Race to Nation across Ethnic Terrain," *Annual Review of Anthropology* 18: 401–44.

———. 1994. "What Determines Where Transnational Labor Migrants Go? Modifications in Migration Theories," *Human Organization* 53: 269–78.

Wong, Bernard. 1998. *Ethnicity and Entrepreneurs: The New Chinese Immigrants in the San Francisco Bay Area.* Boston: Allyn and Bacon.

Yanagisako, Sylvia. 1985. *Transforming the Past: Tradition and Kinship among Japanese Americans.* Stanford, Calif.: Stanford University Press.

Zavella, Patricia. 1988. "Abnormal Intimacy: The Varying Work Networks of Chicana Cannery Workers," *Feminist Studies* 11: 541–57.

Zinn, Dorothy Louise. 1994. "The Senegalese Immigrants in Bari: What Happens When the Africans Peer Back," in Rina Benmayor and Andor Skotnes, eds., *Migration and Identity*, pp. 53–68. Oxford: Oxford University Press.

CHAPTER 6

The Politics of International Migration

How Can We "Bring the State Back In"?

James F. Hollifield

In the disciplines and subdisciplines associated with the study of politics and government, including political science, public policy, public administration and international relations, only recently has migration emerged as a field of study. From the standpoint of intellectual history, why have political scientists and scholars of international relations arrived so late to the study of international migration, in comparison with sociologists or historians, for example? This is an especially surprising fact in a country like the United States, where immigration has had an enormous impact on politics and government.

Given the paucity of theorizing about the politics of international migration, it is therefore not surprising that migration theory tends to be dominated by economic or sociological explanations. Push-pull and cost-benefit analyses are closely associated with neoclassical economics, whereas networks and transnationalism are analytical concepts derived primarily from world systems theory and most often studied in sociology and anthropology. This is not to say that political scientists were totally absent from the study of immigration and international migration in the postwar period. I will cite here the works of many distinguished political scientists in this field, who are today considered pioneers. But only recently, in the 1980s and '90s, the field of study has begun to emerge, which we might call the *politics of international migration*; and theorists are scrambling to see how we can "bring the state back in" to social scientific analyses of migration.[1]

This chapter treats three major themes or questions that have emerged in the study of the politics of international migration. The first major theme revolves around the question of *control*, that is, the role of the nation-state in establishing rules of entry and exit. To what extent can states control their borders? What are the factors that define the capacity and limits of control (Brochmann and Hammar 1999; Cornelius, Martin, and Hollifield 1994;

Freeman 1995; Hollifield 1992a, 1999a)? These questions lead directly to the second major theme of this chapter—the impact of migration on international relations. How does migration affect the sovereignty and *security* of the nation-state? What are the possibilities for controlling or managing migration at the international, as opposed to the domestic, level? What is the relationship between migration, national security, and foreign policy (Teitelbaum 1980; Weiner 1993)? And why do states "risk migration" and accept "unwanted immigrants" (Hollifield 1998; Joppke 1998a; Martin 1994b)? The third theme to be explored is intricately related to the first two. It revolves around the issue of *incorporation*, specifically the impact of immigration on citizenship, political behavior, and the polity itself. How do emigration and immigration affect the political behavior of individuals, natives as well as migrants? What role does the state play in incorporating immigrants into society and the economy? And what is the relationship between social and political citizenship? These questions lead inevitably to discussions of national identity, citizenship, and rights, which are at the heart of the way in which every polity defines itself (Brubaker 1992; Schuck 1998; Schmitter 1979).

The final section of the chapter links these three themes (control, security, and incorporation) together, focusing on political explanations for international migration and the role of the state in encouraging or discouraging migration. Demarcating the politics of international migration is a first and essential step to talking across the disciplines.

FRAMING THE QUESTION

The movement of individuals across national boundaries challenges many of the basic assumptions that social scientists make about human behavior—for example, that individuals tend to be risk averse, that they are always in need of community, or, as Aristotle put it, "man is a social animal." If individuals move long distances, leaving their families and communities behind and crossing national, ethnic, or cultural boundaries, then there must be some extraordinary forces compelling them to do this. Hence, many social scientists, especially economists, begin their study of international migration by pointing out that the vast majority of the world's population is in fact sedentary. At the end of the twentieth century only 125 million people—roughly equivalent to the population of Japan, according to estimates by the International Organization for Migration—live outside of their country of origin. So international migration is the exception rather than the rule. Why then should we bother to study it, if most people are born, live, and die in the same geographic area, if not in the same village?

The answer to the "so what" question is not straightforward. The best answer I can offer is that international migration provokes a sense of crisis and has been steadily increasing as a result of social and economic forces that seem to be beyond the control of states and communities (Massey 1998; Sassen 1996). An anthropologist or sociologist might call it a fear of the other, of the unknown, and of those who are different (Barth 1969; Lévi-Strauss 1952; Schnapper 1998). In this sense, xenophobia could be considered a basic human instinct. An economist or a demographer might argue that international migration places a strain on resources. It can cause a hemorrhage of scarce human capital—a brain drain—from the sending society, if the brightest and most talented people leave their home countries (Bhagwati 1976). If, however, those leaving are the most destitute, least educated, and have low levels of human and social capital, then they may pose a threat for the receiving society. Many economists and demographers have argued in Malthusian terms, that even the wealthiest societies have a limited amount of space (land) and capital, which should be preserved for the national or indigenous population. Overpopulation and overcrowding can strain urban infrastructures and cause environmental damage, while saturated urban labor markets can drive down wages, hurting those who are at the bottom of the social ladder (Bouvier 1992). In those receiving societies with highly developed welfare states, there is a fear that immigrants will become public charges, placing an unfair burden on the public purse (Borjas 1990). Of course, the same arguments can be made in reverse: migration poses no threat to either the sending or receiving society; it is in fact a boon, providing remittances for the sending society and an influx of human capital and entrepreneurial talent for the receiving society (Chiswick 1982; Russell 1986; Simon 1989). In either case, however, the focus is on the abundance or scarcity of resources, the social or human capital of migrants and how well they can integrate into the receiving society.

THE MIGRATION "CRISIS" IN HISTORICAL PERSPECTIVE

In the last decades of the twentieth century, international migration has been increasing in every region of the globe, feeding the fears of some political and intellectual elites, who give voice to a sense of crisis—a crisis which is as much political as social and economic. Yet, the political aspect of international migration has, until recently, received little attention from political scientists; perhaps because the "crisis" is so recent, or because migration is viewed as essentially an economic and sociological phenomenon, unworthy of the attention of political scientists.

It might be wise, however, to remind ourselves that migration is *not* a new phenomenon in the annals of human history. Indeed, for much of recorded history and for many civilizations, the movement of populations was not unusual. Only with the advent of the nation-state in sixteenth- and seventeenth-century Europe did the notion of legally tying populations to territorial units and to specific forms of government become commonplace (Moch 1992). State building in Europe entailed consolidating territory, centralizing authority, controlling the nobility, imposing taxes, and waging warfare (Tilly 1975). The institutions of nationality and citizenship, which would become the hallmarks of the modern nation-state, did not develop fully until the nineteenth and twentieth centuries (Koslowski 1999). Again, the reason for this development, particularly in Europe, was closely related to warfare, to the beginnings of conscription and more fully developed systems of taxation. As modern warfare took on the characteristic of pitting one people against another, nationalism intensified and political elites cultivated among their populations a sense of nationalism or of belonging to a nation and a state (Kohn 1962). The expansion of the European system of nation-states through conquest, colonization, then decolonization spread the ideals of sovereignty, citizenship, and nationality to the four corners of the globe (Said 1993).

In the nineteenth and twentieth centuries, passport and visa systems developed and borders were increasingly closed to nonnationals, especially those deemed to be hostile to the nation and the state (Noiriel 1988; Torpey 1998). Almost every dimension of human existence—social-psychological, demographic, economic, and political—was reshaped to conform to the dictates of the nation-state (Hobsbawm 1990). In looking at recent migration "crises," it is important to keep in mind *la longue durée*, in order to put these crises into historical perspective. Perhaps more than any other social science discipline, historians have a better understanding of what constitutes a crisis and what forms of human behavior are unique and unusual.[2] From a historical perspective, the migration crises of the late twentieth century pale by comparison with the upheavals associated with the industrial revolution, the two world wars, and decolonization, which resulted in genocide, irredentism, the displacement of massive numbers of people, and the radical redrawing of national boundaries, not only in Europe but also around the globe (Said 1993). This process, which Rogers Brubaker calls the "unmixing of peoples," has been repeated with the end of the cold war and the breakup of the Soviet Empire, Czechoslovakia, and Yugoslavia (Brubaker 1996). Does this mean that the latest waves of migration do not rise to the level of a crisis, threatening the political and social order in various regions of the globe?

In *The Global Migration Crisis* (1995), political scientist Myron Weiner argues that the increase in international migration in recent decades poses a threat to international stability and security. This is especially true in those areas of the globe where nation-states are most fragile—the Balkans, Transcaucasia, the Middle East, or the great lakes region of Africa, for example. But Weiner extends this argument to the Western democracies as well, pointing out that the rise in xenophobic and nationalist politics in Western Europe indicates that even the most advanced industrial democracies risk being destabilized politically by a "massive" influx of unwanted immigrants, refugees, and asylum seekers. Weiner postulates that there are limits on how many foreigners a society can absorb. Another prominent political scientist, Samuel Huntington, in a recent article in the influential American journal *Foreign Affairs*, argued that in the post–cold war era, failure to control American borders is the single biggest threat to the national security of the United States (Huntington 1996). These two political scientists echo the sentiments of the historian Arthur Schlesinger Jr., who sees recent immigration and the rise of multiculturalism posing a threat to society and leading potentially to the *Disuniting of America* (1992). In this line of reasoning, nation-states are being threatened by globalization from above and multiculturalism from below.

Whether international migration in the late twentieth century poses a dramatic threat to the sovereignty and integrity of nation-states remains an open question. But clearly the latest waves of migration have led to political crises in many countries in both the developed and developing world. As a result, a new literature in political science is emerging, with a range of research questions, some of which are similar to the questions posed about migration in other social science disciplines. Not surprisingly, at the heart of the political science literature on international migration are concerns about the institutions of sovereignty and citizenship (Fuchs 1990; Smith 1997). If we accept the Weberian definition of sovereignty—which flows more or less directly from the Treaty of Westphalia of 1648—a state can exist only if it has a monopoly of the legitimate use of force in a given territorial area. In this way, states have some protection from interference in their internal affairs (Weber 1947). It would then follow that the ability or inability of a state to control its borders and hence its population must be considered the sine qua non of sovereignty. With some notable exceptions—such as the international refugee regime created by the 1950 Geneva Convention in the aftermath of World War II (Goodwin-Gill 1996)—the right of a state to control entry and exit of persons to and from its territory is an undisputed principle of international law (Shaw 1997). But this political and legal principle, which is one of the cornerstones of the international legal system, immediately raises another question or puzzle: Why are some states willing to accept rather high levels of immigration (or emigration for that matter), when it would seem not to be in their interest to do so (Cornelius, Martin, and Hollifield 1994; Hollifield 1992a; Joppke 1998b)? Does this influx pose a threat to the institutions of sovereignty and citizenship (Pickus 1998; Rudolph 1998; Schuck 1998; Shanks 2000)?

The sovereignty or security issue, then, immediately spills over into a more specific question of migration control, and a large and growing body of literature seeks to address this question. Here, political scientists, sociologists, anthropologists, and economists begin to step on each others' toes, with historians and demographers more or less on the sidelines. To understand the difficulties of controlling (or regulating) international migration, it is essential to understand why individuals move in the first place. Economists and sociologists have developed elaborate models to explain international migration, favoring such independent variables as demand-pull, supply-push and relative deprivation on the economic dimension (Stark 1991; Todaro 1976) and trans-nationalism, networks, and social capital on the sociological dimension (Massey et al. 1993, 1998; Portes 1996).

Only recently have political scientists begun to formulate hypotheses about the political dimension of international migration and specifically the role of the state. For Aristide Zolberg—who was among the first to try to insert politi-cal variables into the equation—by any measure, the state does matter and has the capacity, if not always the will, to regulate migration flows and stocks. Zolberg's argument is that social scientists can measure and observe the inde-pendent effect of state policies for controlling entry and exit (Zolberg 1981, 1999). But, even if we accept this argument prima facie—that politics and the state matter—it does not explain *how* they matter. To understand how poli-tics affects international migration requires us, in the first instance, to theo-rize about politics and the state. This is an essential first step—to agree on some of the categories and concepts that will constitute our independent vari-ables. The next step is to search for a consensus on the dependent variables: What exactly is it that we are trying to explain? The final step, which is the principal subject of this chapter, is to open a dialogue with migration schol-ars in the other social sciences, so that we can talk across the disciplines, see if the objects of our inquiry are the same, and see whether our research find-ings are complementary or contradictory. A new generation of scholars in political science has begun to do the research that will be needed to fill the gap that exists in the migration literature, bringing to bear theories of poli-tics, sorting out dependent from independent variables, and addressing what I see as three major areas of inquiry: the politics of control, national security, and citizenship.

THE POLITICS OF CONTROL

Many political scientists would agree that at its most basic level politics involves "control, influence, power, or authority." If we add to this definition Weber's concerns about legitimacy and the importance of controlling territory, together with Aristotle's more normative focus on issues of participation, citi-zenship, and justice, we have a fairly complete picture of what Robert Dahl (1991) calls the "political aspect."[3] We can see immediately how migration touches on each of these dimensions of politics: the procedural or distribu-tional dimension—who gets what, when, and how; the legal or statist dimen-sion, involving issues of sovereignty and legitimacy; and the ethical or normative dimension, which revolves around questions of citizenship, justice, and participation. Choosing policies to control migration leads us to ask who is making those decisions and in whose interest? Are policies being made in the interest of migrants, workers, employers, or some other group? Are these policies contributing to the national interest of the state and are they just? Does migration weaken or strengthen the institutions of sovereignty and citizenship? At what point should migrants become full members of society, with all the rights, duties, and responsibilities of a citizen?

As in other social sciences, but especially economics, the key concept here is one of interest. But, unlike economics, where the emphasis is on scarcity and efficiency, in the study of politics the primary emphasis is on power, influence, and authority, but with strong ethical and normative overtones, concerning justice, membership, and citizenship (Carens 1989; Schuck 1998; Walzer 1983). In a free market, the allocation of scarce goods and resources takes place according to the logic of the marketplace, that is, the interaction of supply and demand. The exercise of power, however, takes place in the ideational, legal, and institutional confines of political systems. These range from the most autocratic (e.g., North Korea), where decisions are made by a single individual, surrounded by a small clique of military or party officials, to the most democratic (e.g., Switzerland), where decisions are made by "the people" according to elaborate constitutional arrangements and with safeguards often built into the system to protect individuals and minorities from the "tyranny of the majority." Obviously migration is less of a problem in North Korea than in Switzerland. Almost by definition, the more liberal and democratic a society is, the greater the likelihood that migration control will be an issue; and that there will be some level of "unwanted migration" (Hollifield 1992a; Joppke 1998b; Martin 1994b).

Not surprisingly, therefore, almost all the literature on the politics of control is focused on the receiving countries, many but not all of which are liberal democracies. Very little has been written about the politics of control from the standpoint of the sending countries. As the world has become more open and democratic, since the end of World War II and especially since the end of the cold war (Hollifield and Jillson 1999)—from a political standpoint, entry rather than exit is more problematic.[4] With the steady increase in immigration in the advanced industrial democracies in the postwar period (IOM 1996; OECD 1992), many states began to search for ways to stop or slow the influx, while immigration injected itself into the politics of these countries. In traditional countries of immigration, especially the United States, this was not the first time that immigration had become a national political issue; but for many of the states of Western Europe, this was a relatively new phenomenon, which took politicians and the public by surprise. How would these different political systems cope with immigration? Would there be a convergence of policy responses, or would each state pursue different control policies? As political scientists began to survey the politics of immigration control, a central puzzle emerged. Since the 1970s, almost all of the receiving states were trying to reassert control over migration flows, often using similar policies and in response to public opinion, which was increasingly hostile to high levels of immigration. Yet, immigration persisted and there was a growing gap between the goals of immigration policies—defined as outputs—and the results or outcomes of these policies (Hollifield 1986, 1990, 1992a). This argument has since come to be known as the *gap hypothesis* (Cornelius, Martin, and Hollifield 1994). Moreover, if control of borders is the sine qua non of sovereignty and if states are unable to control immigration, does it not follow that the institutions of sovereignty and citizenship are threatened (Castles and Davidson 1998; Sassen 1996; Schuck 1998; Shanks 2000; Soysal 1994)? I shall return to this question below.

With this puzzle and the gap hypothesis in mind and armed with a panoply of theories, political scientists set off in search of answers. Some, like Aristide Zolberg, Anthony Messina, and to a lesser extent Gary Freeman, questioned the empirical premise of the argument. Zolberg argues that liberal states have never lost control of immigration and that the migration crisis itself is much exaggerated (Zolberg 1999). Messina and Freeman pointed to Great Britain as a major outlier—a liberal democracy which has been efficient at controlling its borders (Freeman 1994; Messina 1996). Yet, Freeman concedes that "the goal of a theory of immigration politics must be to account for the similarities and differences in the politics of immigration receiving states and to explain the persistent gaps between the goals and effects of policies as well as the related but not identical gap between public sentiment and the content of public policy" (Freeman 1998b:2). The challenge, therefore, for political scientists is to develop some generalizable or unifying hypotheses to account for variation in (1) the demand for and the supply of immigration policy—whether greater restriction or more liberal admission policies—and (2) the outcomes or results of those policies, as measured in terms of increasing or decreasing flows and stocks. Looking at immigration from the standpoint of the politics of control, these are, in effect, two separate dependent variables.

As in any social science discipline, the choice of independent variables is driven largely by theoretical considerations and the hypotheses flowing from them. This brings us back to our definition of politics (above) and raises the broader question of how political explanations for international migration are related to economic or sociological explanations. If politics is defined primarily in terms of process and the struggle for "influence, power, and authority," then it is a relatively straightforward exercise to develop a theoretical framework for explaining the demand for and supply of immigration policy, as well as the gap between policy outputs and outcomes. This is the approach taken by Gary Freeman, who, following the work of James Q. Wilson on *The Politics of Regulation* (1980), argues that the demand for immigration policy—like any public policy in a democracy—is heavily dependent on the play of organized interests. To understand the politics of immigration control, we must be able to define the distribution of costs and benefits, which will then enable us to separate winners from losers in the policy-making process. Depending on the scarcity or abundance of productive factors (land, labor, and capital), as well as the substitutability of immigrant for native labor, the costs and benefits of immigration will be either concentrated or diffuse. From this simple factor-cost logic, we can deduce what position powerful interest groups, like organized labor and agricultural or business lobbies, are likely to take in debates over immigration policy. Again following Wilson, Freeman associates different cost-benefit distributions with specific "modes of politics," either interest group, clientelist, entrepreneurial, or majoritarian (Freeman 1995, 1998b; Wilson 1980).

Using this essentially microeconomic framework, Freeman predicts that when—as is often the case with immigration policy—benefits are concentrated and costs are diffuse, a clientelist politics will develop. The state will then be captured by powerful organized interests, who stand to benefit handsomely from expansive immigration policies—like fruit and vegetable growers in the southern and southwestern United States, the software and computer industry in the Northwest, or perhaps the construction industry in Germany or Japan. This would seem to explain why many states persist with admissionist or guest-worker policies, even during recessionary periods when the economic conjuncture would seem to dictate greater restriction. If we combine Freeman's "modes of politics" approach with the work of Alan Kessler (1998)—who argues in a similar vein that the demand for immigration policy is heavily dependent on the relative rates of return to factors and the substitutability or complementarity of immigrant and native factors—then we have a fairly complete theory of the politics of immigration control, albeit one that is heavily indebted to microeconomics and may be (like the old push-pull arguments) economically overdetermined.

The reason for this is not hard to see. If we start with a definition of politics that reduces the political process to an economic calculus, then we have in effect defined away some of the more interesting and difficult questions associated with immigration politics. In this formulation, the role of the state is particularly problematic, since the state is merely a reflection of societal interests. By focusing so exclusively on process, we lose sight of the importance of institutional and ideological variation within and among states. Both Freeman and Kessler concede that the supply of immigration policy does not always match demand. Policy outputs are heavily contingent on ideational, cultural, and institutional factors, which often distort the market interests of different groups, to such an extent that some groups (like organized labor, for example) may end up pursuing policies that would seem to be irrational, or somehow at odds with their economic interests (Haus 1995, 1999). Likewise, many employers in Western Europe were initially skeptical of the need to import guest workers (Hollifield 1992a). As Freeman puts it, the drawback of these economic models of politics "is their extreme parsimony. They leave us with generalizations about labor, landowners and capitalists; useful abstractions, surely, but probably too crude for the satisfactory analysis of immigration politics in particular countries, especially highly developed ones" (Freeman 1998b:17). So where does this leave us with respect to our ability to advance generalizable and testable hypotheses about the politics of immigration control?

Freeman offers several solutions. One obvious way to get around the limitations of factor-endowment or factor-cost models is to disaggregate or break down factors into their sectoral components, which would lead us into an industry-by-industry analysis of immigration politics. We also would want to distinguish between the political positions of skilled labor (e.g., software engineers or mathematicians) and unskilled workers (e.g., in the construction trades or service sectors). In the end, Freeman seems to retreat to a position that is a bit more ad hoc, from a theoretical and empirical standpoint. He argues that there is not that much uniformity in immigration policies among the Western democracies. He also draws a sharp distinction between the settler societies—such as the United States, Canada, or Australia—which continue to have more expansionist immigration policies, when compared to the newer countries of immigration in Western Europe. For example, Britain, France, Germany, Switzerland, and the Netherlands are still struggling to cope with the fallout from postcolonial and guest-worker migrations (Freeman 1998a; Joppke 1998b; Thränhardt 1996).

An alternative to Freeman's interest-based approach to the politics of immigration control can be found in my own work, which one reviewer aptly described as the "liberal state" thesis (Schmitter-Heisler 1993). Rather than focusing on politics defined as process, which leads us inexorably into a factor-cost logic, where productive factors in the guise of interest groups are the units of analysis, my work takes the state as the unit of analysis (Hollifield 1992a, 1997a). The dependent variable also differs from that of Freeman and many other political scientists (see, for example, Money 1999), who are more interested in explaining policy outputs (the demand for and the supply of immigration policy) than in explaining policy outcomes (flows and stocks of immigrants across time and space). From a political and theoretical standpoint, it is admittedly more difficult to explain outcomes than it is to explain outputs, because we are compelled to look at a broader range of independent variables. If we want to know why individuals move across national boundaries and if we want to explain variation in those movements over time, it will not be enough just to look at policy outputs and the political process. As I pointed out in the first section of this chapter, theories of international migration have been propounded primarily by economists and sociologists. Economists have sought to explain population movements in terms of a basic push-pull logic, whereas sociologists have stressed the importance of transnationalism and social networks. What's missing from these accounts is a theory of the state and the way in which it influences population movements (Massey 1999b).

The types of push and pull factors identified by scholars may vary, but the logic of looking at individual migrants as preeminently rational, utility-maximizing agents remains the same (see, for example, Stark 1991). Some economists, like George Borjas or Julian Simon, have injected important political or policy considerations into their analysis. Borjas in particular has argued that the welfare state itself can act as a powerful pull factor, which may change the basic calculation of potential migrants. In his formulation, before the rise of the welfare state, individuals chose to emigrate on the basis of their chances for finding gainful employment. However, after the advent of generous social policies in the principal receiving countries, like the United States, even migrants with low levels of human capital were willing to risk the move, confident in the fact that they would be cared for by the host society (Borjas 1990). Gary Freeman also argues that the logic of the modern welfare state is one of closure and that large-scale immigration may ruin public finances, bankrupt social services, and undermine the legitimacy of the welfare state (Freeman 1986). But none of these works has really elevated policy outputs and the state to the status of independent variables. Little systematic cross-national research has been done by economists, with the notable exception of scholars like Philip Martin or Georges Tapinos (Miller and Martin 1982; Tapinos 1974).

Many sociologists and anthropologists have built upon the logic of push-pull, often setting up their work in direct opposition to microeconomics, in order to inject more sociological reasoning into theories of international migration. A pioneer in this regard is Douglas Massey, who was one of the first sociologists to point out the importance of social networks in linking sending and receiving societies (Massey 1987, 1998). In the same vein, Alejandro Portes has developed the notion of transnational communities to explain international migration. Portes—whose work will be discussed at greater length in the last section of this chapter—has done extensive empirical research on the human and social capital of different immigrant groups in the United States. He seeks to explain not only why individuals emigrate but also patterns of immigrant incorporation (Portes and Bach 1985; Portes and Rumbaut 1996). Both network and social capital theory help to explain the difficulty that states may encounter in their efforts to control immigration. Kinship, informational networks, and transnational communities are in effect a form of social capital. As they develop, they can substantially reduce the risks that individual migrants must take in moving from one country to another, thereby stimulating international migration. States must then find a way to intervene in or break up the networks in order to reduce an individual's propensity to migrate.

Still, by their own admission, sociologists have been unable to incorporate political variables into their analysis of international migration. In recent articles, both Massey and Portes lament the absence of a political theory of international migration. Massey writes, "Until recently, theories of international migration have paid short shrift to the nation-state as an agent influencing the volume and composition of international migration" (Massey 1999b:303). Portes argues along the same lines that "detailed accounts of the process leading to major legislation . . . have not been transformed into a systematic theoretical analysis of both the external pressures impinging on the state and the internal dynamics of the legislative and administrative bodies dealing with immigration" (Portes 1997:817).

In response to this challenge, the liberal state thesis draws our attention to a third independent variable—rights—which are heavily contingent upon legal and institutional developments. Rights must be considered in any theory of international migration. Thus, in my formulation, international migration can be seen as a function of (1) economic forces (demand-pull and supply-push), (2) networks, and (3) rights (Cornelius, Martin, and Hollifield 1994; Hollifield 1992a; Hollifield and Zuk 1998). Much of the variation in international migration over time can be explained in economic terms. In the post–World War II period, south-north labor migration started largely in response to demand-pull forces.[5] The major industrial democracies suffered labor shortages, from the 1940s through the 1960s; and foreign workers were brought in to meet the increasing demand for labor. In the United States, these shortages, especially in agriculture, were met in part through the *bracero* program; whereas in Western Europe, *Gastarbeiter* programs were put in place to recruit immigrant and guest workers, thus placing the imprimatur of the liberal state on certain types of (presumably temporary) international migration. But when demand for immigrant and foreign labor began to decline in the 1970s, in the wake of the first oil shock in 1973, powerful supply-push factors came into play. The populations of the sending countries (for example, Algeria, Turkey, and Mexico) were increasing rapidly, at the same time that the economies of these developing states were reeling from the first truly global recession of the postwar period. Networks helped to sustain international migration, even in countries that attempted to stop all forms of immigration, including family and refugee migration. These economic and sociological factors were the *necessary* conditions for continued migration; but the *sufficient* conditions were political and legal. In the last three decades of the twentieth century, a principal factor that has sustained international migration (both south-north and to a lesser extent east-west) is the accretion of rights for foreigners in the liberal democracies, or what I have called elsewhere the rise of "rights-based liberalism" (Cornelius, Martin, and Hollifield 1994:9–11).

Politics affects migration, like many other social and economic phenomena, at the margins. But this does *not* mean that politics (like culture) is simply a residual variable. In any social process, it is often what happens at the margins that is of greatest importance and also the most difficult to incorporate into our analysis. To use a familiar Weberian metaphor, if the speeding train of international migration is fueled by economic and sociological forces, then it is the state that acts as a switching mechanism, which can change the course of the train, or derail it altogether. In the oft-quoted words of the Swiss novelist Max Frisch, who was speaking of the guest-worker program in Switzerland: "We asked for workers but human beings came."

Where do rights come from, and how are they institutionalized? Much of my recent work has been devoted to answering these questions, using comparative and historical analysis. Unlike recent works in sociology, which see rights flowing from international organizations (like the UN or the EU) and from human rights law—a kind of postnational or transnational citizenship (Bauböck 1994; Jacobson 1996; Soysal 1994)—I argue that rights still derive primarily from the laws and institutions of the liberal state and they fall into the three categories originally enunciated by the sociologist T. H. Marshall: namely, civil, political, and social rights (Castles and Davidson 1998; Marshall 1964; Schmitter 1979). My interpretation of "rights-based liberalism" differs from Marshall's in the sense that I do not espouse the same linear and evolutionary sequence, which Marshall first identified in Great Britain. Rather, I argue that rights vary considerably, both cross-nationally and over time. Therefore, the empirical and theoretical challenge for migration scholars is to find a way to incorporate rights, as an institutional and legal variable, into our analysis of international migration.

I have done this in two ways: first, by measuring the impact of specific policy changes (either expanding or contracting rights for immigrants and foreigners) on immigration flows, while controlling for changes in the business cycle (Hollifield 1990, 1992a; Hollifield and Zuk 1998; Hollifield, Tichenor, and Zuk forthcoming); and secondly, by looking specifically at how rights act, primarily through independent judiciaries, to limit the capacity of liberal states to control immigration (Hollifield 1999a, 1999b). Again, the level and unit of analysis is the state; the method is statistical, comparative, and historical. The best way to think about how rights act to limit the capacity of states to control immigration is to envision a time-series curve of immigration flows. The United States is currently well into the fourth great wave of immigration in its history. What is driving this immigration wave? To what extent is it driven by economic or political factors? To answer these questions, Gary Zuk, Daniel Tichenor, and I used time-series analysis to look at the effect of business cycles on immigration flows from 1890 to 1996 (Hollifield, Tichenor, and Zuk forthcoming). We were able statistically to demonstrate the impact of major policy shifts on flows during this time period, net of the effects of the economic conjuncture. The most striking result of our analysis is the gradual weakening of the effect of business cycles on flows after 1945, but especially from the 1960s to the late 1990s. The impact of legislation passed after the Civil Rights Act of 1964 was so expansive that it negates the effect of business cycles; in stark contrast to the period before 1945, when flows were much more responsive to economic cycles. Thus, to explain the politics of control in Western democracies, it is crucial to take account of changes in the legal and institutional environment. It is not sufficient simply to look at winners and losers, or focus on politics defined narrowly in terms of process and interest.

From the works of Zolberg, Freeman, myself, and others, we are starting to get a better picture of how politics matters in driving and channeling international migration. Two theories and their attendant hypotheses have been advanced: (1) the interest-based argument of Freeman, that states are subject to capture by powerful organized interests. These groups have pushed liberal democracies toward more expansive immigration policies, even when the economic conjuncture and public opinion would argue for restriction; and (2) the more comparative, historical, and institutional analysis—which I have summarized as the liberal state thesis—that, irrespective of economic cycles, the play of interests and shifts in public opinion, immigrants and foreigners have acquired rights and therefore the capacity of liberal states to control immigration is constrained by laws and institutions (Hollifield and Zuk 1998). This is not meant to imply that rights, once extended to foreigners, can never be revoked. Laws and institutions can and do change. Like any social, economic, or political variable, rights vary, cross-nationally and over time; we have seen evidence in the past ten to fifteen years that many liberal states have indeed tried to roll back immigrant rights (Hollifield 1999a). But, rights in liberal democracies have a long half-life. Once extended, it is difficult to roll them back, which may explain why many liberal states, especially in Western Europe, are so reluctant to make even small or incremental changes in immigration and refugee law. Governments fear that any move to expand the rights of foreigners could open up the floodgates and that such change (like amnesties or wholesale naturalizations) would send the wrong message to others wanting to immigrate.

Both the more procedural (and mildly rational choice) theory of Freeman and the more institutional and state-centered theory of Hollifield look at policy outputs as well as outcomes. But Freeman tends to focus more on the demand for and supply of immigration policy, whereas Hollifield and colleagues are more focused on outcomes, that is, immigration flows. To this point, my review has barely touched on the core issues of sovereignty and citizenship. If we turn our attention from the politics of control to international relations and the politics of national security, then we can add a third hypothesis concerning the capacity of states to control migration. This is what I call the *globalization thesis,* which, in its original formulation, was developed by sociologists, although some political scientists have contributed to its elaboration and testing (Cornelius 1998; Koslowski 1999; Sassen 1996). Simply put, there is a process of economic globalization at work in the late twentieth century, buttressed by transnational social networks and communities. Globalization has led to a structural demand for foreign labor (at the high and low end of the labor market) and a loss of control of borders, to the point that sovereignty and even citizenship itself may be redundant (Bauböck 1994; Castles and Davidson 1998; Soysal 1994). The next two sections are devoted to an examination of these powerful arguments.

THE POLITICS OF SOVEREIGNTY AND NATIONAL SECURITY

Given the seemingly inexorable increase in transnational movements of goods, services, capital, and people, it is tempting to conclude that migration is simply part of the process of globalization over which states have little, if any, control. From an economic standpoint, it is difficult to separate trade and investment—the movement of goods, services, and capital—from migration (Sassen 1988); but conventional economic wisdom has it that in the long run, trade can substitute for migration through a process of factor-price equalization (Krugman and Obstfeld 1997:160–65; Mundell 1957; Stolper and Samuelson 1941). In the short run, however, historical and empirical studies demonstrate that free trade can lead to increased emigration, especially when disparities in wages and incomes are high, as between the United States and Mexico, for example (Faini, De Melo, and Zimmerman 1999; Martin 1993). When backward economies are exposed to strong exogenous competitive pressures, the agricultural sector can collapse, leading to a rural exodus, which will swell the population of cities and increase pressures to emigrate. Again following the logic of microeconomics—one of the most powerful arguments in the social sciences—we would expect emigration to continue so long as there are economic imbalances in the international economy, or until the process of factor-price equalization is complete. But these basic economic models, like their sociological counterparts, more often than not, ignore the political and legal realities of the Westphalian system, which is based on the principles of sovereignty and noninterference. Without arguing that these principles are eternal, absolute, and immutable, it is nonetheless important to remind ourselves that the world is divided into territorial units over which governments still exercise considerable authority (Krasner 1999). Rather than assuming that states have lost control of their borders—overwhelmed by transnationalism and unable to regulate the movement of goods, capital, and people (Sassen 1996)— a more interesting question is to ask why states risk opening themselves to trade, foreign investment, and immigration, and why such openness has varied considerably over time.

In looking at the politics of sovereignty and national security, we are concerned not just with domestic politics, the play of organized interests, and issues of state autonomy (Hollifield 1992a), but also with foreign policy and the nature and structure of the international system. In addition to immigration policy, we can add to our list of dependent variables the demand for and supply of refugee policy, which has become an increasingly important foreign-policy issue, especially with the end of the cold war (Teitelbaum 1984; Weiner 1993, 1995; Zolberg, Suhrke, and Aguayo 1989). When and under what international systemic conditions are states willing to accept large numbers of refugees or risk large-scale labor migration? Here we are shifting the level of analysis from individuals and interest groups, to the state and the international system itself. Contending theoretical perspectives in international relations (liberalism, realism, and Marxism-Leninism) come into play, each with its own view of the state and the international system. However, the political science literature on migration and international relations (IR) is exceptionally thin, even though a number of younger (and some older) scholars have begun to turn their attention to this field of inquiry (see, for example, works by Andreas 1998; Heisler 1998; Hollifield 1998; Koslowski 1999; Meyers 1995; Miller 1997; Rosenblum 1998; Rudolph 1998; Shanks 2000; Thouez 1999; Uçarer 1997; Weiner 1993, 1995).

How to explain the absence of this area of inquiry from one of the most important subfields in political science is indeed a mystery, worthy of the attention of intellectual historians.[6] In my view, the answer to the mystery is historical, as well as theoretical and methodological. The period from 1945 to 1990 was dominated by the cold war and international relations theorists tended to divide politics into two categories: high and low. In the realist formulation, high politics—the paramount subject of international relations—is concerned with national security, foreign policy, and issues of war and peace, whereas low politics is concerned with all issues relating to social and economic policy. In this framework, international migration, like any economic or social issue, belongs in the realm of low politics and therefore should not be the subject of analyses by scholars of international relations, especially national security or foreign-policy analysts. For IR theorists wedded to the "realist paradigm," the international system, rather than the state or the individual, is the appropriate level of analysis (Waltz 1979). Unless it can be demonstrated that a social or economic phenomenon, like migration, clearly affects relations among states, to the point of upsetting the balance of power, it should be left to economists, sociologists, anthropologists, and other scholars of low politics.

But as the cold war began to wane, during the period of détente in the 1970s, new issues forced their way onto the agenda of IR theorists. Enormous increases in the volume of trade and foreign investment in the 1950s and 1960s and the rise of multinational corporations (MNCs) drew the attention of IR theorists like Robert Gilpin, Joseph Nye, Robert Keohane, and Stephen Krasner. Efforts were made to bring the insights of IR theory to bear on solving some of the basic dilemmas of conflict and cooperation, not only in the area of international security also but in international economics. From the efforts of these and other scholars, a new subfield of international political economy (IPE) was created; and the basic, realist assumptions of IR theory—that the international system is structured by anarchy, and states are the key units of action—were relaxed (Keohane and Nye 1977). With the end of the cold war in 1990 and even before, a cottage industry of new security analysis sprang up, focusing on a wide range of problems: from population control and environmental degradation, to the protection of human rights and combating terrorism. But still, despite the best efforts of some scholars (e.g., Heisler 1992; Hollifield 1992b; Weiner 1993), the issue of international migration did not make it onto the agenda of IR theorists. Only in the mid- to late 1990s and with a new generation of scholars is this beginning to change (Meyers 1995; Rosenblum 1998; Rudolph 1998). The discipline of international relations began to recognize that international population movements can have a dramatic effect on the security and sovereignty of states.[7] But how can we begin to theorize about international migration from the standpoint of IR?

In a recent article (Hollifield 1998), I examine some competing explanations, derived from IR theory, for the continuous rise in international migration. Broadly speaking, there are three schools of thought in IR that might tell us something about migration: (1) realism or neorealism; (2) transnationalism or what I call the globalization thesis; and (3) liberal institutionalism, which is closely associated with IPE and the theory of complex interdependence. In these three theories, much empirical work has been done from the globalization perspective, primarily in the context of the sociology of international relations, following the works of such scholars as Mary Douglas (1986) and John Meyer (1979). The students of Douglas, like Martin Heisler (1992, 1998) and of Meyer, like Yasemin Soysal (1994) and David Jacobson (1996), have been especially prolific in writing about international migration. In political science, Rey Koslowski subscribes to the basic tenets of globalization theory. He has extended his work to look at migration from a constructivist perspective, which holds that concepts such as national security or the national interest are sociological constructs (Katzenstein 1996). Constructivists argue that the national interest cannot simply be deduced, as realists would have it, from the structure of the international system or from the balance of power.

A growing body of work draws upon the insights of IPE to understand why states risk migration. Exemplars of this school include Alan Kessler (1998), Christopher Rudolph (1998), Marc Rosenblum (1998), and Hollifield (1998). As we shall see, they differ from the globalization theorists, who tend to focus more on social networks and transnational communities and less on the state, which they want to deconstruct and de-emphasize (Koslowski 1999; Sassen 1996). IPE theorists follow one of the two approaches delineated in the previous section of this chapter on the politics of control. They focus either on the play of interests (e.g., Kessler) or on ideas and institutions (e.g., Hollifield and Rudolph) to explain why states risk migration.

Finally, the school of thought in IR which has the least to say about international migration is in fact the oldest and most venerable theory: political realism. Myron Weiner (1993, 1995) has been the most consistent advocate in political science for taking a realist approach to understanding international migration. But, like IPE theorists, he tends to mix the levels of analysis, moving back and forth from the individual, to the state, to the international level. In this respect, no one has taken a purely realist approach to the study of international migration. This would require us to infer the behavior of states, as reflected in their policy choices (more or less migration, greater or lesser support for the principle of political asylum), from the structure of the international system (i.e., the distribution of power).

The basic assumption of political realism is that states are unitary rational actors, whose behavior is constrained by the anarchic structure of the international system. States are therefore caught in a security dilemma, forced to be ever attentive to the protection of their sovereignty and searching for ways to enhance their power and capabilities. From this theoretical starting point, we can derive two simple hypotheses. (1) Migration or refugee policy (i.e., rules of entry and exit) is a matter of national security, and states will open or close their borders when it is in their national interest to do so (i.e., when it will enhance their power and position in the international system). We can see rather quickly that this argument is dangerously close to being a tautology, therefore it must be linked to the second hypothesis. (2) Migration policy (and flows) are a function of international systemic factors, namely, the distribution of power in the international system and the relative positions of states. It is their relative position in the system and balance of power considerations that will determine whether states are willing to risk immigration or emigration and whether they will accept large numbers of refugees or turn them back.

We can see the attractiveness of these arguments, if we look at shifts in the politics of international migration before and after the end of the cold war in 1990. During the cold war, it was not in the interest of communist states to allow their people to emigrate (witness the construction of the Berlin Wall); and it was in the interest of the West to support the principle of political asylum and promote immigration from the East. With the end of the cold war, the situation changed dramatically. Now people are freer to move (exit), but not so free to enter. Migration has been redefined in the West as a security threat by national security analysts like Samuel Huntington (1996), whereas the economist, George Borjas puts it succinctly in the title of his best-known work, *Friends or Strangers?* (1990). He argues that mass migration from poor Third World countries constitutes an economic threat, because it depletes or waters down the human capital stock of the receiving societies, transforming them from diamond- to hourglass-shaped societies, with lots of haves at the top and more have nots at the bottom. The middle class is squeezed, which fosters social and economic conditions that are not healthy for capitalist democracies. Finally, the polemicist Peter Brimelow, in his popular book *Alien Nation* (1995), makes a security argument with clear cultural and racial overtones. He sees the influx of nonwhite immigrants into Western societies as a cultural threat that could lead to the political destabilization of the liberal democracies. His argument is reminiscent of the now famous quote, from 1969, by the Tory politician Enoch Powell that, unless colored immigration to Britain is halted, there would be "rivers of blood" in English streets.

All of these works are, in effect, securitizing migration. But, by far the most sophisticated treatment of migration from the standpoint of political realism is that of Myron Weiner (1993, 1995). Weiner is particularly conscious of the destabilizing impact of mass refugee migrations in the Southern Hemisphere, where the legitimacy of newly independent states is extremely fragile. Weiner extends his argument to include south-north and east-west movements, hypothesizing that every society has a limited capacity to absorb foreigners—what the former French President François Mitterrand called a "threshold of tolerance"—and he points to xenophobic backlashes in Western Europe as examples of the kind of security threat posed by uncontrolled migration. Hence, it is imperative that Western governments be prepared to intervene in conflicts that are likely to produce large refugee flows, as the American government did in Haiti and as NATO has done in the Balkans in the 1990s.

Although it is a powerful argument—we cannot ignore the effect of structural or systemic factors on the demand for and the supply of migration policy—the principal weaknesses of realism are that it is politically overdetermined and cannot account for the continued increase in world migration (flows) in the post–cold war era. The globalization thesis, with its strong emphasis on transnationalism, offers a compelling alternative hypothesis. Globalization arguments come in many shapes and sizes, but most are grounded in one way or another in the world systems framework (Wallerstein 1976) and are inspired by works in economic sociology and the sociology of international relations. But all the globalization theorists agree on one point: the sovereignty and regulatory power of the nation-state has been weakened by transnationalism, in the form of the movement of goods, capital, or people (Sassen 1996). With respect to migration, however, the dependent variable in these arguments is the movement of people; and, in contrast to realism, the actors in international relations are not limited, if they ever were, to states. In the globalization thesis, firms, individuals, and transnational communities have found ways to bypass the regulatory authority of sovereign states. In the words of James Rosenau (1990), the world has been "indivdualized." To borrow the expression of another IR theorist, John Ruggie (1998), states have been "deterritorialized."

The globalization thesis stands at the other extreme from neorealist arguments, which stress the role of the nation-state as the primary decision-making unit in international relations. The nation-state is no longer the sole, legitimate actor in international relations, if it ever was. Rather, the tables have been turned against the state, which is unable to control either transnational corporations—especially banks, which move vast sums of capital around the globe—or migrants, who move in search of employment opportunities. The internationalization of capital, we are told, has provoked a radical restructuring of production, as national economies move up (or down) in the international product cycle. Production itself has been decentralized with the rise of new centers of power and wealth, which Saskia Sassen (1991) has dubbed "the global city."

According to Sassen, Portes, and others, the rise of transnational economies has resulted in the creation of transnational communities, as workers are forced to move from one state to another in search of employment, often leaving family members behind. Such communities can be found at both the high and low end of the labor market, as individuals move with more or less ease from one national society to another. A great deal of research has been done to document this practice among Mexican immigrants to the United States. Douglas Massey was one of the first migration scholars to point out the importance of transnational social networks in linking communities in the country of origin to those in the country of destination (Massey 1987). These kinship and informational networks helped to instill confidence in potential migrants, thus raising their propensity to migrate and, in effect, lowering transaction costs for international migration. Alejandro Portes (1996) argues that migrants have learned to use this "transnational space" as a way to get around national, regulatory obstacles to their social mobility. He goes on to point out that changes in Mexican law to permit dual nationality may reinforce this type of behavior, leading to ever-larger transnational communities.

The rapid decline in transaction costs and the ease of communication and transportation have combined to render national migration policies obsolete. Indeed, the entire regulatory framework of the state with respect to labor and business has been shaken by the process of globalization. To compete in the new international marketplace, business and governments in the OECD countries have been forced to deregulate and liberalize labor and capital markets. Moreover, less developed states have been thrown into debt crises, leading to the imposition of painful policies of structural adjustment, which in turn cause more migration from poor to rich states. A case in point is the financial crisis in Mexico in the mid-1990s, which led to the devaluation of the peso and a surge in emigration to the United States in the latter part of the decade (Commission on Immigration Reform 1997).

Politics and the state have been factored out of international relations in these types of globalization arguments. Following on this apolitical logic, both trade and migration (which are closely linked) are largely a function of changes in the international division of labor and states play at best only a marginal role in determining economic and social outcomes. The prime agents of globalization are transnational corporations and transnational communities, if not individual migrants themselves. If states have such a minor role to play, any discussion of national interests, national security, sovereignty, or even citizenship would seem to be beside the point. But at least one group of sociologists has tried to bring politics and law, if not the state, back into the picture.

Recent works by Yasemin Soysal and David Jacobson focus on the evolution of rights for immigrants and foreigners. Both authors posit the rise of a kind of postnational regime for human rights wherein migrants are able to attain a legal status that somehow surpasses citizenship, which remains grounded in the logic of the nation-state. Jacobson, more so than Soysal, argues that individual migrants have achieved an international legal personality by virtue of various human rights conventions, and both authors view these developments as presenting a distinctive challenge to traditional definitions of sovereignty and citizenship (Jacobson 1995). But Soysal in particular is careful not to use the term postnational or transnational citizenship, opting instead for the expression postnational membership. Wrestling with the contradictory nature of her argument, Soysal writes: "Incongruously, inasmuch as the ascription and codification of rights move beyond national frames of reference, postnational rights remain organized at the national level ... the exercise of universalistic rights is tied to specific states and their institutions" (Soysal 1994:157).

Another sociologist, Rainer Bauböck, is less circumspect. He argues simply that, given the dynamics of economic globalization, a new transnational/political citizenship is necessary and inevitable (Bauböck 1994). Bauböck draws heavily on political and moral philosophy, especially Kant, in making his argument in favor of transnational citizenship. Like Soysal, he relies on the recent history of international migration in Europe and the experience of the European Community/Union to demonstrate that migration has accompanied the process of economic growth and integration in Europe. These guest workers and other migrants achieved a rather unique status as transnational citizens. What all three of these authors (Soysal, Jacobson, and Bauböck) are attempting to do is to give some type of political and legal content to world systems and globalization arguments. But like Saskia Sassen (1996), they see the nation-state as essentially outmoded and incapable of keeping pace with changes in the world economy.

What do these theories tell us about migration policy (the opening and closing of societies) and the more or less continuous rise in international migration in the postwar period? At first blush, they would seem to account rather well for the rise in migration. Even though the globalization arguments, which draw heavily upon world systems theory, are neo-Marxist and structuralist in orientation, they share many assumptions with conventional, neoclassical (push-pull) theories of migration. The first and most obvious assumption is that migration is caused primarily by dualities in the international economy. So long as these dualities persist, there will be pressures for individuals to move across national boundaries in search of better opportunities. But whereas many neoclassical economists (like the late Julian Simon) see this as pareto optimal—creating a rising tide that will lift all boats—many globalization theorists (like Sassen and Portes) view migration as further exacerbating dualities both in the international economy and in national labor markets. This variant of the globalization thesis is close to the Marxist and dual labor market arguments that capitalism needs an industrial reserve army to surmount periodic crises in the process of accumulation (Bonacich 1972; Castells 1975; Castles and Kosack 1975; Piore 1979). As migration networks become more sophisticated and transnational communities grow in scope and complexity, migration should continue to increase, barring some unforeseen and dramatic fall in the demand for immigrant labor. Even then, some theorists, like Wayne Cornelius, would argue that the demand for foreign labor is "structurally embedded" in the more advanced industrial societies, which cannot function without access to a cheap and pliable foreign workforce (Cornelius 1998).

The second (crucial) assumption that globalization theorists share with neoclassical economists is the relatively marginal role of the state in governing and structuring international migration. States can act to distort or delay the development of international markets (for goods, services, capital, and labor), but they cannot stop it. With respect to migration, national regulatory regimes and municipal law in general simply must accommodate the development of international markets for skilled and unskilled workers. To talk about the opening and closing of societies, or rules of exit and entry, is simply a nonstarter in a "global village." Likewise, citizenship and rights can no longer be understood in their traditional national contexts (Castles and Davidson 1998). If we take the example of postwar West Germany, nationality and citizenship laws date from 1913 and, until the reforms of 1999, they retained kinship or blood (*jus sanguinis*) as the principal criterion for naturalization (Brubaker 1992). But this very restrictionist citizenship regime did not prevent Germany from becoming the largest immigration country in Europe. Globalization theorists, like Portes, Soysal, and Castles can explain this anomaly by reference to the structural demand for foreign labor in advanced industrial societies, the growth of networks and transnational communities, and the rise of postnational membership, which is closely tied to human rights regimes—what Soysal calls universal personhood. National citizenship and regulatory regimes would seem to explain little in the variation of migration flows or the openness (or closure) of German society.

What can we retain from globalization, as opposed to neorealist, arguments? The biggest shortcoming of the globalization thesis—in contrast to realism—is the weakness or in some cases the absence of any political explanation for migration. The locus of power and change is in society and the economy. There is little place for states and national regulation in this framework. Almost everything is socially and economically determined. By contrast, neoliberal arguments focus on institutions and the state and they share many assumptions with neorealism. Both neoliberal and neorealist theories are heavily rationalist and stress the primacy of interests, the major difference being that neoliberals want to disaggregate the "national interest" and to look at the multiplicity of social and economic groups, which compete to influence the state. For neoliberals, both national and international politics can be reduced to an economic game and ultimately to a problem of collective action. To understand this (means-ends) game, all that is needed is to correctly identify the interests and preferences of social, economic, and political actors (Milner 1997). Not surprisingly, neoliberal theorists focus almost exclusively on politics and policy in liberal states, where the competition among groups is relatively open and unfettered by authoritarianism and corruption. Studying competition among groups at the domestic level, as well as the allocational and distributional consequences of policy, presents a clearer picture of why states behave the way they do in the international arena, whether in the areas of trade, finance, or migration.

Since this approach incorporates both economic and political analysis, it has come to be called international political economy (IPE). IPE theorists are interested in the connections between domestic/comparative and international politics. In addition to focusing on domestic interests, they also stress the importance of institutions in determining policy outcomes. For one of the original IPE theorists, Robert Keohane, international institutions hold the key to explaining the puzzle of conflict and cooperation in world politics, especially with the weakening of American hegemony in the last decades of the twentieth century. Along with Joseph Nye, Keohane argued that increases in economic interdependence in the postwar period have had a profound impact on world politics, altering the way states behave and the way in which they think about and use power (Keohane and Nye 1977). In the nuclear age and with growing interdependence, it became increasingly difficult for states to rely on traditional military power in order to guarantee their security. National security was tied more and more to economic power and nuclear weapons fundamentally altered the nature of warfare. The challenge for states (especially liberal states) was how to construct a new world order to promote their national interests that were tied ever more closely to international trade and investment, if not to migration.

In the first two decades after World War II, this problem was solved essentially by the United States, which took it upon itself to reflate the world economy and to provide liquidity for problems of structural adjustment. This approach was dubbed "hegemonic stability" (Gilpin 1986). But with the gradual decline of American economic dominance in the 1970s, the problem arose of how to organize world markets in the absence of a hegemon. The answer would be found, according to Keohane and others, in multilateralism and the building of international institutions and regimes (like GATT and the IMF) to solve the problems of international cooperation and collective action (Keohane 1984; Ruggie 1993). As the cold war waned in the 1980s, the entire field of international relations shifted dramatically away from the study of national security toward the study of international economics, especially issues of trade and finance. In the last decades of the twentieth century, even domestic politics, according to IPE theorists, has been thoroughly internationalized (Keohane and Milner 1996).

Despite the fact that international migration would seem to lend itself to neoliberal/IPE arguments (migration has a strong political-economic dimension and it clearly contributes to the internationalization of domestic politics), very little has been written about it from this perspective (see, however, Hollifield 1992b, 1998, 2000a). The reasons for this are fairly simple. Until recently, there was little demand for international cooperation (or policy) in the area of migration, with the major exception of managing refugee flows (Teitelbaum 1984). The dependent variable in this framework is the demand for and supply of international policy, in the form of regimes. Even for the relatively weak refugee regime (UNHCR), the numbers were modest until the 1980s and the incentives for cooperation among liberal states were closely linked to the cold war and the bipolar structure of the international system. From the late 1940s through the 1970s, liberal states had little incentive to cooperate or to build regimes for managing labor migration; because there was an unlimited supply of (unskilled) labor available, which could be recruited through bilateral agreements with the sending countries. The German *Gastarbeiter* (1960s) and the American *bracero* (1940s to the '60s) programs are classic examples of these types of bilateral accords (Rogers 1985; Calavita 1992).

With the major exception of the European Union and the Schengen system (Geddes 1995; Guiraudon 1998; Thouez 1999), the situation has not changed that much in the 1980s and 1990s, despite the end of the cold war. There is still an unlimited and rapidly growing supply of cheap labor available in developing countries. What has changed, however, are the goals of immigration and refugee policies among the OECD states. The demand now is for policies to control, manage, or stop migration and refugee flows (Ghosh 2000). The cold-war refugee regime, specifically the United Nations High Commission for Refugees (UNHCR), has come under enormous pressure to manage various refugee crises, from the Cambodians in Thailand, to the Kurds in Iraq, to the Hutus in Zaire (now the Republic of Congo), to the Albanians in Italy. Existing international organizations for dealing with economic migration, such as the International Organization for Migration (IOM) and the International Labour Office (ILO) in Geneva, have not been besieged by demands for action. Western Europe, however, developed its own regional regime for migration— the Schengen system. Otherwise, there has been little effort to regulate international migration on a multilateral basis.

What can neoliberal or IPE arguments tell us about the development of international migration during the postwar period and the willingness of states to risk exposing their economies to the exogenous pressures of trade and migration? The first major hypothesis that we can derive from neoliberal theory is that states are more willing to risk opening their economies to trade (and by extension migration) if there is some type of international regime (or hegemonic power) that can regulate these flows and solve collective action and free-rider problems. However, there is no regime for regulating migration that comes close to the type of regime that exists for trade (GATT/WTO), or for international finance (IMF/World Bank). Yet, we know that migration has increased steadily throughout the postwar period, in the absence of a regime or any type of effective multilateral process. Again, the EU and Schengen constitute important exceptions. If we accept the neorealist assumptions that states are unitary, sovereign actors, capable of closing as well as opening their economies, then other (political) factors must be at work, driving the increases in migration and maintaining a degree of openness to migration, at least among the advanced industrial democracies.

A second (powerful) hypothesis can be derived from neoliberal theory. The maintenance of a relatively open (nonmercantilist) world economy is heavily dependent on coalitions of powerful interests in the most dominant, liberal states. In *Resisting Protectionism* (1988), Helen Milner—a prominent neoliberal theorist—demonstrates how advanced industrial states in the 1970s were able to resist the kind of beggar-thy-neighbor policies that were adopted in the 1920s and '30s. She argues that growing interdependence (multinationality and export dependence) helped to solidify free trade coalitions among the OECD states in the postwar period, thus preventing a retreat into protectionism following the economic downturns of the 1970s and '80s. Government leaders in a range of industrial nations were willing (and able) to resist strong political pressures for protectionism in the 1970s in large part because a powerful constellation of business interests contributed to a substantial realignment within these societies. In some cases polities themselves were creatively redesigned by political entrepreneurs to facilitate the maintenance and strengthening of these new (free-trade) coalitions (Lusztig 1996). Of course, free-trade interests were bolstered by the existence of an international trade regime (GATT) in the 1970s.

From a neoliberal/IPE perspective, the central question with respect to migration is: How did proimmigration coalitions in the key OECD states form, and will they be able to maintain legal immigration regimes with the end of the cold war and in the absence of a strong international migration regime? We cannot discount the importance of international systemic constraints, like the end of the cold war, which clearly has had an impact on political coalitions and alignments in all of the liberal democracies (Meyers 1995). The end of the cold war has had a profound impact on coalitions supporting open migration policies, even more so than in the area of trade. The major difference between trade and migration is in the nature and types of the coalitions that form to support or oppose them. Although related, in the sense that strong economic liberals tend to support both free trade and more open migration policies (Hollifield, Tichenor, and Zuk forthcoming), there is a much stronger legal, ideational, and cultural dimension involved in the making of promigration coalitions than is the case with free-trade coalitions, which tend to be based more narrowly on economic interests. Free-trade policies clearly have important political and social effects, but the arguments about comparative advantage and tariff policies tend to be heavily economic, and the interests are organized along sectoral or class lines. With respect to trade, individuals and groups tend to follow their market interests. But in the making of migration policies, this is not always the case.

If a state can be sure of reciprocity—that other states will abide by the MFN principle—then it is easier to convince a skeptical public to support free trade. With migration, by contrast, economic arguments (about the costs and benefits of migration) tend to be overshadowed by political, cultural, and ideological arguments. National identities and founding myths, what I have called elsewhere "national models," come into play in the making and unmaking of coalitions for admissionist or restrictionist migration policies (Hollifield 1997a, 1997b). Debates about migration in the liberal-democratic (OECD) states revolve as much, if not more so, around issues of rights, citizenship, and national identity than around issues of markets (cf. infra). The coalitions that form to support more open migration policies are often rights-markets coalitions. Debates about sovereignty and control of borders are reduced to debates about national identity—a fungible concept that reflects values, morality, and culture, rather than a strictly instrumental, economic calculus.

THE POLITICS OF INCORPORATION, CITIZENSHIP, AND NATIONAL IDENTITY

If we take a neoliberal approach to understanding the rise of international migration in the postwar era, then we are thrown back onto an analysis of three factors, which together drive national migration policies. The first of these factors is ideational, historical, and cultural. Migration policy, especially in the big three liberal republics (the United States, France, and Germany), is heavily influenced by national or founding myths, which are codified in citizenship and nationality laws. These myths about the national identity are fungible, subject to manipulation, and involve strong elements of symbolic politics. They are reflected in constitutional law and can be analyzed from a historical, sociological, legal, and political standpoint (Hollifield 1997a, 1997b; Schuck 1998; Shanks 2000; Tichenor 1996). They also can be the subject of political struggle and heated partisan debates; and the institutions of sovereignty and citizenship, like the economy, are subject to exogenous shocks. Immigration, as Gary Freeman (1979), Myron Weiner (1995), Martin Schain (1988), Rey Koslowski (1999), Jeannette Money (1999), and others have pointed out, can change the composition of societies, alter political coalitions, disrupt the party system, and transform citizenship and the national identity. The argument therefore can be made, following Koslowski and Money, that migration con-

tributes to the internationalization of local and domestic politics. Multiculturalism is the functional equivalent of multinationalism. If the rise of multinational corporations—as Milner and others have argued—contributed to the
creation of new free-trade coalitions, then the rise of immigration and multiculturalism has contributed to new proimmigration coalitions. As foreigners
gain a legal foothold in liberal societies, rights accrue to them and they become
political actors capable of shaping both policy and polity (Hollifield 1992a;
Ireland 1994; Miller 1981; Schmitter 1979).

But there is clearly a second factor involved in building promigration coalitions. As Gary Freeman argues, businesses that are dependent on foreign
labor—whether skilled, as in the case of the software industry, or unskilled, as
in the case of construction trades or agriculture—can form powerful lobbies.
Under the right conditions, these lobbies can capture parts of the state in order
to maintain access to a vital input (Freeman 1995). The political and economic
history of Western states, since the late nineteenth century when the transaction costs of migration were drastically reduced, is replete with examples of
businesses working with, around, through, or against the state to import labor
(Cornelius, Martin, and Hollifield 1994). Economic interests are always at play
in the making of migration policy, because the profits to be had from importing labor are great (demand-pull forces are strong) and there is an abundant
supply of cheap labor available. Cutting off access to foreign labor for businesses that are heavily dependent upon it is the same thing as imposing high
tariffs on imported raw materials. The industries affected will howl (Cornelius
1998). Both policies are protectionist and have profound allocational effects.

In the postwar period, the third and most important factor in building promigration (as opposed to free-trade) coalitions is institutional. Again to quote
Max Frisch, "We asked for workers but human beings came." Unlike capital
or goods, migrants, qua individuals and sometimes qua groups (e.g., Cubans
in the United States, ethnic Germans and Jewish immigrants in Germany) can
acquire legal rights and protections under the aegis of liberal constitutions and
statutory law. Even when they are not admitted immediately to full citizenship, migrants acquire the rights of membership, which can (depending upon
the state) include basic civil rights, a package of social or welfare rights and
even political or voting rights (Geddes 1995; Hammar 1990; Layton-Henry
1990; Schuck 1998). What is important to keep in mind, however, is that these
rights are anchored in national legal systems. Although they may flow from
constitutional law, they also depend upon increasingly fragile political coalitions, involving left- and right-wing liberals. With the end of the cold war,
these "strange bedfellow" coalitions have become more difficult to sustain,
even in the area of political asylum, a principle which is supported in international law (Goodwin-Gill 1996; Shaw 1997; Zolberg, Suhrke, and Aguayo
1989). As the coalitions weaken, we would expect to see a concomitant decline
in support for admissionist immigration and refugee policies.

But rights have a very long half-life in liberal democracies. Once they are extended and institutionalized, it is extremely difficult to roll them back. Most democracies—especially those like the United States, France, and Germany, which have universalist (egalitarian), republican traditions and strong elements of separation of powers—have a variety of institutional/judicial checks that limit the ability of executive and legislative authorities to change individual rights. To understand the "limits of immigration control" in liberal democracies, as well as the mix of internal and external strategies for control, we must have a clear understanding of the evolution of rights-based politics and of the way in which rights are institutionalized (Cornelius 1994; Hollifield 1998). Even if rights-markets coalitions supporting immigration weaken, this does not mean that migration and refugee policies will change overnight, or that liberal states can quickly and effectively seal their borders.

The neoliberal approach requires us, in the first instance, to look at international institutions and regimes and secondly at the types of coalitions that form to support more open migration regimes. I have identified three factors that influence coalition building: (1) ideational and cultural factors which are closely linked to formal-legal definitions of citizenship; (2) economic interests, which are linked to factor proportions and intensities, that is, land, labor, capital ratios; and (3) rights, which flow from liberal-republican constitutions. Although we have seen a good deal of theorizing in political science about the second factor and how it affects immigration policy (outputs) and actual flows (outcomes), less has been written about the first and third factors. Certainly there is a burgeoning literature on the politics of citizenship, focused on a wide range of issues, such as nationality, naturalization, ethnicity, and identity. Political scientists, along with sociologists, have contributed heavily to debates about the changing nature of citizenship (Brubaker 1989, 1992; Fuchs 1990; Pickus 1998; Smith 1997). But no attempt has been made to link the literature on citizenship with an even broader range of sociological and economic work on incorporation (see, for example Kurthen, Fijalkowski, and Wagner 1998; Portes and Rumbaut 1996). Instead, we have seen the emergence of a small but growing literature on the politics of immigration, by which I mean the effect that immigration has on political behavior in general and voting in particular (DeSipio 1996; de la Garza and DeSipio 1996; Fetzer 1996). Much of the literature on the politics of immigration is comparative in nature, with a regional focus on Western Europe. Many of the works in this field are more interested in the rise of radical right-wing, xenophobic, and anti-immigrant political movements, than in understanding the politics of immigration and citizenship (see, for example, Betz 1994, 1996; Kitschelt 1995; Layton-Henry 1992; Messina 1989; Minkenberg 1992; Money 1999; Schain 1990; Thränhardt 1993, 1996; Wihtol de Wenden 1988). With respect to the tremendously important role that rights play in defining citizenship—who is and is not a foreigner—most of the work has been done by legal scholars, like Peter Schuck (1998), Alexander Aleinikoff and David Martin (1995), or Stephen Legomsky (1987) in the United States, Danièlle Lochak (1985) in France, or Kay Hailbronner (1984, 1997) in Germany. One notable exception to this rule is Patrick Weil, the French political scientist who has written the most comprehensive work on the politics of immigration and the rights of foreigners in France (Weil 1991).

If my analysis is correct—that ideas and institutions play a vital role in determining outputs (the demand for and supply of immigration and refugee policy) and outcomes (the level of flows and stocks)—then it is in the area of immigration politics, involving issues of incorporation, sovereignty, and citizenship where the most work remains to be done. Many questions barely have been posed, but are begging for an answer. (1) What is the relationship between the politics of immigration and incorporation? (2) Is there a link between social and political incorporation? (3) How does the rate of social and economic incorporation affect political behavior and the institutions of sovereignty and citizenship? All of these questions strike at the heart of the state-society relationship and presuppose that immigration has the effect of upsetting or transforming this relationship, which leads inexorably to policy reform and institutional change.

But before we can understand the impact of immigration on the state (and how we can bring the state back into our analysis), we must understand the impact of immigration on society. Theories concerning the social impact of immigration fall into fairly recognizable categories, and each of these theoretical perspectives tends to inform the way in which political scientists think about the political impact of immigration. I would divide these theories into four categories. First is the Smithian or liberal view, which holds that market-oriented societies are incredibly dynamic and capable of absorbing large numbers of immigrants, who, because they tend to self-select, will contribute to the human capital stock and to the overall wealth of society. The works of Julian Simon and Barry Chiswick best reflect this perspective (Chiswick 1982; Simon 1990). Scholars working in this tradition generally accept the proposition that immigrants will assimilate, within one or two generations (Fuchs 1990; Gordon 1964). Ethnic identity and ethnic politics should fade quickly as individuals are absorbed into the mainstream of the political and social life of the host country. From this perspective, there is no need for positive discrimination, affirmative action or bilingual education policies that may prolong the process of acculturation and exacerbate ethnic tensions. If problems arise with the assimilation of immigrants, then naturalization or "Americanization" would be the obvious long-term remedy (Pickus 1998; Skerry 1993).

A second theoretical perspective—at the opposite extreme of Smithian liberalism—is the neo-Malthusian view that every society has limited resources (especially land) and a limited number of jobs. From this perspective, any immigration may be harmful to some or all segments of society and the environment. Some level of immigration may be safe, but a large or uncontrolled influx of foreigners is not in the interests of society. This perspective seems most often shared by demographers (e.g., Bouvier 1992; Coleman 1992), economists (Borjas 1990; Martin 1994a), and by some political scientists (Teitelbaum and Weiner 1995; Weiner 1995). A third perspective is informed by the Marxist notion (already discussed above) that capitalist economies need an industrial reserve army, composed primarily—but not exclusively—of foreign or immigrant workers, in order to overcome periodic crises of accumulation (Bonacich 1972; Castells 1975). In this view, immigration only heightens class conflict and will contribute to a further politicization and ethnicization of the working class (Castles and Kosack 1973; Faist 1995; Miles 1982; Rath 1988; Rex and Moore 1967). Finally, a fourth perspective is what I would call, for lack of a better term, the Durkheimian view, that immigration, like the process of modernization itself, may contribute to a sense of alienation, leading to the fragmentation or even dissolution of society. This perspective is often shared by social or political geographers and demographers, who point to the spatial impacts of immigration. A large concentration of foreigners in specific locales can exacerbate class, ethnic, and racial tensions (Clark 1997; Money 1999; Tribalat 1995).

From the Smithian perspective, the institution of citizenship and the regulatory powers of the liberal state should be dynamic enough to respond to the challenges posed by international migration. The strongest polities are those with strong civil societies and a well-developed "national model" or founding myth around which to organize debates about immigration control and incorporation (Hollifield 1997). The American political scientist and historian, Lawrence Fuchs, argues in Tocquevillian fashion that the strength of American civic culture has helped the United States to overcome racial, ethnic, and even class divisions, leading to what he calls a kind of "voluntary pluralism" (Fuchs 1990). In effect, Fuchs is arguing for American exceptionalism, where the strengths of liberal-republican ideals and institutions have created a pluralist and centrist politics, gradually excluding the extremist politics of the Right or the Left that one finds in other political systems, particularly in Europe. The American conception of citizenship, with its emphasis on individual rights and responsibilities and its aversion to "old-world" notions of class and ethnicity, is most compatible with a liberal society and economy and therefore most open to immigration.[8] Since the adoption of the Fourteenth Amendment, access to citizenship is automatic for anyone born on American territory and naturalization is relatively easy for newcomers who arrive legally in the United States (Schuck 1998). Immigration, as Rogers Brubaker (1989) and others have pointed out, is part of the American tradition of nationhood, whereas in Europe the formation of nation-states did not coincide with waves of immigration. With the partial exception of France (Hollifield 1994, 1999b), European societies from the sixteenth through the nineteenth centuries were exporting rather than importing people (Moch 1992). Most of these European emigrants went to the Americas, with the idea of leaving the "old world" behind forever.

This is the American founding myth, which stood in sharp contrast to European traditions, until the latter half of the twentieth century, when we have seen a rise of immigration in Western Europe and a marked convergence in immigration and citizenship laws and practice (Cornelius, Martin, and Hollifield 1994; Thränhardt 1996). The American political theorist Rogers Smith, while remaining firmly ensconced in the liberal-republican tradition, has criticized the narrow reading of American history offered by Fuchs and others. Smith finds that there are multiple traditions in American liberalism, some more egalitarian than others. For much of the history of the American Republic, ascriptive, hierarchic, and racist views prevailed over more egalitarian or Tocquevillian views (Smith 1997). Clearly racism, through slavery and the Jim Crow system—an American version of apartheid—was built into the American political system from the beginning. In the nineteenth and first half of the twentieth centuries, racism also played a prominent role in the making of immigration and naturalization policy and in the construction of American national identity, from the Chinese Exclusion Act through the National Origins Quota System (King 2000). In the post–World War II period, however, both the United States and the immigrant receiving states of Western Europe have moved away from this ascriptive, exclusionary, or particularlistic approach to immigration and naturalization, in favor of more egalitarian policies (Cornelius, Martin, and Hollifield 1994; Tichenor 1996). In 1999, the German government changed German nationality law, making it possible for anyone born in Germany who has at least one parent who has been in the country for eight years to gain automatic German citizenship. This reform was the culmination of decades of political struggle and debate and was fiercely contested right up to the moment of its passage. Among the liberal democracies, Britain would seem to be the glaring exception to this rule of convergence in citizenship policy and practice. Race has remained a prominent feature of immigration policy making in Britain throughout the postwar era (Freeman 1979; Hansen 2000; Layton-Henry 1992; Messina 1996).

Remaining within the Smithian/liberal-republican tradition, the jurist Peter Schuck (1998) has written extensively on the evolution of American citizenship, carefully documenting changes in law and policy and their effects on immigration and incorporation. Schuck and his coauthor, Rogers Smith, criticized American naturalization policy for contributing to the "devaluation" of American citizenship (Schuck and Smith 1985). Their main concern was that newcomers had little incentive to naturalize and that as a consequence American society and ultimately the polity itself was being weakened. This concern for the solidarity of society and community is echoed in the works of other political theorists, like Michael Walzer (1983) and Joseph Carens (1989), who argue that openness to immigration must be tempered by a willingness on the part of the receiving society quickly to integrate and care for newcomers. To show how expansive and adaptive liberal thinking about citizenship can be, the Canadian political theorist Will Kymlicka (1995) argues that liberal states even can function in a multiethnic or multicultural setting. A uniform (legal) citizenship is not, in his view, inconsistent with the recognition of minority and group rights. The biggest theoretical stretch of all is the argument advanced by the sociologists Yasemin Soysal (1994) and David Jacobson (1995), who see the possibility of a postnational citizenship, where rights flow from international law, organizations, and regimes.

Each of these liberal theorists places great emphasis on ideas and institutions for understanding the impact of immigration on the state-society relationship. Each also points to the contradictions and tensions within liberal theory; but none of them, with the exceptions of Peter Schuck and Daniel Tichenor, seek to include in their theoretical framework more economic, or interest-based explanations for the supply of and demand for immigration policy (Schuck 1998; Tichenor 1996). For most of these political theorists, citizenship is a dependent rather than an independent variable. So there would be no reason to try to link the evolution of rights with changes in immigration policy (outputs) or actual levels of immigration (outcomes). Both Fuchs and Smith, for example, are writing about American political and social development, rather than about immigration per se. But both are intensely interested in how newcomers have fared in different periods of American history and how their identities and legal status have been shaped by the evolution of the institution of citizenship. The issue of incorporation lies just beneath the surface in many of these works on citizenship. But it is not clear how to make the link between the politics of incorporation, immigration control, and citizenship.

Sociologists, like Alejandro Portes and Rubén Rumbaut (1996), focus on immigration (that is, the process of immigrating), settlement, and incorporation. They see citizenship not so much as an institution but as a process whereby newcomers are able to adapt to their new social and political environment, with some groups adapting more quickly than others, depending on their levels of social and human capital. They take issue with scholars, like Glazer and Moynihan (1970) or Fuchs (1990), who see assimilation as a more or less linear process where ethnic identities and attachments fade quickly over time. Instead, they note an increasing tendency toward segmented assimilation, whereby immigrant groups (and especially the second generation) suffer from new forms of discrimination that may delay or impede acculturation and assimilation. The unevenness of the process is linked, in their view, to the advent of postindustrial society, which places a great premium on education and human capital. Earlier waves of unskilled immigrants were able to find employment in traditional manufacturing industries. Their children either followed in the parents' footsteps or (more likely) got a better education and moved into high-skilled jobs. This is the traditional pattern of assimilation as outlined by Gordon (1964) and Alba and Nee (1997). Today, however, according to Portes and Rumbaut (1996), many immigrant groups in postindustrial economies have found themselves trapped in an endless cycle of poverty and discrimination. But despite the difficulties of finding adequate employment, immigrants continue to arrive in the United States in great numbers (legally or illegally) because of poorer opportunities in the countries of origin and because social networks help to sustain high levels of immigration. Many members of the first and second generations find themselves excluded from the mainstream of social and economic life, ostracized or stigmatized by dominant groups in the host society. They are thus denied the benefits of citizenship (Lamont 1998). As a result, they retreat into ethnic enclaves (or ghettos) in search of community, which can lead to deviant behavior, such as joining gangs. This pattern of segmented assimilation reinforces ethnic identity and makes it more difficult for newcomers to incorporate politically.

In this analysis, we can see how the optimistic, liberal view of immigration, incorporation, and citizenship begins to give way to a more Durkheimian, if not Malthusian or Marxist view of the impact of immigration on state and society. As newcomers "fail" to assimilate, a political backlash will build and natives—especially those more marginal members of the majority ethnic group—will come to see immigrants as a threat, demanding that the state do something to alleviate "the problem." Analyses of voting in the California ballot initiative Proposition 187 point to social class as a major predictor of voting outcomes. Higher levels of education and income were correlated with a higher "no" vote (Hollifield and Martin 1996). At the same time, individuals belonging to an ethnic minority or in some other way culturally marginalized (e.g., being young or female) were less likely to support the initiative (Fetzer 1996). The passage of Proposition 187 together with the Illegal Immigration and Immigrant Responsibility Act, approved in 1996 by the U.S. Congress and which severely curtailed immigrant access to certain social programs like Supplemental Security Income (SSI), contributed to a wave of naturalizations in the mid- to late 1990s. A decade earlier Peter Schuck had been writing about the "devaluation of citizenship," but by the end of the 1990s, he was writing about the "revaluation of citizenship" (Schuck 1998).

The newcomers in the United States were naturalizing in great numbers and beginning to organize and participate in a wider range of political activities. Louis DeSipio finds that, while political participation of first-generation immigrants in the United States is low, it is substantially higher for the second generation, although still lower than that of natives. He is cautiously optimistic that new immigrants and their children will not descend into a kind of political ghetto (DeSipio 1999). Likewise, comparative studies of immigrant political behavior show the resilience of the institutions of the liberal state and demonstrate how immigrants are able to take advantage of opportunity structures open to them in the political process. Immigrants then become players in redefining the institution of citizenship itself (Feldblum 1999; Ireland 1994; Miller 1981).

A legitimate question of cause and effect can be raised regarding what triggers such a change in political attitudes and behaviors, in the native as well as the immigrant population. The rather straightforward, Durkheimian thesis is that social change itself is driving politics (Durkheim 1964). As societies "modernize," individuals and groups are displaced. This occurred in Europe during the industrial revolution, which completely disrupted family and community life, leading to anomie and forcing individuals to seek new communities and new identities. In some societies, this type of social change led to a radicalization and polarization of politics—in Germany, for example—whereas in others the institutions of the liberal state were able to control and channel these radical impulses. Britain is the most obvious example (Marshall 1964; Moore 1966). Many political and social scientists see the same thing happening with the advent of postindustrial society, which has created feelings of failure, alienation, and resentment, especially among workers in the most advanced industrial societies, many of whom see immigrants as the cause of their problems (Betz 1994; Kitschelt 1995). All it takes then is some entrepreneurial (usually right-wing) politician to trigger feelings of xenophobia and racism in these segments of the population (Thränhardt 1993). It is not surprising that immigration becomes the focal point of radical right-wing politics (Mayer and Perrineau 1996; Minkenberg 1992), and in some cases, like France, the entire party system may be destabilized (Schain 1988).

As the politics of immigration and incorporation intensify, political institutions in general and political parties in particular, come to center stage. Demands for greater immigration control or changes in nationality or citizenship laws will be channeled through political parties and party systems (Perlmutter 1996; Schain 1990). In this perspective, immigration can be understood as part of the broader phenomenon of globalization, which itself goes hand in hand with the advent of postindustrial society. Social movements, opposed to globalization and multiculturalism, may spring up in the native populations, resulting in a new politics of national identity and citizenship, driven in part by the demand for participation by new immigrant groups (Ireland 1994; Kastoryano 1997). Fierce debates have occurred over whether new immigrant groups should be entitled to special rights and privileges, or whether they should conform to a more individualistic pattern of incorporation (Feldblum 1999; Skerry 1993). As during the industrial revolution, how a society manages this type of change is heavily dependent on the strength of its institutions, especially the welfare state, which is much stronger and better developed today than in the nineteenth century (Bommes and Halfmann 1998; Kurthen, Fijalkowski, and Wagner 1998; Marshall 1964). It is important to note, however, that the level and unit of analysis in these works has shifted, from the state to the individual or the group. In such analyses of political behavior, political scientists are not so concerned with predicting state-level responses to immigration, as with understanding the impact of immigration on the attitudes of individuals and groups in society.

In the analysis of the politics of immigration, the whole panoply of variables for predicting voting behavior (Miller and Shanks 1996) come into play. They can be arrayed along two dimensions: one focused on social class, the other on culture and ethnicity. Hypotheses for explaining the support for anti-immigrant parties and social movements or ballot initiatives, like California's Proposition 187 and English-only movements, tend to stress one or the other dimension (Citrin, Reingold, and Green 1990; Espenshade and Calhoun 1993; Hollifield and Martin 1996; Mayer and Perrineau 1996; McClain and Karnig 1990). The question is whether the roots of xenophobic politics lie primarily in the realm of economic interests or cultural beliefs and attitudes. Scholars are divided in their answer to this question: some stress the importance of ethnicity as a mobilizing factor (Fetzer 1996; Schmitter-Heisler 1986; Tolbert and Hero 1996); others continue to focus on class as the driving force in immigration politics (Bach 1986; Hollifield and Martin 1996; Lamont 1995; Rath 1988). In the general literature on voting in the United States, very little attention has been paid to the impact of immigration on political behavior.[9] Perhaps because immigration has had a much more visible impact on politics in Western Europe, the European voting literature is more extensive (see, for example, Betz 1994; Mayer and Perrineau 1996).

An alternative to the Smithian or Durkheimian arguments draws heavily on social geography and has a distinctive Malthusian ring to it. This is the idea that the spatial concentration of immigrants triggers a xenophobic reaction in the native population, which fears being overwhelmed by "the other." According to Jeannette Money (1997, 1999) limits on resources and space, especially at the local level, will trigger xenophobic and nativist politics. The intensity of local reactions against immigration, as happened in the town of Dreux, France, in the early 1980s, or in Southern California in the early 1990s, forced immigration onto the national political agenda (Clark 1997; Tribalat 1995). Martin Schain (1988, 1990) has analyzed how the French National Front began to make inroads in local politics, often at the expense of the communists, playing on the xenophobic feelings of the native working class vis-à-vis North African immigrants who were having difficulties in acculturating and assimilating. Tolbert and Hero (1996) look at the subtle interplay of class, race, and ethnicity in local voting patterns for and against Proposition 187 in California. In the mid-1990s, it appeared that the California ballot initiative would succeed in putting nativist politics back on the top of the agenda in American politics. But as quickly as the issue inserted itself onto the California agenda, it disappeared as the business cycle in the state improved. The "Golden State" once again found its Midas touch, which would seem to indicate that economic interests play a crucial role in the rise and decline of immigration politics (Hollifield and Martin 1996).

Nevertheless, as I pointed out above, it would be a mistake to reduce immigration politics to the simple play of economic interests. Coalitions that form for or against immigration are held together not simply by narrow calculations of the costs and benefits that accrue to a specific class or group. Rather policy and politics in this area are driven in no small measure by attitudes and beliefs shaped by national cultures and histories. This is why identity politics in the advanced industrial democracies can quickly overwhelm clientelist politics, driving immigration policy either in a more expansive direction (as in the cases of the United States and Germany) or toward greater restriction (as in Britain). Concerns over citizenship, identity, sovereignty, and incorporation can override the market interests of specific groups or classes, creating "strange bedfellow" coalitions, most often of right-wing (free-market or economic) liberals and left-wing (political) liberals—what I have called elsewhere "rights-markets coalitions" (Hollifield 1992; Hollifield and Zuk 1998). What is it that holds these coalitions together?

In the American case, it was the strange conjuncture of the cold war—with its emphasis on national security and the need to resurrect the very old notion of the United States as a land of asylum or refuge—and the civil rights movement. Taken together, they dramatically expanded the civil and social rights of minorities, including immigrants (Tichenor 1994, 1996). In the German case, the cold war also played a role. But more important is what Markovits and Reich (1997) call the politics of collective memory, which helped to shape a new German model of citizenship. This model was based in the first instance on the famous social market economy (*Sozialmarktpolitik*), meaning a strong commitment to the welfare state and to the maintenance of social solidarity in the face of rapid social and economic change. In the second instance, the model derives from the overwhelming burden of German history and the experiences of the Holocaust and the Second World War. In both cases "ideas, institutions and civil society" have worked to limit the capacity for immigration control (Hollifield 1997a, 1997b, 1999a). In neither case were markets for immigrant or foreign labor functioning in a political, cultural, or ideational void. In the German or American cases, any attempt to understand policy outputs or outcomes purely in terms of interest or clientelist politics will not get us very far. This does not mean that powerful anti-immigrant forces were absent in either the German or the American cases; merely that they were unable to overcome strong proimmigration coalitions, built on the dual dynamic of markets and rights.

So where does this leave us with respect to our understanding of the politics of international migration and our ability to theorize about this complex phenomenon? I would like to conclude this chapter by summarizing the various theories and hypotheses reviewed above, with an eye to describing how we can bring politics and the state into or "back into" our analysis of migration. I also will discuss what I see as the major avenues for future research.

CONCLUSION: AVENUES FOR FUTURE RESEARCH

Simply asserting that politics and the state matter in the analysis of international migration does not help us in constructing a theory of the politics of international migration. The challenge for political scientists is to demonstrate how the state and politics matter and to develop theories of international migration that incorporate political variables. Few serious social scientists, irrespective of their home discipline, would disagree with the proposition that politics matters. The trick, as one colleague put it to me, is to bring politics into the analysis in a "nonstylized way."[10] Before we can get to the richness or power of political explanations for migration, we must be clear about the models we are using, as well as the levels and units of analysis. Only then will we be able to develop generalizable and testable propositions.

In the current literature, what is an independent variable for some—the supply of and the demand for immigration policy—is a dependent variable for others. We can therefore identify an immediate schism between those who see their objective as explaining policy, *tout court*, or what I call policy outputs, and those who have a somewhat broader objective of explaining policy outcomes, in this case international migration itself. Most works, however, focus on explaining immigration rather than international migration, for reasons that I have outlined in the first section of this chapter. The receiving countries really are calling the shots with respect to international migration. So not surprisingly much greater attention is given to the politics of immigration (rules of entry) than to the politics of emigration (rules of exit). This points to an immediate gap in the literature, since, with very few exceptions (Russell 1986; Shain 1989; Weiner 1995), scholars have focused most of their attention on political, economic, and social conditions in the liberal, receiving states. One, perhaps false, assumption is that immigration is permanent. But with the rise of transnational communities and dual nationality, this may be even less true today than it was in earlier periods. Clearly more research needs to be done on the politics of emigration and the increasingly transnational nature of migration, one indicator of which is dual nationality.

By contrast, in the study of the politics of immigration, we have only scratched the surface. Much of the literature takes the supply of and the demand for immigration policy as the dependent variable, focusing heavily on the play of organized interests to explain why some states are willing at certain points in time to "risk migration," while others remain closed. Freeman's "modes of politics" approach offers a neat typology for explaining how powerful, proimmigration coalitions form and prevent liberal democracies from reducing immigration, even when the economic conjuncture would seem to dictate greater closure (Freeman 1995). Freeman's is basically a "capture argument," that liberal states are vulnerable to capture by powerful organized interests. If we combine his approach with a factor-cost model (Kessler 1998), then we have a more complete theory of the political economy of immigration, albeit one heavily indebted to microeconomics. In this construction, politics is defined primarily by the play of interests.

In the liberal state thesis, I offered a more cultural and institutionalist approach to answering the question of why states are willing to risk migration, even in the face of a negative economic conjuncture. In this approach, politics is defined more in institutional and legal terms, with a heavy focus on the evolution of rights as the key variable for explaining openness or closure (Hollifield 1992, 1999a). In most of my work, the dependent variable is immigration and policy is an independent variable. The unit of analysis is the state, while the method is comparative, historical, and statistical; and the analysis is done at a macrolevel, using aggregate data. In this framework, the principal challenge is to understand the development of rights (as an independent variable), in their civil, social, and political dimensions. The liberal state is key to understanding immigration and rights are the essence of the liberal state. One problem with this approach, however, is that liberal states are caught in a dilemma. International economics (markets) push liberal states toward greater openness for efficiency (allocational) reasons; whereas domestic political and legal forces push the same states toward greater closure, to protect the social contract and to preserve the institutions of citizenship and sovereignty. How can states escape from this dilemma or paradox?

Some political scientists, like Myron Weiner (1995), argue that states cannot escape from this dilemma; therefore, migration must be understood in the context of political realism. For Weiner, migration is simply another of the many security threats that states must face in an international system, structured by anarchy, where states are the sole/unitary actors. Here, the dependent variables are the rules of entry and exit (supply of and demand for migration policy) and the principal independent variable is national security. In Weiner's framework, migration is above all else a foreign policy issue and the international system or the state (as opposed to individuals or groups) are the appropriate levels of analysis. In making migration policy, states face fundamental, structural constraints that are dictated by the nature of the international system. As in Freeman's theory, politics is defined primarily in terms of the play of interest, but at the international rather than the domestic level.

As with most interest-based arguments in political science, we do not have to look very far to find alternative hypotheses that place more stress on institutions and ideas, if not culture. The globalization thesis has it that states are not the sole/unitary actors in the international system and the dilemma in which they find themselves is a result of a process of social and economic change, over which states have little control (Sassen 1996). Migration is simply one of several transnational forces that buffet states and societies, leading inevitably to the erosion of sovereignty and the system of nation-states. Few if any political scientists would accept the globablization thesis in its purest form, because it is so apolitical. Most would agree that states remain very much at the center of international relations. But, unlike the political realists, those international relations theorists who take a liberal institutionalist approach accept the fact that economic and social change have led to growing interdependence and states have found ways to cooperate and solve coordination problems. The way in which they have done this is through international law and organization and the building of international regimes and institutions.

Liberal institutionalists themselves are split between those who see the rise in migration primarily as a function of the growth of international human rights regimes (Jacobson 1996; Soysal 1994) and those who see the "possibility" for further cooperation among liberal states in building such a regime. As someone who subscribes to the latter view, I argue that in the final analysis rights still derive from the liberal constitutions (and power) of national states (Hollifield 1998, 2000a). Here, politics is defined more in terms of ideas and institutions than in terms of interest. Much work, however, remains to be done in the area of migration and international relations. Scholars have only just begun to specify the conditions under which states may cooperate to solve the problem of unwanted or uncontrolled migration (Ghosh 2000). Not surprisingly, a great deal of attention is being lavished by political scientists on the experience of the European Union, as it attempts to grapple with the rights of third-country nationals (Guiraudon and Lahav 2000; Thouez 1999).

Once again we are thrown back onto an analysis of rights, which raises another set of questions and problems concerning the institutions of citizenship and sovereignty. It is in this area of inquiry where the most work by political scientists remains to be done and where the biggest payoff will be in theoretical terms. Is international migration really eroding the twin pillars of the international system: citizenship (the nation) and sovereignty (the state)? This is a daunting question and we can see immediately that the dependent and independent variables have been reversed. Is migration now a force that has the potential to undermine the institution of sovereignty and transform world politics, as Rey Koslowski (1999) and Yasemin Soysal (1994), inter alia, have put it? Answering this question will require us to look at the relationship between immigration and integration (or incorporation). Very few political scientists have studied immigration as an issue of sovereignty (see, however, Joppke 1998; Rudolph 1998; Shanks 2000). Instead, more have focused on the relationship between citizenship and immigration (Fuchs 1990; Pickus 1998; Smith 1997; Tichenor 1996). Almost no one in political science has studied the relationship between immigration and incorporation—a literature dominated by sociologists and economists (see, however, DeSipio 1996). How, for example, does political incorporation (the final step to formal-legal citizenship) affect the prospects for social and economic incorporation? Does or should one precede the other? Without the data or the theoretical tools to answer these questions, we cannot begin to understand the relationship between immigration and citizenship. Yet, given the rise in immigration in the industrial democracies since 1945 and the development of more expansive notions of citizenship, this relationship is likely to preoccupy students of international migration for decades to come.

Much of the literature on citizenship tends to be atheoretical and heavily formal-legal in orientation, relying primarily on inductive/historical analysis and moral reasoning. Perhaps the most highly developed body of literature in political science is that on voting. But, as in the area of international relations, little attention has been given to the issue of migration, and few attempts have been made to integrate the literature on voting behavior with broader issues in the politics of immigration: control, national security, sovereignty, citizenship, and incorporation. Most studies of immigration, voting and political participation have focused on the rise of extremist political parties and new social movements, again with little attention given to issues of political incorporation or citizenship (see, however, Feldblum 1999). In much of this literature, the nativist and xenophobic backlash against immigration is seen as yet another symptom of postindustrial change, with the losers in struggles over modernization (especially unskilled workers) seen to be the easiest groups to mobilize against further immigration. Jeannette Money (1999) has added a spatial dimension to the analysis, suggesting that heavy concentrations of immigrants in specific locales can exacerbate anti-immigrant politics.

While the literature on immigration, voting, and political participation holds some promise for helping us to understand how and why coalitions form—for or against immigration—it does not address the relationship between immigration and integration. Jeannette Money (1998) argues that the determinants of immigration policy are difficult to grasp because immigration is a two-dimensional policy problem. She returns to the classical distinction made by Tomas Hammar (1985; Hollifield 2000b) between immigration and immigrant policy, arguing that issues of control elicit different types of coalitions than issues of integration or incorporation. These two issues tend to split mainstream political parties, often in very odd ways that are difficult to predict. Much more theorizing and research needs to be done on the relationship between immigration and integration in order to understand the types of coalitions that form.

In this respect, political scientists have their work cut out for them. Historians, sociologists, economists, anthropologists, and demographers have a head start in the study of international migration. These disciplines have a large body of literature and a bigger empirical base from which to work. But given the sheer number of political scientists who are now turning their attention to the study of international migration, we should close the gap fairly quickly.

NOTES

Many colleagues read and commented on earlier drafts of this chapter. I would like specifically to acknowledge the invaluable feedback I received from Wayne Cornelius, Louis DeSipio, Thomas Faist, Miriam Feldblum, Gary Freeman, Barbara and Martin Heisler, Christian Joppke, Rey Koslowski, Marc Rosenblum, Rogers Smith, and Dietrich Thränhardt. Errors, of course, are mine alone.

1. Reference here is to the seminal essay by Theda Skocpol, "Bringing the State Back In" (Evans, Rueschemeyer, and Skocpol 1985). For some recent efforts to theorize about the role of the state in international migration, see Freeman 1998; Weil 1998; and Zolberg 1999.
2. I was once reproached by a colleague in history who said, "You political scientists just lurch from one crisis to another."
3. As defined in one of the most widely used introductory texts in political science (Dahl 1991).
4. Aristide Zolberg pointed out the hypocrisy of liberal democracies, which, throughout the period of the cold war, worked to create a right to exit, but without a concomitant right to entry (Zolberg 1981).
5. The argument here is that international migration in the post-1945 period was stimulated by economic imbalances between the north and the south. We cannot, however, ignore the role of decolonization and refugee movements in this process. The politics of postcolonial and refugee migrations are admittedly different than the politics of labor migration (see Zolberg, Suhrke, and Aguayo 1989; Joppke 1998a).
6. An interesting exercise is to search the index of major texts in international relations. Almost never does one find even a single entry about migration, immigration, or emigration.
7. The section on Ethnicity Nationalism and Migration (ENMISA) is the fastest growing group within the International Studies Association.
8. This liberal view of citizenship underpins the modernization school of political development. At a conference on security and migration at MIT, convened by Myron Weiner, Lucian Pye was asked to comment on the rise of ethnic nationalism in the post–cold war era. He responded that ethnic nationalism is an oxymoron. According to Pye, you either have ethnicity or nationalism. But you cannot have both, because one destroys the other.
9. If we take Miller and Shanks (1996) as the state of the art in this literature, then it is surprising to see no reference whatsoever to immigration in the entire volume and only one reference to ethnicity.
10. The quote is taken from an e-mail exchange with Robert Keohane.

REFERENCES

Alba, Richard, and Victor Nee. 1997. "Rethinking Assimilation Theory for a New Era of Immigration," *International Migration Review* 31: 826–74.

Aleinikoff, Thomas A., and David A. Martin. 1995. *Immigration Process and Policy*. St. Paul, Minn.: West Publishing.

Andreas, Peter. 1998. "The Escalation of U.S. Immigration Control in the Post-NAFTA Era," *Political Science Quarterly* 113/4: 591–615.

Bach, Robert L. 1986. "Immigration: Issues of Ethnicity, Class and Public Policy in the United States" *The Annals* 485: 139–52.

Barth, Fredrik. 1969. *Ethnic Groups and Boundaries: The Social Organization of Culture Difference*. Boston: Little, Brown.

Bauböck, Rainer. 1994. *Transnational Citizenship: Membership and Rights in International Migration*. Aldershot, Eng.: Edward Elgar.

Betz, Hans Georg. 1994. *Radical Right-wing Populism in Western Europe*. New York: St. Martin's Press.

Bhagwati, Jagdish. 1976. *The Brain Drain and Taxation: Theory and Empirical Analysis*. New York: American Elsevier.

Bommes, Michael, and Jost Halfmann. 1998. *Migration in nationalen Wohlfahrtsstaaten*. Osnabrück: Universitätsverlag Rasch.

Bonacich, Edna. 1972. "The Split Labor Market: A Theory of Ethnic Antagonism," *American Journal of Sociology* 37: 1050–87.

Borjas, George J. 1990. *Friends or Strangers: The Impact of Immigrants on the U.S. Economy*. New York: Basic Books.

Bouvier, Leon F. 1992. *Peaceful Invasions: Immigration and Changing America*. Lanham, Md.: University Press of America.

Brimelow, Peter. 1995. *Alien Nation: Common Sense About America's Immigration Disaster*. New York: Random House.

Brochmann, Grete, and Tomas Hammar, eds. 1999. *Mechanisms of Immigration Control: A Comparative Analysis of European Regulation Policies*. Oxford: Berg.

Brubaker, Rogers, ed. 1989. *Immigration and the Politics of Citizenship in Europe and North America*. Lanham, Md.: University Press of America.

———. 1992. *Citizenship and Nationhood in France and Germany*. Cambridge, Mass.: Harvard University Press.

———. 1996. *Nationalism Reframed. Nationhood and the National Question in the New Europe*. Cambridge: Cambridge University Press.

Calavita, Kitty. 1992. *Inside the State: The Bracero Program, Immigration and the INS*. New York: Routledge.

Carens, Joseph H. 1989. "Membership and Morality: Admission to Citizenship in Liberal Democratic States," in Rogers Brubaker, ed., *Immigration and the Politics of Citizenship in Europe and North America*. Lanham, Md.: University Press of America.

Castells, Manuel. 1975. "Immigrant Workers and Class Struggles in Advanced Capitalism: The Western European Experience," *Politics and Society* 5: 33–66.

Castles, Stephen, and Alastair Davidson. 1998. *Citizenship in the Age of Migration: Globalisation and the Politics of Belonging*. London: Macmillan.

Castles, Stephen, and Godula Kosack. 1973. *Immigrant Workers and Class Structure in Western Europe*. London: Oxford University Press.

Castles, Stephen, and Mark Miller. 1998. *The Age of Migration: International Population Movements in the Modern World*. New York: Guilford.

Chiswick, Barry R., ed. 1982. *The Gateway: U.S. Immigration Issues and Policies*. Washington, D.C.: American Enterprise Institute.

Citirn, Jack, Beth Reingold, and Donald P. Green. 1990. "American Identity and the Politics of Ethnic Change," *Journal of Politics* 52: 1124–54.

Clark, W. A. V. 1997. "Scale Effects in International Migration to the United States," *Regional Studies* 30: 589–600.

Coleman, David A. 1992. "Does Europe Need Immigrants? Population and Work Force Projections," *International Migration Review* 26/2: 413–61.

Commission on Immigration Reform. 1997. *Binational Study on Migration Between Mexico and the United States*. Washington, D.C.

Cornelius, Wayne A. 1998. "The Structural Embeddedness of Demand for Mexican Immigrant Labor: New Evidence from California," in Marcelo M. Suárez-Orozco, ed., *Crossings: Mexican Immigration in Interdisciplinary Perspectives*. Cambridge, Mass.: Harvard University Press.

Cornelius, Wayne A., Philip L. Martin, and James F. Hollifield, eds. 1994. *Controlling Immigration: A Global Perspective*. Stanford, Calif.: Stanford University Press.

Dahl, Robert A. 1991. *Modern Political Analysis*. Englewood Cliffs, N.J.: Prentice-Hall.

De la Garza, Rodolfo O., and Louis DeSipio. 1996. *Ethnic Ironies: Latino Politics in the 1992 Elections*. Boulder, Colo.: Westview Press.

DeSipio, Louis. 1996. *Counting on the Latino Vote: Latinos as a New Electorate*. Charlottesville: University of Virginia Press.

_____. 1999. "The Second Generation: Political Behaviors of Adult Children of Immigrants in the United States," paper prepared for the annual meeting of the American Political Science Association, Atlanta, Georgia.

Douglas, Mary. 1986. *How Institutions Think*. Syracuse, N.Y.: Syracuse University Press.

Durkheim, Emile. 1964. *The Division of Labor in Society*. New York: Free Press.

Espenshade, Thomas J., and Charles A. Calhoun. 1993. "An Analysis of Public Opinion Toward Undocumented Immigration," *Population Research and Policy Review* 12: 189–224.

Evans, Peter B., Dietrich Rueschemeyer, and Theda Skocpol, eds. 1985. *Bringing the State Back In*. New York: Cambridge University Press.

Faini, Ricardo, Jaime De Melo and Klaus F. Zimmerman, eds. 1999. *Trade and Migration: The Controversies and the Evidence*. Cambridge: Cambridge University Press.

Faist, Thomas. 1995. *Social Citizenship for Whom? Young Turks in Germany and Mexican Americans in the United States*. Aldershot, Eng.: Avebury.

Feldblum, Miriam. 1999. *Reconstructing Citizenship: The Politics of Citizenship and Immigration in Contemporary France*. Albany: SUNY Press.

Fetzer, Joel. 1996. "Marginality, Economic Self Interest and Voting for Proposition 187," paper prepared for the annual meeting of the American Political Science Association, San Francisco, Calif.

Freeman, Gary P. 1979. *Immigrant Labor and Racial Conflict in Industrial Societies: The French and British Experiences*. Princeton, N.J.: Princeton University Press.

_____. 1986. "Migration and the Political Economy of the Welfare State," *The Annals* 485/May: 51–63.

_____. 1994. "Britain, the Deviant Case," in Wayne A. Cornelius, Philip L. Martin, and James F. Hollifield, eds. *Controlling Immigration: A Global Perspective*. Stanford, Calif.: Stanford University Press.

_____.1995. "Modes of Immigration Politics in Liberal Democratic States," *International Migration Review* 29/4: 881–902.

_____. 1998a. "The Decline of Sovereignty? Politics and Immigration Restriction in Liberal States" in Christian Joppke, ed., *Challenge to the Nation-State*. Oxford: Oxford University Press.

_____. 1998b. "Toward a Theory of the Domestic Politics of International Migration in Western Nations," South Bend, Ind.: Nanovic Insititute, University of Notre Dame.

Fuchs, Lawrence H. 1990. *The American Kaleidoscope: Race, Ethnicity and the Civic Culture*. Hanover, N.H.: Wesleyan University and University Press of New England.

Geddes, Andrew. 1995. "Immigrant and Ethnic Minorities and the EC's Democratic Deficit," *Journal of Common Market Studies* 33/2: 197–217.

Ghosh, Bimal, ed. 2000. *Managing Migration: The Need for a New International Regime*. Oxford: Oxford University Press.

Gilpin, Robert. 1986. *The Political Economy of International Relations*. Princeton, N.J.: Princeton University Press.

Glazer, Nathan, and Daniel P. Moynihan. 1970. *Beyond the Melting Pot: The Negroes, Puerto Ricans, Jews, Italians and Irish of New York City*. Cambridge, Mass.: MIT Press.

Goodwin-Gill, Guy S. 1996. *The Refugee in International Law*. Oxford: Clarendon.

Gordon, Milton. 1964. *Assimilation in American Life*. New York: Oxford University Press.

Guiraudon, Virginie. 1998. "Third Country Nationals and European Law: Obstacles to Rights' Expansion," *Journal of Ethnic Studies* 24/4: 657–74.

Guiraudon, Virginie, and Gallya Lahav. 2000. "A Reappraisal of the State Sovereignty Debate: The Case of Migration Control," *Comparative Political Studies*.

Hailbronner, Kay. 1984. *Ausländerrecht*. Heidelberg: C.F. Müller.

Hailbronner, Kay, David A. Martin, and Hiroshi Motomura, eds. 1997. *Immigration Admissions: The Search for Workable Policies in Germany and the United States*. Oxford: Berghahn Books.

Hammar, Tomas, ed. 1985. *European Immigration Policy: A Comparative Study*. New York: Cambridge University Press.

———. 1990. *Democracy and the Nation-State: Aliens, Denizens and Citizens in a World of International Migration*. Aldershot, Eng.: Avebury.

Hammar, Tomas, Grete Bochmann, Kristof Tamas, and Thomas Faist, eds. 1997. *International Migration, Immobility and Development: Multidisciplinary Perspectives*. Oxford: Berg.

Hansen, Randall. 2000. *Immigration and Citizenship in Postwar Britain*. Oxford: Oxford University Press.

Haus, Leah. 1995. "Openings in the Wall: Transnational Migrants, Labor Unions and U.S. Immigration Policy," *International Organization* 49/2: 285–313.

———. 1999. "Labor Unions and Immigration Policy in France," *International Migration Review* 33/3: 683–716.

Heisler, Martin O. 1992. "Migration, International Relations and the New Europe: Theoretical Perspectives from Institutional Political Sociology," *International Migration Review* 26/2: 596–622.

———. 1998. "Contextualizing Global Migration: Sketching the Socio-Political Landscape in Europe," *UCLA Journal of International Law and Foreign Affairs* 3/2: 557–93.

Hobsbawm, Eric. 1990. *Nations and Nationalism since 1780*. Cambridge: Cambridge University Press.

Hollifield, James F. 1986. "Immigration Policy in France and Germany: Outputs vs. Outcomes," *The Annals* 485/May: 113–28.

———. 1990. "Immigration and the French State," *Comparative Political Studies* 23 (April): 56–79.

———. 1992a. *Immigrants, Markets and States: The Political Economy of Postwar Europe*. Cambridge, Mass.: Harvard University Press.

———. 1992b. "Migration and International Relations: Cooperation and Control in the European Community," *International Migration Review* 26/2: 568–95.

———. 1994. "Immigration and Republicanism in France: The Hidden Consensus," in Wayne A. Cornelius, Philip L. Martin, and James F. Hollifield, eds., *Controlling Immigration: A Global Perspective*. Stanford, Calif.: Stanford University Press.

———. 1997a. *L'Immigration et L'Etat-Nation à La Recherche d'un Modèle National*. Paris: L'Harmattan.

———. 1997b. "Immigration and Integration in Western Europe: A Comparative Analysis," in Emek M. Uçarer and Donald J. Puchala, eds., *Immigration into Western Societies: Problems and Policies*. London: Pinter.

———. 1998. "Migration, Trade and the Nation-State: The Myth of Globalization," *UCLA Journal of International Law and Foreign Affairs* 3/2: 595–636.

———. 1999a. "Ideas, Institutions and Civil Society: On the Limits of Immigration Control in Liberal Democracies" *IMIS-Beiträge* 10 (January): 57–90.

———. 1999b. "On the Limits of Immigration Control in France," in Grete Brochmann and Tomas Hammar, eds., *Mechanisms of Immigration Control*. Oxford: Berg.

———. 2000a. "Migration and the 'New' International Order: The Missing Regime," in Bimal Ghosh, ed., *Managing Migration: The Need for a New International Regime*. Oxford: Oxford University Press.

———. 2000b. "Immigration and the Politics of Rights," in Michael Bommes and

Andrew Geddes, eds., *Migration and the Welfare State in Contemporary Europe*. London: Routledge.

Hollifield, James F., and Calvin Jillson, eds. 1999. *Pathways to Democracy: The Political Economy of Democratic Transitions*. New York: Routledge.

Hollifield, James F., and David L. Martin. 1996. "Strange Bedfellows? Immigration and Class Voting on Prop 187 in California," paper prepared for the American Political Science Association. San Francisco, Calif.

Hollifield, James F., Daniel J. Tichenor, and Gary Zuk. Forthcoming. "Immigrants, Markets and the American State: The Political Economy of U.S. Immigration," Unpublished paper.

Hollifield, James F., and Gary Zuk. 1998. "Immigrants, Markets and Rights," in Hermann Kurthen, Jürgen Fijalkowski, and Gert G. Wagner, eds., *Immigration, Citizenship and the Welfare State in Germany and the United States*. Stamford, Conn.: JAI Press.

Huntington, Samuel P. 1996. "The West: Unique, Not Universal," *Foreign Affairs* 75/6: 28–46.

IOM. 1996. *Foreign Direct Investment, Trade, Aid and Migration*. Geneva: International Organization for Migration.

Ireland, Patrick. 1994. *The Policy Challenge of Ethnic Diversity: Immigrant Politics in France and Switzerland*. Cambridge, Mass.: Harvard University Press.

Jacobson, David. 1996. *Rights across Borders: Immigration and the Decline of Citizenship*. Baltimore, Md.: Johns Hopkins University Press.

Joppke, Christian, ed. 1998a. *Challenge to the Nation-State: Immigration in Western Europe and the United States*. Oxford: Oxford University Press.

———. 1998b. "Why Liberal States Accept Unwanted Migration," *World Politics* 50/2: 266–93.

Kastoryano, Riva. 1997. *La France, l'Allemagne et leurs immigrés: négocier l'identité*. Paris: Armand Colin.

Katzenstein, Peter J., ed. 1996. *The Culture of National Security: Norms and Identity in World Politics*. New York: Columbia University Press.

Keohane, Robert O. 1984. *After Hegemony: Cooperation and Discord in the World Economy*. Princeton, N.J.: Princeton University Press.

Keohane, Robert O., and Helen V. Milner. 1996. *Internationalization of Domestic Politics*. New York: Cambridge University Press.

Keohane, Robert O., and Joseph S. Nye. 1977. *Power and Interdependence: World Politics in Transition*. Boston: Little, Brown.

Kessler, Alan E. 1998. "Distributional Coalitions, Trade and the Politics of Postwar American Immigration," paper prepared for the American Political Science Association, Boston, Mass.

King, Desmond. 2000. *Making Americans: Immigration, Race and the Diverse Democracy*. Cambridge, Mass.: Harvard University Press.

Kitschelt, Herbert. 1995. *The Radical Right in Western Europe*. Ann Arbor: University of Michigan Press.

Kohn, Hans. 1962. *The Age of Nationalism: The First Era of Global History*. New York: Harper & Row.

Koslowski, Rey. 1999. *Migration and Citizenship in World Politics: From Nation-States to European Polity*. Ithaca, N.Y.: Cornell University Press.

Krasner, Stephen D. 1999. *Sovereignty: Organized Hypocrisy*. Princeton, N.J.: Princeton University Press.

Krugman, Paul, and Maurice Obstfeld. 1997. *International Economics: Theory and Policy*. Reading, Mass.: Addison-Wesley.

Kurthen, Hermann, Jürgen Fijalkowski, and Gert G. Wagner, eds., 1998. *Immigration, Citizenship and the Welfare State in Germany and the United States*. Stamford, Conn.: JAI Press.

Kymlicka, Will. 1995. *Multicultural Citizenship*. Oxford: Clarendon Press.

Lamont, Michèle. 1995. "National Identity and National Boundary Patterns in France and the United States," *French Historical Studies* 19/2: 349–65.

———. 1998. *The World in Moral Order: Working Men Define the Boundaries of Race, Class and Citizenship*. Princeton, N.J.: Princeton University Press.

Layton-Henry, Zig, ed., 1990. *The Political Rights of Migrant Workers in Western Europe*. London: Sage.

———. 1992. *The Politics of Race: Immigration, "Race" and "Race" Relations in Postwar Britain*. Oxford: Blackwell.

Legomsky, Stephen H. 1987. *Immigration and the Judiciary: Law and Politics in Britain and America*. Oxford: Clarendon.

Lévi-Strauss, Claude. 1952. *Race and History*. Paris: UNESCO.

Lochak, Danièle. 1985. *Etrangers: de quels droits?* Paris: Presses Universitaires de France.

Lusztig, Michael. 1996. *Risking Free Trade: The Politics of Trade in Britain, Canada, Mexico and the United States*. Pittsburgh, Pa.: University of Pittsburgh Press.

Markovits, Andrei S., and Simon Reich. 1997. *The German Predicament: Memory and Power in the New Europe*. Ithaca, N.Y.: Cornell University Press.

Marshall, T. H. 1964. *Class, Citizenship and Social Development*. Garden City, N.Y.: Doubleday.

Martin, Philip L. 1993. *Trade and Migration: NAFTA and Agriculture*. Washington, D.C.: Institute for International Economics.

———. 1994a. "The United States: Benign Neglect Toward Immigration," in Wayne A. Cornelius, Philip L. Martin, and James F. Hollifield, eds., *Controlling Immigration: A Global Perspective*. Stanford, Calif.: Stanford University Press.

———. 1994b. "Germany: Reluctant Land of Immigration," in Wayne A. Cornelius, Philip L. Martin, and James F. Hollifield, eds., *Controlling Immigration: A Global Perspective*. Stanford, Calif.: Stanford University Press.

Massey, Douglas S. 1987. *Return to Aztlan: The Social Processes of International Migration from Western Mexico*. Berkeley and Los Angeles: University of California Press.

———. 1998. *Worlds in Motion: Understanding International Migration as the End of the Millennium*. Oxford: Oxford University Press.

———, ed. 1999a. *Becoming American, American Becoming*. New York: Russell Sage.

———. 1999b. "International Migration at the Dawn of the Twenty-First Century: The Role of the State," *Population and Development Review* 25/2: 303–22.

Massey, Douglas S., et al. 1993. "Theories of International Migration," *Population and Development Review* 19/3: 431–66.

Mayer, Nonna, and Pascal Perrineau, eds. 1996. *Le Front National à Découvert*: Paris: Presses de la FNSP.

McClain, Paula D., and Albert K. Karnig. 1990. "Black and Hispanic Socioeconomic and Political Competition," *American Political Science Review* 84: 535–45.

Messina, Anthony M. 1989. *Race and Party Competition in Britain*. Oxford: Clarendon Press.

———. 1996. "The Not So Silent Revolution: Postwar Migration to Western Europe," *World Politics*. 49/1: 130–54.

Meyer, John W., and Michael T. Hannan, eds. 1979. *National Development and the World System: Educational, Economic and Political Change*. Chicago: University of Chicago Press.

Meyers, Eytan. 1995. "The Political Economy of International Migration Policy," unpublished Ph.D. dissertation, University of Chicago.

Miles, Robert. 1982. *Racism and Migrant Labour: A Critical Text*. London: Routledge.

Miller, Mark J. 1981. *Foreign Workers in Western Europe: An Emerging Political Force*. N.Y.: Praeger.

———. 1997. "International Migration and Security: Towards Transatlantic Convergence," in Emek M. Uçarer and Donald J. Puchala, eds., *Immigration into Western Societies: Problems and Policies*. London: Pinter.

Miller, Mark J., and Philip L. Martin. 1982. *Administering Foreign Worker Programs*. Lexington, Mass.: D.C. Heath.

Miller, Warren E., and J. Merrill Shanks. 1996. *The New American Voter*. Cambridge, Mass.: Harvard University Press.

Milner, Helen V. 1988. *Resisting Protectionism: Global Industries and the Politics of International Trade*. Princeton, N.J.: Princeton University Press.

———. 1997. *Interests, Institutions and Information: Domestic Politics and International Relations*. Princeton, N.J.: Princeton University Press.

Minkenberg, Michael. 1992. "The New Right in Germany: The Transformation of Conservatism and the Extreme Right," *European Journal of Political Research* 22: 55–81.

Moch, Leslie Page. 1992. *Moving Europeans: Migration in Western Europe since 1650*. Bloomington: Indiana University Press.

Money, Jeannette. 1998. "Two Dimensional Aliens: Immigration Policy as a Two Dimensional Space," paper prepared for a conference on "Migration and the State," The New School for Social Research, New York.

———. 1999. *Fences and Neighbors: The Geography of Immigration Control*. Ithaca, N.Y.: Cornell University Press.

Moore, Barrington Jr. 1966. *Social Origins of Dictatorship and Democracy: Lord and Peasant in the Making of the Modern World*. Boston: Beacon Press.

Mundell, Robert A. 1957. "International Trade and Factor Mobility," *American Economic Review* 47: 321–35.

Noiriel, Gèrard. 1988. *Le creuset français*. Paris: Seuil.

OECD. 1992. *Trends in International Migration*. Paris: Organization for Economic Cooperation and Development.

Perlmutter, Ted. 1996. "Bringing Parties Back In: Comments on 'Modes of Immigration Politics in Liberal Democratic Societies,'" *International Migration Review* 30: 375–88.

Pickus, Noah M. J., ed. 1998. *Immigration & Citizenship in the 21st Century*. Lanham, Md.: Rowman and Littlefield.

Piore, Michael J. 1979. *Birds of Passage: Migrant Labor in Industrial Societies*. Cambridge: Cambridge University Press.

Portes, Alejandro. 1996. "Transnational Communities: Their Emergence and Significance in the Contemporary World-System," in R. P. Korzeniewidcz and W. C. Smith, eds., *Latin America in the World Economy*. Westport, Conn.: Greenwood.

———. 1997. "Immigration Theory for a New Century," *International Migration Review* 31/4: 799–825.

Portes, Alejandro, and Robert L. Bach. 1985. *Latin Journey: Cuban and Mexican Immigrants to the United States*. Berkeley and Los Angeles: University of California Press.

Portes, Alejandro, and Ruben Rumbaut. 1996. *Immigrant America: A Portrait*. Berkeley and Los Angeles: University of California Press.

Rath, Jan. 1988. "Political Action of Immigrants in the Netherlands: Class or Ethnicity?" *European Journal of Political Research* 16: 623–44.

Rex, John, and R. Moore. 1967. *Race, Community and Conflict*. Oxford: Oxford University Press.

Rogers, Rosemarie, ed. 1985. *Guests Come to Stay: The Effects of European Labor Migration on Sending and Receiving Countries*. Boulder, Colo.: Westview.

Rosenau, James N. 1990. *Turbulence in World Politics: A Theory of Change and Continuity*. Princeton, N.J.: Princeton University Press.

Rosenblum, Marc R. 1998. "Abroad at Home: Foreign and Domestic Sources of U.S.

Migration Policy," paper prepared for the American Political Science Association Meeting. Boston, Mass.

Rudolph, Christopher W. 1998. "Globalization, Sovereignty and Migration: A Conceptual Framework," *UCLA Journal of International Law and Foreign Affairs* 3/2: 325–55.

Ruggie, John Gerard, ed. 1993. *Multilateralism Matters: The Theory and Practice of an Institutional Form*. New York: Columbia University Press.

———. 1998. *Constructing the World Polity: Essays on International Institutionalization*. New York: Routledge.

Russell, Sharon Stanton. 1986. "Remittances from International Migration. A Review in Perspective," *World Development* 41/6: 677–96.

Said, Edward W. 1993. *Culture and Imperialism*. New York: Knopf.

Sassen, Saskia. 1988. *The Mobility of Capital and Labor*. Cambridge: Cambridge University Press.

———. 1991. *The Global City: New York, London, Tokyo*. Princeton, N.J.: Princeton University Press.

———. 1996. *Losing Control? Sovereignty in an Age of Globalization*. New York: Columbia University Press.

Schain, Martin A. 1988. "Immigration and Change in the French Party System," *European Journal of Political Research* 16: 597–621.

———. 1990. "Immigration and Politics," in *Developments in French Politics*, in Peter A. Hall et al., eds. London: Macmillan.

Schlesinger, Arthur Jr. 1992. *The Disuniting of America*. New York: W. W. Norton.

Schmitter, Barbara E. 1979. "Immigration and Citizenship in West Germany and Switzerland," unpublished Ph.D. Dissertation, University of Chicago.

Schmitter Heisler, Barbara. 1986. "Immigrant Settlement and the Structure of Emergent Immigrant Communities in Western Europe," *The Annals* 485: 76–86.

———. 1993. "Review of Hollifield, *Immigrants, Markets and States*," in *Work and Occupations* 20/4: 479–80.

Schnapper, Dominique. 1998. *La relation à l'autre*. Paris: Gallimard.

Schuck, Peter H. 1998. *Citizens, Strangers and In-Betweens: Essays on Immigration and Citizenship*. Boulder, Colo.: Westview.

Schuck, Peter H., and Rogers Smith. 1985. *Citizenship Without Consent*. New Haven, Conn.: Yale University Press.

Shain, Yossi. 1989. *The Frontier of Loyalty: Political Exiles in the Age of the Nation-State*. Middletown, Conn.: Wesleyan University Press.

Shanks, Cheryl. 2000. *Immigration and the Politics of American Sovereignty, 1890–1990*. Ann Arbor: University of Michigan Press.

Shaw, Malcolm N. 1997. *International Law*. Cambridge: Cambridge University Press.

Simon, Julian. 1989. *The Economic Consequences of Immigration*. Oxford: Blackwell.

Skerry, Peter. 1993. *Mexican Americans: The Ambivalent Minority*. New York: Free Press.

Smith, Rogers. 1997. *Civic Ideals: Conflicting Visions of Citizenship in U.S. History*. New Haven, Conn.: Yale University Press.

Soysal, Yasemin N. 1994. *Limits of Citizenship: Migrants and Postnational Membership in Europe*. Chicago: University of Chicago Press.

Stark, Oded., 1991. *The Migration of Labor*. Cambridge, Mass.: Basil Blackwell.

Stolper, Wolfgang Friedrich, and Paul A. Samuelson. 1941. "Protection and Real Wages," *Review of Economic Studies* 9: 58–73.

Tapinos, Georges. 1974. *L'Economie des migrations internationales*. Paris: Colin.

Teitelbaum, Michael S. 1980. "Right Versus Right: Immigration and Refugee Policy in the United States," *Foreign Affairs* 59/1: 21–59.

———. 1984. "Immigration, Refugees and Foreign Policy," *International Organization* 38/3: 429–50.

Teitelbaum, Michael S., and Myron Weiner. 1995. *Threatened Peoples, Threatened Borders*. New York: W. W. Norton.

Thouez, Colleen V. 1999. "Theories of International Cooperation: Prospects for a Common Migration Policy for the EU Governing Entry Rules for TCNs," unpublished Ph.D. dissertation. The Fletcher School of Law and Diplomacy.

Thränhardt, Dietrich. 1993. "Die Ursprünge von Rassismus und Fremdenfeindlichkeit in der Konkurrenzdemokratie," *Leviathan* 21/3: 336–57.

———, ed. 1996. *Europe: A New Immigration Continent*. Münster: Lit verlag.

Tichenor, Daniel J. 1994. "The Politics of Immigration Reform in the United States," *Polity* 26/3: 333–62.

———. 1996. "Regulating Community: Race, Immigration Policy and American Political Development," unpublished Ph.D. dissertation, Brandeis University.

Tilly, Charles, ed., 1975. *The Formation of National States in Western Europe*. Princeton, N.J.: Princeton University Press.

Todaro, Michael P. 1976. *Internal Migration in Developing Countries: A Review of Theory, Evidence, Methodology and Research Priorities*. Geneva: International Labor Office.

Tolbert, Caroline J., and Rodney E. Hero. 1996. "Race/Ethnicity and Direct Democracy: An Analysis of California's Illegal Immigration Initiative," *Journal of Politics* 58/3: 806–18.

Torpey, John. 1998. "Coming and Going: On the State's Monopolization of the Legitimate 'Means of Movement,'" *Sociological Theory* 16/3: 239–59.

Tribalat, Michèle. 1995. *Faire France*. Paris: La Découverte.

Uçarer, Emek M. 1997. "Europe's Search for Policy: The Harmonization of Asylum Policy and European Integration," in Emek M. Uçarer and Donald J. Puchala, eds., *Immigration into Western Societies: Problems and Policies*. London: Pinter.

Wallerstein, Immanuel. 1976. *The Modern World System*. New York: Academic Press.

Waltz, Kenneth N. 1979. *Theory of International Politics*. Reading, Mass.: Addison-Wesley.

Walzer, Michael. 1983. *Spheres of Justice: A Defense of Pluralism and Equality*. New York: Basic Books.

Weber, Max. 1947. *The Theory of Social and Economic Organization*. New York: Oxford University Press.

Weil, Patrick. 1991. *La France et ses étrangers: L'aventure d'une politique de l'immigration 1938–1991*. Paris: Calmann-Lévy.

———. 1998. "The State Matters: Immigration Control in Developed Countries," New York: United Nations, Department of Social and Economic Affairs, Population Division.

Weiner, Myron. 1995. *The Global Migration Crisis: Challenge to States and to Human Rights*. New York: HarperCollins.

———, ed. 1993. *International Migration and Security*. Boulder, Colo.: Westview.

Wihtol de Wenden, Catherine. 1988. *Les immigrés et la politique*. Paris: Presses de la FNSP.

Wilson, James Q., ed. 1980. *The Politics of Regulation*. New York: Harper.

Zolberg, Aristide R. 1981. "International Migration in Political Perspective," in Mary M. Kritz, Charles B. Keely, and Silvano M. Tomasi, eds., *Global Trends in Migration: Theory and Research in International Population Movements*. New York: Center for Migration Studies.

———.1999. "Matters of State: Theorizing Immigration Policy," in Douglas Massey, ed., *Becoming American, American Becoming*. New York: Russell Sage.

Zolberg, Aristide R., Astri Suhrke, and Sergio Aguayo. 1989. *Escape from Violence: Conflict and the Refugee Crisis in the Developing World*. New York: Oxford University Press.

CHAPTER 7

Law and the Study of Migration

Peter H. Schuck

Law has always borne, perhaps vaingloriously, the high prestige of a learned, esteemed profession operating at the center of policymaking, indeed legitimating it. The legal academy also boasts antiquity, having been established in English and Italian universities in medieval times. Yet, despite law's distinguished pedigree, American institutions of higher learning long resisted including it among their academic departments. For this reason, American law schools developed first as independent institutions outside the traditional college or university setting. When the universities did deign to include law schools during the nineteenth century, their welcome was usually a cool one—at least until they realized that legal education could be delivered with large classes, no laboratories, and, often, part-time teachers. Better still, it produced prosperous alumni. Thus it could be a "profit center," cross-subsidizing other, less worldly fields of study (Stevens 1983).

The academy's long disparagement of law reflected a number of considerations, some principled, some not. A principled reason was that law is an intensely practical, cosmopolitan, prescriptive discipline seeking to serve lawyers in practice and to influence the daily behavior of courts, legislators, regulators, and private actors. In this view law, unlike many other academic departments, aspired neither to develop new objective knowledge about the world nor to recover old cultural artifacts and meanings.

This view of law was largely true when it was first advanced in the nineteenth century, but even then it ignored a long, rich, and often fruitful tradition of jurisprudential theory. Jurisprudence was concerned with the nature of law, rules, equity, and justice; with the distinction between legal positivism, natural law, and with other normative legal theories; and other foundational legal ideas that together constitute the philosophy of law. These are theoretical questions by any standard.

By the late nineteenth century, legal scholarship had grown more ambitious.

A scientific approach, associated with Harvard Law School Dean Christopher Columbus Langdell, sought to infer the corpus of general legal rules from the reasoning used by courts in deciding a mass of specific case decisions. He hoped to use such reasoning, which the judicial methodology often obscured, to predict outcomes in future cases. Langdell's system was derided by many— most famously, by Oliver Wendell Holmes—as an excessively abstract, deductive system ill-suited to a rich understanding of law. Inspired by Holmes's critique of Langdell's case method, the so-called Legal Realists cut another channel of legal scholarship during the 1920s. Many Realist law professors and judges, who foreshadowed many of today's "critical legal studies" scholars, emphasized the irreducibly political and subjective motives for decisions; they doubted that any theoretically valid science of law could or should be developed.

Some other Realists, however, were committed empiricists who held that carefully gathering facts about legal phenomena in the real world would demystify or even discredit many existing legal rules and theories while perhaps justifying others. They and their successors in the legal academy advanced hypotheses about the conduct and decisions of judges and other legal actors and institutions, and then sought to test the hypotheses against these facts. But this empirical tradition has always been exceptional among legal scholars, most of whom devoted themselves instead to analyzing and assessing caselaw. More than a decade ago, I lamented (and sought to explain) the relative dearth of legal scholarship concerned with the kind of hypothesis testing and cumulative theory building that is commonplace among social scientists (Schuck 1989).

Although such research remains exceptional in legal scholarship, legal academics now do more of it and do it better than ever before (Heise 1999). Theory and theory testing are more prominent in legal scholarship today for much the same reason that my first sentence of this chapter qualified "theory" by "autonomous": academic lawyers and practicing lawyers today increasingly appropriate theories drawn from other disciplines. These theoretical borrowings (often called "Law and . . .")[1] usually rely on economics and political science but they also include sociology, evolutionary biology, literary theory, game theory, history, and other fields. Skeptics doubt their relevance to many legal phenomena, and also doubt whether lawyers, policymakers, and judges have understood and applied them competently (Posner 1999). In any event, the academic study of law, particularly but not exclusively at the elite institutions, is today a highly but eclectic theoretical enterprise depending on other disciplines for many of its foundational concepts, methodological tools, analytical constructs, and predictive hypotheses.[2]

Whatever the intellectual history and lineaments of legal theory, its most important contribution to the study of migration is to provide insights about how legal rules, institutions, processes, and decisions—their nature, behavior, competence, consequences, and legitimacy—affect the movement of people within and across national borders. Because the law in action and the law in people's minds frequently diverge from the law on the books—a trichotomy discussed in the next section—legal scholars' careful descriptions and analyses of legal phenomena can also help to refine, and in some cases debunk, more general social scientific theories, empirical claims, and applications.

Much of this chapter is devoted to explicating how legal analysis can advance this understanding. I first discuss how law shapes the incentives that drive the decisions of potential migrants. I then turn to the more specific modalities, structures, and institutions through which law attempts to influence decisions and behavior. A third section discusses why contemporary immigration law's enforcement mission has faltered, while also suggesting how this ostensible failure actually serves certain latent social functions. Finally, I consider whether Americans perceive much illegal immigration as a victimless offense and discuss how this perception affects immigration enforcement and politics. In the spirit of this book's comparative and theoretical ambitions, I emphasize throughout the general structures and processes of law that influence migration; I discuss detailed doctrines and operational realities of immigration law only insofar as they help to illuminate the more theoretical claims.

HOW LAW AFFECTS MIGRATION FLOWS

Few migrants know much about law and even fewer would point to law as a major factor in their migration decisions. Nevertheless, law influences those decisions at every turn. Most fundamentally, law defines individuals' rights to property and economic activity, political participation, physical security, religious and cultural identity, and family relationships. The content and configuration of these extra-immigration rights help to structure the set of opportunities that people can exploit in their countries of origin. The greater those opportunities, the less individuals will want to migrate, ceteris paribus; the emotional links that hold people in their native land are as powerful as any we know; only deep social convulsions can shatter them. Even when such convulsions occur, the grip of old attachments and the fears of the unknown are powerful reasons to remain; this inertia can only be overcome by the promise of far greater opportunities in possible destination states, opportunities that the law helps to construct. Potential migrants who enjoy the luxury of calculation and choice compare these opportunity sets before deciding whether, when, where, how, and with which others they will migrate.

But law not only shapes individuals' incentives and decisions to migrate; it also constrains them. Some states impose significant restrictions on the right to depart or make it practically difficult for would-be migrants to exercise that right. All states seek to limit immigration and to enforce those limits through legal and extra-legal techniques. Because legal immigrants can naturalize in the United States relatively easily and U.S.-born children of both legal and illegal immigrants enjoy constitutionally protected birthright citizenship (Schuck 1998:185–86), the law defining the categories of legal immigrants, and the law enforcement processes that are used to exclude illegal ones, in effect determine who will constitute the future stock of Americans. In the United States, as in other states, the legal barriers to immigration—and in that sense, to citizenship—have become more restrictive as a matter of both formal law and informal practice (Hailbronner, Martin, and Motomura 1998). In principle, international law protects certain rights of migrants, particularly those of Convention refugees, but these rights are much honored in the breach (Fitzpatrick 1994). Treaties, a species of international law, often regulate important aspects of migration between the subscribing states such as employment, trade, taxation, criminal prosecution, extradition, access to consular assistance, and the like. The international law governing migration, however, is even more difficult to enforce than is domestic law.

Although legal commentators understandably emphasize states' restrictive immigration laws, it is also true that some states use the law to "compete" for immigrants—at least for those who possess valuable skills, investment resources, and attractive political attributes. Industrialized countries like Canada, Australia, and the United States, for example, often target the same groups of potential immigrants—those who possess desired skills in short supply or are willing to invest in job-creating enterprises in the destination country. In a similar spirit, American refugee law traditionally favored those from Communist-bloc countries. Notwithstanding efforts in the Refugee Act of 1980 to eliminate this bias, it still favors those fleeing certain countries for certain reasons (such as China's one-child policy or Russia's treatment of Jews and evangelical Christians).

None of this, of course, is meant to suggest that law is the principal force shaping migration flows—economic and family factors share that distinction—but only that it regulates many (and influences the remainder) of the social conditions that figure so prominently in individual and group migration decisions. Specifically, the kinds of legal systems associated with liberal property, integration, and human rights regimes exhibit powerful tendencies to attract immigration and discourage emigration.[3]

Before discussing how legal rules, institutions, processes, and decisions influence migration, I wish to note an elementary distinction in legal sociology developed by one of the first Legal Realists, Roscoe Pound, between the "law on the books" and the "law in action"—to which I have added a third category, the "law in their minds" (Schuck 1994:904). The importance of distinguishing among these three aspects of legal consciousness in the immigration field can be measured by the immense gaps that separate each of them from the others. This trichotomy reflects the fact that the law as formally enacted ("law on the books") almost always differs from the law as actually implemented ("law in action"). We shall see that this difference, while true to some extent of all legal and social systems, is particularly great in the immigration system. Consequently, many groups of actors in the immigration system see different aspects of the system or see the same aspects differently ("law in their minds").

These perspectival differences affect immigration law and policy in important ways. For example, immigrants view aspects of the immigration experience differently than people in their communities of origin do, despite the close, enduring linkages between the two groups (Levitt 1997). INS officials and the (at least nominally) independent immigration judges constantly differ about the bond levels for detainable aliens (Gilboy 1988) and also about the process and standards for immigrant detention and removal decisions (Schuck 1997). A fundamental mismatch of resources, incentives, and perspectives between the INS and state and local law enforcement agencies seriously compromises the apprehension, processing, and removal of criminal aliens (Schuck and Williams 1999). The State Department consular officials who make initial visa decisions often interpret immigration law differently than do INS and Department of Labor officials; indeed, consular officials differ even with their own bureaucratic superiors (Nafziger 1991). Voluntary agencies on which the INS heavily relies to help administer refugee, amnesty, and other programs view their roles differently than does the INS; legal immigrants and their undocumented co-ethnics often disagree about how the law should be applied (Schuck 1995). Federal trial judges encounter immigration law in a different context than appellate judges. And so forth.

The most important perspectival difference concerns illegal immigration; the law and the INS vigorously condemn it, whereas much of American society countenances it. This radical disjunction of views, I believe, helps to render intelligible much about immigration law and policy that might otherwise seem odd or inexplicable. I explore the implications of this disjunction in the final section of the chapter.

THE FORMS, PROCESSES, AND INSTITUTIONS OF IMMIGRATION LAW

In the complex immigration control system constituted by these different groups, law confers authority in many different forms and deploys that authority in diverse ways. The situations of actual and putative migrants vary enormously, and any rational and humane immigration policy will want to take many of these factors into account in determining immigrants' legal status. For this reason, immigration policymakers have chosen to make the law ambiguous and open-ended on many crucial points, leaving considerable room for interpretation and specialized judgment by the officials who administer the law in the first instance, and, in the event of appeal by appellate administrative tribunals and federal judges. The law thus grants broad discretion to both low-level and high-level decision makers. Even after the enactment of the Illegal Immigration Reform and Immigrant Responsibility Act of 1996 (IIRIRA), a landmark statute that sharply limited INS officials' authority to grant discretionary relief from removal,[4] the INS continues to enjoy enormous discretion. Indeed, even ranking members of Congress who sponsored IIRIRA's harshest provisions—Lamar Smith, for example—are now pressing the agency to exercise more discretion in the interests of a more humanitarian application of the law (Lipton 1999). In August 1999, the INS responded to these pressures by agreeing to release, under administrative criteria, some detainees (including some asylum claimants, as well as some others who cannot as a practical matter be removed) whom the agency previously had insisted could not be released under the rigid provisions of IIRIRA.

Thus, immigration inspectors and enforcement personnel, like police officers, drug enforcement agents, schoolteachers, social workers, and other "street-level bureaucrats" (Lipsky 1980), are the crucial decision makers. As a result, many conventional assumptions about bureaucratic authority, drawn from the Weberian ideal-type, simply do not apply to immigration policy. For example, much of what low-level INS officials do is invisible, both literally and figuratively, to their bureaucratic superiors, and even visible conduct is often uncontrollable through either the ordinary structure of hierarchical rules or the economy of incentives. In effect, power over day-to-day immigration decisions runs bottom-up instead of top-down.

The unusual operational autonomy enjoyed by low-level INS officials is further protected by certain legal principles peculiar to the immigration field. The most important of these is the so-called plenary power doctrine, which was announced by the U.S. Supreme Court announced more than a century ago (*Chinese Exclusion Case* 1889) and has reaffirmed many times since despite the absence of any clear textual basis in the Constitution and despite repeated criticism by legal scholars. The plenary power doctrine holds that Congress's power over immigration policy is comprehensive, complete, and all but immune to judicial review for unconstitutionality (Aleinikoff, Martin, and Motomura 1998:217–18). Invoking this doctrine or relying on other principles of self-restraint or limited jurisdiction, the federal courts have abjectly deferred to immigration officials' decisions (Schuck 1998:29–31). When one adds to this very broad area of autonomy the more general principle of federal sovereign immunity, which largely protects the INS against possible monetary liability for illegal conduct (Schuck 1983),[5] one can easily understand why the INS has become a particularly lawless agency characterized by chronic administrative failures (Schuck 1998:87; Schuck 1999:88; Schuck and Williams 1999). During the early to mid-1980s some federal judges issued injunctions in order to bring the INS into compliance with mainstream constitutional and administrative law principles (Schuck 1998:chap. 2). These judicial interventions, however, were spasmodic at best and of doubtful effectiveness, and appellate courts subsequently rejected some of them. Most important, IIRIRA imposed severe, unprecedented, and possibly unconstitutional limitations on the courts' power to review INS enforcement or discretionary decisions, as well as on judicial power to issue injunctions and entertain class actions against the INS.

The sources of INS operational autonomy over immigration enforcement are not merely legal; they are also political. Until the 1980s, when illegal migration first became a prominent policy issue in Washington, the INS was an obscure agency of little interest to anyone other than the chairmen and key members of the Judiciary subcommittees in Congress that exercised legislative and oversight jurisdiction over immigration matters. Except for the special post–World War II and cold-war refugee programs, no major immigration legislation was enacted between 1924 and 1952; the next major reform was enacted in 1965 and another, lesser change in 1978. Administrative initiatives by the INS were also rare and congressional oversight hearings were rarer still. This inactivity reflected an understanding between key Judiciary Committee members and the INS Commissioner that the agency would do little but serve as the members' malleable instruments of policy and patronage. Not surprisingly, media coverage of immigration issues during this period was limited (Schuck 1975).

All of this changed in the 1980s, of course, but even in the supercharged immigration politics of recent years, the INS has continued to enjoy freedom of action (or inaction), and bureaucratic growth—in budget, legal authority, and personnel—that most of its federal agency counterparts can only envy.[6] Even the agency's chronically illegal conduct and abject administrative failures, however, have not stemmed its dramatic growth during the last decade. Because immigrants are ineligible to vote, immigration politics is conducted through other organized interests—growers, other employers, unions, state and local governments, religious and ethnic groups, immigration lawyers— and the congressional allies of these interests. A remarkably diverse coalition of interest groups concerned with immigration policy exert substantial influence today, predominantly in a proimmigration direction.[7] Despite the autonomy conferred on the government by the plenary power doctrine, some lower federal courts continue to require the INS to extend additional protections to aliens.

THE "FAILURE" OF IMMIGRATION ENFORCEMENT

The INS's relative institutional autonomy has produced a retarded organizational learning process, an attenuated feedback loop that delays responses to change, which in turn contributes to the agency's chronic incompetence and lack of accountability. In a recent study, John Williams and I demonstrate this sluggishness in the context of the INS's much belated and still-inadequate program to remove criminal aliens despite the agency's great advantages: a continuing, clear, and emphatic congressional priority for the swift removal of criminal aliens, the issue's high political profile throughout the United States, and the increased legal and fiscal resources provided to the agency. Although Congress deserves most of the blame for this missed (or delayed) opportunity, the INS's many administrative failures also contributed to the inadequate outcome (Schuck and Williams 1999).

The system's inability to remove most criminal aliens, however, is no isolated occurrence; rather, it should be seen as a particularly egregious instance of a much more pervasive failure by Congress and the INS to design, support, and implement a legal and policy framework equal to the immense challenge of contemporary migration. Immigration control, like most other public policy goals, is a far more complex and intractable problem today than in the past. For a variety of technological, geopolitical, military, psychological, economic, and other reasons, the delicate balance of factors influencing potential migrants' behavior has shifted somewhat in favor of a decision to migrate. More people are moving across national borders, and all but a relative handful lack legal permission to reside in their destination states. Often expelled by their own rulers and assisted by others who hope to profit by smuggling them, migrants have grown bolder, more determined, and more resourceful. Short-term ebbs and flows aside, migratory pressures are bound to increase in response to population growth, better information, social chaos, and economic mismanagement in many source countries, as well as the greater work opportunities, more stable politics, and strong ethnic communities in the leading receiving states.

The control strategies deployed by receiving states, however, have not kept pace with these changes. In recent years, European states have devised new restrictive techniques, including readmission agreements, detention, buffer zones, return policies, agreements to speed (and defeat) the processing of asylum claims, and many others[8] (Hailbronner, Martin, and Motomura 1997, 1998). *Mutatis mutandis,* the United States has done likewise, adopting harsh detention, interdiction, and other control while also dramatically increasing the Border Patrol's physical and technological presence along the long border with Mexico. The flows of undocumented migrants to the United States, however, have not declined significantly, although the flow might have been even greater absent these measures. The number of undocumented aliens in Europe has risen sharply in recent years, and the number residing in the United States has reached to a level probably even higher than in 1986 when Congress, declaring an illegal migration crisis, enacted employer sanctions and other far-reaching enforcement measures.

Today, the obstacles to effective immigration control are even more formidable. Not only are undocumented migrants more numerous and resourceful; the receiving states' ability to respond to the new flows aggressively and effectively is more constrained. The growth of ethnic communities in the receiving states makes enforcement more difficult; these communities are better able to exert domestic political pressure against INS enforcement or in favor of securing legal status for their co-ethnics. Ethnic communities also facilitate illegal migrants' ability to melt into the community where they can live and work illegally without detection by the authorities. New legal constraints limit what receiving states may do in the name of immigration control, as constitutional courts and international tribunals and instruments affirm rights that even illegal migrants can legitimately assert against the destination states (Jacobson 1996).

Most of these new rights are merely procedural in nature; they prescribe the processes that governments must employ before they may remove aliens but seldom entitle aliens to remain. Similarly, refugee law limits a state's ability to return (*refoule*) asylees to another state in which they may face persecution, but this does not confer a substantive right to remain (although as a practical matter it may enable the asylee to do so). Occasionally, however, the law may go farther and grant aliens a new substantive right. One important example is the U.S. Supreme Court's decision holding that Texas could not deny basic public education to undocumented alien children even though this denial was part of an explicit state strategy to discourage illegal migration (*Plyler* v. *Doe* 1982).[9] Other examples are recent laws granting certain undocumented aliens from some Central American countries the right to seek discretionary relief from removal, which Congress eliminated in 1996.

But even "merely" procedural rights can drastically alter migrants' incentive structure. Because it is costly for the INS to undertake effective enforcement proceedings against illegal aliens and even more costly to detain them until their removal can be effectuated, the agency allows many who could be apprehended and removed to remain at large or (which is much the same thing) it apprehends but then releases them pending completion of removal proceedings, whereupon most abscond and disappear into the population. Because their primary objective is to work in the United States, procedural delays and release pending removal enable them to gain most of what they migrated for in the first place (Schuck 1998: chap. 2).

Finally, a growing public acceptance of human rights principles makes it harder for liberal democratic states to remove (or even detain) aliens whose circumstances arouse widespread media attention, public sympathy, or even solidarity expressed through civil disobedience and sanctuary movements. Compared to these compelling political and humanitarian claims, the legalistic arguments advanced by INS officials often seem petty, hollow, even immoral. Confronted by a courageous, hard-working migrant's well-publicized human drama, liberal societies are strongly tempted to make room for one more. Defense of the larger, inevitably anonymous "system" against such heartrending claims falls largely to the beleaguered, often justly criticized immigration bureaucracy. Even today, of course, most migrants do not arouse this kind of public support, but are unceremoniously detained and removed. Still, the relatively few who do manage to beat the system and elicit criticism of the INS for its heartlessness disproportionately weaken the agency's enforcement incentives in future cases.

These new constraints, of course, hardly leave the receiving states defenseless in the face of the rising migratory pressures. Strong domestic economic and political imperatives impel even liberal, democratic polities committed to free trade policies to tightly control migration, protect national labor markets and resist the more speculative, often more diffuse claims of globalism (Hollifield 1998). Stepped-up border enforcement and crackdowns on undocumented workers in the interior are popular policies in all receiving countries, but state implementation of migration controls has nonetheless become far more costly and problematic. Indeed, it is difficult to imagine a politically viable policy approach to the control of illegal migration that the United States has not already tried or seriously considered.

Confronted by these dynamic external conditions, internal social pressures, and political constraints, immigration enforcers must have nimble and flexible regulatory instruments at their disposal in order to pursue optimal control strategies. Yet, flexibility is precisely what the law denies them. In the United States, constitutionally required separation of powers, fierce competition for influence in the immigration policy domain, mutual suspicion among the various participants, a legal-political culture emphasizing individual rights, and mistrust of public authority all combine to favor rigid criteria and procedures designed to limit official discretion. This rigidity is especially perverse in the important area of immigrant labor certification, where slow bureaucratic processes force employers and workers competing in increasingly dynamic labor markets to devise informal, often illegal, stratagems in order to circumvent legal obstacles and get the job done.

Earlier I observed that immigration law gives INS officials much discretion—and so they do, but it is a matter of degree. Canada and some other parliamentary systems, for example, accord immigration officials even broader discretion, allowing them to apply multifactor point systems for some admission categories and then to adjust admissions criteria as political and economic conditions change. This greater flexibility is possible, of course, because the controlling legislative coalition and the political executives are members of the same ruling group, which under a parliamentary system tends to minimize the conflict and suspicion among them and thus facilitates more trust and greater willingness to delegate discretionary authority to administrators.

But to speak of the failure of immigration enforcement in the United States as I have is a bit too facile and glib. Official behavior that appears on its face to be ineffective may actually serve a deeper, more latent social function (to use Robert Merton's phrase). It may help us to maintain certain cherished myths in the face of contradictory facts we are reluctant to recognize. To put it another way, we may prefer to think that we have certain goals and have failed to achieve them than to acknowledge the possibility that these are not really our goals or, worse still, that the goals were not worth striving for in the first place.

Like the wars on drugs and crime, the battle against illegal immigration and the political rhetoric that it inspires lend themselves to this kind of collective self-delusion. Illegal immigration, after all, confers significant benefits on almost all concerned,[10] while the costs of eliminating it (in terms of enforcement resources, opportunity costs, civil liberties, foreign-policy interests, and so on) would be manifestly prohibitive. This means that the socially optimal level of illegal migration—the policy that balances its social benefits and costs—is far greater than zero. Indeed, in a nation of 270 million people, the optimal level of illegal immigration may even exceed today's actual level, conservatively estimated at about 6 million illegal residents, with 250,000 more added each year.[11]

But for the government even to acknowledge that it countenances this amount of illegal immigration, much less that this might be a desirable policy, is politically unthinkable.[12] If so, the "failure" of immigration enforcement serves an important latent function by sustaining the attractive, reassuring, ennobling myth that the rule of law is a paramount, priceless ideal that we relentlessly pursue. At the same time, it obscures the reality that our actual goal is the less exalted one of enriching ourselves by condoning illegality and then concealing this fact beneath a veil of hypocritical high-mindedness.

ILLEGAL IMMIGRATION AS A VICTIMLESS CRIME

I have discussed the limitations on immigration law's effectiveness imposed by legal rules, institutions, processes, and interest group politics. Perhaps the most profound limitation, however, arises out of the tensions created by Americans' complex attitudes toward immigration, their growing attraction to the ideology and imagery of human rights, and the impersonal immigration law on the books.

Americans harbor ambivalent or conflicting attitudes toward immigration and immigrants, attitudes in which they tend to draw subtle but important distinctions. According to survey data, for example, Americans like immigrants more than they like immigration, favor past immigration more than recent immigration, prefer legal immigrants to illegal ones, prefer refugees to other immigrants, support immigrants' access to educational and health benefits but not to welfare or Social Security, and believe that immigrants' distinctive cultures have contributed positively to American life and that diversity continues to strengthen American society. At the same time, they overwhelmingly resist any conception of multiculturalism that discourages immigrants from quickly learning and using the English language. Americans treasure their immigrant roots, yet they are convinced that current immigration levels are too high (Schuck 1998:9).

The law exhibits no such ambivalence.[13] It treats illegal migration as a crime justifying the state in imposing tough, far-reaching sanctions, which may include fines, imprisonment, and permanent exile for such aliens and fines or imprisonment for their employers. Many citizens, however, are reluctant to view ordinary illegal border crossing[14] (as distinguished, say, from smuggling illegal migrants, drug trafficking, or other serious criminal activity) as a reprehensible crime warranting harsh penalties. Indeed, the same illegal immigration that the law categorically condemns may reasonably be regarded by citizens as a socially efficient offense (i.e., one whose aggregate social benefits exceed its social costs) or even a Pareto-superior offense (i.e., one that makes at least some people better off and no one worse off). For the sake of simplicity (though somewhat inaccurately), I shall call both socially efficient and Pareto-superior offenses "victimless" ones.[15]

In an intriguing but unpublished analysis, legal sociologist Robert Kagan identifies some characteristic features of victimless offenses and finds that illegal immigration fits the description well.[16] By definition, a victimless offense is one that violates the law but does not directly harm anyone. Because there are no complainants to demand that the agency punish particular offenders and to provide evidence of the offenses to prosecutors, the offenses are hard to detect. Indeed, employers and landlords who know about the illegal conduct are often the ones who benefit most from it.

In order to detect violations in such cases, proactive methods must be devised. Yet, these tend to be costly for the government and intrude on innocent third parties. Kagan cites examples of such methods in immigration enforcement: patrolling borders, establishing mandatory checkpoints, searching cars, interrogating travelers, and trying to distinguish illegal travelers from legal ones. One might add to this list the practice of workplace raids, which are particularly crude and disruptive, affecting American citizens and legal resident aliens along with the agency's undocumented prey. These effects in turn trigger political criticism of the agency. Since these methods impose high social costs and there are no complainants, the agency is less inclined to take aggressive enforcement action against violators, and is subject to less day-to-day pressure from outsiders to do so. The agency grows less zealous, diverts scarce enforcement resources elsewhere, looks for exceptions that can justify nonenforcement, and generally assumes a passive role, which Kagan calls "retreatism." Because violations are not routinely publicized, the agency can more easily trade leniency for something it values, which invites low-level corruption and nurtures deviant subcultures.

Conduct that creates no victims but that the law on the books makes illegal is morally ambiguous. After all, if the conduct is voluntary, we can presume that it benefits those who engage in it. If no one else is harmed, then the conduct seems unobjectionable. In such a situation, the rationale for any punishment is so elusive that strict enforcement of the law seems pointless, oppressive, even inhumane.[17] Most illegal immigrants are otherwise law-abiding, future-oriented individuals who work hard, attend church, raise strong families, surmount daunting obstacles, love their new country, and exemplify many of our cherished social ideals. Their struggles to participate in the American dream resemble the now-mythic struggles of our own ancestors.

Americans unmoved by purely legalistic arguments may well wonder what justifies the INS in doggedly pursuing such people. The short answer, good and sufficient for legalistic citizens and agencies, is that the immigration statute demands it. The law demands enforcement not because of a particular alien's conduct, which apart from the illegal entry may well be unimpeachable and have only a *de minimis* effect on others, but because of the supposed aggregate, cumulative burdens that tens of thousands of violators wreak on American workers (by taking their jobs, reducing their wages, eroding their labor standards, and weakening their unions), on local communities (by consuming scarce public services), and the national polity (by threatening our sense of sovereignty and control).

But citizens sympathizing and perhaps even identifying with enterprising immigrants whose only offense was to cross the border illegally are unlikely to view the aggregate of such acts with horror or moral indignation. They may be further mollified by empirical studies purporting to show neutral or even positive effects of illegal migration on low-income Americans.[18] Even assuming negative effects, Kagan notes, they would be cumulative and aggregated, not immediate and individual. To punish an individual violator in these circumstances, especially when such violations are ubiquitous, only aggravates the moral dilemma that haunts immigration enforcement. For all of these reasons, then, the agency has strong political, fiscal, and (as we have just seen) moral incentives to avoid investing heavily in the prevention or prosecution of victimless offenses. Scarce resources can almost certainly be deployed elsewhere to greater effect.

Other aspects of the "law in action" make it even more rational for INS officials to view their enforcement efforts as largely futile, which surely demoralizes them (Harwood 1986:118). These aspects include the often long delays in completing removal proceedings; the INS's limited detention capacity and the notorious propensity of non-detained, removable aliens to abscond and go underground before their removal can be adjudicated, much less effectuated; the INS's strong preference for voluntary departure and other swift, low-cost, informal but also low-deterrence sanctions over formal removal proceedings; the "revolving door" resulting from the ease and celerity with which those aliens who are removed or do depart can reenter the country; and the alien's ability to delay the proceedings long enough to build up equities, obtain relief from removal, and adjust status. I have already noted the INS's inability to remove most criminal aliens. The INS has also found it difficult or impossible to remove the hundreds of thousands of aliens, most of them undocumented, to whom the agency has granted "temporary" humanitarian refuge on the express, statutorily imposed condition that they return to their countries of origin once the political, environmental, or economic emergency that brought them to (or kept them in) the United States abates. Indeed, most of them end up staying in the United States indefinitely. The immigration law in action—a combination of domestic politics, ethnic solidarity, foreign policy considerations, and an INS administrative overload that makes the prospect of mass removals impractical and unacceptable—in effect transforms temporary protection into permanent residence (Krikorian 1999). If few illegal aliens are subjected to formal removal proceedings and even fewer are criminally prosecuted (much less convicted), immigration officials' judgments about which few among the many violators will be prosecuted are bound to be arbitrary—and to be regarded as such by the public and the courts.

It is impossible to know how many Americans in fact view ordinary illegal migration as an essentially victimless offense—one to be regretted perhaps or even prosecuted in unusually egregious cases, but not one to be generally reprehended, much less stigmatized. The victimless offense view is quite widespread, judging from the significant number of people who employ workers of whose illegal status they are, or should be, aware; the periodic amnesties that Congress has granted to large numbers of undocumented aliens; the refusal of many city governments to cooperate with INS actions against illegal aliens even in defiance of IIRIRA's cooperation mandate; and the manifest unwillingness of schoolteachers, hospital workers, taxi passengers, social service providers, civil servants, and other Americans not covered by employer sanctions to report suspected illegal aliens to the immigration authorities.

If this is true, it is bound to undermine the vigor and effectiveness of immigration enforcement and to call into serious question the legitimacy of immigration law—its social acceptance as an authoritative set of social norms supporting widely felt moral duties to obey the law and to punish violators.[19] The INS, Kagan predicts, will respond to this dilemma by adhering to a rigid legalism manifested in strict, ritualistic patterns of enforcement, punctuated by spasms of retreatism. This is a fair description of INS behavior over the years.

CONCLUSION

Even today, autonomous theory—that is, hypotheses not largely drawn from theories in other disciplines—does not play a significant role in the law's approach to migration issues. Nevertheless, many of law's characteristic patterns are highly relevant, indeed essential, to any sophisticated understanding of the forces that drive, divert, and blunt migration, and that shape migrants' experiences in destination countries. Legal rules—the law in action, on the books, and in the mind—help to construct the complex array of incentives that individuals and groups take into account in deciding whether, when, how, and where to migrate. Law determines the formal status that migrants may enjoy and the entitlements they may claim, but it also contributes to the normative and cultural settings in which migrants must decide how to behave and find meaning as they seek success in their new homeland. Law must design, discipline, and legitimate the political institutions and legal procedures that regulate the immigration process and the formal statuses through which migrants pass. Law must also join with other social mechanisms to negotiate the terms of their eventual integration into their new society. In all of this, law's inspiring possibilities are yoked to its inherent limitations (Schuck 2000). Both its possibilities and its limitations help to shape the experiences of migrants and their countries of origin and destination.

NOTES

1. The phrase, I believe, was originated by my former colleague Arthur Leff in a meditation on this phenomenon in a characteristically witty, insightful article of the same name (Leff 1978).
2. For a useful discussion of law's methodological relationships to other disciplines, see Rubin 1997.
3. Indeed, some commentators have argued that the economic inequality often found in countries with relatively capitalistic systems tends to attract the more entrepreneurial and highly skilled citizens of more egalitarian countries, while more egalitarian countries tend to attract the less entrepreneurial and skilled citizens of more inegalitarian countries (Borjas 1990).
4. Elsewhere I have characterized this statute as "the most radical reform of immigration law in decades—or perhaps ever. It thoroughly revamps the enforcement process and extends [restrictions adopted earlier in 1996] in ways that even many INS officials find arbitrary, unfair, and unadministrable. For example, it requires the INS to exclude aliens at the border summarily and without judicial review if they seem to lack proper documentation. The IIRIRA makes asylum claiming more difficult and bars the INS from granting discretionary relief from deportation to many aliens even for compelling humanitarian reasons as the previous law permitted. It mandates the detention of many removable aliens—perhaps forever if they come from a country like Vietnam that refuses to take them back. It equates the rights of aliens who entered illegally and live in the United States with those of aliens with no ties in the United States. It limits the rights of illegal aliens to reenter legally. It further expands the category of 'aggravated felon' aliens, who can be deported summarily even if they have been long-term residents of the country. It bars judicial review of INS decisions to deport them. (The definition of 'aggravated felony' is now so broad that it includes almost all drug, weapons, and other nonpetty offenses; it even covers subway fare beating.)" (Schuck 1998:143–44).
5. In a very unusual decision, a federal judge recently permitted asylum seekers detained by the INS to seek money damages against individual INS officials

and contractors based on alleged international human rights violations (*Jama v. U.S.I.N.S.* 1998).

6. This is particularly true of the most politically favored, elite unit within the INS, the Border Patrol. Its resources have increased more rapidly during the last decade than those of almost any other agency in the federal government; they account for most of the growth in the INS as a whole during this period of budgetary stringency elsewhere in the government.

7. Consider that for a decade, the United States has been admitting nearly one million legal immigrants each year, a level that approaches, if not exceeds, historic highs in terms of absolute totals (not, however, as a percentage of the population), and has also tolerated high illegal migration levels. The United States has even accorded legal status to millions of long-resident undocumented aliens, most of whom are low-skilled workers from Latin America, not high-skill workers or the white Europeans who comprised the traditional U.S. migration stream. Even the Republican Party has a powerful proimmigration wing that has succeeded in stifling restrictionist initiatives in Congress. Evidently, the fact that migrants to the United States cannot vote and often have insecure immigration statuses (at least in the short-run) does not deprive immigrant interests of all political influence (Schuck 1998:91–148).

8. Some of these techniques may violate international human rights law (Fitzpatrick 1994).

9. International human rights law also recognizes limited rights even for undocumented aliens, most notably the right of nonrefoulement if the alien would suffer persecution in his home country based on his race, religion, nationality, membership in a particular social group, or political opinion (Convention Relating to the Status of Refugees 1951: Article 33).

10. The "almost" qualification is added in recognition of the possibility, which certianly cannot be ruled out, that some individuals and groups are net economic or fiscal losers from illegal migration. The economic literature has not yet clearly established adverse effects on the most plausible group of victims, inner-city black Americans (Hamermesh and Bean 1998). Another plausible group of victims consists of local communities with high concentrations of illegal aliens requiring public services (Espenshade 1995).

11. The figure is derived from the INS's most recent official estimate of 5.1 million in October 1996, plus an estimated 250,000 more for each of the three years since then.

12. As a result, certain policy options cannot be fully or candidly explored, such as accepting a certain level of illegal migration but compensating those who suffer economic disadvantage as a result, much as Congress has done for some victims of free trade policies.

13. This was not always the case. Until 1986, the law contained the so-called Texas proviso that made it a crime for aliens to enter the United States illegally but precluded criminal liability for the employers who hired them. Congress repealed the Texas proviso in the Immigration Reform and Control Act of 1986.

14. Americans may be somewhat less sympathetic to those illegal aliens—roughly half the total—who originally entered the United States with a legal visa but have violated its terms, but this is purely a matter of conjecture. Needless to say, Americans bear little or no sympathy for those who commit ordinary crimes in the United States (Schuck and Williams 1999:372).

15. Inaccurate because in the case of a socially efficient offense, some may be made worse off (and hence might be considered "victims") even though the offense makes society better off as a whole, as when illegal migration takes away the

jobs of a few American workers but creates many more jobs in the aggregate. See supra note 10 and infra note 18.

16. The observations that follow are drawn from Kagan's unpublished notes for a talk at a panel on regulatory enforcement of immigration law at the Law and Society Association's annual meeting in Philadelphia, May 24, 1988.

17. For example, many libertarians, many economists, and the editors of the *Wall Street Journal* take this view.

18. Hamermesh and Bean 1998. In contrast, some economists, notably George Borjas, claim to have found significant adverse effects on blacks and other low-income Americans (Borjas 1990; Hamermesh and Bean 1998:chap. 2). The taxpayer-as-victim argument for immigration enforcement was weakened in 1996 when the federal welfare reform law made illegal aliens ineligible for almost all federally funded benefits and for some state and local ones (Schuck 1998:199–200).

19. On the question of law's legitimacy, see Schuck 2000:chap. 13.

REFERENCES

Aleinikoff, T., David A. Martin, and Hiroshi Motomura. 1998. *Immigration and Citizenship: Process and Policy.* 4th ed. St. Paul, Minn.: West Publishing.

Borjas, George J. 1990. *Friends or Strangers: The Impact of Immigrants on the U.S. Economy.* New York: Basic Books.

Chinese Exclusion Case (Chae Chan Ping v. United States), 130 U.S. 581 (1889).

Convention Relating to the Status of Refugees, 189 U.N.T.S. 137 (July 28, 1951).

Espenshade, Thomas J. 1995. "Unauthorized Immigration to the United States," *Annual Review of Sociology* 21: 195–216.

Fitzpatrick, Joan. 1994. "Flight from Asylum: Trends Toward Temporary 'Refuge' and Local Responses to Forced Migrations," *Virginia Journal of International Law* 35: 13–70.

Gilboy, Janet A. 1988. "Administrative Review in a System of Conflicting Values," *Law & Social Inquiry* 13: 515–79.

Hailbronner, Kai, David A. Martin, and Hiroshi Motomura, eds. 1997. *Immigration Admissions: The Search for Workable Policies in Germany and the United States.* Providence, R.I.: Berghahn Books.

———. 1998. *Immigration Controls: The Search for Workable Policies in Germany and the United States.* Providence, R.I.: Berghahn Books.

Hamermesh, Daniel S., and Frank D. Bean, eds. 1998. *Help or Hindrance? The Economic Implications of Immigration for African Americans.* New York: Russell Sage.

Harwood, Edwin. 1986. *In Liberty's Shadow: Illegal Aliens and Immigration Law Enforcement.* Stanford, Calif.: Hoover Institution Press.

Heise, Michael. 1999. "The Importance of Being Empirical," *Pepperdine Law Review* 26: 807–34.

Hollifield, James F. 1998. "Migration, Trade, and the Nation-state: The Myth of Globalization," *UCLA Journal of International Law and Foreign Affairs* 3: 595–636.

Jacobson, David. 1996. *Rights across Borders: Immigration and the Decline of Citizenship.* Baltimore, Md.: Johns Hopkins University Press.

Jama v. U.S.I.N.S., 22 F. Supp.2d 353 (D.N.J. 1998).

Krikorian, Mark. 1999. "Here to Stay: There's Nothing as Permanent as a Temporary Refugee." Center for Immigration Studies, Washington, D.C., August.

Leff, Arthur A. 1978. "Law And," *Yale Law Journal* 87: 989–1011.

Levitt, Peggy. 1997. "Transnationalizing Community Development: The Case of

Migration Between Boston and the Dominican Republic," *Nonprofit and Voluntary Sector Quarterly* 26: 509–26.

Lipsky, Michael. 1980. *Street-Level Bureaucracy: The Dilemmas of the Individual in Public Services.* Cambridge, Mass.: MIT Press.

Lipton, Eric. 1999. "As More Are Deported: A '96 Law Faces Scrutiny," *New York Times*, Dec. 21, p. 1.

Nafziger, James A. R. 1991. "Review of Visa Denials by Consular Officers," *Washington Law Review* 66: 1–105.

Plyler v. *Doe*, 457 U.S. 202 (1982).

Posner, Richard A. 1988. *Law and Literature: A Misunderstood Relationship.* Cambridge, Mass.: Harvard University Press.

———. 1999. *The Problematics of Moral and Legal Theory.* Cambridge, Mass.: Harvard University Press.

Rubin, Edward L. 1997. "Law and the Methodology of Law," *Wisconsin Law Review* 1997: 521–65.

Schuck, Peter H. 1975. *The Judiciary Committees: A Study of the House and Senate Judiciary Committees.* New York: Viking Press.

———. 1983. *Suing Government: Citizen Remedies for Official Wrongs.* New Haven, Conn.: Yale University Press.

———. "Why Don't Law Professors Do More Empirical Research?" *Journal of Legal Studies* 39: 323–36.

———. 1994. "Rethinking Informed Consent," *Yale Law Journal* 103: 899–959.

———. 1995. "The Message of Proposition 187," *The American Prospect* 21: 87–92.

———. 1997. "INS Detention and Removal: A White Paper," *Georgetown Immigration Law Journal* 11: 667–708.

———. 1998. *Citizens, Strangers, and In-Betweens: Essays on Immigration and Citzienship.* Boulder, Colo.: Westview Press.

———. 1999. "Current Debates About U.S. Citizenship," in *In Defense of the Alien*, L. Tomasi, ed. 21: 80–98.

———. 2000. *The Limits of Law: Essays on Democratic Governance.* Boulder, Colo.: Westview Press.

Schuck, Peter H., and Williams, John. 1999. "Removing Criminal Aliens: The Pitfalls and Promises of Federalism," *Harvard Journal of Law & Public Policy* 22: 367–463.

Stevens, Robert Bocking. 1983. *Legal Education in America from the 1850s to the 1980s.* Chapel Hill: University of North Carolina Press.

CHAPTER 8

The Economic Analysis of Immigration Law

Howard F. Chang

Legal scholars have increasingly turned to economic analysis to shed light on the effects of laws upon the welfare of those regulated. Numerous textbooks now provide a general introduction to the economic approach to law (Barnes and Stout 1992; Cooter and Ulen 1988; Katz 1998; Polinsky 1989; Posner 1992). Yet, economics has had less influence in the field of immigration law than one might expect. Few legal scholars (other than Chang 1997, 1998–99, 1999; Sykes 1995) have applied economic theory to the analysis of immigration laws. None of the leading immigration law textbooks (Aleinikoff, Martin, and Motomura 1998; Boswell 1992; Legomsky 1997; Piatt 1994) include a basic introduction to the economics of migration, although such an introduction is a standard feature of textbooks in labor economics (Ehrenberg and Smith 1994:346–57) and in international economics (Krugman and Obstfeld 1991:156–61).

The limited role of economics in the study of immigration law is especially striking given the prominent role of economics in immigration policy debates. Concerns about national economic welfare have played a dominant role, for example, in recent public debates over U.S. immigration laws. In 1995, the U.S. Commission on Immigration Reform (CIR 1995:1–3), urged Congress to move radically toward more restrictive immigration laws and introduced its report to Congress with a discussion of the costs and benefits of immigration. The Commission (1995:xii) recommended sweeping changes in long-standing U.S. immigration laws, including a reduction in the overall level of legal immigration into the United States by one-third.[1] The proposed changes included permanent cuts in both employment-based and family-based immigration.[2] Senator Alan Simpson and Representative Lamar Smith soon introduced bills to implement the Commission's recommendations.[3] These radical cuts in legal immigration proved controversial, however, and after heated debate, both the House of Representatives and the Senate ultimately voted to exclude these cuts from their immigration reform bills.[4] Nevertheless, the Commission (CIR 1997:xvii, 59) reiterated its restrictionist recommendations in its 1997 report to Congress, and observers expect restrictionists in Congress to revive their efforts to implement these proposals in the future.[5]

The Commission (1997:59) asserted that its proposals would serve "the national interest," citing a recent report that it had commissioned from the National Research Council (Smith and Edmonston 1997), which presents the most thorough analysis of the economic effects of immigration conducted so far. Yet, Commissioner Warren Leiden dissented from the Commission's proposal to reduce legal immigration, charging that the Commission "can provide no convincing argument for this drastic reduction" because "there is no objective basis for a drastic reduction" (CIR 1995:229). Some basic literacy in the economics of migration is essential if one is to understand and evaluate the economic arguments advanced by restrictionists and by their critics. In fact, I will argue in this chapter that economic analysis of U.S. immigration law strongly suggests that specific liberalizing reforms, which are likely to increase levels of employment-based and family-based immigration by eliminating certain immigration barriers, would raise national economic welfare as well as global economic welfare (Chang 1997, 1998–99, 1999).

I will focus on the implications of immigration for national economic welfare defined narrowly, in terms of the wealth of U.S. natives alone. I take the promotion of the welfare of natives to be our objective, not because I believe that immigration policy should be guided solely by considerations of economic self-interest, but because such concerns have in fact played a dominant role in the public debate over immigration policy and because this objective is commonly thought to provide a strong case in favor of restrictive immigration laws. Economic analysis reveals, however, that even from this narrow perspective, which "stacks the deck" against the immigrant, the United States should allow higher levels of employment-based and family-based immigration than current immigration laws permit. Even if we give zero weight to the welfare of aliens in our policy objectives, our immigration laws should be more liberal than our current laws in most important respects. In particular, although the economic welfare of natives and distributive justice among natives are often advanced as reasons to reduce immigration, I will argue that neither objective provides a sound justification for more restrictive laws regarding employment-based and family-based immigration.

I will begin my analysis with the effects of immigration upon natives through labor markets, setting aside economic effects that operate outside the market. First, I examine how immigrant labor promotes the economic welfare of natives, setting aside questions of income distribution. Second, I will extend the analysis to include issues of distributive justice. Third, I will consider the effects of immigration upon natives through the public treasury. Finally, I examine the implications of my analysis for the reform of U.S. immigration laws. I propose liberalizing reforms for family-based immigration policies, employment-based immigration policies, and guest-worker policies.

GAINS FROM INTERNATIONAL TRADE IN THE LABOR MARKET

We would expect labor to migrate from low-wage countries to high-wage countries in pursuit of higher wages. As a result of this migration, world output rises. Higher wages in the host country imply that the marginal product of labor is higher there than in the source country. That is, higher wages for the same worker mean that the worker produces more value in the host country than in the source country. Labor migration generally leads to net gains in wealth for the world as a whole, because labor flows to the country where it has the higher-value use (Krugman and Obstfeld 1991:158–59). An efficient global labor market would allow labor to move freely to the country where it earns the highest return. Market forces would thus direct labor to the market where its marginal product is highest. For this reason, economic theory raises a presumption in favor of the free movement of labor.

Immigration barriers interfere with the free flow of labor internationally and thereby cause wage rates for the same class of labor to diverge widely among different countries. For any given class of labor, residents of high-wage countries could gain by employing more immigrant labor, and residents of low-wage countries could gain by selling more of their labor to employers in high-wage countries. Immigration restrictions distort the global labor market, producing a misallocation of labor among countries, thereby wasting human resources and creating unnecessary poverty in labor-abundant countries.

The larger the inequality in wages between countries, the larger the distortion of global labor markets caused by migration restrictions, and the larger the economic gains from liberalizing labor migration. Given the large international differences in wages, it should be apparent that the potential gains from liberalized labor migration (and the costs that the world bears as a result of immigration barriers) are huge. In fact, some economists have attempted to estimate the gains that the world could enjoy by liberalizing migration. These studies suggest that the gains to the world economy from removing immigration barriers could well be enormous and greatly exceed the gains from removing trade barriers. For example, Hamilton and Whalley (1984) provide a range of estimates based on various assumptions about critical parameters, but all their estimates suggest that the potential gains are large. Many of their estimates suggest that the gains from free migration of labor would *more than double* worldwide real income, indicating that immigration controls "are one of the (and perhaps the) most important policy issues facing the global economy" (Hamilton and Whalley 1984:70). Even their most conservative estimate suggests that the gains would be a significant fraction (more than 13 percent) of worldwide real income (71–72). Furthermore, their analysis indicates that the free migration of labor would also greatly improve the global distribution of income by raising real wages dramatically for the world's poorest workers (73–74).

Would this labor migration, however, be in the economic interest of natives of the country of immigration? If we examine the impact of immigrants in the labor market, we find that the natives of the host country, taken together, will gain from the immigration of labor. Wages may fall for native workers who compete with immigrant labor, but this loss for workers is a pure transfer among natives: it is offset by an equal gain for those who employ labor, and ultimately for consumers, who obtain goods and services at lower cost. Furthermore, natives gain from employing immigrant workers: they gain surplus in excess of what they pay immigrants for their labor. If they did not gain any surplus from employing immigrants, they would not hire them. Thus, natives as a group enjoy a net gain (Smith and Edmonston 1997:138).

By the same token, immigration restrictions impose costs on natives by driving up the cost of labor, which in turn drives up the cost of goods and services to consumers. Native workers may gain from higher wages, but this gain comes only at the expense of employers in the host country and ultimately consumers. Thus, immigration restrictions not only redistribute wealth among natives but also destroy wealth by causing economic distortions. Restrictions prevent employers from hiring foreign workers even if the value that they would produce exceeds the wage that would be paid to them. Immigration restrictions entail a sacrifice of this "immigration surplus" (Borjas 1995:5).

Borjas (1995) has attempted a rough calculation of the size of the immigration surplus enjoyed by natives in the United States, using a variety of assumptions. Assuming a homogeneous supply of labor, for example, Borjas (1995:7) estimates that immigration into the United States has produced a surplus of $7 billion per year, which he characterizes as "relatively small" compared to the total size of the U.S. economy. The National Research Council surveys similar estimates, "on the order of $1 to $10 billion a year," which "may be modest relative to the size of the U.S. economy, but ... remains a significant positive gain in absolute terms" (Smith and Edmonston 1997:153). As the NRC notes, this gain is still large compared to the economic effects of most other public policies: "Not many changes in policies would produce benefits as large as that number" (Smith and Edmonston 1997:153). Furthermore, if we believe that these gains are too small, then we can increase immigration and thereby enjoy greater gains. We would expect a more liberal policy to produce a much larger immigration surplus for natives.

Furthermore, immigrants into the United States also gain from their migration: they obtain higher wages than they would receive in their source countries and thereby enjoy far larger gains than U.S. natives do from their immigration. In this sense, labor migration represents a form of international trade in which the source country exports labor to the host country. Like international trade in goods, labor migration allows foreign suppliers to sell their services to domestic buyers, allowing both parties to enjoy gains from trade as a result of the transaction.

EFFECTS ON NATIVE WORKERS: EMPIRICAL EVIDENCE

While I have addressed how the effects of immigration in the labor market increase the wealth of natives, I have not addressed the distribution of that wealth among natives. Immigration not only expands wealth but also can have important distributive effects. Those natives who must compete with immigrants in the labor market may find that immigration reduces their real income. Thus, countries often restrict immigration to protect native workers from the unemployment or the wage reductions that the entry of foreign workers would supposedly entail. Borjas (1999), for example, urges more restrictive immigration laws to protect native workers from immigrant competition in the labor market.

Studies of the effects of immigration in U.S. labor markets, however, have shown little evidence of effects on native wages or employment. Borjas (1994:1698), Friedberg and Hunt (1995:42), and the National Research Council (Smith and Edmonston 1997:223), for example, have conducted thorough surveys of this empirical literature and concluded that the evidence indicates that immigration has a weak effect on the employment of natives. They have also found that this evidence indicates a weak relationship between native wages and immigration across all types of native workers, white or black, skilled or unskilled, male or female (Borjas 1994:1697; Friedberg and Hunt 1995:42; Smith and Edmonston 1997:223).

Borjas (1994:1699) criticizes these studies, however, because they compare local labor markets to see if natives in those areas receiving immigrants fare worse than natives in other areas. These comparisons may be misleading if, for example, natives respond to immigration by moving to other areas where there is less competition from immigrants in the labor market. If natives migrate in response to reduced economic opportunities, then the adverse impact of immigration on natives will not be concentrated in just the local labor market, but will instead spread throughout the national labor market. This process could explain why comparisons of local labor markets fail to find much of an effect on native wages or employment opportunities.

Some results, however, are hard to explain using such a theory. Card's (1990) influential study of the effect of the Mariel Cubans on the Miami labor market, for example, is probably the most widely cited analysis of the effects of immigration on native workers. His results are fairly typical. Card (1990: 245) found that the arrival of 125,000 Cubans in 1980, which unexpectedly increased the supply of labor in Miami by 7 percent almost overnight, had "virtually no effect" on the wages and employment opportunities for workers in

Miami, including unskilled whites and blacks, even in the year in which the Cubans arrived. For the migration of natives to account for this striking result, as Borjas (1994:1700) concedes, natives would have had to respond to this immigration by moving virtually instantaneously. This type of rapid adjustment in the labor market is inconsistent with empirical evidence (Blanchard and Katz 1992) that an adverse shock can reduce wages in a state for up to a decade before the interstate migration of workers reequilibrates wages across regions. Thus, Card's study confirms that the evidence of only a weak effect of immigration on native wages and employment is not simply an artifact of the internal migration of natives. Given the small effects of immigration on native wages and employment, restrictionist policies seem particularly misguided.

Why do immigrants have so little adverse impact on the wages and employment of natives? One reason is that the demand for labor does not remain fixed when immigrants enter the economy. Immigrant workers not only supply labor, for example, they also demand goods and services, and this demand will translate into greater demand for locally supplied labor. This increase in demand can offset the effect of increased supply.

Furthermore, the empirical evidence indicates that immigrants and natives are not perfect substitutes in the labor market (Grossman 1982). Thus, immigrants often do not compete for the same jobs as natives. Indeed, immigrant labor can be a complement rather than a substitute for native labor, so that an increase in the supply of immigrant labor will increase the demand for native labor and thus have positive effects on native workers rather than negative effects. In fact, the National Research Council (Smith and Edmonston 1997) finds that labor markets are highly segregated, with immigrant labor concentrated in some occupations while natives are concentrated in others. The NRC reports that immigrants are concentrated in occupations "at both the high and the low end of the educational distribution" and concludes that "the data suggest that the jobs of immigrant and native workers are different" (Smith and Edmonston 1997:218). Immigrants compete with one another far more than they compete with natives. Thus, the NRC reports that immigration does have a more significant negative effect on the wages of other immigrants, who are much closer substitutes for new immigrants: "The one group that appears to suffer significant negative effects from new immigrants are earlier waves of immigrants, according to many studies" (223).

Borjas (1995:10–11) has claimed, "Even though the debate over immigration policy views the possibility that immigrants lower the wage of native workers as a harmful consequence of immigration, the economic benefits from immigration arise only when immigrants *do* lower the wage of native workers." This claim, however, refers only to the immigration surplus enjoyed by natives through immigrant entry into labor markets with native workers. If only immigrant workers take certain jobs, then natives can gain from immigration in these markets without any adverse effect on the wages of native workers.[6] Moreover, if native workers can move into jobs where their competitive advantage (in English language skills, for example) provides a natural barrier to competition from immigrants, then they can enjoy the benefits of immigration and still avoid any adverse effects of immigration in the labor market. Thus, segmented labor markets imply that immigration can produce gains for natives in the labor market without necessarily producing adverse effects for native workers.

It is important to interpret claims in the literature in light of the empirical evidence of segmented labor markets. For example, Borjas, Freeman, and Katz (1997) produce one of the largest estimates of the effect of immigrants on native wages. They estimate that immigration between 1980 and 1995 accounted for 44 percent of the 11 percent decline in the relative wages of high-school dropouts in the United States during this period (Borjas, Freeman, and Katz 1997:53, 62). This result, however, is based on a *simulation* that *assumes* that unskilled immigrants are *perfect* substitutes for unskilled natives (56). That is, this simulation makes an extreme assumption regarding the single most important fact in dispute. Therefore, simulations based on this assumption are biased in favor of finding large effects on natives; thus at best they provide only an upper bound on the potential effect of immigration on the wages of unskilled natives (Friedberg and Hunt 1995:39).

Furthermore, Borjas, Freeman, and Katz (1997:61) simulate what would have happened if we had cut off *both* all immigration *and* all increases in trade flows since 1980. We cannot infer from their study that immigration restrictions alone could have prevented the drop in wages that they identify, because they do not attempt to simulate that counterfactual. Given that immigration and international trade are substitutes, a decrease in immigration would probably cause an increase in trade flows, which would have a similarly depressing effect on the wages of unskilled natives. Borjas, Freeman, and Katz (1997:39) themselves concede, "Examining how immigration affects U.S. workers without recognizing that reduced levels of immigration will create incentives for greater trade (and capital flows) will likely overstate the economic effects of immigration." This trade effect is a second reason that their results overstate the actual effect that immigration policies standing alone would have upon native wages.

INCOME DISTRIBUTION AND THE COSTS OF PROTECTIONISM

Even if present levels of immigration have little effect on native wages in the United States, a more liberal immigration policy might produce more significant effects. As the National Research Council (Smith and Edmonston 1997:220) explains, the wage effects of immigration are small in part because "the aggregate increase in the supply of labor caused by immigration is itself small." Thus, much of the support for immigration restrictions is protection-ist in nature: restrictionists often cite the need to protect U.S. workers from foreign competition. Both quantitative restrictions and the requirement of "labor certification" for employment-based immigrants and temporary work-ers are designed to ensure that immigrants do not "take jobs away" from U.S. workers or drive down their wages.[7]

Labor certification is a determination by the Department of Labor that "there are not sufficient workers who are able, willing, qualified, ... and avail-able ... at the place where the alien is to perform" the work in question and that the employment of the alien "will not adversely affect the wages and work-ing conditions of workers in the United States similarly employed."[8] The U.S. immigration statute requires labor certification for most employment-based immigrants, even aliens "who are members of the professions holding advanced degrees or aliens of exceptional ability," professionals "who hold baccalaureate degrees," and others "performing skilled labor."[9] Through the labor-certification requirement, the U.S. government requires U.S. employers to discriminate against foreign workers: the statute requires an employer to prefer any qualified U.S. worker over any foreign worker, no matter how much better qualified the foreign worker may be. As Legomsky (1997:185) explains, "[T]he employer ordinarily must hire a minimally qualified American over a more qualified alien (or hire no one at all)."[10]

In this sense, immigration barriers, like trade barriers, are protectionist: they are designed to protect natives from foreign competition. Like trade bar-riers, however, immigration barriers sacrifice gains from trade and thus reduce the total wealth of natives as a group. In this sense, protectionism is a costly way to redistribute wealth from some natives to others. We could redistribute this same wealth through tax policies and transfer programs, rather than through protectionism, and thereby make all classes of natives better off, because liberalized immigration produces net gains for natives as a group. That is, concern for the distribution of income among natives does not imply that restrictive immigration laws are in order.

First, concerns regarding income inequality do not justify any restrictions on skilled immigration, because skilled immigrants not only increase total wealth for natives but also promote a more equitable distribution of income among natives. They are likely to have an adverse effect only on competing skilled natives and increase the real wages of everyone else, including less skilled natives, who enjoy the benefits of a greater supply of skilled labor. Therefore, the pursuit of a more equal distribution of income would at most justify concerns regarding unskilled immigration, which could have an adverse effect on real wages of unskilled native workers.

Second, even with respect to unskilled immigration, however, the appro-priate response to these distributive concerns is redistribution through pro-gressive reforms of tax and transfer policies, not immigration restrictions. If we wish to protect unskilled native workers from adverse distributive effects, the less costly solution is not protectionism but redistribution. Optimal policies would liberalize immigration insofar as it increases the total wealth of natives. As long as immigration increases total wealth, then those who gain from immigration can compensate those who lose and still be better off. That is, those who gain by paying lower wages, or by buying products and services at lower cost, can afford to pay enough to compensate those who find their wages fall relative to prices. Redistributive policies can shift the costs of liberalized immigration to the beneficiaries of liberalization.

This redistribution would produce some costly distortions, but the deadweight loss of protectionism would be greater than the deadweight loss from taxes with the same redistributive effects. Protectionism is less efficient than the tax system in producing a desirable distribution of income. Shavell (1981) and Kaplow and Shavell (1994:669) have shown that we can always replace an economically inefficient rule with an efficient rule without making any income class worse off, provided that we make the appropriate adjustments in income taxes. For example, Chiswick (1988:107) notes that if the immigration of unskilled workers reduces the wages of unskilled natives, then raising taxes on those workers with higher incomes and reducing taxes on native workers with the lowest incomes can leave all classes of natives better off than they would be in the absence of immigration. That is, those classes that would pay higher taxes to compensate unskilled native workers bear a still heavier burden under the protectionist alternative, which raises the prices of goods and services for all consumers. Protectionist policies currently impose an implicit tax on these consumers that costs them more than the explicit tax that would be necessary to compensate unskilled native workers for the effects of liberalized immigration policies. Once we recognize that protectionism is merely a disguised tax-and-transfer program, it should be apparent that there is no good reason to favor protectionism over less costly and more efficient redistributive policies.

We can achieve redistribution more efficiently and equitably by expanding redistributive programs already in use under the existing U.S. tax system. We could make Social Security taxes more progressive, for example, or we could increase the earned income tax credit and liberalize its eligibility requirements. These progressive reforms can supplement the income of unskilled native workers if unskilled immigration drives down their real wages. We can thereby reduce deadweight loss while still redistributing the same wealth that we currently redistribute through costly protectionism. Evidence that immigration has only mild effects upon the wages of unskilled natives suggests that modest changes in the tax system may suffice to offset the distributive effects of liberalized U.S. immigration policies.

Economists have suggested immigration, international trade, and technological progress as possible causes of the growing inequality in income in the

United States.[11] Such an effect, however, is no more an argument for restricting immigration or international trade than it is an argument for policies designed to reduce the pace of innovation. As long as a policy increases national wealth, it can (when combined with appropriate fiscal policies) make all economic classes of natives better off.

FISCAL EFFECTS: EMPIRICAL EVIDENCE

The presence of taxes and transfer policies, however, raises additional issues that we have not yet addressed. The foregoing analysis considered the economic effects of immigrants through the labor market alone. Immigrants, however, also have effects that are not internalized by private participants in that market. Taxes collected from immigrants, for example, yields benefits for the public sector, not for the private sector. Indeed, much of the debate over the economic effects of immigration has focused on the effects on the public sector.

The presence of the public sector introduces external effects that must be included in the analysis. These effects include both benefits and costs, so that depending on the immigrant, it is possible for the net external effect to be positive or negative. First, like natives, immigrants pay taxes, including income taxes, social security taxes, sales taxes, and property taxes. All these taxes introduce an additional reason to value immigrants: they increase tax revenues by expanding the tax base. Second, an immigrant also imposes external costs. For example, to the extent that an immigrant receives transfer payments from the government or has access to other public entitlement programs, these transfers will represent a cost to the country of immigration. Immigrants also gain access to public goods when they immigrate. To the extent they are pure public goods, like national defense, immigrants can enjoy the public good without imposing any cost on natives. Immigrant access to other public goods, however, may aggravate problems of congestion. Roads, for example, may become congested more frequently or more severely. These problems may require the construction of more infrastructure to relieve this congestion, and these investments in new infrastructure will require the expenditure of public funds.

Here, the effect of immigrants on natives will depend on whether immigrants pay more in taxes than the costs they impose through the public sector. Thus, the net effect of an immigrant on the public sector may be positive or negative, so that the benefit to a private employer of hiring a foreign worker may understate or overstate the benefit to the "importing" country from the immigration of that worker. Those immigrants who pay the least in such taxes would be the most likely to impose net external costs on natives. Thus, another important reason that countries regulate immigration is to protect the public treasury from the fiscal burden that immigrants may represent.

Calculating the net effect of immigration upon the public treasury is a complex and difficult empirical question. The 1997 study by the National Research Council represents a quantum leap in sophistication beyond any prior study of the fiscal impact of immigration. Past calculations, like that by Borjas (1994:1706–7) have estimated the fiscal effects of immigrant-headed households, for example, but these studies are biased in favor of finding a negative effect. These studies include the cost of educating the children born in the United States to immigrant parents, but they do not include the taxes that these children will pay when they grow up, enter the workforce, and leave the immigrant household. The NRC (Smith and Edmonston 1997:298) notes that a proper accounting of the total fiscal impact of immigration must include the fiscal effects of all the descendants of immigrants.

The NRC conducted the first study to attempt such a comprehensive calculation of the fiscal impact of immigration, using a range of different assumptions. The NRC economists made projections regarding the education and income of future generations and added their fiscal effects to the fiscal effects of immigrants over their own life cycles. The NRC economists find that the descendants of current immigrants into the United States are likely to have a net positive fiscal impact, whether their immigrant forebears are highly educated or not: although the descendants of more educated immigrants tend to have larger positive effects, even the descendants of immigrants with less than a high school education will on average have a significant positive effect (Smith and Edmonston 1997:328). This result emerges because the descendants of relatively uneducated immigrants show substantial upward educational mobility (356–57). The positive fiscal impact of an immigrant's descendants ranges from $76,000 for an immigrant with less than a high school education to $93,000 for an immigrant with more than a high-school education, expressing the average net present value of each fiscal impact in 1996 dollars (334). Once they include the future fiscal impact of an immigrant's descendants, under the most plausible assumptions, they find that the average immigrant will produce a net fiscal benefit of $80,000 overall in net present value in 1996 dollars (334).

Even if the *average* immigrant has a positive fiscal impact, however, *some* immigrants may impose external costs in excess of the taxes they pay. To the extent that unskilled workers tend to have lower incomes, they tend to pay less in taxes and to take greater advantage of public entitlement programs, so that the benefits flowing to the national economy from their immigration may be reduced and may be negative. The NRC found that the average immigrant with less than a high school education imposes a net fiscal cost (334). Once the NRC takes the positive fiscal effect of the immigrant's descendants into account, however, the average immigrant with less than a high-school education imposes only a modest net fiscal cost of $13,000 in net present value in 1996 dollars (334).

Skilled workers, however, tend to have higher incomes and to pay more in taxes, and so it is especially in the national economic interest to promote their immigration. The NRC, for example, found that the average immigrant with more than a high school education pays enough in taxes to produce a net fiscal benefit (334). In fact, once the NRC economists take the positive fiscal effect of the immigrant's descendants into account, they find that the average immigrant with a high school education produces a net surplus of $51,000, and the average immigrant with more than a high school education produces a net surplus of $198,000 (334). As long as these immigrants make a positive contribution to the public sector, there is in general no economic justification for excluding them. These estimates suggest that quantitative and other protectionist restrictions on their immigration should be eliminated. Even if concerns about the fiscal costs of immigration were to justify restrictions on unskilled immigration, these concerns cannot justify any restrictions on the immigration of skilled workers, who tend to have high incomes and pay more in taxes than the unskilled.

Furthermore, the age of the immigrant at time of entry proves to be an important determinant of the total fiscal impact of that immigrant. In general, the younger the immigrant at time of entry, the more working years the immigrant can spend in the United States, the more tax revenues the immigrant will contribute to public coffers prior to retirement, and the more positive the immigrant's overall fiscal impact. Thus, even an immigrant with less than a high school education will have a positive net fiscal impact if the immigrant enters the United States at age twenty-one or younger (Smith and Edmonston 1997:328). Therefore, the fiscal impact of immigration upon natives would justify, at most, concerns regarding the immigration of the unskilled or the elderly.

FISCAL POLICIES AS LESS RESTRICTIVE ALTERNATIVES TO EXCLUSION

Even for unskilled or older immigrants, the optimal response to fiscal concerns would not be exclusion but less restrictive alternatives designed to reduce the fiscal burden that these immigrants impose on natives. If some immigrants have a negative effect on the public sector, the optimal response is not quantitative or other protectionist restrictions on immigration. Rather, the appropriate response is fiscal. Restrictions on alien access to public benefits, for example, can improve the fiscal impact of immigration without excluding unskilled immigrants from the United States. Exclusion is the more costly response for both natives and immigrants, because it excludes immigrants not only from our public benefits but also from our labor market and thereby sacrifices the gains from trade that we and they would otherwise enjoy.

The objective of reducing the burden that immigrants impose on natives through the public sector underlies restrictions on the access of aliens to various entitlement programs. Under U.S. law, for example, even before Congress enacted new restrictions in 1996,[12] aliens were generally ineligible for most public entitlements, including Medicaid, Aid to Families with Dependent Children (AFDC), and food stamps, unless they had been lawfully admitted for permanent residence.[13] Thus, not only unauthorized immigrants but also aliens admitted to the United States temporarily as nonimmigrants, including temporary workers, were ineligible for most public benefits because they were not lawfully admitted for permanent residence. Current law now generally excludes nonimmigrants and unauthorized immigrants from an even broader range of public benefits: with only narrow exceptions, these aliens are ineligible for "any Federal public benefit."[14]

Current law also includes extensive new restrictions on the access of other aliens, including even legal permanent residents, to federal entitlement programs. In particular, an alien admitted for permanent residence after enactment of the new law is ineligible for "any Federal means-tested public benefit for a period of 5 years beginning on the date of the alien's entry into the United States," with only narrow exceptions.[15] Furthermore, these permanent resident aliens are now ineligible for food stamps and for Supplemental Security Income (SSI) without regard to length of residence in the United States, with only narrow exceptions.[16] Finally, the new law also permits states to exclude permanent resident aliens, including current recipients already admitted to the United States, from benefits under other federal programs, including Medicaid and Temporary Assistance for Needy Families (TANF), and under state programs, without regard to length of residence in the United States.[17]

The National Research Council (Smith and Edmonston 1997:339) estimates that by excluding immigrants from various means-tested benefits for their first five years in the United States, the 1996 welfare legislation improves the total fiscal impact of the average immigrant by $8,000 in net present value in 1996 dollars. Moreover, if the new welfare law has the effects predicted by its proponents, then the positive net fiscal impact of immigration will increase still more: the new restrictions would not only reduce the transfers paid to individual immigrants but also discourage the immigration of low-income aliens and thereby raise the income of the average immigrant. Thus, the NRC's estimates of the fiscal impact of immigration are likely to understate the fiscal benefits of future immigrants, given the legislation passed by Congress in 1996. Therefore, liberalized immigration is now even more likely to produce net economic benefits for natives.

IMPLICATIONS FOR FAMILY-BASED IMMIGRATION

Even before Congress enacted new restrictions on immigrant access to public benefits in 1996, our immigration laws sought to ensure that immigrants would have a net positive effect on the public treasury. Although an immigrant may have access to some public benefits after admission to the United States (and full access after naturalization), any alien deemed "likely at any time to become a public charge" may be excluded.[18] In making this determination, consular officers consider the alien's age, health, education, skills, and assets.[19] Based on such evidence, consular officers have broad powers to screen out immigrants expected to have a negative effect on the public treasury.

This inadmissibility ground serves to ensure that family-based immigration as well as employment-based immigration is likely to have a net positive effect on the economic welfare of natives. In fact, in the most careful and complete empirical analysis of the fiscal impact of immigration to date, the National Research Council found that even before Congress enacted new restrictions on immigrant access to public benefits in 1996, immigrants and their descendants are likely to pay more in taxes than they will consume in public benefits. The NRC estimate that the average immigrant will produce a net fiscal benefit of $80,000 is striking because this calculation includes all immigrants, including unauthorized immigrants and refugees (Smith and Edmonston 1997:306, 334), who are not subject to the "public charge" inadmissibility ground and have thus tended to be less educated and poorer than employment-based and family-based immigrants.[20]

To avoid the "public charge" inadmissibility ground, sponsoring relatives have often provided affidavits of support and evidence of their own incomes in order to gain the admission of the sponsored alien.[21] Thus, when the sponsored alien has had a low income, then the income of the sponsor would become relevant: this inadmissibility ground has in effect limited the right to sponsor low-income relatives to those petitioners with adequate levels of income. In short, the "public charge" provision has ensured not only that family-based immigrants impose little burden on the public sector but also that the formal right to petition for low-income family members is likely to prove most valuable in effect for sponsors with relatively high incomes.

Consequently, the availability of these family-based visas serves as an incentive for skilled aliens in particular to choose to accept employment and residence in the United States. That is, the prospect of family reunification may lead skilled aliens to come to the United States who would not otherwise. Thus, the family-based immigration of even unskilled aliens may be in the economic interest of natives insofar as skilled aliens contemplating immigration to the United States take into account the benefits their relatives will enjoy as family-sponsored immigrants. Borjas (1990:188) stresses that "it is *families* who enter the immigration market, compare the various offers, and choose the option that maximizes the household's economic well-being," so that "the family as a whole and individual members within the household take actions that maximize total family income." To consider the fiscal impact of family-sponsored immigrants standing alone overlooks the role of family-based immigration in encouraging skilled immigration and thus producing the fiscal benefits that the skilled sponsor confers on natives. So long as the family as a whole does not impose a net fiscal cost, the immigration of that family is in the economic interest of natives. Thus, the NRC estimates of the fiscal impact of the immigration stream as a whole suggest that current family-based immigration is consistent with the economic interest of natives. Indeed, Borjas (1990:191) has found empirical evidence that family considerations induce more skilled workers to immigrate, suggesting that "[p]olicies that favor the immigration of families ... may actually increase the average skills of immigrants."[22] Furthermore, the presence of a sponsoring relative in the United States improves the likelihood that the sponsored relatives will integrate smoothly into the U.S. economy and will thus yield external benefits for natives rather than costs.

In 1996, Congress imposed still more stringent requirements for family sponsorship that will further limit access to these visas and will tend to reserve them for sponsors with relatively high incomes. The Illegal Immigration Reform and Immigrant Responsibility Act of 1996 requires virtually all family-based immigrants to submit an affidavit of support.[23] An affidavit of support must now be a contract enforceable against the sponsor not only by the sponsored alien but also by a federal, state, or local agency seeking reimbursement for benefits provided to the sponsored alien under a means-tested entitlement program.[24] The affidavit must bind the sponsor "to provide support to maintain the sponsored alien at an annual income that is not less than 125 percent of the Federal poverty line."[25] The sponsor must demonstrate "the means to maintain" at least this level of income for "a family unit of a size equal to the number of members of the sponsor's household (including family and non-family dependents) plus the total number of other dependents and aliens sponsored by that sponsor."[26] Furthermore, under the welfare legislation enacted by Congress that same year, if the immigrant beneficiary of such an affidavit later applies for "any Federal means-tested public benefits," then the immigrant's income and resources will be "deemed" to include the income and resources of the sponsor, until the beneficiary either obtains U.S. citizenship or has worked for a sufficient period of time.[27] Thus, "deeming" will render otherwise eligible immigrants ineligible for public benefits and make them more reliant on their sponsors instead.

The new sponsorship requirements will not only improve still further the effect of family-based immigrants on public coffers but also deter or preclude those of modest means from sponsoring relatives for immigration. In fact, preliminary research sponsored by the Immigration and Naturalization Service found that 30 percent of those who sponsored relatives for immigration in 1994 had incomes below the new standard.[28] These new sponsorship requirements also ensure that the availability of family-based immigration visas will prove most valuable for the immigrants with the most wealth, because the number of relatives an immigrant can sponsor will be directly related to the immigrant's wealth. Furthermore, the legally binding obligations entailed by sponsorship will ensure that immigrants will sponsor only those relatives with whom they have close ties. Immigrants will choose to sponsor only when they consider family reunification very valuable and only when the welfare of the sponsored relative matters a great deal to the sponsor. Thus, legal liability will restrict sponsorship of indigent immigrants to those cases in which family-based immigration will provide the most valuable incentive for a skilled sponsor to immigrate.

Although restrictionists have proposed drastic cuts in family-based immigration, citing the national interest,[29] these cuts may in fact reduce the economic welfare of natives by reducing the incentives for skilled immigration and by excluding valuable workers and taxpayers. Indeed, given the alternative of qualitative restrictions like the "public charge" inadmissibility ground as a device for regulating immigration, it is doubtful that quantitative restrictions on family-based immigration serve a useful purpose at all in the pursuit of national economic welfare. Liberalization or elimination of these quotas would probably serve the national economic interest better than cuts in these quotas.

Liberalized quotas would serve the interests of natives not only by increasing the immigration of valuable workers and taxpayers but also by allowing individual immigrants to enter sooner, thereby increasing the total economic contribution made by each immigrant. Quotas currently create backlogs of millions of family-based immigrants waiting for as long as ten years or more to enter the United States.[30] The National Research Council (Smith and Edmonston 1997:328–35) found that immigrants arriving at earlier ages make a significantly larger net fiscal contribution overall because they will spend more of their working lives—and thus pay more taxes—in the United States. Thus, the U.S. Commission on Immigration Reform (1997:66) observed that the "extended waiting periods" for immigrant visas for siblings of U.S. citizens "mean that most siblings enter well into their working lives, limiting the time during which they can make a contribution to the U.S. economy." Perversely, however, the Commission cited these backlogs for family-based immigrant visas as a reason to eliminate most categories of family-based immigration rather than as a reason to eliminate or liberalize the quotas.[31] Liberalized quotas would reduce these backlogs, improve the fiscal impact of the average family-based immigrant, and would be more likely to promote the economic welfare of natives than the Commission's proposals. The Commission's restrictionist proposals seem particularly misguided, given the important changes in 1996 in the requirements for family sponsorship and in immigrant access to public benefits. Both sets of changes are likely to improve the fiscal effects of the average family-based immigrant. By disqualifying many sponsors, the changes in sponsorship rules are likely both to reduce family-based visa backlogs and to select for wealthier family-based immigrants.

Indeed, the new income test for family sponsorship sweeps so broadly that it applies to the sponsor regardless of the characteristics of the sponsored immigrant. Thus, the test seems overly broad and unduly rigid in that it will preclude the immigration of valuable workers and taxpayers simply because their sponsors have insufficient income. A test that would serve the interests of natives better would exempt sponsors from this test if the sponsored immigrant is likely to have a net positive effect on the public sector. For example, the National Research Council (Smith and Edmonston 1997:334) found that once we take account of the fiscal impact of an immigrant's descendants, the average immigrant with at least a high school education will have a positive fiscal effect. Similarly, the NRC also found that the average immigrant who arrives at age forty or younger will have a positive fiscal effect (335). A liberalized rule that admitted young or educated immigrants regardless of the incomes of their sponsors would be more closely tailored to the national interest.

IMPLICATIONS FOR EMPLOYMENT-BASED IMMIGRATION AND GUEST WORKERS

The categories of employment-based immigration visas under U.S. law are largely designed to select particularly skilled or wealthy immigrants for permanent residence. As a result, the National Research Council (Smith and Edmonston 1997:194) finds that "immigrants admitted under employment-preference visas have substantially greater earnings than those in other categories." Quotas for employment-based immigration allocate most visas to "priority workers," which include aliens with "extraordinary ability," "outstanding professors and researchers," and "multinational executives and managers," to "members of the professions holding advanced degrees or aliens of exceptional ability," and to other "skilled workers" and "professionals."[32] The vast majority of employment-based immigrants enter through these categories (CIR 1995:89).[33] Few unskilled workers can obtain such visas: of the 140,000 visas allocated to employment-based immigration per year, only 10,000 may go to unskilled workers.[34]

Skilled workers can also enter as temporary workers on H-1B nonimmigrant visas, but like employment-based immigrants, these nonimmigrants are also subject to quantitative restrictions.[35] Congress imposed these numerical limits on these temporary workers only recently, in 1990, and these ceilings are among the first quantitative restrictions ever imposed on any category of nonimmigrants (Legomsky 1997:242). So long as fiscal policies, employer sponsorship, and the "public charge" provision ensure that these skilled immigrants and temporary workers are expected to have a net positive economic effect on natives, however, it would be in the economic interests of U.S. natives to admit them without protectionist "labor certification" requirements or quantitative restrictions. The United States should eliminate or liberalize these restrictions.

The NRC estimates indicate that immigrants with at least a high school education have a net positive fiscal impact and that even immigrants with less than a high school education can have a positive fiscal impact if their access to public benefits is restricted. Thus, it is important to recall that aliens admitted on nonimmigrant visas only, including temporary workers, are not admitted as permanent residents and are thus not eligible for most public entitlements and not eligible to naturalize. Only aliens "admitted for permanent residence" may naturalize as U.S. citizens.[36] Therefore, classes of foreign workers deemed likely to have a negative fiscal impact if treated as citizens or as permanent residents can be admitted on nonimmigrant visas without the same adverse fiscal impact. A truly temporary worker, for example, would remain in the United States only while employed and would then return home, imposing even less of a burden on the public treasury than a permanent resident.[37] The NRC report (Smith and Edmonston 1997:315) indicates that immigrants are likely to make a positive contribution to the public treasury during their working years and impose a burden only if they remain in the United States for their retirement years and gain access to public benefits. Thus, temporary workers admitted on nonimmigrant visas, even if unskilled, are likely to have a net positive fiscal impact on natives. There is little reason to restrict their entry.

In fact, most employment-based visas for unskilled workers go to those who enter as nonimmigrants rather than immigrants. Unskilled workers may enter on H-2A visas as agricultural workers, which are not subject to a quantitative restriction, or on H-2B visas for workers who come "temporarily to the United States to perform ... temporary service or labor," which are limited to 66,000 per year.[38] This "double requirement of 'temporariness'" requires the H-2B alien not only to enter temporarily but also to fill a temporary job (Aleinikoff, Martin, and Motomura 1998:395). Furthermore, both visas are subject to labor certification requirements.[39] As a result of these requirements, the demand for each of these visas has remained low, but the liberalization or elimination of these requirements could greatly increase use of these programs.[40]

The alternative to a guest-worker program for many migrant workers is probably entry as an unauthorized immigrant. A liberalized guest-worker program would relieve the pressures in the labor market that generate unauthorized immigration. In fact, the United States brought in hundreds of thousands of agricultural guest workers from Mexico annually for most years of the *bracero* program from 1942 to 1964, and the decline in admissions of such workers was closely correlated with the rise in the estimated number of unauthorized immigrants (Simon 1989:286). Simon (1989:302) concludes that "the bracero program provides solid evidence that a legal temporary worker program will indeed reduce illegal immigration."

In fact, employment-based immigration of unskilled workers into the United States has largely taken the form of illegal rather than legal immigration, with this unauthorized immigrant population currently growing by as many as 300,000 aliens each year (Smith and Edmonston 1997:51). Given that unauthorized immigrants have little access to public entitlements for as long as their presence remains unauthorized, they may make a positive contribution to public coffers under the fiscal policies currently applied to them. Without distinguishing between legal and illegal immigrants, the National Research Council found that once we take the positive fiscal effect of the immigrant's descendants into account, an immigrant with less than a high school education imposes a net fiscal cost of only $13,000 in net present value in 1996 dollars (Smith and Edmonston 1997:334), and that if the 1996 welfare legislation excludes immigrants from seven specified means-tested benefits for only their first five years in the United States, then the total fiscal impact of the average immigrant would improve by $8,000.[41] The NRC figures suggest that if an immigrant *never* has access to such benefits, as would be the case for an unauthorized immigrant who never obtains legal status, then such an immigrant would probably have a positive fiscal impact even if the immigrant is unskilled.

Legalization of these immigrants through a liberalized guest-worker program would serve the interests of the immigrants as well as the interests of U.S. natives. The workers would gain from having a legal alternative to illegal entry and life as an unauthorized immigrant, which leaves them vulnerable to deportation by the government and to abuse by employers. Illegal immigration implies that the unauthorized immigrant must bear the costs of evading detection, apprehension, and deportation by the government. As a result, producers of counterfeit documents, smugglers, and unscrupulous employers can extract significant amounts of revenue from unauthorized immigrants.

Furthermore, admission as a guest worker need not entail permanent status as an alien: the NRC estimates indicate that the United States could allow even an unskilled immigrant to naturalize without generating a net fiscal burden if a sufficient period of alienage without access to public benefits has passed.[42] We could also allow guest workers to obtain permanent residence if they pay a tariff sufficient to cover the present discounted value of any net costs that we expect the worker to impose on natives after the worker obtains U.S. citizenship. A tariff could also take the form of an amount withheld out of income earned as a guest worker. For example, we could collect a tariff from all guest workers and offer a rebate for any guest worker who chooses to return home, retaining only the revenue necessary to cover the cost of any public benefits provided to the guest worker. To avoid a negative fiscal impact, we would only need to retain the tariff from a guest worker who remained in the United States as a permanent resident. For guest workers who wish to remain in the United States permanently, we could offer the option of adjusting their status to permanent residence once they had paid a sufficient tariff. The NRC estimates suggest that a modest tariff may be sufficient to cover the expected net fiscal costs of the permanent residence of an average unskilled immigrant.

The degree of international inequality in wages, the magnitude of unauthorized immigration into the United States, and the fees that unauthorized immigrants are willing to pay to smugglers suggest that a large number of aliens would be willing to enter as guest workers even if this required paying a significant fraction of their income as a tariff. Unauthorized immigrants from Mexico, for example, have recently reported that they receive wages in the United States nearly nine times what they receive in Mexico.[43] Given such large disparities in wages, unauthorized immigrants are willing to pay substantial sums to smugglers for illegal entry into the United States.[44] Through a tariff, the government can collect some of the value that immigrants would enjoy as a result of legal status, including wealth that they would otherwise transfer to forgers, smugglers, and unscrupulous employers. Natives would derive more benefit with this revenue going to the public treasury instead, which would allow a reduction in taxes paid by natives.

CONCLUSION

Thus, an economic analysis of U.S. immigration laws produces important and striking results. I have argued that a fair reading of the economic literature on immigration presents little justification for more restrictive immigration laws in the United States. Indeed, contrary to popular belief, economic considerations point toward liberalizing reforms rather than restrictionist policies. In particular, the following reforms are likely to promote the economic welfare of natives.

First, we should liberalize or eliminate our quotas on skilled immigrants and eliminate the "labor certification" requirements that impose protectionist restrictions on their immigration. We should also liberalize our quotas on family-based immigration, subject to the "public charge" inadmissibility ground, which provides an efficient incentive for skilled immigration while protecting public coffers. Furthermore, we should liberalize requirements for sponsorship of family-based immigrants so that young and educated immigrants are not excluded based solely on the income of their sponsors. Skilled immigration is in the interests of U.S. natives as well as of the immigrants.

Second, we should liberalize our existing guest-worker programs to allow more unskilled aliens to work in the United States. We should eliminate "labor certification" requirements for guest workers, which raise protectionist barriers to their employment. We should also liberalize our quotas on these admissions, our restrictions on the duration of their employment, and our limits on the length of their stay in the United States as workers. A liberalized guest-worker program would be in the economic interest of natives as well as in the interest of the guest workers. One question regarding national economic welfare arises with respect to the costs unskilled immigrants might impose through the public sector if they become permanent residents. To the extent this cost is a concern, the appropriate response would be fiscal: a tariff collected from those guest workers who wish to become permanent residents can ensure that they do not impose a net cost on natives. Even with such fiscal policies in place, a liberalized guest-worker program would be an improvement for the many aliens excluded by existing laws. Unskilled guest workers also raise an issue with respect to the distribution of income among natives, but again the appropriate response is fiscal: to compensate unskilled native workers for any reduction in their real wages, Congress could combine immigration reforms with tax relief for the working poor, such as expansions in the earned income tax credit.

Why has the United States not moved toward such policies? Part of the explanation may be the same protectionist pressures generated by special interest groups that oppose liberalized trade in goods: those who fear foreign competition lobby for protectionist barriers. Unskilled native workers, for example, may oppose the immigration of guest workers. To the extent Congress links a liberalized guest-worker program with subsidies for the working poor, however, progressive tax reforms designed to compensate unskilled labor could help overcome opposition to liberalization. These fiscal policies could ensure that all income classes share in the economic benefits produced by liberalized immigration.

Part of the problem, however, may be the xenophobia and intolerance that have unfortunately always exerted a powerful influence on the formulation of immigration policies. Immigration restrictions, like laws mandating racial segregation in the domestic context, have excluded those who are different in order to satisfy the intolerant preferences of some citizens. One could extend the concept of economic benefits to include the satisfaction of these intolerant preferences, so that one would view immigration restriction as a policy that produces the "public good" of segregation along the lines of national origin. These intolerant preferences, however, are fundamentally morally objectionable in ways that preferences for conventional economic goods are not (Chang 1997:1210–21).

This issue suggests that ultimately one cannot generate normative conclusions using the tools of economics alone, without addressing the moral issues analyzed by political philosophers (Ackerman 1980:93–95; Barry and Goodin 1992; Carens 1987). Economic analysis raises questions regarding what welfare objective we should assume. Should we seek to maximize a measure of economic welfare that includes the satisfaction of intolerant preferences? Should we seek to maximize the welfare of natives alone, or does the welfare of immigrants count as well? Should we seek to maximize national economic welfare or global economic welfare? Different welfare objectives will imply different optimal policies (Chang 1997). Although economists can tell us what policies would maximize any given welfare objective, the choice of that objective is ultimately a moral decision. In this chapter, I have assumed the economic welfare objective commonly assumed in public debates over immigration, which focus on the economic welfare of natives and do not consider the satisfaction of intolerant preferences explicitly as an economic benefit. I have assumed this objective for the sake of argument, to show the valuable contribution that economics can make to the debate over immigration laws as that debate is usually framed. While economics is an essential component of a normative analysis of immigration law, however, a truly comprehensive analysis must go beyond economics as well.

NOTES

Parts of this chapter have appeared previously in articles by Chang (1997, 1998–99, 1999).

1. See Robert Pear, "Change in Policy for Immigration is Urged by Panel," *New York Times*, June 5, 1995, A1.
2. The U.S. Commission on Immigration Reform (1995: xii) proposed permanent reductions in the numerical limits for employment-based admissions (from 140,000 to 100,000 per year) and for family-based admissions (from 480,000 to 400,000 per year). The Commission (1995: xviii) also proposed the complete elimination of all family-based immigration categories other than nuclear family admissions.
3. See H.R. 2202, 104th Cong., 2d Sess. (1995) (the Smith bill); S. 1394, 104th Cong., 1st Sess. (1995) (the Simpson bill).
4. See "House Approves Immigration Bill After Removing Legal Immigration Restrictions," 73 *Interpreter Releases* 349 (1996); "Senate Approves Omnibus Immigration Bill After Removing Exclusion Provisions," 73 *Interpreter Releases* 601 (1996).
5. See William Branigin, "Immigration Issues Await New Congress: Surging Legal Influx Will Be Among Topics of Renewed Debate," *Washington Post*, Nov. 18, 1996, A1.
6. As the NRC (Smith and Edmonston 1997: 220) explains, "the economic benefits of immigration that operate only through lower prices, without displacing or disadvantaging competitive domestic labor, add to the positive effects of immigration." Furthermore, if immigrants generate a benefit for the public sector in the form of tax revenues, then natives can gain from immigration even if there is no effect on wages at all.
7. Employment-based immigration is normally capped at 140,000 visas, 8 U.S.C. § 1151(d) (1994), but the qualitative restrictions are so stringent and the "labor certification" requirement so burdensome that this ceiling has not in fact been binding. In the 1996 fiscal year, for example, the United States admitted only 117,346 employment-based immigrants (CIR 1997:3).
8. 8 U.S.C. § 1182(a)(5)(A) (1994).
9. 8 U.S.C. § 1153(b)(2)–(3) (1994); see 8 U.S.C. § 1154(b), 1182(a)(5)(D) (1994). The requirement also applies to temporary agricultural workers on H-2A visas, see 8 U.S.C. § 1188(a)(1) (1994), and other temporary workers on H-2B visas, see 8 C.F.R. § 214.2(h)(6)(iv) (1998).
10. The statute requires the U.S. worker to be "equally qualified" only in the case of an alien who "is a member of the teaching profession" or "has exceptional ability in the sciences or the arts." 8 U.S.C. § 1182(a)(5)(A) (1994).
11. For example, Borjas, Freeman, and Katz (1997) estimate the share of the decline in the relative wages of high school dropouts that can be attributed to immigration and

international trade, and Burtless (1995) surveys the literature addressing whether international trade or technological change is the primary cause of rising inequality in the United States and other industrialized countries.

12. See Personal Responsibility and Work Opportunity Reconciliation Act of 1996, Pub. L. No. 104–93, 110 Stat. 2105.

13. See 42 U.S.C. § 1396b(v) (1994) (limiting the eligibility of aliens for Medicaid benefits); 42 U.S.C. § 602(a)(33)(1994) (limiting the eligibility of aliens for AFDC benefits), 42 U.S.C. § 1436a (1994) (limiting the eligibility of aliens for public housing assistance); 7 U.S.C. § 2015(f) (1994) (limiting the eligibility of aliens for food stamps).

14. 8 U.S.C. § 1611(a) (Supp. II 1996). Furthermore, the new law also prohibits states from providing "any State or local public benefit" to unauthorized immigrants unless the state subsequently enacts a law that "affirmatively provides for such eligibility." 8 U.S.C. § 1621 (Supp. II 1996). The new law also makes explicit the exclusion of aliens from the earned income tax credit if they are not authorized to work in the United States. See 26 U.S.C. § 32 (Supp. II 1996). Thus, unauthorized immigrants are ineligible for the earned income tax credit.

15. 8 U.S.C. § 1613(a) (Supp. II 1996).

16. 8 U.S.C. § 1612(a) (Supp. II 1996). One exception applies to legal permanent residents who have "worked for 40 qualifying quarters." 8 U.S.C. § 1612(a)(2)(B) (Supp. II 1996). Thus, under this law, a permanent resident alien must work for a sufficient period of time to earn an entitlement to these benefits.

17. See 8 U.S.C. § 1612(b) (Supp. II 1996) (allowing states to restrict alien access to designated federal programs), 8 U.S.C. § 1622 (Supp. II 1996) (allowing states to restrict alien access to state public benefits). Each provision features exceptions that include legal permanent residents who have "worked for 40 qualifying quarters." 8 U.S.C. §§ 1612(b)(2)(B), 1622(b)(2) (Supp. II 1996).

18. 8 U.S.C. § 1182(a)(4) (Supp. II 1996).

19. See 8 U.S.C. § 1182(a)(4)(B)(i) (Supp. II 1996).

20. Smith and Edmonston (1997:194) note that among legal immigrants, "refugees or asylees and their spouses have the lowest occupational earnings." Similarly, Fix and Passel (1994:5, 31, 34, 37) present evidence that unauthorized immigrants and refugees tend to have less education and lower incomes than other immigrants. Those seeking admission as refugees are not subject to the "public charge" inadmissibility ground. See 8 U.S.C. § 1157(c)(3) (1994). Furthermore, as Fix and Passel (1994:63) note, "The only major immigrant population eligible to participate broadly in the nation's welfare state from date of entry is refugees." Their data indicate that refugees receive welfare at far higher rates than other immigrants (63, 65).

21. See, e.g., Kohama, 17 I. & N. Dec. 257 (Assoc. Comm'r, Examinations 1978).

22. Borjas compares the incomes of single immigrant men with those of married immigrant men; he also compares the incomes of men who immigrated alone with those of men who immigrated contemporaneously with relatives. In both cases, immigrants with more family ties had higher incomes. He infers that "family ties increase the average skill level of the immigrant flow" (1990:191).

23. The new law states that any alien seeking admission as a family-based immigrant, with only very narrow exceptions, is inadmissible unless the alien's sponsor executes an affidavit of support. See Illegal Immigration Reform and Immigrant Responsibility Act of 1996, Pub. L. No. 104–208, sec. 531(a), § 212(a)(4)(C), 110 Stat. 3009–546, –647 (codified at 8 U.S.C. § 1182[a][4][C] [Supp. II 1996]).

24. See 8 U.S.C. § 1183a (Supp. II 1996).

25. 8 U.S.C. § 1183a(a)(1)(A) (Supp. II 1996).

26. 8 U.S.C. § 1183a(f)(1)(E), (6)(A)(iii) (Supp. II 1996). The law allows a sponsor who fails to meet this requirement to recruit another sponsor who can satisfy the require-

ment by accepting joint and several liability. 8 U.S.C. § 1183a(f)(2), (5) (Supp. II 1996). This legal liability, however, is likely to deter all but close relatives from serving as sponsors.

27. Personal Responsibility and Work Opportunity Reconciliation Act, sec. 421, 110 Stat. at 2270 (codified at 8 U.S.C. § 1631 (Supp. II 1996).

28. See Celia W. Dugger, "Immigrant Study Finds Many Below New Income Limit," *New York Times*, Mar. 16, 1997, § 1, 1. Another study by the Urban Institute found that 40 percent of immigrant families and 26 percent of natives in the United States in 1993 had incomes below the new standard.

29. The U.S. Commission on Immigration Reform (1995:70–71), for example, recommended the complete elimination of most family-based admission categories, including not only siblings of U.S. citizens but also adult sons and daughters of U.S. citizens and of legal permanent residents. The Smith and Simpson bills sought to implement these recommendations. See H.R. 2202, *supra* note 4; S. 1394, *supra* note 4.

30. For example, as of January 1997, 1.5 million siblings of U.S. citizens were on the waiting list for immigrant visas, and those currently eligible to enter applied at least ten years ago (CIR 1997:66). Sibling immigrants from oversubscribed countries had to wait even longer: those admitted from the Philippines, for example, applied nearly twenty years ago (CIR 1997:66).

31. The U.S. Commission on Immigration Reform (1997:66) pointed to "the extraordinarily large waiting list for siblings of U.S. citizens, and to a lesser extent, adult children" and concluded that "[a]n end to extended [family] visa categories is justified."

32. 8 U.S.C. § 1153(b)(1)–(3) (1994).

33. Smaller numbers of visas are available for unskilled workers, see 8 U.S.C. § 1153(b)(3)(A)(iii), (B) (1994), for "qualified special immigrants," 8 U.S.C. § 1153(b)(4) (1994), and for foreign investors, who must invest at least $1 million in a new commercial enterprise that will create at least ten jobs in the United States, 8 U.S.C. § 1153(b)(5) (1994).

34. See 8 U.S.C. §§ 1151(d)(1)(A), 1153(b)(3)(A)(iii), (B) (1994).

35. See 8 U.S.C. § 1101(a)(15)(H)(i)(b) (1994).

36. 8 U.S.C. § 1427(a) (1996).

37. Sykes (1995:189) notes, "Temporary workers are even less likely than permanent immigrants to be a net drain on the public sector, given that these workers pay taxes just like anyone else, federal funds cannot be used to provide them with public safety net benefits, and their right to remain in the country generally depends on continuing employment." (Footnote omitted.)

38. 8 U.S.C. § 1101(a)(15)(H)(ii) (1994); see 8 U.S.C. § 1184(g)(1)(B) (1994).

39. See 8 U.S.C. § 1188(a)(1) (1994); 8 C.F.R. § 214.2(h)(6)(iv) (1998).

40. Admissions under H-2B visas has remained below one-third of the quota limit in recent years, and admissions under H-2A visas have been similar (Aleinikoff, Martin, and Motomura 1998:393, 395). Aleinikoff, Martin, and Motomura (1998:395) state that "demand would be much higher but for the double 'temporariness' requirement." Similarly, Sykes (1995:189) reports that "[a]dmissions under the H-2 categories have been modest in recent years, on the order of 35,000 for the two combined" and explains that "because of the transaction costs of obtaining a visa coupled with the limited certifications for labor shortages in the agricultural sector, employers often find that these visas are not worth the effort to procure."

41. Smith and Edmonston (1997:339) arrive at this figure, assuming that these programs include "SSI, AFDC, food stamps, non-emergency Medicaid, energy assistance, rent subsidies, and public housing."

42. Nor would a guest-worker program produce a hereditary class of alien residents in

the United States, because the Fourteenth Amendment of the U.S. Constitution confers U.S. citizenship on anyone born in the United States, including the children of nonimmigrants. See U.S. CONST. amend. XIV, § 1 ("All persons born or naturalized in the United States, and subject to the jurisdiction thereof, are citizens of the United States and of the State wherein they reside."); *United States* v. *Wong Kim Ark*, 169 U.S. 649, 676 (1898).

43. See "Mexican Deportees Report Good Treatment," UPI, Apr. 21, 1996, available in LEXIS, Nexis Library, UPI File (reporting that Mexican immigrants received an average of $278 per week in the United States, compared with $30.81 per week in Mexico).

44. See Somini Sengupta, "Crackdowns Have Smugglers Trying New Routes, Officials Say," *New York Times*, June 1, 1998, B6 (reporting that the prices that Chinese immigrants currently pay to be smuggled into the United States range from $40,000 to $45,000).

REFERENCES

Ackerman, Bruce A. 1980. *Social Justice in the Liberal State*. New Haven, Conn.: Yale University Press.

Aleinikoff, Thomas A., David A. Martin, and Hiroshi Motomura. 1998. *Immigration and Citizenship: Process and Policy*, 4th ed. St. Paul, Minn.: West Publishing Co.

Barnes, David W., and Lynn A. Stout. 1992. *Cases and Materials on Law and Economics*. St. Paul, Minn.: West Publishing Co.

Barry, Brian, and Robert E. Goodin, eds. 1992. *Free Movement: Ethical Issues in the Transnational Migration of People and of Money*. University Park: Pennsylvania State University Press.

Blanchard, Olivier J., and Lawrence F. Katz. 1992. "Regional Evolutions," *Brookings Papers on Economic Activity* (1): 1–61.

Borjas, George J. 1990. *Friends or Strangers: The Impact of Immigrants on the U.S. Economy*. New York: Basic Books.

———. 1994. "The Economics of Immigration," *Journal of Economic Literature* 32: 1667–1717.

———. 1995. "The Economic Benefits from Immigration," *Journal of Economic Perspectives* 9 (2) (spring 1995): 3–22.

———. 1999. *Heaven's Door: Immigration Policy and the American Economy*. Princeton, N.J.: Princeton University Press.

Borjas, George J., Richard B. Freeman, and Lawrence F. Katz. 1997. "How Much Do Immigration and Trade Affect Labor Market Outcomes?" *Brookings Papers on Economic Activity* (1): 1–67.

Boswell, Richard A. 1992. *Immigration and Nationality Law: Cases and Materials*. 2d ed. Durham, N.C.: Carolina Academic Press.

Burtless, Gary. 1995. "International Trade and the Rise in Earnings Inequality," *Journal of Economic Literature* 33: 800–16.

Card, David. 1990. "The Impact of the Mariel Boatlift on the Miami Labor Market," *Industrial and Labor Relations Review* 43: 245–57.

Carens, Joseph H. 1987. "Aliens and Citizens: The Case for Open Borders," *Review of Politics* 49: 251–73.

Chang, Howard F. 1997. "Liberalized Immigration as Free Trade: Economic Welfare and the Optimal Immigration Policy," *University of Pennsylvania Law Review* 145: 1147–244.

———. 1998–99. "Migration as International Trade: The Economic Gains from the Liberalized Movement of Labor, *UCLA Journal of International Law and Foreign Affairs* 3: 371–414.

————. 1999. "The Economic Effects of Immigration and the Case for Liberalizing Reforms," *Bender's Immigration Bulletin* 4: 497–521.

Chiswick, Barry R. 1988. "Illegal Immigration and Immigration Control," *Journal of Economic Perspectives* 2 (3) (summer 1988): 101–15.

Cooter, Robert, and Thomas Ulen. 1988. *Law and Economics*. Glenview, Ill.: Scott, Foresman and Co.

Ehrenberg, Ronald G., and Robert S. Smith. 1994. *Modern Labor Economics: Theory and Public Policy*. 5th ed. New York: HarperCollins.

Fix, Michael, and Jeffrey S. Passel. 1994. *Immigration and Immigrants: Setting the Record Straight*. Washington, D.C.: Urban Institute.

Friedberg, Rachel M., and Jennifer Hunt. 1995. "The Impact of Immigrants on Host Country Wages, Employment and Growth," *Journal of Economic Perspectives* 9 (2) (spring 1995): 23–44.

Grossman, Jean B. 1982. "The Substitutability of Natives and Immigrants in Production," *Review of Economics and Statistics* 64: 596–603.

Hamilton, Bob, and John Whalley. 1984. "Efficiency and Distributional Implications of Global Restrictions on Labour Mobility," *Journal of Development Economics* 14: 61–75.

Kaplow, Louis, and Steven Shavell. 1994. "Why the Legal System is Less Efficient than the Income Tax in Redistributing Income," *Journal of Legal Studies* 23: 667–81.

Katz, Avery W. 1998. *Foundations of the Economic Approach to Law*. Oxford: Oxford University Press.

Krugman, Paul R., and Maurice Obstfeld. 1991. *International Economics: Theory and Policy*. 2d ed. New York: HarperCollins.

Legomsky, Stephen H. 1997. *Immigration and Refugee Law and Policy*. 2d ed. Westbury, N.Y.: Foundation Press.

Piatt, Bill. 1994. *Immigration Law: Cases and Materials*. Charlottesville, Va.: Michie Co.

Polinsky, A. Mitchell. 1989. *An Introduction to Law and Economics*. 2d ed. Boston, Mass.: Little, Brown.

Posner, Richard A. 1992. *Economic Analysis of Law*. 4th ed. Boston, Mass.: Little, Brown.

Shavell, Steven. 1981. "A Note on Efficiency vs. Distributional Equity in Legal Rulemaking: Should Distributional Equity Matter Given Optimal Income Taxation?" *American Economic Review Papers and Proceedings* 71: 414–18.

Simon, Julian L. 1989. *The Economic Consequences of Immigration*. Oxford: Basil Blackwell.

Smith, James P., and Barry Edmonston, eds. 1997. *The New Americans: Economic, Demographic, and Fiscal Effects of Immigration*. Washington, D.C.: National Academy Press.

Sykes, Alan O. 1995. "The Welfare Economics of Immigration Law: A Theoretical Survey with an Analysis of U.S. Policy," in Warren F. Schwartz, ed., *Justice in Immigration*, pp. 158–200. Cambridge: Cambridge University Press.

U.S. Commission on Immigration Reform. 1995. *Legal Immigration: Setting Priorities*. Washington, D.C.: U.S. Commission on Immigration Reform.

————. 1997. *Becoming an American: Immigration and Immigrant Policy*. Washington, D.C.: U.S. Commission on Immigration Reform.

Contributors

Caroline B. Brettell is Professor and Chair of the Department of Anthropology at Southern Methodist University. She has conducted research and published on the topic of Portuguese migrations in historical and contemporary contexts in both Europe and North America. She has also worked on issues related to immigrant women. Among her books are *We Have Already Cried Many Tears: The Stories of Three Portuguese Migrant Women* (Waveland 1995); *Men Who Migrate, Women Who Wait: Population and History in a Portuguese Parish* (Princeton 1986); and *International Migration: The Female Experience* (coedited with Rita James Simon) (Rowman and Littlefield 1986).

Howard F. Chang is Professor of Law at the University of Pennsylvania Law School. He has published articles applying economic analysis to diverse areas of the law, including immigration law and international trade law. He is an economist as well as a lawyer, and his scholarship has appeared not only in law reviews but also in economics journals.

Barry R. Chiswick is Research Professor and Head of Economics at the University of Illinois, Chicago. His specialties are in the areas of labor economics, human resources, the economics of immigration, the economics of minorities, and income distribution. His most recent book is an edited volume, *The Economics of Immigrant Skill and Adjustment*.

Hasia R. Diner, the Paul S. and Sylvia Steinberg Professor of American Jewish History at New York University, holds a joint appointment in History and Hebrew and Judaic Studies. She is the author of three books: *In the Almost Promised Land: American Jews and Blacks, 1915–1935; Erin's Daughters in America: Irish Immigrant Women in the 19th Century;* and, most recently, *A Time for Gathering: The Second Migration 1820–1880*. She is currently working on a book with the working title *Memories of Hunger: Food and the Creation of Immigrant Identity*.

James F. Hollifield is the Arnold Professor of International Political Economy and the Director of International Studies at Southern Methodist University. Jim is the author of *Searching for the New France* (with George Ross), and *Immigrants, Markets and States, and Controlling Immigration* (with Wayne Cornelius and Philip Martin). His most recent work looks at the rapidly evolving relationship between trade, migration, and the nation state.

Charles B. Keely is the Donald G. Herzberg Professor of International Migration in the School of Foreign Service at Georgetown University. His current research focuses on refugee production and the interaction of globalization and international personnel movements, with a particular focus on firm behavior and strategic planning for skilled personnel and knowledge transfer.

Barbara Schmitter Heisler is Professor in the Department of Sociology and Anthropology at Gettysburg College. Her long-standing interests in issues of citizenship and the integration of newcomers in advanced industrial societies began with her 1979 University of Chicago dissertation "Immigration and Citizenship in Germany and Switzerland." She has published numerous articles in a range of scholarly journals and, as a comparative sociologist, has often drawn comparisons between the post–World War II European experience of immigration and the historical experience of the United States.

Peter H. Schuck joined the faculty of the Yale University Law School in 1979 and has been Simeon E. Baldwin Professor of Law since 1986. His most recent books are *Citizens, Strangers, and In-Betweens: Essays on Immigration and Citizenship* (Westview Press 1998) and *The Limits of Law: Essays on Democratic Governance* (Westview Press 1999). He is coauthor (with Rogers Smith) of *Citizenship without Consent: Illegal Aliens in the American Polity* (Yale University Press 1985), and has also written widely on torts, administrative law, and public policy. He is a graduate of Cornell University and holds advanced degrees from Harvard University and New York University.

Index